**DO NOT REMOVE**
**CARDS FROM POCKET**

THE CIVILIZATION OF THE AMERICAN INDIAN SERIES

# The Tzutujil Mayas

# The Tzutujil Mayas

## CONTINUITY AND CHANGE, 1250-1630

*By Sandra L. Orellana*

UNIVERSITY OF OKLAHOMA PRESS : NORMAN

Library of Congress Cataloging in Publication Data

Orellana, Sandra L. (Sandra Lee), 1941-
  The Tzutujil Mayas.

  Bibliography: p. 261
  Includes index.
  1. Tzutuhil Indians—History. 2. Acculturation—Guatemala. 3. Indians of
Central America—Guatemala—History. I. Title.
F1465.2.T9073   1984                972,81'0497                83-47837

Publication of this work has been made possible in part by a grant from the
Andrew W. Mellon Foundation.

The paper in this book meets the guidelines for permanence and durability of
the Committee on Production Guidelines for Book Longevity of the Council on
Library Resources, Inc.

*To Juan Ajtzip Alvarado
and the people of Santiago Atitlán*

# *Contents*

# Illustrations and Maps

# *Tables*

# *Preface*

The purpose of this work is to reconstruct Tzutujil Maya culture
as it existed in aboriginal times and to examine the changes brought
about by the Conquest. By focusing on the lives of the people
of one area of Mesoamerica, it is possible to illuminate the general
patterns of acculturation that took place among all the native
populations of the New World. Although several studies have established the broad outlines of this process, few have dealt in
depth with changes that occurred within individual groups, especially those beyond the centers of the great Indian empires.

The Tzutujil Mayas provide a clear example of New World
acculturation because only two sets of actors played primary roles
in the culture contact: Indians and Spaniards. The meeting and
interaction of these two different cultures previously unknown to
each other must be one of the most dramatic instances of culture
contact ever recorded.

The pre-Hispanic Tzutujil Mayas shared many features of Mesoamerican culture with groups within and beyond the Guatemala
area. They belonged to an exotic world whose features were irre-
vocably changed by Spanish domination. The Spanish crown attempted to impose similar institutions and policies on Indians
wherever they found them, but some differences in application
resulted as officials responded to local realities. The process of
adaptation that characterizes the Tzutujils may then be seen in
its general outlines as the same one that affected other New World
peoples. Their story also provides data on how a specific group
adjusted to the reality of conquest and incorporation into a foreign
imperial system. Such data may be useful to those engaged in
comparative studies of culture change in the New World.

Part One of this book deals with pre-Hispanic Tzutujil culture
and is based primarily on archaeological and documentary information. Archaeological data are essential in establishing such basic

features of precontact Tzutujil life as settlement pattern, material culture, and cultural development in the period not covered by the documents, which tend to focus on the late precontact period. Such archaeological data as exist have been utilized, but explorations have been rather brief and superficial in the Tzutujil region. Thorough excavation could provide many details on the early Tzutujils, and such information could also help confirm or disprove interpretations of late precontact history made solely on the basis of written sources.

Part Two deals with the Conquest and the colonial period and is based primarily on written and ethnographic sources. An abundance of documentary information is available on the aboriginal and colonial Tzutujils. A discussion of some of the documentary materials available for the study of highland Maya cultural groups has been presented by Robert M. Carmack.[1] There are no long native manuscripts that focus only on the Tzutujils, but a good deal of material written by Indians and Spaniards after the mid-sixteenth century is extant. Major accounts of closely related native groups, such as the *Popul Vuh* of the Quichés and *The Annals of the Cakchiquels,* also contain quite a bit of information about the Tzutujils. The lack of a comprehensive narrative describing pre-Hispanic Tzutujil legend and history has made it necessary to fill in important gaps in the data by analogizing from nearby peoples, such as the Quichés and the Cakchiquels. This procedure does not provide an ideal reconstruction and is followed only when the information points to shared features. It is clear that some things cannot be known from presently existing sources.

Ethnographic studies are also invaluable in ethnohistorical work because a good knowledge of the contemporary situation is necessary in gauging the accuracy of the documents.[2] Recent observations can provide information not contained in the documents, especially in an area as culturally conservative as that of the Tzutujils. Direct observation allows the ethnohistorian to work from the known back to the unknown—a process termed "upstreaming."[3] From 1971 to 1979, I spent about six months living among the Tzutujils of Santiago Atitlán and worked for another six months in archives in Guatemala City and Seville, Spain.

Ethnohistory is uniquely suited to cultural reconstruction and processual analysis, for many native cultures were the subjects of Spanish and Indian written accounts from Conquest times until the end of the colonial period. Despite the availability of documentation, few ethnohistorical studies of Mesoamerican groups have examined both the aboriginal and the colonial cultures. France

V. Scholes and Ralph L. Roys wrote such an account of the Chontal Mayas of the Acalan-Tixchel area of Yucatán, Ronald Spores provided an account of the Mixtecs, and Roys wrote on pre-Hispanic and colonial Yucatán.[4] Most ethnohistorical works have focused on either the aboriginal or the colonial period. Examples of studies that are primarily aboriginal are S. W. Miles on the Pokomans and Carmack on the Quichés.[5] Important colonial studies of central Mexico have been carried out by Charles Gibson and of the Mayas by Francisco de Solano and Silvio Zavala.[6] This book examines both time periods and from a close study of the Tzutujils draws some conclusions about the process of acculturation in the Tzutujil area.

Present-day visitors to the Tzutujil region observe many remnants of native culture. Most of the people live in houses whose style has not changed substantially since late-precontact times, wear typical native dress, farm by ancient methods, and practice a form of Catholicism that contains aboriginal and Spanish beliefs. The native language is still spoken, and many geographical features surrounding Lake Atitlán bear names of pre-Columbian origin. The Church of Santiago Atitlán, one of the oldest churches in Guatemala, dates to the late sixteenth century and is a reminder of the many years of Franciscan domination.

Modern Tzutujil society has its roots in both the pre-Hispanic and the colonial periods. The location of communities, the town-government system, economic practices, social organization, and religious beliefs are all the products of developments over a long period of history. Tzutujil society was profoundly modified by the Spaniards, but despite some 450 years of European domination the native culture has survived and represents an example of the adjustment of the two traditions.

I wish to thank the many individuals, funding agencies, and institutions who generously assisted me during the preparation of this manuscript. I received grants from the Cora Black Fund at the University of California at Los Angeles and from the Del Amo Foundation that made it possible for me to carry out archival research in the Archivo General de Centroamérica, in Guatemala, and the Archivo General de Indias, in Seville, Spain. The Latin-American Library in the University of Texas supplied me with a map of Santiago Atitlán of 1585, and the Special Collections of the University Research Library in the University of California at Los Angeles provided me with the illustrations from the *Lienzo de Tlaxcala*. Fred Folger prepared one of the drawings, and Libby Hayes, of the University of California at Los Angeles, made the maps. William Douglas, Stan Rother, and Nicolas Chiviliu allowed me to look at archival documents in their possession.

Several persons generously gave of their time and read portions of this book. Robert M. Carmack, of the State University of New York at Albany, read most of the manuscript, and Murdo MacLeod, of the University of Pittsburgh, gave many helpful suggestions on Part Two. Gary Elbow, of Texas Tech University; John Fox, of Baylor University; Lyle Campbell, of the State University of New York at Albany; James Butler, of the Summer Institute of Linguistics, University of Oklahoma, Norman; and H. B. Nicholson, of the University of California at Los Angeles, made many useful comments.

Acknowledgments are also made to Clyde Woods, who gave me my initial opportunity to go to the Tzutujil area on the UCLA Guatemala Project; to Carlos Orellana, who helped me carry out the archaeological survey of 1971; and to Patricia Anawalt, Keith Swan, Benjamin Paul, and Earl Yin Jew, for their constant encouragement and helpful information. I am grateful to Barbara Goldfus and Heather Chronert for typing the final draft of the manuscript.

I especially wish to thank the people of Santiago Atitlán for their help during my fieldwork. My special appreciation goes to Juan Ajtzip Alvarado and Nicolas Coché Sapalu, who accompanied me on archaeological explorations and gave me valuable insight into Tzutujil culture.

*Los Angeles*                                                     SANDRA L. ORELLANA

PART ONE

# *Pre-Hispanic Tzutujil Society*

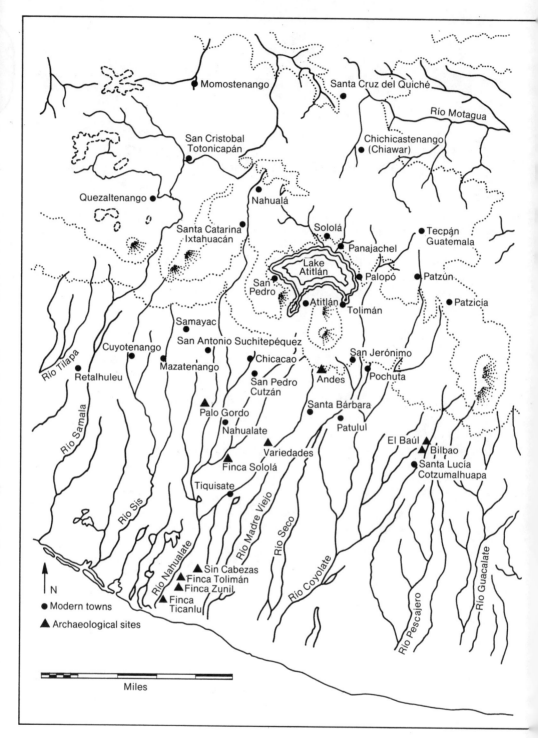

Fig. 1. *Southwestern Guatemala. Adapted from McBryde 1947, map between pp.* 2 *and* 3.

## CHAPTER 1

# The Tzutujils and Their Region

The Tzutujil Mayas of today inhabit the south, west, and north-west region surrounding Lake Atitlán, a picturesque volcanic lake in the middle-western highlands of Guatemala. In pre-Columbian times their kingdom extended from the lake to the adjacent coastal lowlands. The Tzutujils competed with other powerful groups, primarily the Quichés and the Cakchiquels, for control of valuable lands and resources. Today Santiago Atitlán is the largest town in the Tzutujil region.

## The People and Their Language

Munro Edmonson calls the Tzutujils "the third important 'nation' of the central Guatemalan highlands," after the Quichés and the Cakchiquels.[1] *Tz'utuj* means "to be on the point of blooming (of flowers of cane or corn),"[2] and the name Tzutujil appears to be of totemic origin. The *Relación Tzutujil* makes reference to *amac-tzutuhile*,[3] which means "settlement of the Tzutujils" or "the Tzutujil people."[4]

Tzutujil belongs to the Quichean group of languages, along with Cakchiquel, Quiché, Pokom, Uspantec, and Kekchi.[5] It is most closely related to Cakchiquel, with which, along with Quiché, it forms a branch of the Quichean group.[6] Today Tzutujil speakers inhabit the lake towns San Lucas Tolimán, Cerro de Oro, Santiago Atitlán, San Pedro la Laguna, San Juan la Laguna, San Pablo la Laguna,[7] and Santa María Visitación (fig. 2).

Nahua words were also in use in the highlands of Guatemala owing to contact with the Pipils (native Guatemalan Nahua speakers) and to the Nahua background of the early Quiché, Cakchiquel, and Tzutujil dynasties. According to the *Relación geográfica Atitlán*, the Tzutujils were acquainted with Nahua: "Some of them understand a corrupted [version] of the Mexican language [Na-

3

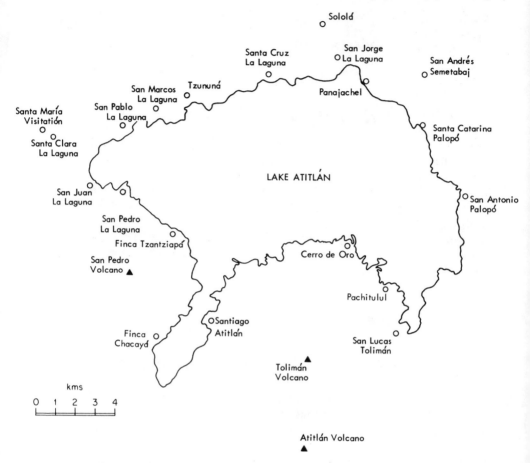

Fig. 2. *Modern settlements of Lake Atitlán. Adapted from Tax 1968, foldout before p. 11.*

huatl], but they do not speak it with as much elegance as do the natives of México."[8] Nahuatl words came into general use after the Conquest because the Spaniards and their Mexican allies were more familiar with that language.

Atitlán is often written Atitan, the Pipil form of the name, in colonial sources. *Atl* means "water" in Nahuatl, *ti* is a connective, and *tlan* is a suffix indicating proximity. Therefore, Atitlán means Near to Lake. The equivalent in Tzutujil is Chiya', the modern spelling, of Chíaa, as it was written in the *Relación geográfica*

Atitlán, in 1585.[9] Ancient terms may sometimes be incorrectly interpreted because the scarcity of sixteenth- and seventeenth-century Tzutujil texts makes it difficult to reconstruct pre-Hispanic phonology accurately.

The pre-Hispanic Tzutujil leader was called Ajtz'inquinajay, or He of the House of the Bird.[10] Ajtz'iquinajay, or Tz'iquinajá, is often used to designate the ancient capital.[11] This confusion arises because some writers have misinterpreted phrases like "those of Tz'iquinajá" as meaning that Tz'iquinajá was the name of the place of habitation when the reference was actually to people of the house of Tz'iquinajay. The name is properly Chiya' or, in Nahuatl, Atitlán. Further confusion has resulted from the name of the hill upon which the ruins of Chiya' lie, today called Chuitinamit. The name probably derives from the Tzutujil word *ch(i)-wi,* meaning "on," and the Nahua word *tinamit,* meaning "fortified town."

## Geography of the Region

*Volcanoes:* The middle-western highlands centering around Lake Atitlán lie parallel to the Pacific coastal plain and rise from it in a steep ascent. On the south the highlands are bordered by several geologically young, active volcanoes of the composite variety. The volcanoes constitute a barrier to travel and strictly limit the number of passageways from the Lake Atitlán basin to the lowlands.

San Pedro has not erupted in pre-Hispanic or recent times, and Tolimán has not erupted within historic times (see fig. 2).[12] Atitlán (also referred to as Patulul or Suchitepéquez in the older sources) has erupted several times since 1469, when Indian oral tradition recorded a violent outburst.[13] Other eruptions may have occurred in the sixteenth and eighteenth centuries.[14] The *Relación geográfica Atitlán* mentions two eruptions of Atitlán, one about 1505 and the other in 1541, the year in which Agua Volcano destroyed the old capital of Guatemala (now called Cuidad Vieja).[15] Ximénez reported continuous volcanic activity during the years 1717 to 1721.[16] The effect of these eruptions was frightful. Ashes and smoke spread over the towns, loud explosions and fire emerged from the mouth of the volcano, and earthquakes caused buildings to collapse. Intermittent activity continued between 1826 and 1853.[17]

Atitlán is called Huncat (Junc'at), or One Cargo Net, in the *Relación geográfica Atitlán.*[18] Tolimán, north of Atitlán, was called

Oxiqahol (Oxic'ajol), or Three Sons. The ancient name of San Pedro is not given, but in modern times it has been called Nimajuyú,[19] Big Mountain.

*Climate:* Three basic climatic divisions are found in the Tzutujil region. The first is the *tierra fría* ("cold land"), at elevations above 2,000 meters with average annual temperatures of less than 15°C. These higher valley and plateau areas are covered with pine-oak forests.

The second division is the *tierra templada* ("temperate land"), at elevations between 1,000 and 2,000 meters. This region contains hills covered with pine forests, as well as monsoon forests in the piedmont *(boca costa).*[20] The average annual temperature is between 15° and 20°C. During the day temperatures may be mild, and nights are usually cool, but daytime temperatures may exceed 35°C in the dry season (November to April).[21]

The third division is the *tierra caliente* ("hot land"), at elevations below 1,000 meters. It lies entirely within the Pacific coastal plain *(la costa),* and is characterized by park-savanna vegetation. Average annual temperatures are between 25° and 30°C during the day and between 20° and 25°C at night.[22] The daytime temperatures are high, and the nights are cool.

The climate of the Lake Atitlán basin is in the border zone between tropical and mesothermal, winter-dry.[23] In 1585 the basin climate was described as the best in the region because it was not too cold or too hot and received some humidity from the lake. Rainfall, usually occurring from midday throughout the afternoon, varies from year to year.[24]

The winds come up from the north and sometimes blow violently from midnight to 8:00 A.M. The south wind *(xcomel)* begins to blow around 8:30 A.M., making lake navigation in small crafts dangerous. The strong winds determine the peak times of lake use. The navigational skill of Tzutujil boatmen has been acclaimed since pre-Hispanic times. Most lake travel is carried on in the morning hours, when buyers visit the markets. The lake has facilitated trade and transportation among surrounding settlements, which are somewhat isolated from each other overland because of the difficult terrain.[25]

The piedmont has a tropical rainy climate.[26] The area receives between 1,500 and 2,000 millimeters of rain annually and has a few weeks of low rainfall between December and March.[27] The heaviest rains occur from June through September, but there may be a short dry period in midsummer *(canícula)* during July and

August.[28] The coastal plain is also tropical, with dry winter months (November to April).[29] In general, it receives less rainfall than does the piedmont; however, at some locations in a narrow strip about 60 kilometers inland from the coast and parallel to it unconfirmed oral reports have been made of more than 6,000 millimeters of rainfall annually.[30] This abundance of rain is caused by upslope winds, which stimulate afternoon thundershowers.

*Soils:* The soils of the Tzutujil region range from volcanic in the Atitlán basin to alluvial in the coastal plain.[31] The volcanoes have provided fertile soil in the highland area, where small-plot farming has been common since pre-Hispanic times.[32] The soils, composed of basalt, are loamy and yellowish to dark brown. Piedmont soils are composed of reddish loam over pumiceous, ashy subsoils and in the past served mainly as cacao lands. At altitudes below 700 meters the soils are primarily alluvial. At altitudes from 100 meters to sea level the soil is black silt.[33] The lower coastal plain has not been used for agricultural purposes in historic times.

### The Lake Atitlán Basin

Lake Atitlán is the second-largest lake in Guatemala, after Lake Izabal.[34] Several theories have been advanced to explain the formation of the lake. One theory supported by early geographers of the region, such as Karl Sapper, A. Dollfus, and E. de Mont-Serrat, held that Lake Atitlán was formed when drainage was dammed by lava flows erupting from the volcanoes along the southern shore.[35] Atwood described the lake as a caldera.[36] Williams, however, said:

It is believed that the basin originated by collapse along ring fractures as a result of magmatic movements at depth. If this is the correct interpretation, then the basin of Lake Atitlán should be spoken of as a cauldron subsidence. It should not be called a caldera, because . . . it was not produced by collapse of the tops of preexisting volcanoes.[37]

The average diameter of Lake Atitlán is 24 kilometers, and the maximum depth is said to be around 330 meters. The level of the lake fluctuates somewhat with the seasons and variation in annual rainfall.[38]

Samuel E. Lothrop divided the region surrounding Lake Atitlán into three areas: (1) the steep-walled rim of the basin on the north and east, (2) the lower slopes of the volcanic plain between Santiago Atitlán and San Lucas Tolimán, and (3) the western side of

the lake fronting on San Pedro Volcano. The first area is characterized by ridges rising steeply from the water's edge. Escarpments
alternate with small valleys largely composed of huge river boulders. Land suitable for agriculture is scarce, with relatively large
plots available only near the water's edge at San Pablo and on a
stream delta at Panajachel.[39]

The dominant feature of the second area is Tolimán Volcano
(3,134 meters high),[40] which is surrounded by rich volcanic slopes.
Much of the area contains good farming land, and towns stand on
nearby plateaus close to the lake's edge. Another significant geological feature of this area is the dome of Cerro de Oro, or Hill
of Gold (1,892 meters), reputedly so named because of the popular
belief that it contained buried treasure.[41] San Lucas Tolimán is
favorably situated near the southeast passage into the lowlands,
which makes it an important market center, as it probably was
in ancient times.

The western side of Lake Atitlán is not extensively populated
today, and probably was not in past times. San Pedro Volcano
(3,020 meters) rises sharply from the lake, and few areas are suitable for settlement or agriculture. The only farming land is near
San Pedro and San Juan at one end and Chuitinamit (altitude 1,695
meters) and Finca Chacayá at the other.[42] Santiago Atitlán and the
ruins of Chiya' stand near the important southwestern passageway
into the lowlands. This favorable location stimulated the growth of
the area as a regional commercial center, having a large population of merchants,[43] a situation existing since pre-Hispanic times.

*Highland Ecology:* Maize *(Zea mays)* has always been the major
crop of the highland Tzutujil region and was extensively traded,
especially in the lowlands, for piedmont and coastal products.[44]
The *Relación geográfica Atitlán* mentions several other crops
grown in the highlands in the sixteenth century that were common
in pre-Columbian times: squash *(Cucurbita* spp.); kidney bean
*(Phaseolus vulgaris);* avocado[45] *(Persea americana);* mombin, or
native plum (jocote; *Spondias* sp.); green sapote *(zapote ingerto;
Calocarpum viride);* Mexican sapote *(nahuazapote);*[46] and *quauhxonequile,* a tree bearing fruit with a cottony white flesh and green
kernels. The Indians also grew chili pepper *(Capsicum* spp.); sweet
potato *(camote; Ipomoea batatas);* potato *(Solanum tuberosum),*
cassava, or manioc *(yuca; Manihot* spp.); annona (Cherimoya; *Annona cherimoya);* tomato *(Lycopersicon* spp.); and chia *(Salvia
hispanica).*[47] An oil extracted from chia was mixed with toasted
maize to make a cooling drink.[48]

Chaparral and oak-pine vegetation predominate around Lake Atitlán.[49] Pine trees (*Pinus* spp.) grew abundantly on the slopes of the volcanoes, and the wood was used in houses and for other purposes. A white resin obtained from the pine trees was used as a medicinal poultice and probably for *ocotes,* pitchpine splints used for starting fires. Pine products were also made into a tar used for caulking ships.[50] Oak, alder, and strawberry trees *(madroños)* also grew in the area.

After the Conquest the Spaniards introduced several crops into the region around Lake Atitlán: fig, quince, grapefruit, pomegranate, plum, apple, peach, orange, sour lime *(limón),* sweet lime *(Citrus limetta),* and citron *(C. medica).* Anise *(Pimpinella anisum),* chick-pea (garbanzo; *Cicer),* and broad bean *(Vicia faba),* were other introduced crops.[51]

Fishing provided food and a marketable commodity for the lake settlements. Pickled *olomina (Fundulus guatemalensis)* and crab *(Potamocarcinus guatemalensis)* were marketed in the sixteenth[52] and seventeenth centuries,[53] a continuation of pre-Hispanic custom. Today small fish are strung on thin sticks, usually four or five on a stick, and toasted before they are taken to market.[54] Francisco Vásquez reported seeing small fish prepared in that way in the seventeenth century.[55] He also noted that places for catching crabs and pescaditos (*Peocilia sphenops* c. and v.) were roped off in the water and separated from each other.[56] In aboriginal times lineage heads may have assigned such holdings to families.

Traps have been used in recent times, in addition to the hook and line, to catch fish and crabs in Lake Atitlán. The traps of San Marcos and Santa Catarina Palopó were the most complex (these towns may have always relied heavily on fishing owing to the lack of farmland in their vicinities). The traps were enclosures formed of lake weeds and were constructed against the shore. They had two openings.[57] Lothrop also saw two fairly complex fishing traps in Santiago Atitlán. One was constructed of wattlework; the other was made of sod and stone.[58] The men would go out into deep water and begin splashing to drive the fish toward shore and into the trap.[59] Crabs were caught by young boys along the lakeshore and by older males, who went out on the lake in canoes and fished for them with baited lines.[60]

The highlanders hunted and domesticated animals such as deer, rabbits, wild pigs, armadillos, pacas, quail, jaguars, foxes, coyotes, coatis, turtle doves, wild pigeons, turkeys, two or three species of parrots, eagles, and macaws.[61] For the most part, however, these animals did not play a major role in the diet of highland communities. McBryde reported that small animals, especially armadillos, have been hunted with dogs in modern times at Tzununá.[62]

Wild ducks were once abundant in the lake area and were hunted by the men of Santa Catarina Palopó and Santiago Atitlán.[63] After the Conquest chickens were introduced and became an important food and tribute item in the Tzutujil area. Cattle and pigs have also been kept since colonial times.

### The Piedmont and the Lower Coastal Plain

The lowland area adjacent to the Lake Atitlán basin is divided into two main areas: the piedmont *(boca costa)* and the lower coastal plain *(la costa)*. The piedmont, an elevated zone whose boundaries roughly follow the 1,000-to-200-meter contours, is covered with the dense vegetation typical of a tropical monsoon forest.[64] Mahogany, sapote, ceiba, tropical-fruit, and palm trees grow along with many other trees, bushes, and vines. The land is mountainous, with ridges dividing swift-flowing rivers. During the rainy season the rivers overflow, making travel extremely hazardous and inhibiting communication with the highlands. In ancient and colonial times the piedmont was primarily given over to cacao groves, but today coffee is the major product.

The coastal plain, with an average width of about 35 to 60 kilometers, lies between the Pacific Ocean and the 200-meter contour.[65] Many streams originating on the volcanic slopes flow in torrents to the coastal plain, cutting deep, narrow ravines in the mountain slopes.[66] Some small streams flow across the area and merge with larger rivers running north to south. The Nahualate River, southwest of the Lake Atitlán basin, and the Madre Vieja, Seco, and Coyolate rivers, the last flowing east of the basin, are among the important in the Tzutujil portion of the coastal plain.

Along the Pacific shore are many rivermouths, hooks, spits, and sandbars. Today as in ancient times the inhabitants engage in fishing and making salt from seawater by the evaporation process. The rest of the coastal plain is swamp, gallery forest, or open grassland interspersed with tall trees.[67] The general vegetation pattern is one of park savanna, as opposed to the monsoon forest of the piedmont.[68] During the colonial period the Spaniards often used the savanna lands for pasturage. In the rainy season the outer lowlands become swampy, inhibiting travel in the area and discouraging settlement there.

*Lowland Ecology:* The major product of the lowlands in pre-

Columbian times was cacao *(Theobroma cacao),* but cotton *(Gossypium* spp.) was also grown there and was purchased for weaving in highland towns.[69] Patulul, a Tzutujil settlement in the fifteenth century, was a cotton producer in the period just after the Conquest.[70] Chicochín, another Tzutujil town, was a producer of a large quantity of cotton in the seventeenth century.[71]

Other crops were grown in the lowlands to provide fruit and vegetables for the tables of the lords and for the market. The land of Xeoj (San Bartolomé; see chap. 4, fig. 6) was fertile, and each year the inhabitants harvested three crops of maize in nearby forests.[72] Cacao, mombin, avocado, several varieties of sapote, banana, *quauhxonequile,* annona, mammee, and pineapple *(Ananas comosus)* were also harvested.[73]

Although there were no level fields in the Tzutujil colony Quioj (San Andrés; see fig. 6), the natives managed to harvest, in addition to cacao, maize, avocado, mombin, sapote, green sapote, nance *(Brysonima crassifolia),* and annona. Sweet potato, potato, Mexican sapote, guava *(Psidium guajava),* banana, chili, beans, squash, and cassava were other staples.[74] Tobacco and the stimulant herb contrayerva *(Dorstenia contrayerva)* were reportedly used by the Indians of the highlands and the lowlands, but the two plants may not have been grown in the Tzutujil area.[75]

The people of San Francisco, on the south side of Atitlán Volcano, planted many of the same crops (see chap. 11, fig. 11). They planted maize twice a year, depending for one crop on natural rainfall and for the other on irrigation by a method called *tonalmilley* (from *tonamil,* "winter crop").[76]

In 1579, Juan de Estrada, speaking of the Zapotitlán and Suchitepéquez areas, said that many fruits and vegetables were grown there and that in places where the thick forests were cut down crops grew abundantly. He also mentioned that achiote, or annatto *(Bixa orellana),* was mixed with cacao to make a chocolate drink and that there were many herbs and medicinal plants.[77] Melons were growing on the coast in 1579 and may have been aboriginal.[78]

Estrada also said that, after the Conquest, apples, figs, and wild grapes were grown in the lowlands along with the native plants, but most Spanish fruits did not do well there because of the heat.[79] Oranges, sweet and sour limes, and citron were also grown in some of Atitlán's lowland dependencies.[80]

Many varieties of animals were hunted as game in the lowlands. The skins of some may have been exchanged for highland products.[81] Jaguars, wild pigs, and tapirs were dangerous and may have been hunted mainly by members of the elite. Gourd and cord traps, nets, and dogs were probably used by commoners to catch birds, iguanas, and other small animals; for the larger animals the nobles probably used bows and arrows.[82] Turkeys, partridges, pheasants, quail, pigeons, chachalacas, parrots, deer, ducks, coyotes, martins, foxes, badgers, squirrels, armadillos, rabbits, eagles, macaws, coatis, iguanas, and pacas inhabited the lowland area and were probably hunted.[83] The Indians also ate domesticated native dogs.[84] Some birds, such as parrots, eagles, and macaws, were domesticated and raised for their feathers—the colored plumes were used in costumes for dance ceremonies.[85] In post-Conquest times chickens, sheep, goats, and cattle were raised in the lowlands.[86]

Fish from the rivers and tributaries served as supplementary food and items of trade. Mojarras *(Cichlasoma guttulatum)* and trout *(tepemechines)* were good fish but were available in only small quantities. In 1579 a few natives were observed fishing with hooks and nets, but only a few fished full time.[87] In recent times Tzutujil Indians have caught small fish, shrimp, and crabs in the Cutzán River, using hand nets for the rapids and cast nets for the pools. Larger shrimp were caught with split-bamboo funnel traps. The traps were set out at night in a line attached to a horizontal pole, with a vertical pole fence across the stream around them, with the wide ends facing upstream, and the trapped shrimp were removed the next morning.[88] During the late sixteenth century the Indians of Xeoj and Quioj also ate crabs and shrimp, which they probably caught in the same fashion in the streams near their towns.[89] Indians living on the lower coastal plain may have engaged in fishing and salt making in pre-Hispanic times, but little agriculture was practiced there.[90]

Such was the geographical and ecological setting in which Tzutujil society developed. Since ancient times the Tzutujils have tenaciously clung to their homeland surrounding Lake Atitlán, though the coastal area has been gradually removed from their control. Many of the same foods and trade products that were utilized in aboriginal times continue to be important today, along with those introduced by the Spaniards.

## CHAPTER 2

# The Archaeological Background

This chapter examines the archaeological remains in the Tzutujil region and establishes the pre-Hispanic sequence of cultural development. Documentary evidence relating to aboriginal Tzutujil settlement patterns and history will be discussed in the following chapters.

It is not always possible to relate archaeological information to that contained in written accounts,[1] but both kinds of data are necessary in gaining an understanding of life in ancient times. Archaeology primarily involves the excavation of nonperishable remains, such as ceramics and lithic objects. Such items are not usually the focus of the written sources, which generally concentrate on political and dynastic history.[2] Documents on the Tzutujil Mayas deal with the last two or three centuries before the Conquest, and it is necessary to rely on archaeology for information on earlier periods.

## Early Descriptions of the Ruins

Few of the sixteenth-century writers or later colonial historians mention any of the ruins in the Tzutujil area. For Chiya' that is not too surprising, for the capital was moved to the present site in the mid-sixteenth century because of the difficulty in reaching the pre-Hispanic location.[3] After the capital was moved, few Spaniards went to the old, no longer inhabited site. Other ruins were covered by new towns or were not noteworthy enough to be mentioned. Despite these problems, some documentary sources do mention the ruins.

The earliest description of Chiya' comes from Pedro de Alvarado, the Spanish conqueror of Guatemala, who wrote in the year 1524. After defeating the Quichés and the Cakchiquels, he marched on the Tzutujils: "I knew from the lords of [Iximché, the Cakchi-

quel capital] that seven leagues from here was another city . . .
and that they made war by the strength of the lake and canoes
they had." Alvarado described his first view of the Tzutujil capital:
"I went with thirty horsemen through the country at the shore of
the lake. . . . We came to an inhabited rock, which stood out in
the water."[4] Bernal Díaz del Castillo confirmed Alvarado's description: "The chiefs of [Iximché] informed [Alvarado] that in
their neighbourhood was a nation called the Altitans, who possessed several strong fortresses on the side of a lake, and who
refused to come in and make submission."[5]

In 1585 there were no fortresses or strong places in the highland Tzutujil territory other than the lake and some stone walls
in narrow places on the roads.[6] In the lowlands the same types
of walls were found.[7] The *Relación geográfica Aguacatepec*, also
written in 1585, contains a description of a pre-Hispanic temple
in Xeoj, a lowland dependency of Chiya': "In a large *qu* [temple]
where they made their idolatries and sacrifices to the demon,
there was a huge avocado tree in a corner of the said *qu* and
house of sacrifice which they had then, and thus the name [of
the town] became attached to it."[8]

Some colonial historians mentioned that Atitlán was the court
of the Tzutujil rulers, but they did not describe any ruins. Some
merely repeated Alvarado's description or that of Bernal Díaz.
Late in the seventeenth century Francisco Antonio de Fuentes y
Guzmán wrote an extensive account of pre-Hispanic Tzutujil history,[9] but he did not elaborate on the ruins beyond saying that
the palace and court were situated in "Atziquinijai" (Chiya') and
describing the site as "well defended like a strong plaza with
moats and castles, with large fortresses and prisons."[10]

Many nineteenth-century travelers described Lake Atitlán and
the contemporary towns, but they did not note any ruins. Most
took boats from Panajachel directly to Santiago Atitlán. The ruins
were usually on the outskirts of town and were in a very poor state
of preservation. They probably did not attract attention.

### Excavation in the Tzutujil Area

Don Carlos Luna, who visited the ruins on top of Chuitinamit in
the early twentieth century, was the first person to conduct excavations and provide a general description of the site. He said
that it was a true fortress, "with immense walls of stone which,
because of the brush and earth, could not be discovered from the

surface of the lake." Luna observed: "The southern part of the plateau is constructed higher up, and there is a platform there where undoubtedly vigilance was exercised. . . . From the northern part up to the platform there is a flight of stairs with huge worked stones. . . . In the center . . . there was a huge truncated pyramidal mound. . . . there are twenty-three more mounds in different parts of the plateau."

In an article originally printed in *El Heraldo* in 1910, Luna stated: "Judging by the vestiges which remain in Santiago Atitlán, San Pedro la Laguna, San Andrés, San Lucas and Santa Catarina la Laguna, these towns have been since times prior to the Conquest cities of much importance." He based his conclusion on the many worked stones in Santiago Atitlán and its environs as well as in neighboring towns. He mentioned seeing, besides carved stones, burials, stone walls, and a huge sacrificial stone.[11]

Luna made some excavations, but it was Samuel K. Lothrop who, in 1933, published the first archaeological report on the area. Lothrop was aware of Luna's excavations and provided further information on the artifacts that his predecessor had recovered. Lothrop first visited the ruins of Chuitinamit in 1928 and described the kinds of constructions that he found there. He saw "rough partly-shaped stones set closely together. In places, remaining fragments indicated that walls had once been stucco coated."[12]

It was not until 1932 that Lothrop was able to do more intensive work in the Lake Atitlán vicinity. In that year he surveyed much of the territory surrounding the lake and found about thirty sites.[13] He also carried out excavations at Chukumuk and Chuitinamit. The excavations were limited owing to time limitations and lack of cooperation by local landowners, but he was able to describe some interesting finds and establish the basic archaeological sequence for the Tzutujil highland area: Chukumuk I, Chukumuk II, and Chuitinamit.[14]

No comparable excavations have been carried out in the part of the piedmont and coastal plain that was dominated by the Tzutujils in the immediate pre-Conquest period. Edwin Shook has surveyed parts of the south coast and made sporadic excavations in the region. Excavations were also carried out by Sir J. Eric S. Thompson at El Baúl and by Lee A. Parsons at Bilbao, two sites just east of Tzutujil territory (fig. 1).[15]

During the summer of 1971, I conducted a cursory archaeological survey in the lake area between San Lucas Tolimán on the east and San Juan on the west. The goal of the survey was to

fill in information on smaller sites and to observe the condition
of the ruins Lothrop had described and excavated about forty
years before.

## Location of the Ruins

*The Highlands:* Today the most densely populated region of the
highland Tzutujil homeland is the southwestern side of Lake
Atitlán. Santiago Atitlán stands there, and smaller towns dot the
lakeshore west and east of the capital (fig. 3). Several reasons
lie behind this settlement pattern, which is similar to that of ancient times.

First, Lake Atitlán is the only permanent water source in the
highland Tzutujil area, and all the modern towns are within half
a kilometer or so of the lakefront. In 1585 the inhabitants of
Santiago Atitlán lived close to the lake, and it was their only
source of water.[16] Intermittent volcanic streams (mostly dry) near
Atitlán and Tolimán may flood the valley areas during the rainy
season. Many fill up only every seven or eight years, according
to modern residents. That water supply would be inadequate
for a large group of people and would also discourage construction of residences in the flood area. Such flooding may also have
been a factor in the choice of settlement locations in ancient times,
but evidence exists that some of the streams have shifted course
since the Conquest. For example, one stream now flows into
Chukumuk, and that site is not presently occupied.

Modern towns stand on rocky plateaus unsuitable for agriculture, and many of these areas were also inhabited before the
arrival of the Spaniards. Good agricultural land must have been
scarce in late pre-Hispanic times, when the population in the lake
region was around 48,000.[17] That the land surrounding Chuitinamit, Santiago Atitlán, and San Lucas was intensively cultivated
is clear from the remains of many ancient terraces.

One settlement factor important in pre-Conquest times was
defense. Plateaus and hilltops were good defensive locations, and
such considerations were important in the immediate pre-Conquest period, when warfare was endemic among the Quichés,
Cakchiquels, and Tzutujils. Chiya' was an excellent natural fortress, and the residents had a clear view in all directions, making
the site nearly immune to surprise attack. Xikomuk, another large
settlement between Santiago Atitlán and Cerro de Oro, is completely protected on the lake side, standing high on a rocky es-
carpment.[18] After the Conquest defensive considerations were no

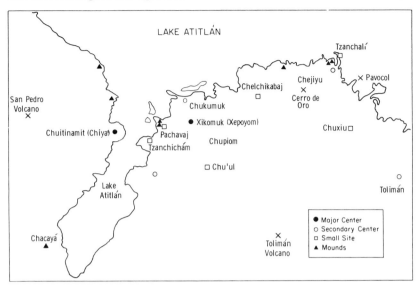

Fig. 3. *Pre-Hispanic archaeological sites of southwestern Lake Atitlán. This map is based upon sites mentioned in Lothrop 1933 and sites visited during the author's archaeological survey of 1971.*

longer important. The Xikomuk and Chuitinamit areas were not reinhabited after Santiago Atitlán was established by congregating inhabitants from ancient sites on both sides of the bay. The population was also much reduced by that time, and additional sites were no longer needed.[19]

Another important factor in determining the residential sites of the Tzutujils is the locations of the two passes into the lowlands. In Late Postclassic times (A.D. 1200-1524) piedmont lands south of Chiya' belonged to the Tzutujil elite and were important for cacao cultivation.[20] The passes were the major trade routes between the highlands and the lowlands. The lowland goods were drawn off by the highland nobility, and luxury items went to the Quiché, Cakchiquel, and Tzutujil courts from their respective lowland domains. Cacao was the most valuable product. Other important trade items were skins, feathers, and maize. Today the lowlands continue to provide income for the highlanders, who go there to trade or to work on coffee plantations.[21]

One of the lowland passes lies on the southwest, between San Pedro and Atitlán volcanoes, on the Nahualate River. It was in Tzutujil control at the time of the Conquest. The other pass lies on the southeast, between Tolimán and Fuego volcanoes, on the

Coyolate and Seco rivers. The Cakchiquels fought the Tzutujils for control of the southeastern pass. The Cakchiquels' drive along the eastern side of the lake to Palopó and Tolimán and their capture during the late fifteenth century of piedmont lands as far west as Patulul meant that the Tzutujils lost control of the pass.[22] That made the southwestern pass all the more important to the Tzutujils. The prime cacao lands were between San Antonio Suchitepéquez and Patulul,[23] and the major Tzutujil settlements, Chiya' and Xikomuk, flanked the southwestern pass into the vital cacao territory.

Because of these circumstances archaeological remains in the Tzutujil area tend to occur in a definite pattern. Lakefronts were never inhabited owing to the rocky terrain and the possibility of flooding. People probably went to the lakeshore to draw water and wash clothes just as they do today, and some pottery and obsidian are scattered throughout these areas, especially near large settlements. Isolated lakeshore areas are not presently used for anything, and that was most likely true in pre-Hispanic times as well.

Peninsulas less than one kilometer from settlements usually had some structures such as houses (Tzanchichám), mounds (Pachavaj), or possibly small fortresses guarding entrances to towns (Tzanchalí). Although these areas may presently be subject to flooding, as is true of Tzanchalí, that may not have been a problem in aboriginal times, when the lake was about ten meters lower.[24] Peninsulas farther than one kilometer from inhabited sites contain only a few sherds and pieces of obsidian.

All lower valley slopes are presently under cultivation and are prime maize land. Remains of obsidian, pottery, houses, and terraces are found throughout much of this area, near Santiago Atitlán, San Lucas, and Cerro de Oro.[25] Upper slopes near these towns contain a lighter scatter of artifacts and a few structures that may have been houses or possibly lookout posts. The absence of a firm chronology makes it difficult to say how many of the house mounds, lookout posts, large mounds, and possible fortresses were contemporary. It is clear, however, that the area was inhabited in ancient times.

The pattern of habitation in the highland Tzutujil region as reflected in the archaeological remains is somewhat different from the modern arrangement. Residential dwellings are now concentrated in focal towns, and defensive lookout posts and fortresses like Chiya' have disappeared. The upper and lower slopes are unoccupied, and two major archaeological sites, Chiya' and Xikomuk, have remained uninhabited since Conquest times. The entire highland domain of the Tzutujils has contracted. Tzutujil speakers now extend only from San Pablo to San Lucas, and today the latter town is more Cakchiquel than Tzutujil. The contemporary residential pattern is similar to the pre-Hispanic one in that most of the population continues to inhabit plateaus, and the greatest density is close to the southwestern pass.

*The Lowlands:* It is more difficult to describe the location of the ruins in the piedmont and coastal zones because we lack a thorough archaeological survey of the area once under Tzutujil control. According to the documentary sources, most settlements were small, and the inhabitants tended cacao groves for their lords.[26] Larger populations may have resided in Suchitepéquez and Nagualapa (fig. 6). Nagualapa had two caciques, or Indian rulers, in the early sixteenth century, but, like Suchitepéquez, it was probably subject to the Ajtz'iquinajay in pre-Columbian times.[27] It is not possible to say how large these settlements were, but they were probably somewhat larger than the other dependencies in the piedmont. One difficulty in describing pre-Hispanic settlements in this area is that some became extinct in colonial times (see chapter 4), and the inhabitants of others were congregated into new towns in the mid-sixteenth century.

The archaeological sites discovered by Edwin M. Shook in 1965 in the region below Lake Atitlán were clustered south of Tiquisate between the Nahualate and Madre Viejo rivers and dated from the Early to Late Classic periods (A.D. 300-1000). A few other scattered sites north of Tiquisate were for the most part from the same time period, but some Late Postclassic remains were found. Documentary evidence seems to indicate a shift in settlement to the area north of Tiquisate in Late Postclassic times, but it is impossible to say how many people continued to reside in the lands farther south.

## The Archaeological Sequence

*The Preclassic Period:* At the end of the Pleistocene, hunters and gatherers following a Paleo-Indian way of life may have inhabited parts of coastal and highland Guatemala.[28] These groups eventually settled down and engaged in simple farming. Such peoples may have wandered through territory that later became identified with the Tzutujils. No Early Preclassic (1500-1000 B.C.) sites have been found in the highland part of this region, but portions of the south coast near the Nahualate River may have been occupied. It is likely that simple Ocós-type villages stood all along the Pacific coast of Guatemala during this time. Such villages were small, lacked large structures, and concentrated on utilizing marine and estuary products along with simple farming.[29]

More information is available on the Tzutujil homeland from the Middle (1000-600 B.C.) and Late Preclassic (600 B.C.–A.D. 300) periods. The exact chronology of Chukumuk, a site east of Santiago Atitlán (fig. 3) excavated by Lothrop, is not clear, but it appears to have been inhabited by Middle to Late Preclassic times.[30] By the Late Preclassic Period, as Michael D. Coe and Kent V. Flannery noted, a population decline had occurred in the Ocós area, on the coast near the Mexican border, when settlement shifted to the piedmont. The major developments of the period took place in the piedmont and highlands.[31]

In some highland Middle Preclassic sites earthern structures may have appeared, especially at large centers like Kaminaljuyú.[32] Lothrop did not discover any structures at Chukumuk comparable to those at Kaminaljuyú,[33] but it is possible that small earthen constructions are buried beneath Santiago Atitlán. An important diagnostic of the period is Usulután pottery, which originated in eastern El Salvador and is decorated with reverse or negative wave- or cloudlike designs.[34] Lothrop found few Usulután sherds (about 2 percent of the total sherds recovered) at Chukumuk.[35]

Lothrop surveyed the lakeshore between Atitlán and San Lucas and found that much of the area close to the former was covered with the remains of ancient houses. He estimated the population density to have been well over 100 within 0.8 kilometer of Chuku-muk, but it is not known whether the houses were contemporaneous, or even whether they are Preclassic (as opposed to Classic). They are definitely ancient because houses similar to those built in historic times were not constructed until the Postclassic Period. Lothrop reported:

Each house covers a space of approximately 40 × 60 feet (12 by 18 m.) which is subdivided into several rooms. . . . The walls are of stone laid without mortar or adobe, and measure from 3 to 6 feet (1-2 m.) in thickness. . . . Present-day houses of the zutugil are of a different type of construction and are smaller than the ancient ones. They are invariably of frame construction lashed together with shredded bark, . . . and the roofs are thatched. The walls may be of stone, either with or without mortar . . . , but they do not support the roof, which rests on upright wooden posts. . . . In Santiago Atitlan the roof usually is capped by an inverted bowl. . . . in San Pedro a row of broken vessels covers the crest of the roof.[36]

It is difficult to confirm Lothrop's estimate of house-mound density because modern farmers have destroyed some ancient structures close to Atitlán, Cerro de Oro, and San Lucas. Many stones from ancient house walls have been removed and used to construct boundary markers separating fields.

Most of Lothrop's information on Chukumuk involved pottery analysis, from which he was able to make certain chronological deductions: "Near the surface of the ground at Chukumuk . . . there are found fragments of trade pottery also encountered at sites known to have been occupied at the time of the Conquest. Hence we feel certain that Chukumuk was inhabited until the Sixteenth Century, but the depth and variety of remains indicate many years of occupation before that time."[37] Although the Usulután sherds at the site place Chukumuk in the Middle Preclassic Period,[38] there was probably a larger occupation in the Late Preclassic. Most of the pottery found at Chukumuk (92 percent) was made locally, which demonstrates that the site was somewhat isolated or provincial, but it was inhabited by commoners, and perhaps a greater amount of trade and luxury wares will appear when other areas are excavated. Most of the trade pieces found at Chukumuk came from other parts of the highlands.[39]

Shook indicated that in the lowlands several sites lie between the Nahualate and Coyolate rivers.[40] Four have piedmont locations: Andes, Palo Gordo, Finca Sololá, and Variedades. The others are farther south, on the coastal plain: Finca Tolimán, Finca Zunil, Finca Ticanlu, and Sin Cabezas. Some of these, such as Sin Cabezas, may have been inhabited in Early or Middle Preclassic times.[41] Variedades was settled in the Late Preclassic Period, but no large structures date from that period. Remains of houses were found along with pottery, manos, metates, obsidian, and stone artifacts.[42] Most information on the area comes from later times, and the other sites will be considered in the appropriate periods.

*The Early Classic Period:* During the Early Classic Period (A.D. 300-700) new developments were made in agriculture, most notably in the construction of terraces.[43] Ancient terraces can be seen between Chuitinamit and Santiago Atitlán and between the latter and San Lucas Tolimán. They continue to exist because they are still in some use by contemporary farmers. The population gradually increased during the Late Preclassic and Early Classic periods, making it necessary for the Indians to use the volcanic slopes for fields; terraces prevented water from running off while preserving topsoil. A. L. Smith's archaeological survey of parts of the western highlands (reported in 1955) demonstrated an increase in the number of sites in the area during this time, but he did not include the Lake Atitlán region in his work.

No monumental architecture has been found associated with Chukumuk II, but that may be due to lack of excavation. An important feature linking Chukumuk with other highland Early Classic sites is the burial of bodies seated in a flexed position or covered with stones. Lothrop also described infants buried under an inverted bowl and a mass burial containing eight decapitated individuals of different sexes and ages, possibly all belonging to the same family. It appeared that the bodies had been placed in the grave, along with pottery, after which the entire grave had been covered with stones and earth. The skulls were found piled up in one corner of the burial.[44] It does not seem likely that the bodies were those of enemies taken as war captives because there were men, women, and children in the grave. The significance of the burial is unknown.

The Early Classic Period throughout the Maya highlands and the Petén lowlands is noted for the influence of Teotihuacán, a large site in central Mexico. This influence shows up strongly at such important Guatemalan centers as Kaminaljuyú and Tikal. Teotihuacán characteristics are hardly noticeable at such peripheral sites as Chukumuk, though molding is evident on some pottery sherds.[45]

Teotihuacán influence was greater in the piedmont lowlands. The Mexicans were probably interested in cacao, which may have been used as a drink and a medium of exchange as early as Olmec times and was well established by the Early Classic Period.[46] Control of the excellent piedmont cacao lands would have been important to an expanding power like Teotihuacán. Teotihuacán-style pottery, especially the cylindrical tripod with slab feet, has been unearthed in burials at Finca Tolimán.[47] The piedmont peoples may not have had Teotihuacán residents living among them, but they were probably dominated by Teotihuacanos or their retainers who were living at Kaminaljuyú.

Most of the Early Classic sites that Shook found in the piedmont lie between the Madre Vieja and Nahualate rivers. He was able to distinguish Early and Late Classic structures at these sites, and they seemed to be similar: ". . . an earth fill surfaced with

adobe floors and plaster, often bearing an over-all red paint."
Early Classic burials were found in the fill of pyramidal structures
and platforms and in open areas. Unlike the bodies in the Chukumuk
burials, these bodies were usually laid out in an extended position with objects placed around the heads and shoulders. Because
Shook also found some flexed and cross-legged burials as well as
mass interments, it is possible that at Chukumuk most of the dead
were laid out in an extended position.[48] Lothrop's excavation area
was not extensive, and his sample was small.

Trade ware was found in piedmont sites, mainly ware from the
highlands and the Petén lowlands. Parsons reported finding one
Early Classic sherd of pottery at Bilbao that was probably a trade
piece from Chukumuk.[49] It is identical to sherds illustrated by
Lothrop.[50] This would indicate that there may have been some
limited trade between the two areas. Also found at Chukumuk
were Patulul and Tiquisate wares from the Cotzumalhuapa region
dating from Middle Classic times.[51]

*The Late Classic Period:* Differences between the Early and the
Late Classic periods (A.D. 700–1000) cannot be distinguished by
the limited amount of archaeological excavation and survey that
has been carried out around Lake Atitlán. Chukumuk continued
to be inhabited during this period and remained on the periphery
of highland cultural developments.[52] One item of note is the possible reappearance of mushroom stones in the Atitlán area during
Late Classic times.[53] These stones have been found at a number
of sites in the central and western highlands, as well as in the
Pacific coastal area,[54] but it is not clear whether they are of Early
or Late Classic origin.

An important development at the close of the Early Classic
Period was the withdrawal of Teotihuacán as an influence in
Guatemala. The decline of Teotihuacán power was followed by
a new wave of influence emanating from the Tabasco-Veracruz
region. A Nahua-speaking people invaded the Pacific coastal and
piedmont areas of Guatemala in Late Classic times. They are
referred to as Pipils in early colonial documents.[55]

The Pipil intruders, who dominated the area from Palo Gordo
on the west to La Nueva on the east until 900, introduced a
new art style called Cotzumalhuapa into the piedmont.[56] Bilbao
and its nearby archaeological zone was the cultural center of the
Cotzumalhuapan style. Stone sculptures included ball-court panels,
stelae, monuments, and stone heads, and pottery types included

San Juan Plumbate and Tiquisate ware.[57] Mushroom stones were also found in the Cotzumalhuapa area; one from Finca Sololá is illustrated in Shook.[58]

Urn burials were found at Finca Ticanlu and Finca Tolimán, but this form of burial has not been found at Chukumuk.[59] Again, that may be due to lack of excavation, for urn burials have been found at other highland sites, Nebaj and Zaculeu.[60] Shook made the observation, however, that such burials seem to have occurred only sporadically in the highlands.

It is difficult at this point to determine the exact nature of the influence the Pipils had on the southern Lake Atitlán area. The Chukumuk area contained commoners, and a much closer relationship with the Pipils might be revealed by further excavations, particularly under the modern town. Ethnohistorical sources indicate that the Pipils and the Tzutujils were allies in Late Postclassic times,[61] and this relationship may have had greater depth than can be presently demonstrated.

*The Early Postclassic Period:* During the Early Postclassic Period (A.D. 1000–1200) much of the Guatemala highlands came under a new influence that may be linked with Toltec Chichén Itzá. Mexican artistic motifs and architectural forms were introduced or adopted at various sites. Some of these characteristics were long buildings, round or oval-shaped temples, round pillars of colonnaded buildings, and I-shaped ball courts.[62] During this time there was also increased movement away from open and undefended valley sites to hilltops and mountain slopes.[63] The lower slopes of the Tzutujil area probably had less population after this time.

John Fox, who surveyed Chiya' in 1972, included it among the acropolis sites settled in the Early Postclassic Period. Chiya' possessed several of the features of those sites. It had two plazas, one situated on an acropolis (fig. 4). A pyramidal temple stood in the center of the main plaza. This temple lacked the abrupt *talud-tablero* balustrades of Late Postclassic temples of the Quichés and had one stairway on each of the four sides. An administrative complex inhabited by the elite once was adjacent to the main plaza. The site was oriented 25 degrees east of north, whereas most acropolis sites are oriented from north to south, but it is not far off north-south. Intermediate-sized rectangular platforms composed the sides of the main plaza.[64] Other Mexican features noted at Chiya' were an I-shaped ball court situated on the plaza side opposite the administrative residential complex; a long, colonnaded

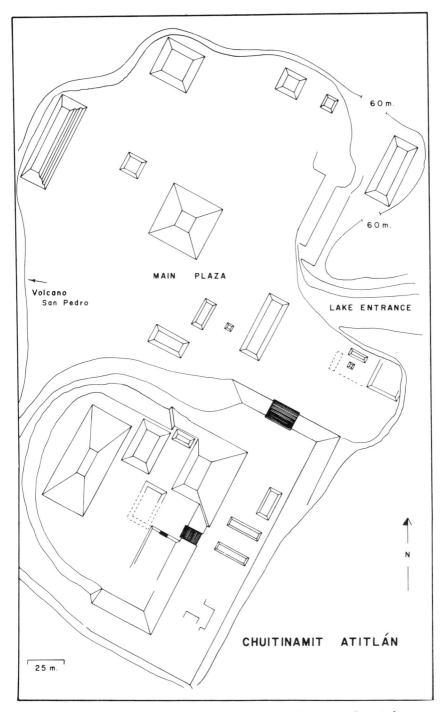

60 m.

60 m.

MAIN     PLAZA

Volcano
San Pedro

LAKE  ENTRANCE

N

CHUITINAMIT   ATITLÁN

25 m.

Fig. 4. *Chiya', a compass-and-pace sketch map. The main plaza is lower than the southern group of structures. The former has a large central pyramid surrounded by square and rectangular structures. The upper group has another pyramid and possibly the remains of a temple complex. From Fox 1978, p. 116.*

building in the complex;[65] and a carved-stone serpent.[66] Lothrop
noted the similarity of some carved stones at Chiya' to those at
Chichén Itzá.[67]

Fox believes that the most likely explanation for such Mexican
influence at these sites was the subjugation of the highland peoples
by small groups of warriors from the Gulf area. The highland
polities ruled by these Gulf peoples recognized cultural ties with
Chichén Itzá, but the distance between the centers led to cultural
differences and explains the absence of many Toltec features from
the highlands.[68] It may also be, however, that highland Guatemalans simply adopted some aspects of Mexican culture through
contact and were never actually conquered by invaders.[69]

Lothrop was unable to establish a fixed chronology for Chiya'
but said that most painted pottery found at the site was of the Late
Postclassic type (red and black on a white slip).[70] One sherd of
Tohil Plumbate, a common Early Postclassic diagnostic ware, was
found.[71] Fox, however, says that carved ware found at Chiya',
which is "characterized by red to orange slip, with a panel around
the vessel containing heavy-line incised or carved decoration, often
painted white," is of Early Postclassic date.[72] This pottery continued to be used at the site throughout the Late Postclassic
Period. Robert M. Carmack believes that Chiya' is probably Middle
Postclassic but that further archaeological excavation is necessary
to demonstrate whether this dating is correct.[73]

Significant changes took place on the south coast at the end
of the Late Classic Period. Many of the major Cotzumalhuapan
sites were abandoned, and there appear not to be any Early Postclassic sites in the coastal area at elevations from 0 to 300 meters.
Above 300 meters many small sites remained.[74] Tohil Plumbate
has been found in the Tiquisate region,[75] but little information is
available on the actual number and characteristics of Early Postclassic settlements in the piedmont.

*The Late Postclassic Period:* At the beginning of Late Postclassic
times (A.D. 1200–1524) another wave of Mexican influence swept
over the Guatemala highlands, apparently coming once again from
the Tabasco-Veracruz area.[76] The documents say that small migrant
warrior groups entered Guatemala during this period and that
they were the ancestors of the Quichés, the Cakchiquels, and
possibly the Tzutujils as well. These peoples were said eventually
to have established capitals at K'umarcaaj (Utatlán), Iximché, and
Chiya', respectively.

Late Postclassic sites were usually chosen for their defensive advantages, for reasons of religious symbolism, or to reserve bottomlands for agriculture.[77] They were the homes of the elite, their servants, and their administrators. The common people lived in small hamlets or were scattered on the slopes or in surrounding territory, close enough to the capitals to be able to reach them quickly in times of crisis.

Chiya' was a fairly typical hilltop settlement. In 1933, Lothrop described evidences of occupation, including terraces, retaining walls, mounds, plaster floors, pictographs, and huge quantities of rubbish, found chiefly on the southern and eastern slopes. His report is valuable because it provides the first drawings of these features and of the site. He also discovered through comparison of the Chiya' (Chuitinamit) ceramics with those of Chukumuk that the former were much more elaborately designed and painted than were those across the bay: "This disparity of types quite possibly may be due to social inequality, for Chuitinamit was a royal residence."[78] There may not have been as much disparity between Chiya' and Xikomuk, another large Postclassic site near Chukumuk.

Writing of Iximché, the Cakchiquel capital, Jorge F. Guillemín said that an artificial moat enclosed the center in which the nobility lived. The commoners lived outside the moat.[79] This description tends to support Lothrop's supposition that Chiya' was inhabited mainly by nobles. Some house mounds and the remains of what may have been small temples are still seen on the ridges of Chuitinamit, but between Chiya' and Chacayá only terraces were seen. This confirms that most of the population lived across the bay, as Lothrop hypothesized.

Lothrop described three structures on the eastern edge of the main plaza at Chiya'. According to popular legend, these were supposed to have been the residences of the Tzutujil ruler, his guards, and his retainers. The outerside of the three structures rested on stone terraces, and one had a white cement floor. A large temple stood near these buildings: "The most obvious feature of the main plaza is a large pyramidal substructure . . . made of adobe and rubble. . . . This probably was the principal temple of the city, and the discovery of bodies near the northwestern corner suggested that human sacrifice had taken place there."[80] This temple may have been similar to the one mentioned in the *Relación geográfica Aguacatepec.*[81] According to Lothrop, excavations in the upper terrace revealed that "stone and adobe buildings painted red once stood upon the mounds. . . . To the north there are traces of retaining walls and a stairway of stone."[82]

Today the foundations of the residential structures and of the main pyramid remain, but the entire site has suffered from the effects of cultivation.

Noteworthy artifacts at Chiya' described by Lothrop were carved boulders, some having circular pits or rectangular basins on the upper surface, which were probably used to collect human sacrificial blood.[83] He also included drawings of pictographs in the Mixteca-Puebla style characteristic of the Late Postclassic Period.[84] Murals in the same style were found by Guillemín at Iximché.[85] Today most of the pictographs reported by Lothrop have disappeared.

Xikomuk—probably the Xepoyom of *The Annals of the Cakchiquels*—was another major center in Late Postclassic times. No exact chronology has been established for the site, but most of the pottery found there was late. Some sherds, however, date from earlier times. According to Lothrop, the ruins at Xikomuk "consist of a number of mounds and house foundations, being the largest conglomeration of this kind we saw on the south shore of Lake Atitlan, with the exception of Chuitinamit." It was a large center, with many mounds, an enclosed court, terraces, and residential buildings, most of which are now in a poor state of preservation.[86] Traces of ancient walls, terraces, streets, and refuse were found throughout the Chukumuk-Xikomuk area.[87]

Fox argues that Xikomuk resembles the administrative plazas built by the Quichés at subjugated acropolis sites.[88] If that is true, Xikomuk may have been constructed during the late fourteenth or early fifteenth century. If future excavations demonstrate the presence of Quiché artifacts, then the Quiché conquest of the Tzutujil at that time will be substantiated.

Lothrop described the location of several mounds, house foundations, terraces, and carvings at Chicayal (Chacayá), Pachiuak (Pachavaj), Tzanchichám, and Cerro de Oro. He also noted the presence of several other mounds between Chuitinamit and San Pedro.

On the steep, forested slopes of the western side of Lake Atitlán between Finca Tzantziapá and Chuitinamit are two isolated mounds. The first, a mound of yellow earth, is about 100 meters from shore "on the next to last ridge of the Volcano San Pedro visible to the north from the summit of Chuitinamit. Around 0.8 kilometer northeast is the second mound, at Finca Tzantziapá, just behind a small bay.[89] I visited the last-mentioned mound in 1971 and observed that obsidian and pottery sherds surrounded it for a distance of about 7 meters. From these mounds it is possible to see across the lake in three directions. They would have been good defensive outposts flanking the capital, or they may have been temples; it is difficult to determine their function without excavation, and it is possible that they were constructed in different time periods. If they were built before Postclassic times, when defensive considerations may have been less important, they could have been temples.

Cerro de Oro (Chejiyu) also provides an excellent view of the entire lake region. Lothrop was told that there were remains on the hilltop and base on the inland side,[90] and that was later verified by a resident priest at Santiago Atitlán, who climbed the hill and observed a stone altar there. The altar, could, however, be a post-Conquest shrine.

On the northwest side of the Tzanchichám Peninsula, Lothrop found terraces and house foundations and a group of boulders carved with pictographs.[91] In 1970 construction was begun at the site, and the carved boulders were used as building material for a new chalet. Only the house foundations and terrace walls remained in 1971, and most of those are probably gone by now.

Lothrop also described a carved boulder at Pachavaj similar to boulders found at Chiya'. It was no longer to be found by 1971, but two mounds, each about two meters high, seen in 1932, were still standing. The carving Lothrop described was about two meters long and appeared to have a jaguar on top with a hole in the middle of its back. The tail and limbs were carved with rows of horizontal lines. Such lines were also observed by Lothrop on boulders at Chiya'; thus the Pachavaj boulder is very likely of Late Postclassic date.[92]

Structural remains similar to those found on Tzanchichám, though fewer, were also found on Tzanchalí, a peninsula north of Cerro de Oro. The structures consisted of one or two rectangular rooms enclosed in low walls of rocks or boulders. The buildings stood on the highest part of the peninsula and may have been a small fortress guarding the entrance to the settlement. No pictographs or carved boulders were found at the site. Two mounds can be seen halfway between the modern town and the lakefront. The mounds, completely covered with brush, appear much as they did in Lothrop's time. They probably date from the late period. The hamlet had a small population in pre-Hispanic times, and today Cerro de Oro is still a dependency of Santiago Atitlán with only a small population.[93]

Presently, only a few pottery sherds are found on Pavocol Peninsula, confirming similar observations made there by Alfred V. Kidder and Earl H. Morris in 1932.[94] Such artifactual scatter characterizes all the peninsulas in the highland Tzutujil area that are more than one kilometer from major and secondary centers.[95]

San Lucas Tolimán, San Juan, San Pedro (Chi-Tzunún-Choy), and San Antonio Palopó show evidence of pre-Conquest occupation, and they gained in population after the Conquest, when new towns were formed (fig. 5). Gerardo Aguirre observed miniature pyramids at several locations in the vicinity of San Pedro.[96] Several mounds were near the lakefront, about 1.6 kilometers east of town.[97] These mounds were still visible in 1971. I also saw a partly covered wall about 2 meters high and 6 meters long composed of shaped stone blocks. A second wall stood about 16 meters from the first. Aguirre also said that he saw certain remains of past construction of San Pablo (Chupalo), and local tradition says that the town was once situated north of the modern location.[98]

Near of the modern town of San Juan (pre-Hispanic name unknown), Lothrop found five mounds ranging from 1.8 to 4.6 meters high. Four of the mounds formed a small plaza, while the fifth stood apart. Stone sculpture was visible in the plaza of San Juan in 1932; one sculpture was carved from the same kind of stone used for the statues at Chacayá. Another had the same parallel lines cut on the limbs as those on the animal figure from Pachavaj.[99] The design places the carving in the Late Postclassic Period.

In modern-day San Pedro, Santiago Atitlán, and San Lucas obsidian chips and pottery sherds are scattered all over the streets, an indication that those locations were inhabited in pre-Hispanic times. When the foundations were sunk for a rectory in Santiago, a stone serpent head was unearthed. Farmers continually turn up small statues and other objects in fields near the modern towns. It is difficult to determine exactly the kinds and numbers of structures that stood on the plateaus in ancient times, but it is likely that they were more than simple house mounds. The type of statuary found at or near these locations indicates the existence of larger buildings of religious or administrative nature that were subsidiary to Chiya'. San Pedro, San Juan, San Pablo, and San Lucas remain fairly small towns today, and they probably never attained the concentration of population of the southwestern corner of the lake.

The region between San Antonio Palopó and San Lucas has no visible structural remains. The documents indicate that it was a

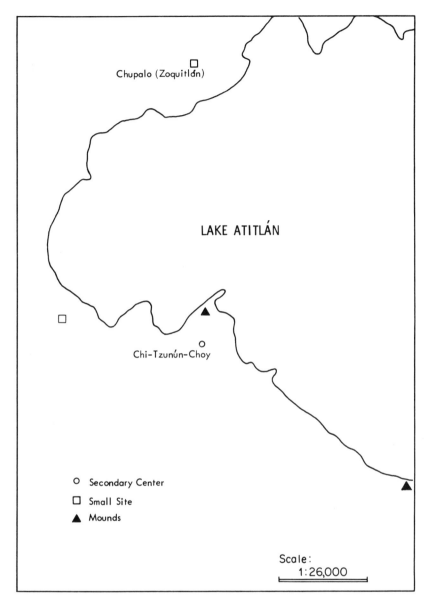

Fig. 5. *Pre-Hispanic archaeological sites of northwestern Lake Atitlán.*
*The unnamed box marks the ancient site of San Juan. Map based on*
*author's archaeological survey of 1971; Carrasco 1967b, p. 318; Lothrop*
*1933, pp. 100-101; Aguirre 1972, pp. 40-43.*

frontier area and that Palopó was a Tzutujil outpost that was
finally captured by the Quichés.[100] Cakchiquel speakers were living there when the Spaniards arrived. Because of the lack of
thorough excavation in the Tzutujil area there is no good chronology for the smaller highland sites. Therefore, they have been
discussed in the Late Preclassic Period, but some of the remains
may be earlier.

Very little information exists on Late Postclassic archaeological
remains in the piedmont area. Shook mentioned finding textile-
marked pottery sherds from the period at Andes, on the south slope
of Atitlán Volcano. These sherds were remnants of comales (tor-
tilla griddles); similar sherds have been found at Variedades and
other nearby sites, which had a Late Postclassic occupation.[101]

Variedades is the only site of Late Postclassic date in the area
that has been partly excavated. As mentioned earlier, Shook found
pottery, manos, metates, and obsidian, and stone artifacts. Variedades was not a very impressive site, probably having comprised
mainly structures built of perishable materials. Fragments of burned
adobe containing impressions of small poles indicated that there
were once houses at the site.[102]

Little is known about the ruins of former Tzutujil coastal dependencies. Many of the locations have been forgotten, and no
survey has been made of the region to determine their location
and condition. Most of the information that we have comes from
the documentary sources and will be discussed in chapter 4.

In summary, the modern Tzutujil settlement pattern around Lake
Atitlán is similar to the pattern of ancient times. Many of the
factors that helped determine the pre-Hispanic configuration continue to be important today. The lake is still the major source of
water, rocky plateaus are inhabited, and most of the Tzutujils still
live near the southwest passage, to facilitate trade with the lowlands. Defensive considerations, paramount in Postclassic times,
are no longer important, and the people are not scattered throughout the upper and lower slopes as they were in Preclassic and
Classic periods.

Today the piedmont area is not primarily Tzutujil, and the
settlement pattern has changed considerably since pre-Conquest
times. Less information is available on ancient sites in the coastal
area owing to lack of surveys and excavations. The earliest coastal
settlements were farther south than those of later times.

Most of the early information about the Lake Atitlán area centers on Chukumuk, which was inhabited by commoners. No monumental architecture of the Preclassic and Early Classic periods has been found in the highland Tzutujil area. Most pottery was local, but Usulután ware was present, possibly indicating trade with other areas as early as the Middle Preclassic Period.

During Early Classic times Guatemala came under the domination of Teotihuacán. Chukumuk shows only traces of this influence, but it is prominent in some of the coastal sites lying between the Madre Vieja and Nahualate rivers. Lowland settlements may have been important in cacao production. There may also have been some contact between the piedmont and Chukumuk during this time, but trade wares are scarce in both areas.

At the close of the Early Classic Period the piedmont was invaded by people from the Tabasco-Veracruz region who produced an art style now called Cotzumalhuapan. Although the Pipils dominated the lowland area, it is not possible to say at this time whether the highland area came under Pipil influence.

In Early Postclassic times much of the Guatemala highlands region came under Mexican influence that may have stemmed from Chichén Itzá. It is possible that Chiya' was constructed at this time, because the site contains some structures and artistic motifs that are similar to those of Chichén. Archaeological excavation is necessary to confirm such an early date of occupation. Many Cotzumalhuapan sites had been abandoned by that period, and the piedmont settlement pattern of the time is not well known. That the Tiquisate region continued to be occupied is indicated by the presence of Tohil Plumbate, a diagnostic of Early Postclassic times, at several small sites there. The outer coastal area was abandoned.

In the Late Postclassic Period another wave of influence arrived, again probably from the Tabasco-Veracruz area. Documentary information tells of small invading warrior groups, but their presence has not been confirmed by excavation in the Tzutujil area. Chiya' became the capital of the highlands, with secondary centers at San Pedro, Santiago Atitlán, and San Lucas. Xikomuk, another important site, may have been constructed by the Quichés after they conquered the Tzutujils.

Defense continued to be important because of frequent warfare, and it is possible that outposts were constructed on peninsulas and upper slopes near Chiya' and flanking the entrance to the southwest pass. All the constructions may, however, be of earlier date and could be isolated temples or other structures. The Late Postclassic configuration cannot be properly interpreted without further excavation and survey.

Practically no archaeological information exists on the piedmont during this time, though it is clear from documentary sources that the area was controlled by the Tzutujil rulers and that cacao was the most important product of the region.

## CHAPTER 3

# Aboriginal History

We have some documents containing legends, myths, and factual data relating to the Tzutujils and their history before the Conquest. These refer mainly to Postclassic times and were written in the early sixteenth century by Quichés or Cakchiquels. Nothing is presently available in the Tzutujil language, with the exception of the *Título San Bartolomé,* which apparently describes events occurring in the early sixteenth century.[1]

## The Beginnings of Tzutujil History

Information relating to early Tzutujil history is contained in a small *título* used by the nineteenth-century Maya scholar Charles Étienne Brasseur de Bourbourg. This document tells something of the history of the Tzutujils before their arrival in the Guatemalan highlands. According to the account, the Tzutujils and other highland groups were once part of a powerful people who lived "on the other side of the seas," probably somewhere in the Tabasco-Veracruz area. They engaged in warfare with nearby groups and were defeated. Pursued by their enemies, the defeated warriors and their families left their homeland in boats, embarking from Wucub Pek, Wucub Ciwan (the Seven Caves and the Seven Ravines), another name for Tula, or Tollan, the great Toltec capital.[2]

The migrants went to a place called Xenimain and settled there in deserted areas. In time they became strong again and founded various states, the one called Tula being the most important. The location of Xenimain is not known, and the settlement called Tula may have been different from the one mentioned in *The Annals of the Cakchiquels* and in the *Popol Vuh.* The name Tula may have been used by many peoples to designate an important capital, or legend may have identified a settlement in the deserted locality with the Tula at Chichén Itzá. *Tolan* means "solitude" or "desert" in the Quichean languages; the meaning may account for the use of the word as a name. War eventually broke out again, and the migrants were driven out of the area and arrived in the Guatemalan highlands.[3]

Much more information on this period appears in the *Annals* and in the *Popol Vuh,* which describe the arrival of the Tzutujils in Tula along with several other groups.[4] Carmack has demonstrated that these small warrior bands were Mexicanized Mayas who migrated to the Guatemalan highlands from the Tabasco-Veracruz region.[5] The Quichés migrated east around 1225-50,[6] and the Tzutujils may have done so about the same time. Eventually the Mexicanized groups conquered highland Maya peoples who spoke Quichean languages. Many of them married Guatemalan women and were gradually absorbed by the people they conquered, even to the point of losing their own language, which was probably Chontal.[7]

According to *The Annals of the Cakchiquels,* which concentrate on the history of that group, the Tzutujils were the first of the "Seven Tribes" to arrive at Tula. The Cakchiquel group, composed exclusively of warriors, arrived last.[8] Other native documents also name the groups that arrived in the Toltec capital, among them the Quichés, the Tamubs, the Ilocabs, the Rabinals, the Cakchiquels, the Tz'iquinajays, and the Tzutujils.

According to the *Annals* these peoples arrived in Tula and gave the ruler tribute, including precious green stones, metal, garlands fastened with green and blue feathers, cacao, paintings, and weapons. This group of gifts may have been a special offering and does not necessarily imply that these peoples regularly paid tribute to Tula. That city was considered the seat of political authority, and gifts were given by visitors in exchange for commissions as legitimate colonizing groups. According to the *Annals,* the ruler of Tula commanded them to "go to where you will see your mountains and your valleys; there on the other side of the sea are your mountains and your valleys. . . . These are the gifts I shall give to you, your wealth and your domain."[9] The *Título Tzutujil* also mentions that the groups left Tula because of "new dissensions" that led to fighting and the expulsion of the migrant warrior groups from the area.[10] Again, however, this Tula may have been different from the Tula of the *Annals* and the *Popol Vuh.*

The Cakchiquels also received at that time the "idols of wood and of stone," and the Quichés received "the substitutes [idols], reminders of Former for you, and Shaper for you." Former (Tz'akol) and Shaper (Bitol) were the twin creator-gods of the Quichés.[11]

Presumably the rest of the groups also received idols. In later times the main god of Chiya' was Sakibuk, or White Smoke.[12]

With their new gods and vested Toltec authority the colonizing groups set forth to seek new domains. They remembered the words of the ruler of Tula: "Truly, your glory shall be great. . . . You shall become great with the wealth of the wooden shields. Do not sleep and you shall conquer."[13] They fought enemies called the Nonoualcas and the Xulpitis, "who were found on the shore of the sea and were in their boats." The migrant bands originating in the Tabasco-Veracruz region must have been skilled in sea warfare because they defeated their enemies and used their canoes to cross the sea.

The migrants reached a city called Zuiwa and attacked the inhabitants. This "formidable city" can probably be identified with Xicalango, on the Laguna de los Terminos, a great commercial trading center in Postclassic times. This time they were defeated, and they decided to go their separate ways in search of new lands: "We dispersed in the mountains; then we all departed, each tribe took its road, each family followed its own."[14]

On the basis of archaeological evidence Fox argues that the migration described in the documents actually consisted of at least three distinct movements. The first may have taken place at the end of the Classic Period, around A.D. 900. A second migration into the Guatemalan highlands may have occurred during the Early Postclassic Period, while Chichén Itzá was still dominant in Yucatán. This migration is of specific interest to the Tzutujils' history if, as Fox states, they entered the highlands at this time and constructed an "acropolis site" on top of Chuitinamit. Around 1200-50 the third group came, including the Quichés, the Rabinals, and the Cakchiquels.

Fox also hypothesizes that these last migrants may initially have been subordinate to the acropolis groups, such as the Tzutujils.[15] Later the Tzutujils were conquered by the Quichés and given a place in Quiché history. If it is correct that Quiché invaders built Xikomuk, then it is possible that this was the time when the Tz'iquinajay lineage, which may have been related to the Quiché lineage of the same name, came to dominate Chiya'. Wallace and Carmack point out that no documentary evidence is available to support this interpretation.[16] Only a more thorough excavation of Chiya' can resolve the question of its antiquity.

Stephen F. Borhegyi believed that the Cakchiquels and Tzutujils followed a different route into the highlands from that of the Quichés. He believed that they went along the Grijalva and Jatate rivers through Chiapas and entered the Guatemalan highlands somewhere in the northwestern part of the modern Department of Huehuetenango. The Quichés went southward along the Usumacinta River and its tributaries. He does not say that the Tzutujils preceded the Cakchiquels, however.[17] Carmack mentioned a similar route for the Quichés but did not mention a separate route for the Cakchiquels and the Tzutujils.[18]

According to the native chronicles, the groups arrived at a mountain called Council (Chipixab),[19] where they deliberated together. The *Popol Vuh* describes what happened when they arrived:

> They gathered themselves together there,
> All the Quiche peoples
> And Tribes,
> And there they all took counsel
> As they deliberated together.[20]

The migrants divided up the highland territory among themselves.

An event of major importance that took place while the Quichés were on top of Chipixab was "the dawning" *(sakiribal),* or ritual of the morning star. All the groups participated in this event, which centered on the moon, the stars, and, most important, the appearance of Venus, the morning star, before the rising of the sun. After the sun rose, the people made sacrifices, burned incense, danced, and sang.[21] Carmack thinks that "the dawning" may be similar to the Aztec ceremony beginning the fifty-two-year cycle.[22] All the groups observed this ceremony, demonstrating that by that time they were probably settled in their own lands. For example, the Cakchiquels celebrated "the dawning" at Pantzic and at Paraxóne, a mountain some distance from their final capital, Iximché.[23]

Sometime after the first "dawning" (around 1250), the Quichés moved to Jakawitz and constructed a fortified hilltop center there.[24] From this settlement they began the conquest of peoples in the surrounding region. The rest of the migrant groups gradually expanded to other areas. The move from the Quiché center was not a sudden large-scale migration but a slow occupation of the lands near Jakawitz.[25] This period was characterized by a great increase in militarism, as Mexican methods of warfare and settlement patterns were introduced or intensified in the highlands. A greater tendency toward urbanism developed, as many of the older open land and valley settlements were abandoned. One reason for the increase in warfare was the new groups' need for sacrificial victims for the gods.[26] They sought as well to conquer new lands and to extract tribute from subject peoples.

It was also a time of great movement as each group searched for a place to settle. The Tzutujils appear to have reached Lake Atitlán before the Cakchiquels.[27] The Cakchiquels had wandered all around, even passing by Chi-Tzunún-Choy, but they did not stay there.[28]

Sometime between 1325 and 1350 the Quiché leader C'ocaib journeyed back to Tula.[29] The *Título Totonicapán* explains the reason for this trip:

"The time has arrived to send ambassadors to our father and lord Nacxit: that he will know the state of our affairs; that he will furnish us means so that in the future our enemies shall never defeat us; that they shall never belittle the nobility of our birth; that he will designate honors for us and for all our descendants; and that, finally, he will send public offices for those who deserve them."[30]

The Cakchiquels also sought new symbols of political authority from the Toltecs and visited another ruler named Nacxit, this one in Valil, which may have been another name for the Nahua-speaking town Acasaguastlan, in the Motagua Valley: "They came before the sons of *Valil* . . . ; they came before *Mevac* and *Naxcit*. . . . Then they entertained them, and the Ahauh Ahpop and Ahpop Qamahay were chosen. . . . the Lord Nacxit said: 'Climb up to these columns of stone, enter into my house. I will give you sovereignty.'"[31] There is no record that the Tzutujil leaders ever made a return trip to Tula. If they did not, they would have had less political status than that of the Quichés and the Cakchiquels. When C'ocaib returned to Jakawitz, all the groups, including the Ajtz'i-quinajay lineage, met together at the center to rejoice at the insignia brought from Tula.[32]

It has been suggested that the Quichés, Cakchiquels, Rabinals, and Tzutujils had a loose confederation during these early times.[33] One reason for the Quichés' dominance over the others was that they had received the most powerful god during the original visit to Tula. The main reasons, however, were their military successes and the symbols of authority that they had received during the second visit to Tula. The Tzutujils were second in rank in the confederation because they were the first to enter Tula, along with the Quichés.[34] They were also culturally more distinct from the Quichés than were the Rabinals and the Cakchiquels, who enjoyed less independence from Quiché dominance.[35]

There are references to Quiché-Tzutujil marriages from this period, and since many Quiché lineages were represented among the Tzutujils in later times, the practice was probably a long-

standing one.[36] Such marriages would facilitate military alliances
and maintain ties among the groups of the confederation. Information is also available on Tzutujil-Cakchiquel marriage ties.
According to the *Annals,* the Cakchiquels wandered about until
they reached the northern shores of Lake Atitlán. They crossed
the lake and agreed to divide it in half, sharing it with the Tzutujils, who had previously built their hilltop center, Chiya', on the
western shore. The Cakchiquel warriors needed wives and were
willing to fight the Tzutujils for women, but the Tzutujil ruler
decided to exchange wives without fighting.[37] According to the
*Título Xpantzay 3,* the wives of the Cakchiquel Xpantzay ancestors were called Xkuhay and Xtziquinajay and were referred to as
"our mothers and grandmothers."[38] According to Pedro Carrasco,
X, which is sometimes used as a feminine indicator, here designates the female counterparts of the Tzutujil Ajcojay and Ajtz'i-
quinajay lineages.[39] This account of the division of the lake and
the giving of wives may be a mythical explanation for the increasing pressure from the Cakchiquels on the northeastern and eastern
portions of Lake Atitlán. Dividing the lake and forming marriage
alliances with the Cakchiquels kept the peace.[40]

Another dawning ceremony appears to have occurred about this
time (1325-50), and the *Annals* specifically mentioned the Tzutujils as witnessing this ceremony in Tzala (Sololá): "The Zutuhils
wished to see their dawn in *Tzala,* but the tribes had not finished
making the fire when the sun rose . . . in the sky and, mounting
above the place called *Queletat,* spread its light and came to *Xepoyom.*" After the ceremony, "the warriors and the tribes quickly
abandoned [those places] because they wished to go immediately
to be united again and to live on the shores of the lake."[41]

## *The Period of Quiché Expansion*

The Quichés founded a new capital at Pismachi soon after C'ocaib
returned from his journey to Tula.[42] The ruins of this center are
slightly south of the modern Santa Cruz del Quiché. The Cakchiquels' main settlement was Mukbalsib Bitol Amak', in southwestern Chichicastenango.[43] From that time they no longer chose their
wives from the Tzutujil Ajcojay and Ajtz'iquinajay lineages.[44] This
custom seems to have stopped because of Quiché pressure; during
the time of K'ucumatz members of the Quiché nobility became the
preferred marriage partners of the Cakchiquels.

The establishment of Pismachi down on the plain indicates that
the local inhabitants were sufficiently subdued to allow the Quichés

to expand from their hilltop center. The new capital was constructed with adequate defenses, however.[45] Fox interprets this movement as representing a shift of power away from earlier acropolis centers to the Quiché invaders.[46] The second journey to Tula was probably tied to the establishment of a new capital and the need for new offices and symbols.

Quiché power was greatly expanded during the Pismachi period under two important leaders, C'otuja (1375-1400) and K'ucumatz (1400-25). It is not clear whether these rulers were actually the same man, as Carmack has previously argued, or two successive rulers. They are regarded as two rulers in the following discussion.[47]

By this time the Cakchiquels and the Tzutujils were definitely under Quiché hegemony. Cay Noj and Cay Batz, who were made Cakchiquel rulers by the Quichés, served as tribute collectors among the Tzutujils. At that time each subject group gathered tribute items and gave them to appointed officials like Cay Noj and Cay Batz when they appeared in town: "All the people brought them the tribute when they went to receive it." The Tzutujils were among the peoples visited for tribute collection. The Ajtz'iquinajay was not content with paying tribute to the Quiché ruler, however. He devised a scheme to gain possession of the treasure that Cay Noj and Cay Batz had already received.

Previously the Ajtz'iquinajay had preserved peace between his people and the Cakchiquels by agreeing to give wives to the Cakchiquel warriors. This time, however, the Tzutujil ruler had to resort to trickery to obtain such a favorable marriage. While marriage was a means of alliance, it was also used as a means of subordination:

. . . none of the lords went to see Caynoh and Caybatz. These two were afraid that it might occur to someone to come and steal their treasure during the night by means of the daughters of the lords. And so it occurred, that the vessels of treasure were stolen while they slept. They were the daughters of the lords *Zunqun Ganel Mayahuah* and *Puzi Ahuah*, and Caynoh and Caybatz made them their wives. One was called *Bubatzo* and the other *Icxiuh.*

Cay Noj and Cay Batz were very frightened upon finding that the treasure had been stolen while they slept, but the Ajtz'iquinajay assured them that the Quiché ruler would say nothing.[48] Perhaps the Ajtz'iquinajay thought that the lord would consider the lost tribute as a bride price because gifts were customarily given for wives at that time.[49] Yet the loss of tribute was very serious, and the two collectors decided to hide from their lord's wrath. The Ajtz'iquinajay proved to be right, however, because the Quiché lord, whom Carmack has identified as K'ucumatz, forgave them.[50]

C'otuja also married a Tzutujil girl, the daughter of the lord of Malaj. The marriage represented a Quiché strategy to gain influence and territory in the eastern lowland area. The Quichés were successful in this attempt, and Quiché vassals began settling "in the hills and valleys of the people of Tzutuhil, and their sons increased." This precipitated a battle between those of "Ah-Tziquinahá" and the Quiché invaders. The Tzutujils were defeated in this confrontation, and two of their leaders were captured. C'otuja rewarded the Tzutujils of Malaj by giving them special offices so as to "give offense to their enemies, particularly those of the lake."[51]

Two documents used by Francisco Antonio de Fuentes y Guzmán stated that the Quiché ruler Acxopil had two sons, Xiuhtemal and Acxoquauh.[52] Carmack identifies Acxopil with C'otuja-K'ucumatz.[53] Acxopil made his sons rulers over the Cakchiquels and the Tzutujils and may have accomplished this by marrying women from those two groups. His domain included the Tamubs, the Ilocabs, the Cakchiquels, the Tzutujils, and other groups.[54] According to the account, both of Axcopil's sons tried to expand their territories and fought each other. Neither was able to gain power over the other, but during this period Acxoquauh managed to extend Tzutujil control over the cacao lands of the southern piedmont. Because of this, the Tzutujils became wealthy and exchanged their cacao for gold and silver. When Acxopil died, the account says, Xiuhtemal became the next Quiché ruler.[55]

By 1400, C'otuja was dead, and K'ucumatz had become ruler of the Quichés. Around the same time K'umarcaaj (Utatlán), the last Quiché capital, was constructed. It stood about three kilometers from present-day Santa Cruz del Quiché.[56] By the time of K'ucumatz, Quiché power was widespread, and although the Tzutujils remained nominally independent, they were subordinated through marriage alliances and regarded the Quiché ruler as the highest lord in the land. Some Quichés may have lived in Xikomuk to watch over the Tzutujils.

Q'uik'ab, the son of K'ucumatz, assumed rule over the Quichés in 1425 and expanded the empire to its farthest limits.[57] Around 1470 a great feast was held in the Quiché capital to determine what was to be done, for the thirteen peoples of Vukamag and many others were beginning to take vengeance. All the groups under Quiché domination were convoked and divided into two categories. Those considered to be Quiché were placed in one group, and the "enemy peoples" were placed in the other. Among the latter were "the peoples that came from Tziquinahá." All these groups came to K'umarcaaj "to hold their ceremonies, showing the feeling they had for those whom Qikab-Cavizimah[58] [previously ordered] killed."[59]

The Tzutujils demonstrated their hostility toward the Quichés at this feast by taking part in an attempt to assassinate Q'uik'ab: "Those called Tzololá, Ahachel, Cooní and Lapoyoi also arrived with the Zutuhil in order to kill . . . Quicab."[60] Possibly these Tzutujils sought revenge because Q'uik'ab had taken some of their territory. The revolt also gave some of the "enemy peoples," such as the Tzutujils, the opportunity to regain a measure of independence. Q'uik'ab himself, humbled but still alive, even advised the Cakchiquels to found a new capital at Iximché to escape the rebels.[61] He died, having been stripped of much of his former power, around 1475.[62]

## Independent Kingdoms

Because of the power vacuum created by the decline of Q'uik'ab, the Tzutujils and several other highland groups began hostilities against the Quichés. Fuentes y Guzmán described the event[63] that was said to have initiated a long series of battles between the Quichés and the Tzutujils: the abduction of a Quiché princess by the Ajtz'inquinajay.[64] This ruler is probably the first Jo'o' Cawok (Five Lightning) mentioned in the *Annals*.[65]

Carmack reported that bride capture is practiced among the modern Quichés, and it has also survived among the Tzutujils.[66] It is most likely that the abduction was not the real reason but only the excuse for hostilities. The true reasons were related to the Quichés' desire to retain control over former dependencies and the Tzutujils' wish to expand their own territory and power.

Fuentes y Guzmán's account of the Tzutujils provides a great deal of information on warfare, history, and geography and names some Tzutujil lords.[67] Unfortunately, his discussion is based on his own interpretation of important documents, some of which are no longer in existence.[68] The wars involving the Tzutujils are not described in as detailed a fashion in other documents, and the reliability of the documents that Fuentes y Guzmán used rests on his ability to interpret what the Indians wrote. He made some mistakes, and it is not always possible to identify persons mentioned by him with those named in other sources.

Fuentes y Guzmán said that the Tzutujils and the Quichés remained at peace throughout the reign of Xiuhtemal's successor, and no fighting is mentioned in the documentary sources between the two groups until around 1485.[69] Until the stealing of the princess the Ajtz'iquinajay was supposedly on good terms with his cousin Balam Acam (Balam Ak'ab), the Quiché ruler.[70] The Tzutujil lord was joined in his deed by a friend, a member of the Ilocabs, who carried off another girl, the niece of Balam Acam. Fuentes y Guzmán described the Ajtz'iquinajay as the kind of man who did not restrain his passions.[71]

To avenge the theft of the girls, Balam Acam gathered an army under the command of Majucutaj, who was eventually to succeed him as ruler. The army set out for Tzutujil territory accompanied by Balam Acam, richly dressed and carried in a litter.[72]

In the war that followed, the Tzutujils allied with the Pipils and the Mams against the Quichés and the Cakchiquels. These two groups joined the Tzutujils out of common interest: all three had been losing territory to the Quichés and the Cakchiquels. The Ajtz'iquinajay also asked the lords of Zapotitlán and Soconusco for aid, but they demurred, saying that they had wars within their own boundaries.[73]

The Quiché army first attacked and conquered Palopó, killing the Tzutujil lord of that fortress and many others. The Quichés then moved to the lowlands to attack the Tzutujil town Chicochín. It was more difficult to conquer because of its moat, but the Quiché army finally prevailed. The victors sacked Chicochín, carrying off its many riches and the daughter of the lord to K'umarcaaj. The battle moved to the lake, and the Tzutujil army met the Quiché host but was defeated. The Ajtz'iquinajay's Ilocab friend was killed in that battle.

In a second encounter the Tzutujils and the Pipils were defeated by the Quiché army, which may have been primarily composed of Cakchiquel mercenaries. The Ajtz'iquinajay shut himself and the remnants of the Tzutujil army inside the walls of Chiya'. Some time afterward the Tzutujils and the Pipils attacked the area around Totonicapán and destroyed the crops. Then the Tzutujils and the Mams fought the Quichés. During this phase of the fighting Balam Acam was slain in his litter by a Tzutujil spear.[74]

Majucutaj became ruler of the Quichés. The Tzutujils attacked their enemies, but, being unable to take any Quiché towns, they besieged Xelaju (Quezaltenango). Many Tzutujil nobles were killed there; the moat that surrounded the city made it difficult to conquer. The lord of Samayac, who aided the Tzutujils, also died in the battle.

According to Fuentes y Guzmán, the Tzutujils suffered such serious defeats that their ruler died of continued profound melancholy.[75] The *Annals,* however, inform us that he was killed in battle around 1493. The Ajtz'iquinajay, Jo'o' Cawok, prepared to fight "the king called *Belehe Quih* [Belejeb Quej, Nine Deer], who was a neighbor." This ruler was Quiché. When the Cakchiquels heard of this, they suspected that they too might be attacked and killed by the Tzutujil leader: "Actually Caoké was courageous, and it was easy to kill him because he went down thirteen times to the city and tried his luck thirteen times in a day." This Jo'o' Cawok is probably the Ajtz'iquinajay who stole the Quiché princess, for both the *Annals* and Fuentes y Guzmán describe him as a daring individual.

The next Ajtz'iquinajay, a nineteen-year-old lord, again took up the battle against the Quichés; he is the second Jo'o' Cawok mentioned in the *Annals.*[76] The Quichés attempted to recover Tolimán and Palopó, which had been retaken by the Tzutujils, and were successful. Majucutaj, the Quiché leader, died soon afterward, "being old and sick," and was succeeded by a new ruler, Iq'ui Balam.[77]

The *Annals* mention one encounter that occurred during the rule of the second Jo'o' Cawok: "The Zutuhils were killed in *Zahcab* on the day 1 Ahmak [July 10, 1495]. . . . Only the lord Voo Caok [Jo'o' Cawok], the Ahtziquinahay, did not surrender, but his heart was full of evil intentions toward the Cakchiquels."[78] The fighting among the Quichés, Cakchiquels, and Tzutujils continued until 1501. The Tzutujils lost land in the piedmont, and Patulul was conquered during this time.[79]

The next Ajtz'iquinajay probably came to power after 1497, for Jo'o' Cawok was still alive in that year, according to the *Annals.* According to Fuentes y Guzmán, this successor became ill during a campaign and died after a fairly short rule, but the Tzutujil army continued to advance into Quiché territory under its lieutenant general. The lieutenant general was killed in battle with a blow of a Quiché war club, and the Tzutujil army fled back to Chiya'.[80] The *Annals* say that "the Zutuhils were exterminated by those of Xeynup and Xepalica. . . . *Zakbin* and *Ahmak* perished on the day 13 Ahmak [October 26, 1501]."[81]

The Pipils introduced the fighting into Cakchiquel territory and fought long and hard until their leader decided to make peace. As a condition of peace the Cakchiquels made them promise not to help the Tzutujils any longer but to fight on their side and to allow Cakchiquel armies safe passage through Pipil territory. This peace came to involve the Tzutujils and the Quichés as well and put an end to the endemic strife that had lasted from 1485 to 1501.[82] As a result of these wars the Quichés and Cakchiquels captured Patulul, Pochuta, Samayac, Ixtahuacán (San Miguel), settlements of the Mams, Palopó, and many other towns.[83] The Tzutujils kept as well as the southern and western areas of Lake Atitlán.

Although Fuentes y Guzmán was confused about names, titles, and dynasties, his work provides a good general outline of the warfare and gives an account of the lands that were lost by the Tzutujils. Attempts to correlate his information with passages in other sources must be somewhat speculative and may be confirmed or denied if further data come to light.

No mention is made of fighting involving the Tzutujil area from the peace of 1501 until the year 1521. The Quichés, Cakchiquels, and Tzutujils were successful, however, in keeping the Mexicans from conquering Guatemalan territory beyond Soconusco.[84] This fighting evidently did not occur in Tzutujil territory. Some years earlier the Cakchiquel ruler Hunyg had married Lady Ixk'ekac'uch, a Tzutujil woman, and in 1521 one of their sons, the Ajpop Achí Tzían, became ruler of the Cakchiquels.[85] Twenty days after the new Cakchiquel ruler, Ajpop Achí Tzían, came to office, on September 2, the Ajtz'iquinajay faced an internal revolt. According to the *Annals,* "The chiefs, the Ahtziquinajay and Qitzihay, came to Yximché seeking assistance; they came to recruit soldiers."[86] Since the Cakchiquels and Tzutujils were at peace, the Tzutujils asked their allies for help in putting down the revolt. The Cakchiquels sent two branches of their people, the Tzotzils and the Tukuchés, to aid the Ajtz'iquinajay:

". . . the Zotzils and Tukuchés killed the [rebel] Zutuhil tribes; all those of Tziquinahay [rebel Ajtz'iquinajay] died. They took many prisoners. And for this reason the Zutuhils, fearing death, surrendered their jewels and money and the city of *Xepoyom* [Xikomuk] was captured. Afterwards the kings Tepepul Ahtziquinahay and Qitzihay returned to their homes."[87]

Perhaps some of the Tzutujils who apparently lived in the Xikomuk region had felt strong enough to challenge the rule of the dominant Ajtz'iquinajay lineage. They may have persuaded some of the ruler's own group to go along with them, for the *Annals* say that "all those of Tziquinajay died," possibly meaning all those of his group who sided with the rebel group and were traitors.

This attempted rebellion sounds very similar to the one carried out against Q'uik'ab in earlier times. In the revolt against Q'uik'ab in 1470 the Quiché ruler was defeated by his vassal warriors and two of his sons.[88] Other groups visiting K'umarcaaj joined the uprising, which was successful. Q'uik'ab lost much of his power and was forced to share his wealth with his sons. The revolt against the Ajtz'iquinajay was, however, unsuccessful. The rebel Tzutujils also seem to have been soldiers and their supporters according to a passage in the *Annals:* "Many Zutuhils arrived at the city, wishing to make war against the people of Tziquinahá [Chiya'] and of *Pavacal,* they wished to be united among themselves because the soldiers had been insulted by those of Pavacal."[89]

Not long after the events described above, warfare again erupted between the Cakchiquels and the Tzutujils. The Tzutujils allied with a rebel lord.[90] Although the Cakchiquel ruler seems to have put down the revolt, the two groups were still engaging in hostilities when Pedro de Alvarado entered Guatemala in 1524.

Table 1 shows the rulers of the Tzutujils, the beginning dates of their reigns, and the dates of their deaths.

In summary, although it is not yet clear whether the Tzutujils preceded the Quichés and the Cakchiquels in their migrations into the Guatemala highlands, they seem to have been established around Lake Atitlán by 1250 and possibly earlier. Around 1250 the Quichés began gaining control of the highlands, where, with the other migrant warrior bands, they settled down, introducing (or intensifying) Toltec cultural patterns among the surrounding native populations. The Quichés, Cakchiquels, Rabinals, and Tzutujils formed a confederation that was mainly a military alliance and intermarried to strengthen dynastic ties. During this early period the Cakchiquels were preferred marriage partners of the Tzutujils, though they probably exchanged spouses with the Quichés as well.

The Quichés' power was greatly expanded during the fourteenth century. Quiché leaders weakened the control of Chiya' over its lowland dependencies through a policy of intermarriage, incorporation, and settlement in Tzutujil territory. The Quichés' power peaked at the end of the century, during Q'uik'ab's reign. The Tzutujils joined other subdued peoples who paid tribute and offered sacrifices in K'umarcaaj. A revolt against Q'uik'ab signaled the end of Quiché hegemony in the highlands and gave the former

Table 1. *Tzutujil Rulers*

| | Source | | |
|---|---|---|---|
| Years of Rule | Fuentes y Guzmán | *The Annals of the Cakchiquels* | Carrasco |
| Ca. 1420 to ? | Acxoquauh[a] | | |
| ? to ca. 1493 | Tzutujil Pop | Jo'o' Cawok[b] | |
| Ca. 1493 to ca. 1497 | Rumal Ajaw | Jo'o' Cawok[c] | |
| Ca. 1498 to ca. 1501 | Chichialhtulú[d] | | Wajxaki' Quiej |
| Ca. 1501 to 1540 | | Tepepul | Jo'o' No'j Quixcáp[e] |
| 1540 to 1547 | | | don Juan |
| 1547 to ca. 1630 | | | don Bernabé[f] |

[a] Acxopil probably made his sons Xiuhtemal and Acxoquauh rulers over the Cakchiquels and Tzutujils in his later years. He died in 1425, and thus 1420 is a reasonable date for Acxoquauh to have begun his rule over the Tzutujils.

[b] According to the *Annals* the elder Jo'o' Cawok was killed sometime around 1493, and his son was in office by 1495 (1967, pp. 106, 110). The former ruler was in power by 1485, when, Carmack estimates the Quiché-Tzutujil wars began (1981, p. 139).

[c] The year of the death of the second Jo'o' Cawok is not clear, but he was still alive in 1497, according to the *Annals* (1967, p. 110). Fuentes y Guzmán erroneously referred to him by the Quiché phrase *rumal ajaw,* which means by the lords (Carmack 1973, p. 78).

[d] It is not clear whether there were two reigns, by father and son, or whether only the son ruled. I have regarded it as one reign. This ruler died before the end of the fighting in 1501. Wajxaki' Quiej means Eight Deer, and this is probably also the meaning of the name (incorrectly spelled) given to this ruler by Fuentes y Guzmán.

[e] Jo'o' No'j Quixcáp (Five Earthquake Quixcáp) was ruler when the Spaniards entered Guatemala and was baptized as don Pedro (Carrasco 1967b, p. 321).

[f] The exact date of don Bernabé's death is not known, but he was still alive in 1630, according to Fray Bernabé Cobo (in Vásquez de Espinosa 1944, pp. 195-96). Don Juan and don Bernabé were both Ajtz'iquinajay.

components of the empire a chance to become independent.

The period from around 1485 to 1501 was one of continual warfare among the most important highland groups. Each attempted to gain ascendency over the others. There is no record of fighting involving the Tzutujils from 1501 until 1521, when they suffered an internal revolt. Although the revolt was unsuccessful, it left dissatisfactions that were to rise to the surface after the Spaniards took over Guatemala.

The Tzutujils did not gain significantly from their battles with the Quichés and the Cakchiquels. Although the latter two groups fought against each other from time to time, they also combined forces against the Pipils, the Mams, and the Tzutujils. This alliance allowed them to gain significantly in the eastern area of Lake Atitlán and in the lowland piedmont.

CHAPTER 4

# Tzutujil Territory

Archaeological remains demonstrate that during the Postclassic Period the highland Guatemalans increasingly tended to establish their settlements on hilltops.[1] This move to higher places was not a sudden one but seems to have begun in the Early Classic Period and was accelerated during Classic and Postclassic times.[2]

The mountain or hilltop center, or *tinamit,* was the home of the ruler as well as a military and ritual-administrative capital.[3] Amak', or secondary centers, were smaller and less important than the *tinamit* and were probably the homes of the lineages.[4] Fray Francisco Ximénez described the *amak'* as "a small town extended like the legs of a spider . . . differentiated from the *cabecera* or town inhabited by lords, which was called *tinamit,* which means, city or court."[5]

The Late Postclassic coastal pattern seems to have involved scattered *amak'* (fig. 6). Several documents state that the Tzutujil ruler owned plantations in the piedmont region and that settlements there paid him tribute.[6] Gerardo G. Aguirre found documentary evidence that San Pedro once extended from Santa Clara on the north to Atitlán and included lowland territory bordering on Nahualá and San Antonio Suchitepéquez (figs. 1, 6, 7).[7] Nobles living in Chiya' or San Pedro may have owned these lands.

## The Highland Territory

The northern shore of Lake Atitlán was always under only tenuous Tzutujil control. Tzololá (Sololá) and Ajachel (Panajachel) are linked with the Tzutujils in the *Título Xpantzay 2* and may have been subordinate to them in the early fifteenth century.[8] After 1440, under their ruler Q'uik'ab, the Quichés applied increasing pressure to the north-shore area. The *Título Santa Clara* mentions a Quiché military drive that extended as far east as Tzololá.[9] Q'uik'ab took

49

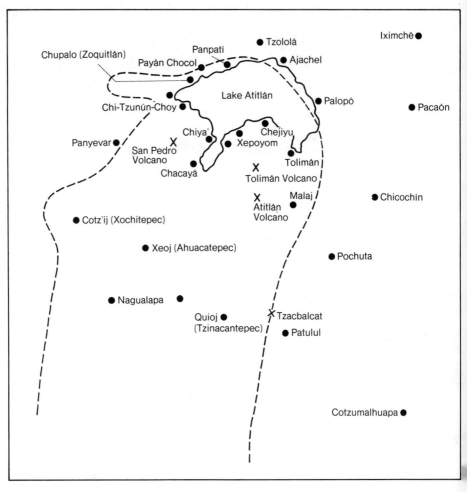

Fig. 6. *The Tzutujil kingdom at the time of the Conquest. The circle above Quioj marks the ancient site of San Francisco. The circle across the bay from Chiya' marks the ruins of present-day Santiago Atitlán. The circle above Chi-Tzunún-Choy marks the ancient site of San Juan. Map constructed on the basis of the documentary and archaeological evidence summarized in chapters 2 and 4.*

Fig. 7. *Pre-Hispanic and modern capitals. Adapted from maps in Tax 1968, front, and in Carmack 1973, p. 243.*

all of the territory north of Tzololá and occupied Xajxac and Kozibal-Caculha, present-day hamlets of Tzololá.[10] Eventually he also captured Tzololá itself, along with Coón (Pacaón, present-day Patzún) and Payán Chocol (near modern-day San Marcos):

The warriors of the king Quicab took the towns of Cumatz and Tuhal. The Lords arrived at Chiavar Tzupitakah where there was no one who could bother them. They were there and afterwards they occupied the cities of the zutujiles, Tzololá, Coón, and Payán Chocol, and no one could conquer them because they were wizards.[11]

After that the Tzutujils of Tzololá paid the Quichés tribute.

The same document says that the inhabitants of Tzololá during these times were the "sons of Atziquinahá."[12] The "Ahpo-Tzololá" was listed in the *Título Totonicapán* as one of the "peoples that came from Tziquinahá, a people of the lake."[13] Others associated with the Tzutujils in the *Título Xpantzay 2* were "those called . . . Ahachel, Cooní and Lapoyoi."[14] The location of the Lapoyois is not known, but a lineage or family named Lapoyatz was listed in church records from Atitlán dating from the seventeenth century.[15] It was probably somewhere northeast of the lake.

Another pre-Hispanic north-shore settlement belonging to the Tzutujils was Panpatí. This settlement is cited in a passage in the *Annals* referring to the time when the Tzutujils and Cakchiquels divided Lake Atitlán between them: "From there they went toward the places called *Panpatí* and *Payan Chocol,* practicing magic arts."[16] Panpatí was near modern-day Santa Cruz,[17] and is usually mentioned in the written sources with Payán Chocol.

Some archaeological remains north of San Pablo[18] may be identified with the Çuquitlan (Nahuatl, Zoquitlán), or Chupalu (Chupalo, from a word meaning "in the lake") mentioned in letters of *encomienda* dated 1529 and 1532. In 1563 the town was called San Pablo Çuquitan,[19] and the aboriginal name appears to have been dropped by the end of the sixteenth century.

Much of the northeastern region of Lake Atitlán was occupied by the Cakchiquels in the late fifteenth century after a revolt against Q'uik'ab.[20] Large numbers of Cakchiquel speakers settled there and by the time of the Conquest apparently outnumbered the Tzutujils at Tzololá.[21] After the Tukuchés, a Cakchiquel group, lost their bid for power in a rebellion in 1493, some of their lords went elsewhere to live. Several of them went to Tzutujil territory and mingled with their former vassals.[22] The implication is that some Tzutujil lands had already come under Cakchiquel control and that these lands were probably in the Tzololá-Ajachel region.

Settlements west of Tzololá and "Qizqab" remained Tzutujil.[23]

Part of the northwestern area of the lake was conquered by the Quichés in Q'uik'ab's time. He probably took possession of Santa Clara[24] and Panyevar, the latter now an *aldea* of San Juan.[25] There the Quiché-Tzutujil boundary remained. Other areas along the Quiché-Tzutujil border are mentioned in the *Título Santa Clara*.[26] The ancient sites of San Juan and Tzununáa remained in Tzutujil hands and are still Tzutujil today (Tzununáa is not to be confused with Tzununá, a modern *aldea* of San Marcos, but refers to Chi-Tzunún-Choy, the ancient name of San Pedro.)[27] The only other area of occupation along the western side of Lake Atitlán south of Chi-Tzunún-Choy, except for a few isolated structures (now mounds), was Chiya'.

Chacayá, Pachavaj, Chukumuk, Xikomuk, Chejiyu, and eventually Tolimán, all situated along the southern shore of the lake, remained firmly under Tzutujil control. It is not clear whether the Tzutujils had control of Tolimán and Palapó at the time of the Conquest. It is likely, however, that they maintained their influence in Tolimán but lost Palapó to the closer Cakchiquels. Tolimán is mentioned in only one of the documents dealing with the pre-Conquest period, the account of Fuentes y Guzmán. Juan de Estrada mentioned it in 1579:

Tulimán is a place which is near Lake Atitlán and is on the banks of that lake. In the shoals a good type of round reed grows which is used to make tumplines for sacks and because this reed is called tule, two places which are near the lake are called Tulimáns, and to differentiate them, there is upper Tolimán and lower Tolimán.[28]

*Tul* is from the Nahua *tollin,* meaning "rush."[29] Lower Tolimán refers to San Lucas, and Upper Tolimán to San Antonio Palopó.[30] The Cakchiquels eventually won control of Upper Tolimán, but at the time of the Conquest, Lower Tolimán was inhabited mainly by Tzutujil speakers.

There were a few other Tzutujil settlements that cannot presently be identified. During a revolt against the Ajtz'iquinajay in 1521 "those of *Xecaká Abah* [Xequiakabaj]" fled and took refuge among the Cakchiquels.[31] Munro Edmonson has translated Xequiakabaj as under Red Rock.[32] A Tzutujil settlement called Naqal on the north of the lake was said to be "under the red rock."[33] Naqal and Xequiakabaj may have been the same or neighboring settlements. Tzala was a Tzutujil town said to be near Cakchiquel territory. Chuitzala is a Tzutujil name for Sololá, and Tzala probably refers to that town. Tzala was an important ritual site, and it is likely that it was situated at or near modern-day Sololá.

The *Annals* refer in one passage to the "women of *Tzununaa*, of *Tzololaa*, and *Ahachel* and *Vaiza*."[34] The first, as explained above, is Chi-Tzunún-Choy, and the next two are Tzololá and Panajachel. Vaiza is also mentioned in the *Título Xpantzay 3*. There it is called Pulchich Vayz Amag and is said to have been located "in the town of the *atziquinahay*,"[35] which probably means that it was a smaller settlement near Chiya'. It may refer to the area of contemporary Santiago Atitlán. The plateau contains pre-Hispanic remains, and the old name is not known.

From this discussion it can be seen that all of the land surrounding Lake Atitlán probably belonged to the Tzutujils before the Quichés' expansion during Q'uik'ab's time. After 1470 much of the northern and eastern sides of the lake was lost to the Quichés and the Cakchiquels. When Alvarado entered Guatemala, the Tzutujils controlled the Lake Atitlán area from slightly east of Panpatí westward all the way around the lake to Lower Tolimán and were trying to regain land on the northwest and the northeast.

## The Lowland Territory

The Tzutujil kingdom also included territory in the coastal lowlands between the Coyolate and Nahualate rivers.[36] Estrada described the piedmont settlement pattern as it existed in 1579 and in pre-Hispanic times:

This coast is moderately populated with Indians although it is said that there were more in other times, and that the cause was that in the time of their greatness, it was not prohibited [for them] to have as many women as they wanted. Also, before they were conquered, they lived scattered at their will and without order.[37]

In the *Relación Tzutujil* two lowland dependencies are mentioned that date from pre-Hispanic times and continued to remain subject to the Tzutujils after the Conquest. These were Xeoj (San Bartolomé) and Quioj (San Andrés).[38] The boundaries of the settlements were not clearly defined, for many of the Indians were dispersed throughout the hills.[39] Although the existence of nucleated settlements, temples, and idols indicates that some of the people must have been concentrated, most of the population may have been spread out over the countryside. For example, in Quioj, "in the time of their infidelity, there were eight hundred Indians living in the woods in different parts and places. . . . The site where they were settled in ancient times . . . was in the high mountains, where the soil was rough and rocky."[40]

Another lowland settlement stood near post-Hispanic San Francisco. It does not, however, appear to have been a separate *amak'* in pre-Hispanic times but was considered part of Chiya'. Both had the same god.[41]

Both Suchitepéquez and Nagualapa probably belonged to the Tzutujil kingdom. The *Título San Bartolomé,* written in Tzutujil in San Antonio Suchitepéquez sometime in the sixteenth century, demonstrates that Tzutujil was still spoken there at the time of the Conquest.[42] In Q'uik'ab's time Suchitepéquez may have come under temporary Quiché control, but with the decline of his power the Tzutujils regained control over the area.

Thompson says that "Zapotitlán comprised the area east of the Tlilapa River to a point slightly east of Zamayaque, and that . . . whole territory was Quiché. To the east of it lay Xuchitepequez which was Zutuhil."[43] In the early nineteenth century Domingo Juarros said that Tzutujil was spoken in Suchitepéquez,[44] as did Teodoro Mendizábal, *cura* of San Antonio, who wrote in 1769. Some Tzutujil speakers lived in Cuyotenango,[45] which was securely within the Quiché orbit after the Conquest; the *Título Nijaib 2* includes the lord of Cuyotenango in a list of those attending the investiture of don Francisco Izquín Nijaib.[46] Perhaps a small Tzutujil colony settled there in pre- or post-Hispanic times.

Nagualapa was about one league from Xeoj, and Xeoj was about four leagues from Atitlán.[47] In a document of 1563 cited by Pedro Carrasco, two *caciques* of Nagualapa were present to help resolve a political dispute among the lords of Atitlán.[48] That would seem to indicate that the town was part of the Tzutujil kingdom.

Malaj was another pre-Conquest Tzutujil settlement.[49] It was somewhere on the coast, probably slightly south of Tolimán. The *Título Santa Clara* mentions "all those of Malah under the pataxte and cacao trees."[50] The mention of these trees is evidence that Malaj was in the lowlands. Fuentes y Guzmán said that there were cacao lands south of Tolimán.[51]

In 1523, Tzacbalcat was on the eastern border between the Cakchiquels and the Tzutujils in the piedmont. In a document dated 1587 the testimony of several witnesses in a jurisdictional dispute between the residents of Patulul and Atitlán demonstrates that Tzacbalcat was a hostile frontier zone under Tzutujil control when the Spaniards arrived.[52] The Tzutujils had once controlled Patulul, Pochuta, and Chicochín but had lost these settlements in the fighting of the late fifteenth century.[53] The Cakchiquels eventually took control of the southeastern lowland area. Thompson reasoned that the Tzutujil and Pipil territories may have been adjacent until the end of the fifteenth century.[54] They were often allies, and the Pipils may even have come under Tzutujil control before the Cakchiquels conquered the area.

The western boundary between the Tzutujils and the Quichés was clearly defined in Q'uik'ab's time and was probably just west of Suchitepéquez.[55] Many of the place-names used in the *Título Santa Clara* to define this boundary are no longer identifiable. For example: "They left there and arrived at the ravine of Chopi, at Zaki Oca. They arrived at Ynup, at the great pyramid. They left there and ascended to the crossroads of Zaká above Zakqak, near Galibal Abah. They arrived later at Omuch Cakhá."[56]

From the foregoing discussion it can be seen that shifting boundaries markedly affected the extent of the Tzutujil kingdom in pre-Hispanic times. Areas in which large numbers of Quichés or Cakchiquels settled, such as Tzololá, Coón, and Santa Clara in the highlands, were lost to the Tzutujils. The Quichés and Cakchiquels took over most of the northern and eastern areas of Lake Atitlán. The Tzutujils in those areas either left or were soon absorbed. The remote northern and eastern highland Tzutujil areas were less secure. Large numbers of Quiché and Cakchiquel speakers filtered in and finally outnumbered the Tzutujil speakers. Victories in war allowed the Quichés and Cakchiquels to absorb these areas permanently. At the time of the Conquest the Tzutujils retained control over lands containing primarily Tzutujil speakers. Their weakest areas of control in both the highlands and the piedmont were the lands bordering Quiché or Cakchiquel speakers, and they continued to lose control of lands in these areas right up to the time Alvarado entered Guatemala.

CHAPTER 5

# *Warfare and Tribute*

Among the Quichean groups conquest and colonization were the major means of incorporating and holding territory. The documents demonstrate that from the time they left Tula in search of a new homeland the warriors' success in establishing new dominions was due to their superior military organization.[1] According to the *Popol Vuh,* warfare first erupted in the Guatemala highlands when the Quichés began offering as sacrifices to their gods members of surrounding groups.[2] In reality, warfare had been common among the native Guatemalans but increased in Late Postclassic times. C'otuja initiated the large-scale expansion of the Quiché empire that was to reach even greater proportions in the reigns of his successors K'ucumatz and Q'uik'ab. By that time the primary motive of warfare was the incorporation of land and tribute rather than the acquisition of sacrificial victims, though captives were still used for that purpose.

### *The Goals of Warfare*

Some of the impetus for conquest during the fourteenth century came from expansion of the Quiché nobility, which stimulated a greater demand for the luxury items that were most easily obtained through tribute.[3] The Tzutujil lowlands were a prime target because of the cacao groves there. During Q'uik'ab's time many towns in that area became subordinate to the Quichés: "By [Q'uik'ab's] order all of the thirteen tribes gathered in Gumarcaah, to repair and make ready their bows and their shields, and they went to conquer all the small towns and the large towns . . . and in this way augmented the glory of the king Qikab."[4]

Besides tribute, booty, and sacrificial victims, another major goal of warfare was the capturing of enemy gods.[5] Sakibuk, the main idol of Chiya', played an important role in Tzutujil warfare:

When the rulers and lords of this town wanted to know if there would
be wars, [they] and their nobles designated persons who were especially
chosen for this ceremony, who after they had offered sacrifices to [Saki-
buk] consulted with [him about] whatever they wanted to know. . . .
When there was to be war, [the idol] showed himself to them with a bow
and arrow in his hands.[6]

The Tzutujils evidently carried Sakibuk into battle, just as the
Quichés carried Tojil,[7] for Tzutujil gods were mentioned by the
Cakchiquels who fought the inhabitants of Chiya': "For seven
days the [Cakchiquel] warriors encountered Zaqui Voc and for
thirteen days . . . Cakix Can."[8] Cakix Can was another important
Tzutujil deity.

## Battle Strategy

Fortifying towns with walls or moats, an important defensive strategy in the highlands, had been practiced since the thirteenth century. The Quichés built a wall around Jakawitz and defeated their
enemies by setting dummies dressed like warriors on top of the
wall.[9] Chiya' was a walled fortress, and the lowland Tzutujil settlement Chicochín had a moat.[10] Because of such defensive constructions siege was a common method of warfare in the Quiché
area. The Quichés captured Chicochín by siege. The Tzutujils, in
turn, laid siege to Xelaju (Quezaltenango), which had a moat, and
burned the fields of towns near that settlement.[11] When the Tzutujil army suffered defeat in the field, the Ajtz'iquinajay would
retreat to Chiya' and lock himself up inside the fortress,[12] which
was never taken by enemies in pre-Hispanic times.

Another important strategy was the settling of trusted groups
in conquered lands. After C'otuja married the princess of Malaj,
he settled groups loyal to the Quichés in the nearby lowlands
belonging to the Ajtz'iquinajay.[13] The Tzutujils also had trusted
servants and administrators in the lowland cacao areas south of
Chiya',[14] but they do not appear to have been as successful as
the Quichés in implementing this tactic. They were unable to conquer and maintain control of major enemy towns in the fighting
that followed the decline of the Quiché state.

Bartolomé de las Casas described the warfare strategy that was
common in the highlands in the years just before the Conquest:
"Concerning warfare they proceeded with the greatest caution,
principally with regard to secrecy: they determined when and
whom, the number of people, suppliers, arms, without raising any

suspicions." He went on to say that when war was imminent the ruler called his people to the palace. There the leaders "provided them their bows and arrows, spears and shields, with their standards of very beautiful feathers and their banners."[15] Probably most of the weapons, banners, and standards were stored in the capitals along with other items captured in previous battles and received in tribute.[16] That appears to have been true in the time of K'ucumatz as well, for he gave the Cakchiquel mercenaries their arrows and shields when he ordered them to fight for the Quichés.[17] It is not known whether all of Las Casas's information applied to the Tzutujils; his accounts usually refer to the people of Verapaz or to the Quichés. The Tzutujils, however, probably employed strategies and military procedures similar to those of their enemies.

### Weapons and Battle Dress

The earliest reference to the battle dress and weapons of the Quichean groups dates back to the fight against the Nonoualcas and Xulpitis, which occurred before their migration into the Guatemala highlands:

"Verily, war is near: adorn yourselves, cover yourselves with your finery, dress yourselves with feathers, uncover your gifts." . . . We uncovered our gifts, the presents which we had, the feathers, the plaster [to paint the face], the arrows, the shields, and the coats of cotton.[18]

In 1585 the Tzutujil elders described the costumes and weapons used by the warriors in pre-Hispanic times:

The arms that they wore for wars against other rulers . . . were a jacket without sleeves which came to the waist which they called *escahuypiles.*[19] It was made of doubled *mantas* with layered cotton in between and then back-stitched with thick heavy cord so that no type of arrow could pass through, nor would a *macana* of knives cut through it. They carried shields of rods and thin pita fiber, twisted and closely woven. These *escaopiles* . . . resisted the arrows and fire-hardened sticks the enemy threw at them. On the sides of the *macanas* they had their knife blades that were sharp enough to cut a man in half like a sword. They also carried sharp fire-hardened sticks [and] slingshots of cord with which they threw stones.[20]

Estrada also mentioned swords made of flint.[21] Fuentes y Guzmán described the weapons used by the Tzutujils when they fought the Spaniards:

Swiftly and with a terrible din of shouting they attacked with huge spears [*lanzas*], arrows [*saetas*], and swords [*espadas*] two hands long made out of obsidian; they also had other types of weapons which penetrated deep and were made out of the same stone [knives?] which being thrown caused fear because of their poisonous wounds.[22]

It was customary for the army to attack with as much noise as possible to inspire fear in the enemy. Sometimes the warriors played musical instruments, such as flutes, conch-shell trumpets, and drums.[23]

The warriors were also distinguished by their insignia:

When the rulers and lords of this town went to war, they carried various devices and insignia on their shields. Some carried eagles made of feathers, others jaguars, and others figures of birds and animals, in such a manner that the . . . lords and rulers of each kingdom and province were known by the devices that were different from each other.[24]

These devices were used along with the standards and banners mentioned by Las Casas.[25] A painting from the *Lienzo de Tlaxcala* shows the battle dress and weapons of the Tzutujil warriors during the battle of Atitlán (fig. 8).

## Organization of the Army

Among the Quichés the highest-ranking lords held offices that had both military and administrative functions *(ajpop, k'alel)*. The Tzutujils had similar offices, such as *pop* and *k'alel*, which no doubt had related functions.[26] The Tzutujil ruler and his closest friends or relatives often led the army in battle, and in Quichean culture warfare was considered the most important part of a noble's life.[27] One lord who fought for the Tzutujil lord was killed in battle after having spent twenty-six years in various campaigns.[28] The Quiché ruler Balam Acam was also described as having been well schooled in military matters from the time of his youth.[29]

There is evidence in the *Relación geográfica Atitlán* for the existence of elite corps among the Tzutujils like the Eagle and Jaguar warriors of central Mexico. The Tzutujil elders described the elite warriors:

The rulers and lords who governed the four capitals[30] of this kingdom . . . would gather the lords in their land and name two captains to command the army and take charge of the warriors. One . . . was called *Quauhtli,* . . . or eagle. He wore the insignia of the eagle over his . . . cotton armor. The second captain was called *Ocelotl,* . . . or jaguar, . . . and wore the insignia of the jaguar over his cotton armor.[31]

Fig. 8. *Panel 28 from the* Lienzo de Tlaxcala *(1892), showing the Battle of Atitlán (Chiya'). The top caption, Tecpanatitlan, should be Atitlán. Tzutujil warriors (upper and lower right) are depicted defending the city from the Spaniards and their allies, the Tlaxcalans. The place-glyph above the Tzutujils consists of a twisted red-and-white headband combined with what is apparently the symbol for water. The former stands for Tecpán (Palace, or Government Building), and the latter for Atitlán (Place at the Water) (Nicholson 1967, p. 82). Four Tzutujil warriors, with their shields, defend the rock (Chuitinamit) and shower the enemy with arrows (see Villacorta Calderón 1938, p. 342). Another Tzutujil warrior (below right), wearing his shield on his left arm and swinging a club with his right hand, attacks the Spanish soldier on horseback, who is about to lance a fallen Tzutujil. Beside the Spaniard are two Tlaxcalan warriors, each with a shield and bearing an elaborate standard. One of the Tlaxcalans carries a Spanish sword.*

All of these warriors were nobles from the highest ranks, and each of the highest lineages may have had members who were Eagle and Jaguar warriors. Tzutujil battle commanders are often mentioned in pairs and may represent the Eagle and Jaguar leaders. Fuentes y Guzmán said that the name Ajtz'iquinajay meant Eagle House and was taken from the leader's battle headdress, which was made of quetzal feathers in the form of an eagle.[32]

The Tzutujil commanders Welpan and Xucutzin, who were defeated by C'otuja's warriors, may also have been Eagle and Jaguar leaders. When they were defeated and captured, the rest of their men took fright and withdrew.[33] It was not uncommon for an army to panic when the leaders were taken.[34] The Cakchiquels also defeated two Tzutujil lords in 1494 and 1501: "The Zutuhils were killed and annihilated, and their chiefs *Nahtihay* and *Ahquibihay* surrendered. . . . During the eighth year after the revolution, the Zutuhils were exterminated. . . . *Zakbin* and *Ahmak* perished."[35] The *Título C'oyoi* describes the Quiché Eagle warriors as those "who take the land with bow and arrow."[36] The Tzutujil elders did not say whether that was also true of the Eagle warriors of Chiya'.

In early times the Quiché vassals served as foot soldiers *(ajlabal)* for the lords without titles, but by Q'uik'ab's time some of the vassals had become specialized warriors called *achij* ("the men").[37] It is possible that the Tzutujils created similar offices for their most important vassals, but it is doubtful that they had as complex a hierarchy as that of the Quichés.

Commoners comprised the main force of the army. The *Annals* say that the Cakchiquels' foot soldiers were called *ajchay*,[38] meaning those who carry obsidian weapons, but there is no information about what the Tzutujil rank and file were called. Las Casas also mentioned permanent and deputy war captains and other subordinates who were like sergeants. There were ensigns who carried the banners and other officials in charge of distributing food and drink to the soldiers. These or others provided firewood and prepared the camps. Perhaps the Tzutujil army was organized in a similar fashion.[39]

The Tzutujils' field army, like that of the Quichés and the Cakchiquels, appears to have been divided into three regiments *(tercios)*, one group perhaps composed of men armed with slingshots *(honderos)*, another of men with lances *(lanceros)*[40] and fire-hardened sticks *(varas tostadas)*, and the third of bowmen *(flecheros)*.[41] The men armed with *macanas* and probably those with battle-axes, appear to have fought with the spearmen. Among the Quichés, warriors from each settlement were grouped under captains according to the weapons they carried.[42] There were shield bearers *(ajpocob),* lancers *(tzununche),* bowmen *(ajch'ab),* and hand-to-hand fighters *(tz'olaj).*[43]

If warriors lost a battle and returned home in defeat, they performed a ritual to demonstrate their sorrow and disappointment: "They broke their arrows, war clubs, and fire-hardened sticks and undid their feathers and threw fragments of their shields into the air, cursing them."[44] If they were successful, they sacrificed their enemies. In Chiya', "men whom they killed were sacrificed to [Sakibuk]. . . . [The victim's] breast was opened with a large knife like a cleaver, and the blood taken out and offered to this idol, smearing its face with it. . . . they ate the flesh of the Indians . . . sacrificed."[45] The lords captured in battle were usually sacrificed, while commoners were kept as slaves or shared a similar fate.[46]

Even though the Tzutujils did not gain significantly from the wars they engaged in immediately before the Conquest, they had the satisfaction of having successfully defended their capital:

The *Sotojiles* had for defense and strength a rock which was very imposing near the lake of the court of [Chiya'] and a large number of canoes, in which they conducted war, . . . sheltering them close to the rock; for this reason they were more invincible than the others, there not being much opportunity to surround them by land due to the roughness of the hills around them.[47]

Canoes were, therefore, important tools of the Tzutujils' military strategy and contributed to their ability to hold several sites around the lake. Xikomuk, Tolimán, and Palopó were not as invincible as Chiya' and, along with such lowland settlements as Pochuta, Chicochín, and Patulul, were attacked or conquered during the late fifteenth and early sixteenth centuries.[48]

## Tribute

Tribute was closely bound up with warfare. Most conquered peoples kept their lands but were obligated to pay a certain amount of goods to the victorious overlords. During the early part of their history the Quichean groups were subordinate to Tula, and they gave tribute to the lord of that city when they first arrived there:

First the seven tribes paid the tribute, and afterwards the warriors paid the tribute. But this consisted only of precious stones [jade], metal, garlands fastened with green and blue feathers,[49] and paintings and sculptures. They offered flutes, songs, ritual calendars, astronomical calendars,[50] *pataxte,* and cocoa. Only with these riches the warriors went to pay tribute to Tulán during the night. Only arrows and shields of wood were the riches they gave as tribute when they came to Tulán.[51]

The visiting groups received symbols of political legitimacy and their gods, as well as arms, and were told by the ruler of Tula that they would also receive tribute from the peoples whom they would conquer: "Thus shall they pay tribute to you of bucklers, riches, bows, shields, feathers and white earth,[52] . . . precious stones [jade], metal, green and blue feathers, . . . paintings, sculptures, ritual calendars, sidereal calendars, flutes, [and] songs."[53] The small militaristic colonies were urged to go forth and win the right to tribute from newly conquered peoples. Evidently the tribute was to be collected on a regular basis, because the month of Tacaxepual (March) was fixed by the Quichés for tribute payment.[54]

The beginning of a more regularized system of tribute in the Guatemala highlands probably dates from the reign of C'ocaib (1325–50), after Quiché control had been extended over a fairly wide area. There is no specific information about the items paid in tribute until the reign of C'otuja and K'ucumatz. By that time there were official tribute collectors: "Caynoh and Caybatz . . . were sent . . . to collect tribute, and they went to collect tribute from the people. . . . There in the east they were paid with precious objects: metal,[55] cloth."[56] After the reigns of C'otuja and K'ucumatz the Quichés expanded their control, and "all the tribes came to give themselves up."[57] Members of conquered groups had to go to K'umarcaaj periodically and spend one month serving the Quichés.[58] Las Casas described a similar practice from later times:

They ordered the town to give a portion to celebrate religious ceremonies and sacrifices to their idols and for the feasts and banquets . . . five or six times a year. . . . Half of this was exhausted by the rituals and what remained went to the lord as tribute and service from the towns.[59]

When the lords married their children, the groups took to the capital offerings of gold, feathers, cacao, and turkeys. Such celebrations were also held in Chiya', and at those times vassals probably took tribute to the main gods and to the Ajtz'iquinajay.

We have some information about items that the Tzutujils gave to Q'uik'ab. When the great Quiché leader arrived with his army at the shores of Lake Atitlán, the Tzutujils presented him with fish, crabs, green stones, jewels, and money (gold?).[60] It is not clear whether this was a special gift offered as a sign of loyalty and submission or a regular payment that was collected by Q'uik'ab in person. Nor is it known whether the items were sent from Chiya' or were given by the Tzutujil lords of Tzololá.

Spoils of war were part of the tribute delivered to the capital by the war leaders. There they made their reports and gave the best part of the booty to the ruler.[61] No doubt the Ajtz'quinajay received the same kinds of offerings; Fuentes y Guzmán mentioned towns being sacked of riches during the wars of 1485 to 1501.[62]

Las Casas described several kinds of tribute given in the highlands in the years just before the Conquest: "The general tribute . . . that they gave their rulers and lords was building their houses in common and cultivating and gathering and putting in their storehouses cotton and cacao . . . and all other things they needed for their households." Tribute was given every eighty days and also five or six times a year on important religious and ceremonial occasions. It was a common practice to give eighty items of one kind after an eighty-day period.[63] The Tzutujils and other tributary groups probably paid tribute to the Quichés at such intervals, and their own vassals must have paid them tribute at the same time.

The *Relación geográfica Atitlán* described the same kind of tribute given to the Ajtz'quinajay and his nobles in late times:

They paid their tribute to [the lords] and gave them other personal services, repairing and building their houses, answering their calls, [and] following their orders. . . . They also paid them tribute of *mantas,* honey, and cacao as well as quetzal feathers. They worked and planted their plots of maize, chili peppers, beans, . . . and other vegetables, as was befitting such hereditary lords and rulers.[64]

The people of Xeoj also gave the rulers gold, cacao, quetzal feathers, slaves, jade necklaces, and foods.[65] The *Relación Tzutujil* adds:

They had their servants and domestics as well as those who gave to them and sent tribute, men and women as slaves, precious stones called *chalchivitl* [jade] among them, gold and cacao, feathers, turkeys, honey, and many plots of maize and cacao plantations. They also made their houses.[66] . . . They gave . . . to all the said lords and also to many officials of different offices who were in their kingdom and in their service as carpenters, bricklayers, painters, and feather workers. . . . They gave it to those lords for arms and they used them for defense of their kingdom.[67]

The "said lords" were the Ajtz'iquinajay and his most important nobles.

An official called the *lolmay* served as tribute carrier in Chiya' in late pre-Hispanic times. He was a noble chosen by the lords to carry messages and orders to other areas and probably delivered tribute to the capital at specified times. Another Tzutujil official, the *ajuchan,* was responsible for collecting and storing gifts presented to the ruler.[68] Las Casas said that among the Quichés such officials either were paid out of the tribute they collected or were given some payment by the lords,[69] and that may have been true among the Tzutujils as well.

Another element of the tribute system mentioned by Las Casas was the individual gifts and services given by those who came to see important rulers: "It is a general rule that no one comes before the lord to negotiate anything without bringing something of service according to his means." Merchants gave "a small part of what they gained to the lord, or they brought some new thing not found in the land."[70] The *Relación Tzutujil* states that people came from other places to see the court at Chiya', and some of these visitors probably brought presents to the Ajtz'iquinajay, especially if they had requests to make.[71] In 1522, when the coastal Tzutujils visited Hernán Cortés in Mexico to ask him to settle a boundary dispute, they carried a gift of eight loads of cacao.[72]

We have seen that the main goals of warfare among the Quichean groups were tribute, sacrificial victims, captured enemy gods, and territorial control. During the fourteenth and most of the fifteenth centuries the Quichés gained territory and were successful in making other highland peoples tributaries. The Tzutujils were subordinate to the Quichés until late in the fifteenth century, when they and others established independent kingdoms in the highlands. The Quichés, Cakchiquels, and Tzutujils had similar patterns of warfare and organization of fighting units. Although military conflict was often disruptive, it also provided some impetus for cooperation among former enemies. Hostilities also stimulated dynastic alliances that tended to reinforce the shared cultural patterns of the highland groups. Therefore, warfare ultimately had an integrative effect and was one means of maintaining contact and cultural similarity among Quichean peoples and their allies.

The tribute system depended upon success in warfare and supplied the elite with luxury goods, over which they had a monopoly. It helped maintain the basic class divisions by setting off tribute receivers (lords) from tribute payers (vassals). There were officials among the Tzutujils who were responsible for delivering tribute to the capital and storing gifts presented to the ruler. Paying tribute was a sign of subordination, and for much of their pre-Hispanic history the Tzutujils were a tributary unit in the powerful Quiché state. During the last few decades before the Conquest they broke away from that domination and were able to form their own independent kingdom and keep for themselves all of the tribute supplied by their vassals.

## CHAPTER 6

# Production and Exchange

In pre-Columbian times foodstuffs and craft products were primarily exchanged among groups through tribute and the system of local and regional markets. The tribute system focused on luxury goods, which were monopolized by the elite, but items of lesser value were also sent to important centers to help support nobles, administrators, servants, and others who did not directly engage in agriculture. The market system involved the exchange of items of value as well as everyday products.

## Production

The sections on ecology in chapter 1 give an idea of the range of products available for tribute and trade in the Tzutujil highland and lowland areas. Some commodities were common to both regions, while others were not. Rare items and the best varieties of fruits and vegetables were exchanged more widely than were the more common items.

Tzutujil nobles obtained much of the food for their tables as tribute from their vassals. These subordinates planted the lords' plots of maize, chili peppers, beans, and other crops, in addition to cultivating their own fields.[1] Some of the vassals lived in the lowlands at Xeoj (San Bartolomé), Quioj (San Andrés), and the pre-Hispanic site of San Francisco. In the late sixteenth century Diego de Garcés, a Spanish official living in the lowlands, said that the inhabitants of Atitlán had cacao fields in lowland towns and that they also raised cotton, seeds, and vegetables.[2] One Tzutujil lord, don Jerónimo Ajpopolajay, who wrote a will dated in 1569, owned cacao lands in Xeoj and Quioj. The boundaries of his lands reached "Nawala" (Nahualá?), and he also owned lands near the lake.[3] In more recent times many highland Tzutujils have rented supplementary maize fields in the lowlands or have purchased land in that area to increase their harvests.[4]

Among the Quiché commoners land was worked by individual families but was probably owned by lineages.[5] Since the Tzutujils were also organized into lineages (see chapter 7), it is likely that ownership of land was vested in those groups. The small fields of the commoners (called *sementeras de maíz* in sixteenth-century documents) contrasted with the larger lowland holdings of the lords (referred to as *heredades de cacao* in the same sources).[6]

The farmers prepared the fields by the slash-and-burn *(roza)* method of cultivation.[7] The *Annals* report, "We cut down the trees, we burned them, and we sowed the seed."[8] Today in the highlands the cornstalks are cleared from the maize fields in the period from September to November, and the burning takes place in late January. Planting is done in February and in May, during the rains, and the principal harvest precedes the clearing of the fields, from August to December.[9] In Atitlán land is planted to maize annually for five to ten years in lower areas and from three to four years in higher elevations.[10] That may also have been the pre-Hispanic practice.

Lowland maize has always been inferior to that of the highlands. Felix W. McBryde reported that in modern times in the piedmont the first planting was done after the first heavy rains, which occur in late March and April. The crop was harvested in July and August. A second planting, sometimes in the same field, took place in September.[11] During the sixteenth century, and probably in pre-Hispanic times, the farmers of Xeoj were able to gather three harvests of maize a year owing to the fertile soils,[12] but two harvests were more common. The maize fields often contained other staple crops, such as squash and beans, which grew among the maize stalks. Fruits were also important supplementary crops.

In pre-Hispanic times farmers used simple tools such as hoes made of stone or wood and perhaps digging sticks and stone axes.[13] McBryde reported that the coastal Indians used long, pointed, fire-hardened poles, which they held vertically in both hands.[14] Because the volcanic soil of the highlands is porous and fairly easily worked, the digging stick was not used as widely there as it was in the lowlands.[15] Lakeside garden plots may also have been cultivated in pre-Hispanic times. Today such plots *(tablones)* are worked by the women, while the men continue to tend the maize fields.

Some items and craft specialties produced in the highlands were traded within the Tzutujil area and in other nearby markets. Atitlán has probably been a center of woven textile manufacture since pre-Columbian times, and *mantas* made there may have been traded for cotton in the lowlands.[16] Canoes and rush mats *(petates)* have been made in Atitlán in contemporary times[17] and were probably pre-Hispanic specialties as well. There were copper deposits near Chiya',[18] and some of this metal may have been traded or given in tribute. Atitlán was also an important honey-producing center in the sixteenth century (see table 7), and probably in earlier times as well. The people of Tolimán specialized in making tumplines owing to the abundance of a species of reed *(tul)* that grew near the town.[19]

The people of Chi-Tzunún-Choy (San Pedro) and Chupalo (San Pablo) may have specialized in making such articles as hammocks and ropes from maguey fiber, just as they do today. Maguey grows abundantly along the northwestern shores of Lake Atitlán, but there is some evidence that the best varieties were introduced from Mexico after the Conquest.[20] If that is true, maguey-fiber products may have been only a small industry in the two settlements in pre-Columbian times. In modern times canoes have also been made at San Pedro, but it is not known how far back the industry dates.[21]

Cacao was the major crop in the lowlands in pre-Columbian times, but cotton and food crops were also produced for tribute and exchange. The cacao groves were owned by the highland nobles and were tended by their retainers.[22] Because the young cacao shoots were sensitive to sunlight, another tree, *coxote,* or "mother of cacao" *(Gliricidia sepium),* was planted among the cacao trees to provide shade. *Coxote* wood was also used by the Indians for making furniture, doors, windows, planks, and beams because it was rot-resistant and very strong.[23] Another, inferior grade of cacao, *pataxte (Theobroma bicolor),* was sometimes used as a shade tree for cacao.[24]

The upper-elevation limit for cacao was about 650 meters; above that elevation the climate was too cold. Cacao also required a plentiful amount of water, but during the rainy season, beginning in April or May, when the waters came down most violently, the young cacao plants often rotted.[25] Windstorms also destroyed the groves from time to time.[26] Various insect pests threatened the harvest, and there were certain diseases to which cacao was susceptible.[27] Martens and *tecotles* (owls?) sometimes destroyed the cacao plants by eating the fruit.[28] All of this meant that the groves had to be constantly watched and that skilled overseers were necessary to guarantee a good harvest.

After the cacao was harvested, some of it may have been treated and stored in warehouses, while the rest was sent to the highlands for the lords to use as a drink or as a medium of exchange. Cacao was valuable and allowed the Tzutujil lords to purchase luxury goods from distant capitals.

Fish were traded and given as tribute in pre-Columbian times.[29] There were no large fish appropriate for commercial trade in the highland area, and the fishing industry was probably a minor one around the lake, mainly supplying supplementary food or trade items for small-scale merchants. Fish and crabs must have had some value, however, because those products were presented to Q'uik'ab along with jewels and money when he arrived in Tzololá.

The most important fish trade was in pickled *olomina*, small fish on sticks *(pescaditos)*, and crabs. Although the many rivers in the lowlands contained fish, crabs, and shrimp, the fishing industry seems to have been relatively unimportant there as well. In 1579, Estrada wrote that few people fished full time,[30] perhaps because the emphasis was placed on producing more important items, such as cacao and cotton.

It appears that highland animals did not play a very important role in trade or tribute, but they may have provided individuals with some items to sell in the market. The skins of some lowland animals were valuable and may have been important tribute and market items. Feathers were also important products; parrots, macaws, and other birds with brilliant plumes frequented both the highlands and the lowlands. Tzutujil featherworkers probably utilized a variety of feathers to make such items as dance costumes.[31] The Verapaz towns Cajabón, Chamelco, and Tucurú were the most important feather-collecting centers, but the Tzutujil lowlands were another important source.[32]

## Exchange

*Merchants:* Three kinds of merchants traded in aboriginal times: professional merchants, petty traders, and individual retailers. The professional merchants made long-distance trading expeditions. Quiché merchants traveled several times during the year, mainly dealing in luxury goods. They often stayed with the lords of the towns, where they conducted their business. In Quiché they were called *ajbeyom* ("merchant" or "rich man") and *yacol* ("men who served the table of lords"). The second term indicates that the merchants were not drawn from among the highest lords. Through their profession they became wealthy and powerful and may have formed a privileged group between the vassals and the lords.[33]

Although there is no direct reference to pre-Hispanic Tzutujil merchants in the documents, they must have been active in trading such items as cacao, copper, feathers, and honey to other areas. Such merchants would have exchanged cacao and feathers for gold, jade, and other nonlocal products. While they probably acted independently, they may have occasionally conducted business for the lords. They must have dealt primarily in large quantities and may even have conducted trade in markets beyond Guatemala.[34] In 1579 it was reported that the piedmont was a trade center for Spanish merchants, who went to Mexico with cacao and brought back cloth and other goods.[35] In pre-Hispanic times Indian merchants had brought back such items as metals and turquoise.[36] Quiché, Cakchiquel, and other merchants crossed Lake Atitlán in canoes, bringing their wares to exchange for Tzutujil products. In the late 1930s, Sol Tax observed large canoes capable of holding fifteen to twenty men or more leaving Santiago Atitlán for the markets at Sololá and Tecpán.[37] In ancient times Tzutujils traveled to such important markets as Iximché, K'umarcaaj, Rabinal, and Cobán. Markets in Soconusco provided access to trade goods from Mexico.

The petty traders ordinarily made short trips within their own market districts. These merchants dealt in one or two items from their local area, such as maize, vegetables, fruits, and simple craft goods. The petty merchants were called *ajc'ay*, ("sellers") in Quiché,[38] and may have had a similar name in Tzutujil. They carried their goods on their backs, just as many traders do today. The traders probably wore carrying frames over their backs similar to the contemporary *cacastes* (Nahuatl, *cacaxtli*) and may have carried loads weighing up to about 50 kilograms, just as they do in modern times.

Individual retailers, primarily women who dealt in small quantities of goods for household consumption, sold their products in local markets.[39] Most of the items the women took to market were products they had grown, prepared, or gathered themselves, as is true in contemporary lake markets.

*The Market System:* Las Casas described the organization of the pre-Hispanic market in Verapaz, and Tzutujil markets may have been similar. He said that the markets were near the temples.[40] The merchants may have lived nearby.[41] Until recently the market of Santiago Atitlán was in an open courtyard next to the church.[42] According to Las Casas, in the Verapaz market a judge set the prices of articles for sale and ruled on disagreements arising among buyers and sellers. In the contemporary market system of the Lake Atitlán area prices are not predetermined but are established through the interaction of buyers and sellers. There are not enough buyers to set a price, and the sellers do not control enough of the supply to affect the price.[43] Sellers are organized in groups, all of those marketing the same product being in one location. This structure, which also helps keep prices uniform,[44] may have characterized Tzutujil markets in ancient times as well. Perhaps the more important markets, such as that at Chiya', had market judges like those of Verapaz.

In Verapaz there were also craftsmen who traded their products. Among them were silversmiths, painters, featherworkers, and makers of copper axes.[45] Among the Tzutujils were the same kinds of craftsmen,[46] who no doubt traded their wares in the local markets. The women of Verapaz, and probably those of Chiya', sold their woven cloth in the market, which served as an outlet for individually produced items as well as for luxury items.

Las Casas also described the manner in which goods were exchanged in Verapaz:

All had great help in supplying their needs in the markets, . . . held near the temples. Their means of carrying out business is to exchange some things for others, . . . giving maize for beans and beans for cacao and especially salt which in many lands is a very precious commodity. They bring . . . chili . . . and game and fruits and all the things they find to eat. They exchange *mantas* of cotton cloth for gold and for copper axes, gold for jade and turquoise and feathers which are the most valued goods.[47]

Although Verapaz is some distance from the Tzutujil area, this description probably characterized transactions there and in many other important Guatemalan markets as well.

The passage from Las Casas above also demonstrates that it was common to use some medium of exchange in trading rather than rely exclusively on barter. Cacao, an important trade medium, was exchanged in standardized amounts. One *carga*, or load, of cacao was composed of 3 *xiquipiles* (Nahuatl), or about 24,000 beans (one *xiquipil* equaled about 8,000 beans).[48] These measures

were used for large purchases and for expansive items. Petty
traders and individuals engaged in sales involving small amounts
of cacao beans, perhaps 20 or fewer.[49]

Salt was also used for small transactions[50] and was no doubt
worth more in areas lacking nearby salt deposits. It appeared in
the marketplace in loaves or bags.[51] The Tzutujils probably obtained most of their salt for exchange from the coastal plain near
Xicalapa.[52] Another product that was a medium of exchange was
the tribute *manta,* a strip of cotton cloth. There were also other
kinds of *mantas,* some larger than the tribute *manta,* all of which
may have served as mediums of exchange for market purchases
as well as tribute.[53]

Pre-Columbian centers were probably linked in a system of
markets similar to those of the middle-western highlands today.[54]
People daily visited the major ancient regional markets, such as
those at Iximché, K'umarcaaj, Rabinal, Xelaju, and possibly Chiya',
to exchange goods from all over the middle-western highlands, the
entire Guatemalan area, and external regions. Because the Tzutujils controlled some of the best cacao lands and were advantageously
situated on a major highland-lowland trade route, Chiya' must
have been an important market, drawing merchants from a wide
area.

Most settlements of any size probably had a local market held
on a scheduled day of the week and specializing in certain products, as in modern times. Certain towns, such as Chi-Tzunún-
Choy, may not have had markets but depended on the market at
Chiya', just as today San Pedro depends on the market at Atitlán.[55]
In modern times San Lucas Tolimán has one of the largest markets
on the lake,[56] and it may have had one in aboriginal times as
well, owing to the town's favorable location on the southeast pass
into the lowlands.

*The Highland-Lowland Exchange:* Although the Tzutujils exchanged
goods with peoples beyond their borders, most of the information
that we have on trade and tribute relates to the flow of goods
between Atitlán and the piedmont area in the late sixteenth century. The *Relación geográfica Atitlán* states that "nothing is raised
on [this land] except a little maize because in many parts of the
town it cannot be grown. The supply of maize comes through trans-
port, the inhabitants of this town buying it in other regions."[57] Pre-
Columbian production of maize probably equaled or exceeded
that of more recent times, and disruptions associated with the
Conquest may have been responsible for the decline in production
in the late sixteenth century.

In the pre-Hispanic period maize was imported into the high-lands at certain times and exported to the lowlands at others. Highland-Tzutujil maize was exported to the lowlands mainly from November to December, when there was plenty to exchange. Low-land grain probably went to the lake region between August and October and again in late February to March, when maize became scarce in some areas.[58] Early frosts often destroyed highland maize, and famine resulted.[59] Although farmers in some areas of the low-lands, such as the Xeoj region, produced three harvests, they still had to import maize at certain times:

Since the earth is overly damp, the maize to be harvested is no good after two months, more or less, because if kept longer, it rots and turns to flour. For this reason most of the year the maize needed by the natives is transported from other towns in the region that are found in the cold land of the mountains."[60]

Although many of the same or similar crops were grown in the highlands and the lowlands, the quality of any one crop varied with the region. The area producing the better crop usually traded it more widely within and beyond the Tzutujil borders. The high-land merchants brought to the lowlands products from all over the upper region, exchanging them for items not found in their own areas. The lowlanders specialized in cacao, which did not grow in the cool highlands, and probably also produced enough food to feed themselves, sell in the market, and provide for the lords.[61] Fuentes y Guzmán reported that the Tzutujils profited from their fields of cacao and achiote and exchanged those products for gold and silver.[62] *Pataxte* was traded too; in 1579 it was worth one-half the price of cacao.[63] Both cacao and *pataxte* were exchanged among pre-Hispanic nobles.[64]

The Ajtz'iquinajay and the other Tzutujil lords received some tribute items that must have been obtained through trade, for they were not produced in Tzutujil territory. This demonstrates the interconnection of the trade and tribute systems in moving products from the lowlands to the highlands and from more distant regions. The lowland Tzutujil settlement at Malaj gave dower gifts to the Quiché ruler C'otuja when he married the daughter of the local lord. The gifts—*quvals* (green stones), *pataxte,* cacao, pacayas (edible palm-tree flowers), *girnallas* (garlands), chili, and small birds—were the girl's dowry and were probably also trade items from that lowland center.[65]

In summary, it seems clear that, by controlling an ecologically diverse and productive area, the pre-Hispanic Tzutujils were able to participate successfully in the regional market system and that the nobles obtained the full range of tribute items. The highland area specialized primarily in the production of maize and other foods, while the lowland area concentrated on cacao, cotton, animal skins, and feathers. Local specialization existed in both areas and stimulated a thriving system of highland-lowland trade carried out by professional merchants, petty traders, and individual retailers. Luxury goods were handled only by the most important merchants, who often brought them from distant centers, while the tribute system channeled most local items of value into the hands of the nobles. The petty traders and individual buyers and sellers dealt mainly in craft items and foodstuffs for the commoners.

The aboriginal market system operated in much the same way that the contemporary market functions in the middle-western highlands. Local markets, held on particular days, specialized in items grown or produced locally. Larger regional markets, which were open daily, exchanged items from a far-ranging area. The market and tribute systems moved the best products of any given region beyond the local centers of production and increased the availability of products to individuals and groups throughout Guatemala.

The market system was also a major factor in highland cultural integration. It stimulated movement of people to various market centers and brought members of different cultural groups together. Going to external markets was an important means of gaining information on nonlocal events and becoming familiar with the customs of people living within the highland-lowland trading region.

CHAPTER 7

# *Class and Lineage*

Pre-Hispanic Tzutujil society was composed of two major groups: the lords, who received tribute and services, and the vassals, the tribute payers. Among the Tzutujils *ajaw* was the general title used to designate a lord.[1] The term for vassals is unknown; it may have been similar to the Quiché *al c'ajol.*[2]

## *Class Stratification*

*Lords and Vassals:* The lords held the most important state offices. The vassals served in the army, tilled the fields of the nobles, and built the nobles' houses.[3] The vassals, who comprised the majority of the population, were the merchants, farmers, laborers, fishermen, lesser artisans, slaves, conquered subjects, and sons and daughters of the lords' commoner and slave wives.

The lords had special symbols or emblems of office and insignia on the standards that they carried into battle.[4] The *Popol Vuh* lists the symbols of leadership that C'ocaib brought back from Tula: canopy and throne, nose bone and earring, jade labret, gold beads, panther and jaguar claws, owl and deer skulls, an armband of precious stones, a snail-shell bracelet, a royal-crane panache, a parrot-feather crest, inlaid and filled teeth—and the custom of bowing to the lords.[5] These symbols of status belonged to the highest Quiché lords. The Tzutujils must have had similar regalia.

In 1585 the elders of Atitlán reported that the nobles wore sleeveless jackets called *xapo't* in Tzutujil (Nahuatl, *xicolli*) and cotton loincloths. The *xapo't* of the lords reached to the middle of the thigh; the commoners' jacket came to a point below the navel. The women wore short cotton blouses, called *po't* in Tzutujil (*huipil* in Nahuatl), and cotton petticoats. The Tzutujil lords' costumes were made of colored cotton, and they may have had many fine furs fashioned from valuable animal pelts obtained in the nearby lowlands. The lords received in tribute quetzal feathers, gold, jade, and other precious stones, and these items were used in making jewelry and headdresses.[6] Only the lords could drink the chocolate beverage made from the valuable cacao, and they ate finer foods than the commoners did.

The most important Tzutujil lords lived in Chiya', the *tinamit*. Most of the vassals were dispersed throughout the countryside, living in the dependencies or *amak'*. From time to time the lords ordered their vassals to populate other regions. The Indians of Xeoj, originally from the Chiya' area, moved to the lowlands on command of their lords.[7]

*Middle Class:* Among the vassals was a small middle class composed of professional merchants, skilled artisans, and lesser government and religious officials. Some of these individuals were able to gain wealth and power. As mentioned earlier, important Quiché merchants stayed in the towns of the lords where they conducted business, and Tzutujil merchants may have done the same thing. A merchant ate at the lord's table and was invited to amuse himself "in accordance with the prestige of each merchant." They knew how to read, write, and play the musical instruments of the lords. They paid tribute nonetheless, and they were not received as members of the noble class.[8] It is likely that Tzutujil merchants were well received by the Tzutujil lords, considering the value their lowland products must have had in highland markets. In 1585 merchants were still active in trading goods in the highlands and lowlands. They were wealthy and could afford to dress better than most of the other commoners, and that may have been a continuation of the pre-Hispanic situation.[9]

Artisans had wealth and prestige in accordance with their lineage, rank, and the craft they pursued. The highest-ranking craftsmen among the Quichés were called *ajtoltecat*,[10] a term suggesting Mexican origin. Some artisans seem to have been the younger sons or relatives of lords holding the highest offices, and they paid tribute in kind to the lords. They were neither lords nor vassals.[11] *The Annals of the Cakchiquels* named some of the Quiché craftsmen: *ajxit* (jeweler), *ajpuvaq* (silversmith), *ajtz'ib* (scribe), and *ajq'ot* (engraver).[12] The *Popol Vuh* mentions others:

|            |               |
|------------|---------------|
| Gemcutter, | Ah Q'uval,    |
| Jeweller,  | Ah Yamanik,   |
| Carver,    | Ah Ch'ut,     |
| Sculptor,  | Ah Tz'alam,   |

| Green Plate Spirit, | Ah Raxa Laq, |
| Blue Bowl Spirit, | Ah Raxa Zel, |
| Incense Maker, | Ah Q'ol, |
| Craftsman, | Ah Toltecat, |
| Grandmother of Day, | R Atit Q'ih, |
| Grandmother of Light | R Atit Zaq.[13] |

These titles were probably used by Tzutujil craftsmen as well. According to the *Relación Tzutujil,* several other kinds of craftsmen practiced at Chiya': carpenters, featherworkers *(ajpixol),* stonemasons,[14] and painters *(ajtz'ib).*[15]

Among the enemy peoples from the lake region was listed an *ahpova,* who was the Tzutujils' counterpart of the Quichés' *ajpuvaq.*[16] In a confessional list from Santiago Atitlán dating from the seventeenth century the names Ajtz'ib and Ajq'ot are shown.[17] The first designates the office of the scribe, and the second the office of the engraver.

*Commoners:* The great majority of the population was composed of commoners, who tilled the soil, fished, and made simple craft goods. There is little information in the documents concerning their lives other than statements describing their subsistence activities and services to the lords.[18]

*Serfs and Slaves:* Las Casas said that the lords rented land to poor people at a low price and married slaves who paid them tribute, worked in the fields, and gathered firewood and pine torches.[19] The Tzutujil lords also had commoners and slaves who worked their lands.[20] Probably there were also conquered groups who had been incorporated into Tzutujil territory and were similar to the *mayeques* of Mexico, who were inherited with the land. In the Quichean region these serfs were known as *nimak achi* ("big people"), a name suggesting that some of them were important individuals.[21]

Zorita spoke of *mayeques* among the Cakchiquels:

"In Tecpán Guatemala, . . . I knew a lord who had succeeded his brother. The son of the deceased lord was living, and I knew him well. He held the patrimonial lands and mayeques, but his uncle had the lordship. It was said that this had been done because the ruler's son was blind, and so the ruler gave the chieftainship to his brother."[22]

The *mayeques* he referred to were probably *nimak achi.* A "Nimak-achí" group was living in San Pedro in the seventeenth century, and thus they existed among the Tzutujils as well.[23] Some of the more important *nimak achi* may have assumed positions of trust and authority within the conquering kingdom.[24] The Tzutujil rulers may have depended upon them rather heavily for the management of the vital lowland cacao plantations.

Slaves formed the lowest class in Tzutujil society. A domestic slave *(muni)* worked primarily in the household and fields of the lords.[25] Among the Quichés, vassal prisoners, criminals, poor vassals sold by kinsmen or lords, vassals who married slaves, slaves who were purchased, and children born of slaves comprised the category of domestic slaves.[26] Carmack described three other categories of slaves among the Quichés: *cana,* or "those who are won," just as animals are won in the hunt; *teleche,* or slaves who were "dragged from one place to another"; and *tz'i',* or dogs, which probably referred to nobles taken in battle who were destined for sacrifice.[27] Las Casas said that those captured in war were the most-preferred slaves; lords who had to buy slaves in effect admitted that they were unable to obtain them in battle.[28] Since the Tzutujils participated in the same warfare system and had a similar military ethic, they must have had the same categories of slaves.

In the late sixteenth century the lords of Atitlán complained of their loss of status owing to heavy tribute demands by the Spaniards. They said that they were in great need and were "forced to carry loads and eat fruit and tree roots, . . . and our wives grind and serve for us, and to maintain our households we are used as our slaves were once used by us."[29]

### The Lineage System

The most important kinship units of pre-Hispanic Quichean society were the unilineal descent groups, or patrilineages, which traced their descent back to the original warlords. Their members were united as brothers and sisters, fathers and fathers' sisters, and children.[30]

*Lords:* There were sixteen important lords among the Tzutujils during the mid-sixteenth century, including the Ajtz'iquinajay.[31] These were the lords of the leading lineages (see table 2). This compares with the twenty-four principal lineages of Quichés at K'umarcaaj, the twenty-two of the Tamubs at Pismachi, and the eighteen of the Ilocabs at Mukwitz Pilocab.[32] The Tzutujils' founding ancestors are unknown.

Table 2. *Leading Tzutujil Lineages*

| | |
|---|---|
| Ajtz'iquinajay | Ajc'abawil |
| Cabinjay | Coonі́ |
| Najtijay | Ajpopolajay |
| Ajcojay | Tzununá |
| Ajquiwijay | Lapoyoi |
| Ajqitzijay | |

The Tzutujils were similar to the Tamubs in that both groups had moietal divisions. The moieties of the Tzutujils were the Ajtz'iquinajay, which was dominant, and the Tzutujil, which, though subordinate, gave its name to the people as a whole. The Ajtz'iquinajay may have been related to the important Tz'iquinajay lineage among the Caweks at K'umarcaaj. Perhaps they became dominant when the Quichés established control over much of the highland area in the early fifteenth century. After the Conquest the Ajtz'iquinajay and Tzutujil moieties participated in rule; it appears that the latter group began contesting the former's dominance shortly before the Conquest.[33]

We have some information about the most important Tzutujil lineages. Two painted cloths *(lienzos)* described in 1563 showed the most important lords of Atitlán. The cloths, dating from pre-Conquest times, were pictorial representations of the highest lord, the Ajtz'iquinajay, and the fifteen lords subject to him. All these lords possessed their own lands but were subject to the Ajtz'iquinajay. There was probably one cloth for each moiety.[34]

The Ajtz'iquinajay, or Bird House lineage, was thus the most important lineage at Chiya'. The *Relación Tzutujil* mentions several other names of high-ranking Tzutujil nobles: Najtijay (Far House), Ajcojay (Strong House), Ajquiwijay (?), Ajqitzijay (?), and Ajc'abawil (Idol House).[35] In the document of 1563 analyzed by Carrasco, the same lords are listed as Natihay, Acohay, Quibihay, Aquizihay, and Acapuhil.[36]

A Nalitihá lineage is mentioned in the *Título Totonicapán*.[37] The spellings Atziquinahay, Atzcavail, Natzihay, and Atzkibitzay appear in a list of names from Atitlán dating from 1683 to 1700.[38] Ajtziquinajay and Ajquivijay were mentioned in the seventeenth-century *Libro primero de matrimonios* of San Pedro.[39] An Ah Qiba Haa lineage is mentioned in the *Popol Vuh*. It seems to have been originally a sublineage of the Cakchiquel Ah Ch'umila Haa (Star House) lineage[40] and may have become established at Chiya' when some of the Cakchiquels stayed behind with their Tzutujil wives.[41] Edmonson translates the name as Chest House.[42]

As mentioned above, the members of the Tzutujil Ajcojay lineage were at one time preferred marriage partners for the Cakchiquels.[43] Along with the Ajqitzijay they are called Ah-Cula-Quichá in the *Título Totonicapán*.[44] The "chiefs . . . Ahtziquinahay and Qitzihay" are also mentioned in *The Annals of the Cakchiquels*.[45]

In the document of 1563 the adjunct lord, or assistant ruler, was the most important lord after the Ajtz'iquinajay and was named Cabunay or Cahunay,[46] which should probably be Cabinjay. This lord served as a close adviser to the ruler, and his lineage may originally have been part of the Ajtz'iquinajay lineage at Chiya'. Carmack has indicated that most of the leading lineages contained secondary, or minimal, lineages, whose members served as lower-echelon political, ritual, military, and economic functionaries. Among the Quichés the minimal lineages of the principal patrilineages gradually came to assume more importance in the political structure.[47] Evidently at some point the Ajtz'iquinajay lineage was able to elevate one of its minimal lineages to principal status. Its members then came to fill the adjunct role.

There were some other Tzutujil lineages which, according to legend, migrated into the Guatemala highlands. Two of these were the Zaq Ahib (White Corns) and the Lamakib (Barriers).[48] These groups apparently did not travel as far south as Lake Atitlán. The former settled at Salcaja, near Xelaju, and the latter at Xolchún, just east of Sacapulas.[49] They were absorbed by the Quichés.

The Tzununá (Hummingbird) lineage was the most important one at Chi-Tzunún-Choy. A "Mayuc Ajtzun(unija)" lineage was one of the original lineages to migrate into the highlands, according to the *Título C'oyoi*.[50] The Cooní lineage may have been one of the sixteen important Tzutujil lineages. This group appeared in the *Título Xpantzay 2*, along with the Lapoyoi lineage.[51] It was among the twelve most important *chinamit* of San Pedro listed in the seventeenth-century *Libro primero de matrimonios* of that town (see table 3).[52]

Another possibly important Tzutujil lineage was that of Ajpopolajay (Counselor House). After the Conquest, don Jerónimo de Mendoza, the Ajpopolajay, made a will dated 1569 leaving lands in the coastal and highland areas to his sons and wife.[53] Since only the most important lords owned such lands, this lineage was probably one of the sixteen painted on the cloths.

Each of the highest lords had his own lands in the highlands

## Table 3. *Tzutujil Chinamit*

| Thirteen Principal Chinamit of San Pedro la Laguna* | |
| --- | --- |
| Tzununá | Ajquivijay |
| Koní | Nimakachí |
| Ajtz'iquinajay | Julo Loquol |
| Uaytza | Chicbal |
| Nikachi | Queuaki |
| Taual Ulujay | Nijakí |
| Ajchavajay | |

| Families Comprising the Tzununá Chinamit* | |
| --- | --- |
| Ajcac | Chicbal |
| Ajpantzay† | Chouaj |
| Ajpixolá | Peneleu |
| Colín | Petzey |
| Cox | Pop |
| Culán | Tziak |
| Cumatz | Tzicay |
| Chacón | |

*The lineage names are taken from the *Libro primero de matrimonios* of San Pedro, which begins with the year 1647. This list is very late and probably represents the amalgamation of remnants of several groups. It is impossible to determine how many of the thirteen principal *chinamit* of San Pedro were among the leading pre-Hispanic *chinamit* at Chiya'.

†An important Cakchiquel lineage.

and lowlands, clearly indicated by boundary markers (Spanish, *mojones*). Each may also have maintained a house in Chiya' where he spent most of his time. Lands owned by the lords could be willed to descendants, as in the case of Ajpopolajay. Carrasco also mentioned one Cakchiquel lineage, the Pacal, that passed lands from fathers to sons for five generations.[54] Both of these examples date from post-Hispanic times, however, and it is not clear whether this was invariably the custom in aboriginal times. Among the Quichés the principal lineages were closely associated with the buildings in which they conducted formal ceremonies. These were called *nim ja* ("big houses").[55] Such structures may also have existed in Chiya'. The important lineages may have had their own temples, gods, and priests as well.[56]

It is not possible today to associate lineages with specific lands. Control of lands was probably originally vested in the lineages, and the lineage head apportioned it to heads of households, but the highest lords seem to have obtained control over conquered

lands. This was the case for some lands in the lowland area, and
the *Relaciones geográficas* state that the dependencies were "always subject to the lords and rulers of the head town."[57]

*Vassals:* There is no documentary information on the organization
of the Tzutujil vassals. They were probably organized into lineages
that were not as highly ranked as those of the lords. Commoner
vassals probably married girls from local vassal lineages. Even
today most Tzutujils in the Lake Atitlán area choose their spouses
from families in their own towns.[58]

The lords and vassals were integrated by means of the *chinamit*
(a Nahua word meaning "fenced-in place"), a common form of
territorial organization in the Quiché region. Not all the people
forming a *chinamit* were necessarily related, but they lived in a
common territory and were subject to the same leader.[59] The sixteen principal Tzutujil lords shown on the two painted cloths may
have been the heads of separate *chinamit,* which were called by
the lineage names.

Among the Quichés the *chinamit* was also the unit of tribute
and personal-service obligations, judicial and ritual processes, and
soldiers fought within *chinamit* units. Most administrative details
of the Quiché *chinamit* were handled by the minimal lineages,
which worked closely with the main lineages.[60] Representatives
from the important lineages in the *tinamit* probably also resided
in important *amak'.* This organizational structure must have been
common throughout Quichean society. There were other territorial
divisions besides the *chinamit.* One was the *calpul* (Nahua, *calpulli,*
"group of houses"), a territorial unit composed of intermarrying
commoner lineages.[61] While the *chinamit* was a territorial unit
associated with a major settlement, or *tinamit,* and secondary
centers like Chi-Tzunún-Choy, the *calpul* was a larger and more
distant territory.

The *calpules* probably represented conquered lands that were
too far from the *tinamit* to be easily incorporated. They were
colonies organized along territorial divisions already established
by the conquered peoples.

To oversee the more distant *calpules,* the lords sent officials
from their lineages.[62] Xeoj and Quioj appear to have been *calpules*
having some measure of independence from Chiya'. They had
their own temples and idols, and perhaps officials from Chiya'
had the responsibility of supervising the cacao groves and delivering tribute to the highland lords. San Francisco, which may not
have had a separate name in pre-Hispanic times, was considered

an integral part of the *tinamit* and was incorporated into the *chinamit* structure of the capital. The town had no separate temple or idol.

The Tzutujil moiety leaders, despite their secondary position, probably had some lands in the highlands and lowlands. Whether they shared in the governing of any specific area other than Xikomuk, however, is not known.

After the Conquest, *cabezas de calpul* ("heads of *calpul*") were listed for Atitlán (see table 10). Some of these post-Conquest leaders were principal lords using the Spanish title *don.* Unfortunately, it is not possible to link these *calpul* leaders with specific lineages because native names are not given in the documents. It appears that the *cabezas de calpul* of Atitlán were really leaders of pre-Hispanic *chinamit* rather than of the distant *calpules.*

*Marriage:* One of the most important functions of the lineage system was the regulation of marriages.[63] Individuals had to marry outside their lineages, and women went to live with their husbands, becoming part of the husbands' lineages after the bride price was paid.[64] Today in Tzutujil towns the bride still customarily moves into the home of her husband's parents after marriage, but the couple may establish its own residence when children are born.[65] In Atitlán most households are now nuclear, being composed of a married couple and their children.[66] A payment is made by the groom's household, but it is not considered a bride price. The money is supposed to be used by the bride to buy material to make her trousseau and a set of clothes for her future husband.[67] In pre-Conquest times, Las Casas said, it was customary for the towns to contribute to the weddings of the lords.[68] The groom's lineage sometimes helped pay the bride price;[69] today in Atitlán this function has been assumed by the household.

Las Casas said that if a woman was widowed she was still considered a member of her husband's lineage, and she usually married one of his near relatives.[70] The levirate may have ended with the decline of the lineage system in the Tzutujil area. Today widows do not customarily marry relatives of their spouses.[71]

The elders of Atitlán stated that in pre-Hispanic times the lords of Chiya' had ten to fifteen wives or more. The first wife was respected by all the other wives and was the one most cherished and loved by the lord. The "lesser Indians" had two to four wives.[72] According to the elders, "When the Indians married, they were about forty years of age, more or less, and the women were about twenty-five or thirty."[73] These ages seem rather old, and the Quiché ruler C'otuja married a very young bride.[74] Las Casas reported, however, that the men usually did not marry until they were thirty or more,[75] which tends to confirm the elders' statement.

The procedures followed by the highest lords in matters of marriage are illustrated by the example of C'otuja:

Wishing to wed a daughter of the lord of . . . *Malah*, [C'otuja] sent two of his men whose mission it was to ask [for her in marriage] according to the instructions of Nacxit. He ordered them to take some rabbits and birds, which they were to put on a height where the lord of Malah lived, and warned them to take great care not to be seen.

The men carried out their lord's orders and found a green stone *(quval)* in place of the rabbits and birds. The envoys were eventually seen and were led before the ruler of Malaj and invited to drink cacao. They asked for the girl and then returned to C'otuja to inform him of her father's consent. C'otuja sent four lords to Malaj to escort the princess to K'umarcaaj. They carried litters painted yellow, a red *petate* (rush mat), and some sandals. When his young bride arrived in K'umarcaaj, C'otuja received gifts from the girl's father.[76] This account demonstrates that the lowland Tzutujils of Malaj followed the same marriage customs as those of the highland Quichés. The highland Tzutujils, being part of the dynastic alliance system, must have followed the common customs.

We have little information regarding marriage practices among the commoners. Perhaps the leader of the boy's lineage asked for the girl's hand on behalf of the groom, as was the practice among the Pokomans in the early seventeenth century.[77]

Slaves usually married other slaves. If a free woman married a slave, her children were slaves.[78] The *Título Xpantzay 3* mentions a marriage between a lord and a slave, after which the kingdom was invalidated.[79] Marriages between high-ranking lords and slaves must have been rare.

Only the offspring of high-ranking lords and equally ranked wives were entitled to inherit and rule. That is why the first wife was respected the most. Both lords and well-to-do commoners probably kept slaves as concubines, but the sons of such unions could never rise to be lords. That was no doubt the custom among the Tzutujils as it was among other Quichean peoples. The lineage system thus determined whom one could marry and at what level and indicated social status. Only the highest members of the highest-ranked lineages could fill the most important political and military offices, rule as lords, own lands, and receive tribute.

Dynastic alliances, such as that between the Quichés and the

Tzutujils of Malaj, served to connect the nobility and strongly reinforced the maintenance of a shared sociopolitical framework among the members of Quichean society. Perhaps the ruler of Malaj felt that by joining the Quichés, K'umarcaaj being farther away than Chiya', he could in fact retain more independence. With his daughter married to C'otuja, he could expect to have some influence at the Quiché court.

Dynastic alliances also helped cement political alliances. In the early sixteenth century a Cakchiquel ruler at Iximché became a widower and chose his second principal wife from among the Tzutujils. She was Lady Ixk'ekac'uch, who was said to be an Ajtz'iquinajay woman.[80] The marriage took place during a time when the two groups were on good terms, and the union assured an alliance between the Cakchiquels and the Tzutujils. Not long after the marriage the Ajtz'iquinajay went to Iximché to recruit soldiers to help him put down an internal revolt.[81]

The Tzutujils intermarried with other Cakchiquel lineages. A member of the Cakchiquel Pacal lineage, Pacal Ixtziquinajay, inherited the highest office of that group early in the sixteenth century. His mother was probably a Tzutujil woman, perhaps from Tzololá. A Qomuyuc Tzutuhil was also mentioned; he may have been born of a mother of the subordinate Tzutujil moiety.[82]

While dynastic marriages ordinarily had positive benefits, elopement or bride stealing could lead to a deterioration of relations. Fuentes y Guzmán said that the Quiché ruler Balam Acam had the utmost confidence and trust in the Ajtz'iquinajay until that lord stole the princess.[83] In view of the long subsequent wars, however, there were probably serious underlying problems between the Quichés and Tzutujils.

Today among the Tzutujils elopement or bride stealing occurs, as in other cultures, when the young couple face objections from their parents or other obstacles. The girl is taken with her consent. Often two or more young men arrange to elope with their brides on the same night, echoing the elopement of the Ajtz'iquinajay and his companion back in the fifteenth century.[84]

It has been seen that the basic divisions in Tzutujil society were the lords, who received tribute, and the vassals, who paid it. The lords traced their descent back to the original migrants, held the most important offices, and had a monopoly on luxury goods.

There was a small middle class of merchants, artisans, and lesser government and religious officials. Despite their vassal status, some of the merchants achieved considerable wealth and power.

High-ranking craftsmen belonged to important lineages but were younger sons or relatives of the leading lords. They paid tribute in kind but appear to have been neither lords nor vassals.

The vassals were the commoners who comprised the major part of the population; serfs, some of whom performed important functions such as tending the cacao lands of the lords; and slaves. The serfs were inhabitants of conquered lands. Slaves were purchased, captured in warfare, born into slavery, made slaves because they were criminals, or were married to slaves. They formed the lowest stratum of Tzutujil society.

Lineage determined a person's rank, and descent usually passed through the male line from father to son, though brothers could also inherit. The Ajtz'iquinajay and the fifteen other highest lords of Chiya' were also the lords of the leading lineages and held the most important offices in the Tzutujil kingdom. They were the leaders of the most important *chinamit,* and they also had under their jurisdiction the more distant *calpules.*

The lineage system determined whom one could marry. Important lords often married high-born women from other groups, and such dynastic alliances linked the nobility of Quichean society, often strengthening political alliances. Many lineage names were the same among the Quichés, Cakchiquels, and Tzutujils as branches became established in distant *tinamit.* This practice helped maintain a shared culture within Quichean society despite warfare and dissension. Vassals tended to marry within their own local areas and were closed off from the nobility. Some marriage practices, such as bride price and elopement, still exist among the Tzutujils while others, such as the levirate and dynastic marriages, do not.

## CHAPTER 8

# The System of Political Offices

All the Quichean groups had a similar system of political offices that both allowed for status recognition and regulated government life. The concept of office was extremely important, and offices belonging to major lineages are frequently mentioned in the native sources.[1] All classes were assigned offices, and the desire to rise in status by gaining more power for one's office provided another stimulus to warfare, which was the major means of gaining personal recognition. A brilliant military record could also mean appointment to a higher office.

## Tzutujil State Offices

*Tzutujil Pop:* The most important positions of state in Tzutujil society were filled by the sixteen lords of the highest-ranking lineages. The leading office was that of the Tzutujil *pop,* and the leader of the Ajtz'iquinajay lineage occupied that position. Lineage names can usually be identified by the ending *jay,* which means "house." Ajtz'iquinajay was the lineage name, and Tzutujil *pop* the office name, which corresponded to the Quiché *ajpop* and the Cakchiquel *ajpoxajil* or *ajpotzotzil.*

As lord and ruler of the kingdom, the Tzutujil *pop* had ultimate say over all that transpired within his domain. If the other lords wanted to make human sacrifices or punish someone, they first had to ask his permission.[2] According to the *Popol Vuh,* the Quiché office titles, which seem to have served as models for the Cakchiquels and the Tzutujils, dated from the Quichés' second visit to Tula:

> "Nacxit was the name of the great lord . . .
> And it was he who gave out the signs of authority,
> All the insignia . . .
> And then came the sign of the power

And authority
Of Counsellor [*ajpop*]
And Step House Counsellor [*ajpop c'amja*]. "³

The *Relación Tzutujil* states that the other Tzutujil offices were called "Lolmay, Atzihuinac, Calel and Ahuchan" and that "these were their agents, accountants and treasurers."⁴ Carrasco used the "Barela" (Varea) and Coto dictionaries to define the functions of these officials, who had counterparts among the Quichés and the Cakchiquels.⁵

*Lolmay:* The *lolmay* was a lord who was sent by the rest of the lords on business of the kingdom or to carry tribute.⁶ In the *Título Totonicapán* enemy list a "lolmet-Cuminay" was included,⁷ and in *The Annals of the Cakchiquels* it was stated that in 1565 "Don Pedro, . . . *Qavinay* of the Zutuhils, died."⁸ Cabinjay was the lineage that held the position of highest *lolmay* in the Tzutujil capital.

The *lolmay* was the most important lord after the Tzutujil *pop* and "was like a father and confidant of the . . . *acequinajay* and [the lords] went to him with their business matters and matters of war and justice and sacrifices so that he [the *lolmay*] might intercede with him for them." He could also assume the position of regent if the Tzutujil *pop* was too young to rule.⁹

Among the Tzutujils the office of *lolmay* may have been similar to that of the *ajpop c'amja* ("receiving house") the second in command among the Cawec Quichés. There is no evidence of an *ajpop c'amja* office among the Tzutujils, but it may have existed. It seems that the office of *lolmay* was the second-highest office in any case. That was also the situation for the Ajaw Quiché branch of the Quichés, in which, according to the *Popol Vuh*, the *ahav lol met* was the second-most-important lord.¹⁰

The Varea and Coto dictionaries defined *lolmay* as "messenger" or "porter" of the lords.¹¹ Both meanings probably refer to the *lolmay*'s primary task of carrying and overseeing valuable tribute items, such as cotton *mantas*. Las Casas reported that there were lords who collected tribute, divided it up, and sent it to the ruler and other lords.¹² Among the Tzutujils the *lolmay* was probably one of the lords who did this. The office also existed among the Cakchiquels: an Ahau Francisco Hernández Lolmay was one of the signers of the *Título Xpantzay 1*.¹³

*Ajuchan:* The *ajuchan* ("treasurer" or "speaker") was responsible for collecting and keeping gifts.¹⁴ He may have kept presents brought to the Tzutujil *pop* by those having specific requests or as booty from conquests. This office may have been similar to those priests called Tepew and K'ucumatz by the Quichés. They were stewards who were responsible for collecting and storing similar offerings.[15] The lineage associated with the office of *ajuchan* is not known. The office was still occupied in 1569, for a Francisco Quiej Ajuc'an signed don Jerónimo Mendoza's will in that year.[16] Quiej means Deer and was probably a calendar, not a lineage, name.

K'alel: The office of *k'alel (calel)* mentioned in the *Relación Tzutujil*[17] corresponds to the Quiché office of *k'alel* ("courtier"). Among the Quichés the *k'alel* attended the *ajpop* in public matters, acting as a chief judge and counselor. His role was to explain, question, witness, and denounce and to assist the ruler in making decisions.[18] The office of *k'alel* also existed among the Cakchiquels, and was filled by the son of the adjunct lord.[19]

*Atzij Winak:* The office of *Atzij winak* ("speaker") was described by Coto as similar to the *lolmay,* the *atzij winak* also being a lord who was sent "with business to negotiate." In the Quiché hierarchy this official was another counselor to the *ajpop.*[20]

*Ajc'abawil:* The *ajc'abawil* ("he of the idol") was the head priest of Chiya'. He probably officiated at major ceremonies and played a role similar to that of the Aj Tojil and Aj K'ucumatz among the Quichés. The Tzutujil priests advised the lords on religious matters and exercised influence over important events through their ability to translate the wishes of the gods.[21] All the other religious officials were subordinate to the head priest. There was another priest of the idol Jun Tijax, or One Flint, in Chiya'. He was called Ajaw Jun Tijax and may have been one of the highest lords.[22] There was probably another priest for the idol Cakix Can.

*Ajpopolajay:* The *ajpopolajay* ("he of counselor house") seems to have been an officeholder as well as a lineage leader. This lord may have served a role similar to that of the Quiché *popol winak,* who was a special adviser to the *ajpop.*[23]

*Tzutujil Moiety:* The Tzutujil moiety must have had offices similar to those of the Ajtz'iquinajay moiety, though they may have lacked the highest office, Tzutujil *pop.* The secondary Quiché Tamubs were able to gain the *ajpop* title late in their history, but the

Tzutujil moiety was still trying to achieve equality with the Ajtz'i-quinajay moiety at the time of the Conquest.[24] Therefore, it is possible that it did not have an office similar to that of Tzutujil *pop*. Beyond this, the sources do not provide any information on the leading offices of the subordinate moiety, though they were probably similar to some offices of the Ajtz'iquinajay.

*Council:* The Ajtz'iquinajay probably had a council, composed of the highest-ranking lords subordinate to him.[25] Las Casas said that the main lords were in the council of the ruler and convened with him when he called them together. They discussed religious, military, and state matters of importance to the kingdom. The lords of the council acted as judges and advisers, and the council also called upon specialists to provide information on certain activities.[26] Even though the judgment of the Ajtz'iquinajay was paramount in Chiya', he consulted the other lords in ruling the kingdom. The *lolmay cabinjay* interceded for the other lords concerning matters requiring a ruling from the Ajtz'iquinajay. The Tzutujil council probably exercised powers similar to those described by Las Casas.[27]

The council must have witnessed important matters, such as the investiture of a new ruler and the transfer of an office upon the death of the incumbent. In the 1560s the lords of the town council of Atitlán witnessed the will of don Jerónimo Mendoza, and that appears to have been a continuation of a pre-Hispanic practice.

The council judged criminal cases involving those of high rank. If a complaint was made against a lord and he was found guilty of wrongdoing, his lands and family were taken as payment for his crime.[28] Among the Tzutujils the criminal was punished according to his crime. The Ajtz'iquinajay sent an official to investigate charges made against lords. This official received a salary of half of everything owned by any lord found guilty of a serious crime. The Ajtz'iquinajay had his prison, gallows, and executioners who carried out sentences, and there was no appeal from his verdict.[29]

According to Las Casas, some of the most serious crimes were treason, adultery with a lord's wife, incorrigible thievery, sorcery, murder, and killing of the valuable quetzal birds.[30] Such crimes were probably considered capital offenses among all Quichean groups. Lesser offenses were customarily punished by fines. Repeated offenses may have been damaging to the prestige of a lineage and, whether the offender was a noble or commoner, probably brought down the wrath of the lineage head.

The fifteen lords who were subordinate to the Ajtz'iquinajay could mete out justice in their areas, but if they wanted to make a sacrifice or punish anyone for a serious crime, they had to obtain the ruler's permission.[31] Las Casas said that minor crimes were handled by the lineage heads: "Less serious crimes were judged, condemned, or pardoned, by the heads of families because in addition to the leading and lesser lords . . . there were heads of families who had limited jurisdiction."[32] The Tzutujil lineage heads could probably make complaints against a lord if he abused his power, as was true among the Quichés.[33] They would probably notify the council in Chiya', and the Ajtz'iquinajay would send an official to investigate.

### Subordinate Officials

Many officials served in capacities subordinate to those of the top sixteen lords. Among these were lineage, or estate, heads, called by the Quichés *utzam chinamital* ("head of the estate members") and *aj tz'alam* ("wall official," referring to the walls of the estates). These officials administered the affairs of the lineage and their estates *(chinamit).*[34] The *Relación geográfica Atitlán* says that "Indian *tequitlatos*" helped prepare that document by telling what they knew about the aboriginal period.[35] *Tequitlato* is Nahuatl for "assigner of tasks," and Carrasco believed that such officials may have been similar to the *aj tz'alam* of pre-Hispanic times.[36] Therefore, *aj tz'alam* probably existed among the Tzutujils.

The office names used by the highest lords were not confined to the most important lineages, the rank of an individual being determined by both his office and his lineage name. Thus, the *lolmay cabinjay* was the second-most-important lord in the Tzutujil kingdom, but there were others with similar functions who were members of lesser lineages. According to the Varea dictionary, one *lolmay* was in Atitlán. Coto said that each *chinamit* elected one official called *pop qamahay.* This name was taken from the phrase *lomay quipop quiqamahay ahava,* according to the Varea dictionary. The phrase may be translated as "messenger" or "porter of the lords"; thus these officials had functions similar to those of the highest *lolmay.* The title *pop qamahay* was widely used in Atitlán for lesser officials.[37] It was customary for all the lineages to have certain offices with functions like those of the higher lords, but lineage name determined an individual's rank in society.

### Succession to Offices

Generally in Quichean society the same lineages monopolized certain offices, and the inheritance of titles usually passed from father to oldest son.[38] If an older son was not fit to succeed, a brother of the ruler might inherit the office.[39] *The Annals of the Cakchiquels* describe the process of succession in the Xajil branch of the Cakchiquels:

Then Caynoh and Caybatz said: "Let our government be completed as our fathers commanded us. Let two of our sons enter into the government," they said. Whereupon one son of the king Caynoh entered and they made him Ahuchán Xahil of the kingdom; and a son of the king Caybatz entered also and came to be the Galel Xahil of the kingdom. . . . The Galel Xahil and the Ahuchán Xahil entered [the government], and soon after the kings died. At once their substitutes succeeded them. . . . The two sons of the king Caynoh were proclaimed Ahpop Xahil and Ahuchán Xahil. And the sons of the king Caybatz entered as Ahpop Qamahay Xahil and Galel Xahil.[40]

This passage clearly indicates how the succession occurred among the Cakchiquel Xajil. Cay Noj was the *ajpoxajil,* and Cay Batz the *ajpop qamajay* (*ajpop c'amja* in Quiché). While they were alive, their oldest sons were given the next-highest offices, which put them in line to succeed their fathers. Cay Noj's son became *ajuchan,* and Cay Batz's son *k'alel,* the fourth-highest office. Their second sons succeeded their older brothers to the offices of *ajuchan* and *k'alel* upon their deaths.

There is further information on Tzutujil succession procedures in the document dated 1563, which was analyzed by Carrasco. It, however, dealt with post-Hispanic times, when the succession to office had been affected by the early deaths of the members of the Ajtz'iquinajay lineage:

The governor was then . . . Don Pedro. However, the ruler was really Don Bernabé who was still a youth, and Don Pedro was governor until Don Bernabé came of age. The grandfather of Don Bernabé was the Ah Tz'iquinahay, . . . Vahxaki Queh. His son was Voo Noh Quicap. This person was king when Alvarado arrived and was baptized Don Pedro. . . . the son of Don Pedro and father of Don Bernabé . . . would be Don Juan, ruler and governor of Atitlán from 1540 to 1547.[41]

From this it can be seen that among the Tzutujils leadership was passed down in one lineage from father to son. In the case of don Bernabé, the ruler was too young to fulfill his duties at the time of his father's death, and don Pedro Cabinjay served as regent until the boy could assume the role of leader.

Once the new officeholder assumed the title, important ceremonies were held to confirm him in office. The Quiché lords were ranked against each other, and the highest four were set apart by the right to use canopies made of rich feathers on state occasions.[42] The custom of using canopies appears to have existed among both the Cakchiquels and the Tzutujils.[43]

The investiture ceremony for the highest lords was an important state event and usually involved seating the lord on a bench or throne made of stone or wood and giving him the symbols of authority.[44] Stone benches found in Chiya' may have been used for investiture ceremonies.[45]

It can be seen that the system of political offices was fundamental to the hierarchical ranking of Quichean society. The highest-ranking lineages also held the highest political offices, and office determined status and prestige. Those offices reflected the most prestigious occupations in Tzutujil society, primarily leadership, warfare, advising, collection and storing of tribute, and religion. This political organization functioned throughout all periods of Late Postclassic history.

In order to know a person's rank, it was necessary to couple his lineage name with his office. Because the Tzutujils followed the same general model as that followed by other highland groups, it is possible to discuss most of their important offices despite scant data. It is not possible to determine all the offices filled by the highest lords, but those of *ajuchan, k'alel, atzij winak, ajc'abawil,* and *ajpopolajay* certainly existed at Chiya'.

Like other Quichean rulers, the Tzutujil ruler probably had a council composed of the highest lords to help him govern the kingdom and administer justice. The fifteen highest lords could exercise justice in their areas but had to ask the ruler's permission before making a sacrifice or punishing anyone for a serious crime.

Succession to office among the Tzutujils usually descended from father to son. There were important ceremonies of investiture for the highest lords, and those held at Chiya' were probably similar to state rituals in other Quichean centers.

CHAPTER 9

# *Religion*

Before the Conquest the highland Mayas worshiped many gods
with distinctive characteristics, and these were often represented
as idols. There was a tendency for this array of gods to increase
because each one had several manifestations, and each manifesta-
tion might be represented as a different idol. The pre-Hispanic
Quichean peoples also worshiped diverse spirits and believed in
hidden, impersonal forces (such as fate), magic, sorcery, and divination.[1] The most important gods, however, were the patron deities of the highest lineages. It was these gods who were represented
as idols and were the focus of highland temple and cave cults.
They were related to nature and may have been totemic.[2] They
served as symbols of identification for the members of each lineage
and helped to differentiate the lineages. The gods were believed to
give aid in times of need and provided psychological security for
their people. The idols were carried into battle and could be captured and held hostage by the victors.[3]

## *Idols*

The most important pre-Hispanic idols were large and were made
of clay, wood, or stone. They were kept in temples and caves.
Small representations, which were probably ancestral commemorations (fig. 9), were made of clay or stone and were usually five
to twenty-five centimeters long. They were worked on the front
side only, the back being flat. In modern times Indians have been
known to carry them as charms in their shoulder bags or to set
them up in their homes and pray to them as icons. Edmonson said
that many small stone and pottery figurines that have been found
in the Guatemala highlands date back as far as the Classic Period.[4]
Las Casas said that people often had images in their homes and
called them the guardians of the houses. Such an idol was called

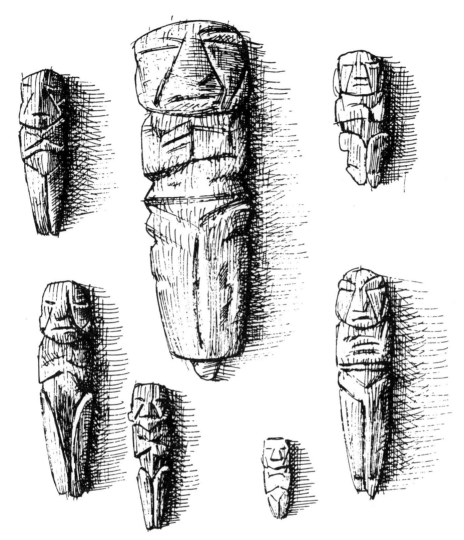

Fig. 9. *Ancestral commemorations. Drawings based on Schultz-Jena 1933, plate 5.*

*chajal* ("guard" or "guardian") by the Cakchiquels,[5] and it may have been a representation of the lineage god.

In more recent times the people of Santiago Atitlán made an idol called Maximón from wood of the sacred *pito* tree *(Erythrina corallodendron)*, which appears to be a continuation of the pre-Hispanic idol tradition. In Tzutujil legend the *pito* tree is reputed to be able to speak,[6] and the people may have used its wood to make idols in ancient times.

According to *The Annals of the Cakchiquels* and the *Popol Vuh,* the main idols were given to the migrating Quichean groups when they were in Tula. It is said that when "they were descending toward Tulán Xilbalbay, . . . they were given the idols of wood and of stone."[7] At Tula the idols were brought into the city in rank order, and Tojil was the first.[8] Therefore, the most important highland gods were derived from those of the Toltecs, and Tojil, as the god of the leading Cawek lineage, became the leading god of the Quichés.[9] When the Tzutujils and the Cakchiquels separated from the Quichés, their own lineage gods superseded Tojil in importance in the local areas, but he was the most important god in the highlands during the period of Quiché dominance (1350-1470). During that time subordinate peoples participated in important Quiché celebrations and brought tribute and sacrifices to Tojil.[10]

By Late Postclassic times the most important god in Chiya' was Sakibuk.[11] Cakix Can was another important god.[12] Vásquez also mentioned a Lord Jun Tijax who was probably a priest of that idol in Pre-Hispanic times.[13] Probably many others were also honored, but Sakibuk was paramount over them all.

Some of the lowland dependencies had their own gods and priests. The goddess of Xeoj was Taluc (Female Goddess) and that of Quioj was Cinquimil (Nahua for Twenty Plants).[14] There may have been other important gods in such places as Nagualapa, Chi-Tzunún-Choy, and Tolimán. The idol of Sakibuk was set on an altar high up in the main temple of Chiya' and was reached by steps.[15] Taluc probably stood in the main temple in Xeoj, and Cinquimil was no doubt housed in a similar temple in Quioj.[16]

Sakibuk was made of stone and was three-quarters of a vara (about 0.75 meter) high.[17] Taluc was about one vara tall, and Cinquimil one and half varas.[18] The *Título Xpantzay 3* mentions that the bath of Sakibuk was at the foot of the hill of the lake (Chuitinamit).[19] This area was evidently considered sacred to the god, and perhaps other idols had such holy places beyond the temples where they usually sat.

Cave worship was widespread in the Guatemala highlands, and

idols were often kept inside the caves.[20] Lothrop found a cave at Chuitinamit that appeared to have been used for ritual purposes. It contained evidence of sacrificial ceremonies, with the remains of armadillos and the skulls of sheep or goats scattered around. The remains were post-Conquest but not recent: "The growth of grass around the bones, absence of footprints in the loose soil and of soot on the cave walls indicate that the cave has not been visited for a long time."[21] The rituals practiced there may have been similar to those of pre-Hispanic times.

Cave worship may have been connected to the belief that the earth gods lived under mountains and that caves were the entrances to their homes.[22] Caves may also have been important because many of them were remote from large centers of population, providing places of safety for the idols in times of attack.[23] Las Casas also said that the Indians kept their idols in caves because this practice demonstrated greater reverence than would be shown by keeping them constantly on view.[24] Most of the idols in the Tzutujil area seem to have been kept in temples, however, not in caves. Besides caves and temples, lesser highland idols were placed in shrines at the entrances to settlements and in homes.[25]

## Rituals and Ceremonies

Aboriginal ceremonies included fasting, ritual purification, abstinence from sexual relations, sacrifice, confession, drinking, and dancing to music. Las Casas said that during times of general celebration the idols were dressed for the festivities and sacrifices. They were decorated with the most precious garments and jewelry that the people possessed.[26] Today the images of the saints in churches and sodalities of Tzutujil towns are dressed in native garments. One particular idol in Santiago Atitlán, Maximón, mentioned earlier, has many items of clothing, offerings from the followers of his cult.[27] During the Holy Week celebrations the clothes are washed, and a specially appointed sodality official, the *telinel*, assembles and dresses the idol. In the sodalities of San Antonio, Concepción, and Santiago officials called *jaloneles* are responsible for dressing the images.[28] This practice appears to be a continuation of a pre-Hispanic ritual, with specific priests who function in similar roles.

Sometimes the idols were carried in procession from the caves to the temples, though in later times many seem to have been kept in the temples permanently. That appears to have been the case with the most important idols in the Tzutujil area, according to the *Relaciones geográficas* of Atitlán and its dependencies.

Idols kept in temples or caves were given sacrifices.[29] It was customary to smear the blood of sacrificial victims on the face and mouth of the idol, probably with the idea that it fed on this offering.[30] In Chiya' sacrifices were made to Sakibuk and the other gods by opening the breast of a victim with a large stone knife and removing the heart. The priest smeared the face of the idol with the victim's blood and burned it with resin (probably rubber) in braziers as incense. After the hearts were removed, the bodies of victims sacrificed to the idols were discarded some distance from the ceremony. Flesh of sacrificial victims was eaten by the captors.[31]

The Mayas believed that the gods would aid their people if they were properly paid, usually in the form of sacrifice.[32] In return for sacrifices the people asked for such rewards as long life, health, children, and sustenance. If their requests were not granted, it was customary among the people of the highlands to confess their sins and perform penance.[33]

Las Casas described two forms of sacrifice among the Mayas, general and private, which appear to have been common throughout the highlands. General sacrifice was offered five or six times a year during important celebrations and also during times of misfortune, sickness, or war. On those occasions everyone performed sacrifices to the gods.[34] Among the Quichés the people from all the lineages dispersed throughout the towns took part in the ceremonies, which thus served as a means of unifying the various segments of society throughout the kingdom.[35] Before Q'uik'ab's death the Tzutujils and others gathered at K'umarcaaj for the ceremonies.[36] The ruler and all the highest nobles became intoxicated on these ritual occasions:

> They danced and leaped in the presence of the idols and gave them the best wine they had to drink. . . . They got drunk, . . . for no other reason than religious zeal. They believed they were performing a great service to their god, and the main people to get drunk were the ruler . . . and the principle lords. . . . others did not get drunk . . . because they had to govern the town and land, . . . while the ruler was busy with his devotion, drinking.[37]

Such ceremonies must have been common in all highland capitals in the centuries immediately preceding the Conquest. The priests may also have danced with the idols during the important celebrations. This practice is still followed in the Tzutujil sodality of Santa Cruz in Atitlán today.[38]

The dance held to commemorate the sacrifice of war captives to the gods was called *loj-tum* in the Tzutujil area. The dance was accompanied by music played on long trumpets. In the early seventeenth century the dance was still being performed in Nagualapa and Suchitepéquez:

It [the *loj-tum*] was a representation of an Indian who was taken in war and was sacrificed and offered to the [idol] . . . by the elders. . . . He was tied to a hitching post and those who attacked him to kill him were four figures . . . a tiger, a lion, an eagle, and another animal. . . . The rest of the ceremonies . . . of the dance . . . were timed to a terrifying and sad sound made by long trumpets twisted like trombones, which caused fear in those who heard them.[39]

Fuentes y Guzmán, mentioning the same dance, called it *oxtum*.[40]

Private sacrifices were also offered on various occasions throughout the year. The inhabitants of the Tzutujil area made personal sacrifices by cutting their ears, penises, and the muscles of their arms and offering up their blood to the idols. These sacrifices were made on special days; for example, in Xeoj they were made on the day in October when the flowers began blooming in the cacao groves. At that time the people also made sacrifices at crossroads, setting up stones and offering their blood for good weather.[41] Mendelson reported hearing that in recent times there were twelve crosses in Santiago Atitlán, most placed at street corners.[42] The location may represent a survival of the ancient preferences for crossroads.

Before taking part in the collective rituals, the people made elaborate preparations. In Verapaz the men remained in the temples for 60, 80, or 100 days. They abstained from bathing and sexual relations, blackened their faces with soot from pine torches as a sign of penitence, and sacrificed their blood.[43] Black had a certain magical quality for the Indians of Mexico and Central America, signifying death, violence, or sacrifice.[44] Idols were also blackened with smoke.[45] According to the *Popol Vuh,* the Quiché lords fasted for 180 days, burned offerings, and then fasted 260 days more (eating dried fruits—mammee, soursop, and custard apples). Sometimes they fasted for 340 days. They made vows, abstained from sexual relations, and remained in the temples.[46] Even today Tzutujil religious and medical practitioners abstain from sexual relations for specified periods of time while performing sacred activities. The midwife abstains for four days before and after a delivery.[47] When the *naybesil* of San Martín, a sodality official associated with particular rituals revolving around this modern-day deity, dances with the sacred San Martín bundle, he is supposed to be ritually pure.[48]

Among the pre-Columbian Tzutujils, when the lords wanted to know something — whether there would be a good harvest or a war or a pestilence — they chose a noble of a prominent family to consult with the main idol. The noble fasted for 260 days, eating only once a day. He sometimes ate toasted whole cacao *(pataxte)* and at other times turkey. At the beginning of the fast he performed sacrifice. At the end of the fast he made another sacrifice of incense and blood and then consulted the idol. During the period of the fast he did not return to his house or have sexual relations with his wife.

The ruler also spent much of his time in the temple during this period. He could return to his home on clear days, but on cloudy days he remained in the temple. If the idol appeared withered and sad, a drought was impending; if it appeared happy, times were to be good. If war was coming, the idol appeared with a bow and arrow in its hands, and if there was to be a pestilence, it appeared with a rope around its neck.[49]

After the idol appeared to the noble chosen to speak with it, the noble reported to the lords what he had learned. Then some of the elders of the settlement gathered together and brought out paintings, which were used as calendars. They threw lots on the paintings and divined the time when the event indicated by the idol would occur.[50] William Douglas described how contemporary shamans *(ajkun)* in Atitlán use the calendar, sacred divining objects, and bean or maize counters:

In many cases the *ajkun* carries as part of his divination implements a set of beans and/or a set of corn kernels which are cast on the table, then counted in sets of twos, threes, or fours. . . . The count is usually, but not always, in terms of the [calendar] and may be repeated as many as three times to verify the count.[51]

Other important rituals that characterized the Tzutujil area were volcano worship and various native dances. In pre-Hispanic times young girls were fed to Atitlán Volcano: "When the volcano thundered and cast forth fire and smoke, [the Indians] were persuaded that it was hungry and asking for food and that its favorite food was Indian girls whom they had also sacrificed in their gentility. They threw them into the burning mouth of that pyre." The priests *(ahquihes)* chose by lot the persons to be sacrificed.[52]

We have little specific information about the dances, other than the *tun,* that were performed by the Tzutujils, though the *Relación geográfica Atitlán* mentions that the Indians danced with snakes.[53] That dance was probably similar to the "Dance of the Snake," which is occasionally performed in highland communities today.[54] Mendelson observed the "Dance of the Jaguar" and the "Dance of the Deer" in Atitlán in recent times.[55] These dances are performed by the members of the sodality of San Juan, named for the patron saint of the animals.

Lothrop said that the "Dance of the Deer" was one of the most common dances in Quiché towns and symbolized human beings' control over the animals. In the dance the deer is told that it must submit to being hunted by dogs and killed and eaten by people.[56]

## Priests

The *ajc'abawil* was the leader of the idol cult of Chiya', and the office of high priest was one of the most respected posts. Other important priests were those of Cakix Can and Jun Tijax. The *ajc'abawil* must have had assistants in the capital, while other, lesser priests resided in the dependencies. Among the Quichés, priests were referred to as *ajq'uixb* and *ajcajb* ("sacrificers").[57] The term is written *achque* in Las Casas[58] and *ahquihes* (or *ahquijes*) in Vásquez, who referred specifically to Atitlán.[59]

The most important priests presided over major ceremonies, consulted with the idols, and spent much time fasting and performing sacrifices. They also interpreted the sacred books, which contained the calendar and the divination charts.[60] The elders who cast lots to divine the date of future events would be among this group.[61] Today in Atitlán the role of the *ajk'ij*, or "he of the day," has merged with that of the *ajkun* ("curer").[62] In pre-Hispanic times the *ajk'ij* was a separate practitioner. A man named Ahkik was listed in church records from Atitlán in the seventeenth century.[63] Among the Cakchiquels a calendar specialist was called *aj may wuj* ("he of the 400-day calendar book")[64] and *aj chol k'in* ("he who counts the days," that is, of the 260-day calendar).[65] These may have been other priests who worked with the *ajk'ij*, and perhaps they also existed in Atitlán.

The 260-day divinatory calendar exists in fragmentary form among the contemporary Tzutujils of Santiago Atitlán. It is still used in divination, and Douglas provides a table showing the calendar as it existed in 1965-66. The day of an individual's birth, which is thought to be ruled by a particular day lord, indicates his abilities, fate, companion animal, and personality. The calendar also indicates lucky and unlucky days for each person. Today the people of Atitlán feel that, even though a person's destiny is fixed, he or she may have periodic phases of good and bad luck.[66]

Several kinds of religious practitioners still function in Atitlán, and it is somewhat difficult to distinguish the roles of each. The *ajkun* ("he of medicine," from *kun,* "medicine") diagnoses and cures illnesses by means of prayers. Douglas said the Tzutujils of Atitlán differentiate two kinds of *ajkun:* (1) those who function primarily as priests and pray for such things as good crops and good fortune and (2) curers, who diagnose and treat illness. These were probably two distinct kinds of specialists in pre-Hispanic times.[67]

In Atitlán the *ajkuns* appear to be the counterparts of the pre-Hispanic Quiché *ajq' uixb.* Sorcerers, called *ajits* ("witches"), have the power to do harm to people owing to the circumstances of their birth: although powerful, they are destined to use their power only for witchcraft and black magic by means of harmful prayers.[68] Sorcery was feared in aboriginal as well as modern times, and Las Casas said that the punishment for sorcery was death by burning.[69]

Other contemporary specialists, the *ajkomanel* ("master curers"), treat illness without the use of prayer. The *ajkomanel* are believed to have knowledge by which they treat illness as a physiological condition. They also know about medicine and use special techniques in treating illnesses. *Ajkomanel* treat patients in their homes.[70] Perhaps the physician referred to in Las Casas was a specialist of this kind, since he made house calls.[71]

Today in Atitlán there are also snake- and spider-bite specialists (*ruki kamats* and *ruki'om*), bonesetters *(rukoy bak),* and midwives *(iyom).* All of these specialists and many others may have had independent roles in pre-Hispanic times, but their functions have tended to merge with those of the *ajkun* except for the more practical medical personnel, bonesetters, midwives, bite specialists, and *ajkomanel.*[72]

In pre-Hispanic times important religious offices were filled by members of the nobility. The *ajc'abawil,* the priest of Cakix Can, and that of Jun Tijax were noblemen. The *ajkun* seems to have been similar to the *ahicom* of the Pokomans, whose office was open to all.[73] Certain other practitioners may also have been drawn from noble lineages, but most were probably from the middle and lower classes. Las Casas seems to imply this in his discussion of pre-Hispanic medicine. He says that lords always had a medical practitioner near their household but that this was not true for commoners. That practitioner could have been a noble but may also have had an office similar in importance to that of the merchants, who also served the lords.[74] Commoners treated commoners.

## Beliefs

Estrada reported that the Indians around Zapotitlán and Suchite-péquez believed in naguals. He said that the Indians believed that all good and bad came from "hatred of an evil one called among them *naguale*."[75] Among the Quichean peoples "nagual" had several meanings. In one meaning, the nagual was an animal into which certain persons could transform themselves and in whose form they could become malevolent.[76] In pre-Hispanic times the ability to transform was usually attributed to powerful men who were believed to be magicians, such as the Cakchiquel ancestor K'akawitz.[77] Today in Atitlán the transforming witch *('isom)* is said to have the ability to change into an animal by using special prayers and ritual, and such persons possess this ability owing to their fate *(suerte)*. Closely associated with the belief in transformation is the belief in the *tonal (ajelbal* in Tzutujil), or companion animal. Strong persons such as *ajkun* and witches have large, strong animal counterparts, while other people have smaller, weaker ones.[78] Although all persons may have companion animals, it is commonly believed in the highlands that only bad persons transform into their *tonals* and harm others.[79] Fuentes y Guzmán mentioned such beliefs among the Quiché groups in colonial times.[80]

Another meaning of "nagual" refers to the ancient ones, who were believed to have extraordinary powers. The Quiché ancestors, for example, were called "nahuales."[81] In general, the term is used to designate something old, ancient, or historical and implies power because of age.[82]

The belief in animals that foretold disaster was widespread in aboriginal times. An owl and a parakeet prophesied doom for the Cakchiquels in Tula, but the people refused to listen to the omens.[83] In the *Popol Vuh* several owls were mentioned as demons and messengers: Knife Owl, 1 Leg Owl, Parrot Owl, and Skull Owl, the messengers of hell *(xibalba)*.[84] The owl on a red tree was also a symbol of disaster among the Cakchiquels.[85] Vásquez wrote of Atitlán: "They lived in their idolatries, speaking and conversing with serpents and evil animals in whom the demon gave them their oracles by means of their *ahquijes,* or priests."[86]

Edmonson also mentioned certain prophets who lived among the Quichés, and similar persons may have practiced among all

the highland groups. *Hiq' vachinel* ("far seers") were prophet diviners with second sight who could "see at a distance" or "scruti-
nize" *(niq'oh)* and "peer into" *(vachih)* things. *Labahinel* (from
*labah,* "dream") were the diviners of omens. There were also
dream diviners *(ichiq'anel); ilol,* or seers, who interpreted omens;
and *ah xulu,* or gleaners, who asked their bodies divinatory questions and received answers by twitches in various parts of their
bodies.[87] Although none of these are specifically mentioned for
the pre-Hispanic Tzutujils, such prophets may also have lived in
the lake area.

Today the Tzutujils continue to believe in "signs" *(retal),* events
indicating that something unusual is occurring or is about to occur.
They may be signals that a person receives while going about his
or her day-to-day life, or they may be dreams. Dreams are believed
to be observations made by the soul while it is out of the body.
The correct interpretation of the sign or dream can be made only
by a divination specialist.[88]

In modern religious rituals vestiges remain of the pre-Columbian
significance of the four points of the compass. Lois and Benjamin
D. Paul reported that the midwife of San Pedro made a ritual
progression around the delivery room, offering prayers at each of
the four corners.[89] Mendelson also described the Holy Week ritual
in Atitlán, in which counter-clockwise processions were made to
four temporary chapels.[90]

While the pre-Hispanic nobles focused their ritual activities
around the major lineage gods, the common people must have
felt closer to the spirits of the earth, wind, and rain. Today the
Tzutujils of Atitlán believe that every aspect of nature has a supernatural master *(dueño)* who regulates its progress and its role in
the agricultural cycle. The main supernatural master who rules
this spirit complex is San Martín, a velvet-wrapped bundle containing sacred objects.[91] Mendelson connected the worship of the
San Martín bundle to the wearing of sacrificed human skin by the
priests of the god Xipe, but he also acknowledged that the shirts
may be copies of the fleece worn by John the Baptist in Roman
Catholic iconography.[92]

Sacred bundles *(pizom)* are definitely pre-Columbian and in
aboriginal times were believed to have great power. They were
said to be in the possession of the most powerful ancestors.[93]
After the Conquest the Christian saints seem to have absorbed
many of the functions attributed to the ancient nature deities,
but other spirits continue to exist for the people of Atitlán, and
some are probably aboriginal. These spirits are divided into two

categories: human *(anima)* and nonhuman *(jawal)*. The first group includes the souls of persons living and dead; the second includes many spirits derived from the Catholic hierarchy and spirits of animate and inanimate objects in the natural world.[94]

Aboriginal Tzutujil religion was thus a complex system. On the state level it involved temple cults dedicated to idols representing important lineages. The idol Sakibuk was the main god of Chiya', but there were others in the capital and the dependencies attended by priests devoted to their cults. Religion permeated all aspects of Tzutujil society. People fasted, prayed, and sacrificed on all important occasions in addition to performing private sacrifice. At times human sacrifices were made. The gods went into battle with their people and, through the priests, gave advice on matters of importance.

Alongside the state cults, individuals maintained their own idol cults at home and used small images in daily rituals. Local "part-time" religious practitioners performed rituals and cures for the commoners as the higher class of priests and doctors did for the nobles. A variety of specialists practiced curing, divining, witchcraft, and prophecy.

Certain beliefs were common in all strata of society, especially those relating to nagualism, oracles, the four points of the compass, sacred bundles, and spirits. The most important idols served as oracles, but there were other, lesser sources of omens, which were interpreted by seers and diviners.

The hierarchy of deities paralleled the lineage structure and thereby supported the sociopolitical system, which was based on lineage and office. Religion was a major force in Quichean society as a whole and provided a common focus of interaction that was shared by all the social components irrespective of their stratum or territorial location.

In the foregoing pages I have sought to establish the ecological and territorial setting for pre-Columbian Tzutujil society and to define the basic military, economic, sociopolitical, and religious structures which characterized that group. Archaeological and ethnohistorical data have been used to outline Tzutujil history and describe their evolution into an independent kingdom by the end of the fifteenth century. Despite the Tzutujils' eventual achievement of freedom from Quiché hegemony, they and other closely related highland groups remained securely within the Quichean cultural orbit. Dynastic marriages among the nobility, the system of regional markets frequented by all members of society, similar cultural patterns, and a common historical framework all served to integrate the highland groups.

Along with these shared characteristics there were rigid social and political boundaries. Lineage determined class as well as the individual's role in society. A bride marrying into a different kingdom became a part of her husband's lineage and was no longer considered a relative by her father's group. If a woman's husband died, she was married again to one of his close relatives. Commoners ordinarily married within their own towns and were socially closed off from commoners in other towns and outside the kingdom. The nobles of all groups had more in common with each other than with their own vassals, but the *chinamit,* the *calpul,* and general religious celebrations joined all levels of society.

Throughout the highland territory political boundaries were defined by markers. These boundaries shifted over time, however, with the fortunes of war and politics. Control of conquered lands depended on a combination of military force and effective administrative policies. Tribute was the primary goal of conquest, and the boundaries of any kingdom could be reconstructed on the basis of its tributary units. At the time of Spanish contact the Quiché, Cakchiquel, and Tzutujil kingdoms were still independent but were contesting one another's frontier areas. Although none was powerful enough to conquer any of the others, the Cakchiquels were gaining in strength at the expense of the Quichés and the Tzutujils.

A common political framework based on recognizable offices regulated contacts within the Quiché state and later among the independent kingdoms. The system of political offices provided internal cohesion and organization and was buttressed by the lineage and religious systems.

After the Conquest important changes were made in the upper levels of the Tzutujil sociopolitical structure, warfare was prohibited, and territorial boundaries gradually shifted. There were also, however, continuities that tended to maintain the Tzutujils' cultural and territorial integrity throughout the sixteenth and early seventeenth centuries. The present configuration of Tzutujil habitation and their contemporary sociopolitical structure is derived from aboriginal patterns and the introduction of post-Conquest Spanish institutions into Tzutujil society. Part Two examines the changes that came about as a result of the Conquest.

# Post-Conquest Tzutujil Society

## CHAPTER 10

# Post-Conquest History

*The Annals of the Cakchiquels* described a calamity at the end of the year 1521 that warned of impending events:

It happened that during the twenty-fifth year the plague began. . . . First they became ill of a cough, they suffered from nosebleeds and illnesses of the bladder. It was truly terrible, the number of dead there were in that period. . . . The people could not in any way control the sickness. . . . Great was the stench of the dead. After our fathers and grandfathers succumbed, half of the people fled to the fields. The dogs and the vultures devoured the bodies. The mortality was terrible.[1]

This disease, which was no doubt plague, was probably contracted from Mexican Indians who had already been in contact with Spaniards.[2]

## The Arrival of the Spanish Conquerors

There is evidence that the first meeting of the Tzutujils and the Spaniards occurred in 1522, before Pedro de Alvarado's entrance into Guatemala. The *Título San Bartolomé* contains an account of a land dispute between the Indians of Xeoj and those of Nagualapa. To resolve the conflict, the Indians of Xeoj sent a delegation to Hernán Cortés to ask him to help them define their boundaries. They carried with them eight loads of cacao to be used as payment for title to the lands in question. The Indians met Cortés and Alvarado on the plains of Centla, Tabasco, near Campeche. Alvarado assured them that when he reached Guatemala the lands would be theirs. After the conqueror arrived, according to the document, he sent his nephew Juan de Alvarado to measure off the lands and set up boundary markers. The Indians of Nagualapa were called in to witness the boundaries along with those of Xeoj.[3]

Other facts substantiate an early-sixteenth-century date for the

events described in the *título*. The Indians of Xeoj stated that
they had been baptized by the priests "Nicolas" Díaz and "Ramón"
de Olmedo. At the beginning of 1522, Juan Díaz (his correct name)
was ill in Mexico, and in October, 1522, Bartolomé de Olmedo
was also in Mexico. If the Indians were evangelized by these two
priests, they must have gone to Guatemala with the emissaries of
Cortés, who preceded Alvarado in Guatemala at the end of 1522
or the beginning of 1523. If that is the case, in light of the account in the *Título San Bartolomé,* they must have visited the
lowland Tzutujils of Xeoj and were probably the first priests in
the country.[4] The fact that their first names are given erroneously
cannot destroy the basic credibility of the document. In *The Annals
of the Cakchiquels,* Spanish names are often distorted; for example, Maldonado is spelled Mantunalo, and Juan Rogel is spelled
Juan Roser.[5]

Although some of the claims made in the *Título San Bartolomé*
may be false, the fact that Alvarado's nephew is also named perhaps tends to lend credibility to this account.[6] The document
also seems to indicate that the Tzutujils were going to the Spaniards for validation of their land claims before Alvarado's conquest of the country. The journey is somewhat reminiscent of
earlier journeys to the east by Quichés and Cakchiquels for symbols of political authority and legitimization. The Tzutujils were
aware of this pattern of behavior and evidently joined the delegation of Indians who sought out Cortés after the fall of the Aztec
Empire. They traveled to Mexico carrying gifts and encountered
Cortés and Alvarado before the actual conquest of the highland
area.

In February, 1524, Alvarado entered Guatemala and proceeded
to the lowland piedmont area. He conquered the Quiché strong-
hold Xelaju and went on to take K'umarcaaj.[7] When the Quichés
learned of the entrance of the Spaniards into Guatemala, they
sent messengers to the Cakchiquels and the Tzutujils asking them
to attend a conference to decide on a proper course of action.
The Cakchiquels refused to come, and the Tzutujils replied that
they could defend themselves without any help.[8] The hostile feel-
ings among the three groups were too strong to allow for military
collaboration against the Spaniards.

Alvarado sent messengers to the Cakchiquels and the Tzutujils
asking them to join the Spanish cause. The Tzutujils responded
by killing the messengers, but the Cakchiquels sent warriors to
help Alvarado destroy the Quichés. After the capture of the Quiché
capital the Spaniards marched to Iximché. There they were well

received by the Cakchiquels, who were more than happy to see the downfall of their former masters. Alvarado then asked the Cakchiquels who their remaining enemies were and learned that they were the Tzutujils.[9] The Ajtz'iquinajay had incurred the wrath of the Cakchiquel ruler by aiding the *ajpoxajil* who had led a rebellion of some important Cakchiquel settlements.[10] The Tzutujils of Chiya' helped the *ajpoxajil* by making night raids into Cakchiquel territory by canoe.

In 1525, Alvarado decided to send two more Indian messengers to the Tzutujils to ask them to surrender peacefully:

And I told them [the Cakchiquels] that I would send [messengers] to call [on] them [the Tzutujils] on the part of our lord the Emperor, and that if they should come I would command them not to make war nor do anything wrong in this land, as they had heretofore done, and if they did not come, I would go with them to make war and punish them.

The Tzutujils also killed those messengers. Soon afterward, on April 18, Alvarado himself set out from Iximché with 60 horsemen, 150 infantry, and a large body of Cakchiquels led by their nobles. They arrived in Tzutujil territory on the same day and approached the fortress of Chiya'. They saw that it could be entered only by a narrow causeway. The Spaniards attacked and gained possession of Chiya'. Many Indians jumped into the lake, swam to a nearby island, and thereby escaped death. They were able to do this because the Cakchiquel auxiliaries, who were on their way by canoe, arrived late.

That evening the victors made camp in a maize field. On the next day, April 19, Alvarado managed to capture three Tzutujils. He sent them to the Tzutujil lords, saying that if they did not surrender the battle would be continued. With this ultimatum the Tzutujils surrendered, saying that until that time "their land had never been broken into or entered by force of arms."[11] Alvarado built a fort and left 418 men among the Tzutujils under the command of Héctor de Cháves and Alonso de Pulgar.[12] Leaving his forces "safe and peaceful," he returned to Iximché. Three days later the most important Tzutujil leaders came to Iximché with presents for the Spaniards. Alvarado gave them some jewels in return and sent them back to Chiya' "with much affection, and they are the most pacific that there are in this land."[13]

## Alvarado's Rule of Guatemala, 1524-41

In Iximché, in July of 1524, Alvarado founded the city of Santiago

de los Caballeros de Guatemala, the first capital of the new colony.[14] The Spaniards were still fighting Indians, and the city was
primarily a camp rather than an urban nucleus. Alvarado immediately began demanding tribute from the Cakchiquels, and the
amounts were so excessive that rebellion soon broke out:

Then the Cakchiquels began hostilities against the Spaniards. They dug
holes and pits for the horses and scattered sharp stakes so that they
should be killed. At the same time the people made war on them. Many
Spaniards perished and the horses died in the traps for horses. The
Quichés and the Zutuhils died also.[15]

The *Relación geográfica Atitlán* says that Alvarado used the Tzutujils as soldiers against the Cakchiquels: "Don Pedro de Alvarado
. . . took out of the town many people, sometimes six hundred
Indian soldiers, to make war on the Indians of the town . . . of
Tecpan Cuauhtemala . . . and other rebellious provinces."[16]

The Cakchiquels retreated to the hills, and in 1526 the Spaniards
burned Iximché.[17] In 1527 the Spaniards moved the capital of the
colony to a better location. A new city, Santiago de los Caballeros
de Guatemala, was founded in the Valley of Bulbuxyá (from a word
meaning "spring" or "gushing water"), at the foot of Agua Volcano.
This valley, called Almolonga by the Mexican auxiliaries of the
Spaniards, is today called Ciudad Vieja.[18]

In 1526, Alvarado went to Mexico City, and his brother Jorge
arrived to take over the rule of the colony. It was Jorge who
laid out the new capital and assigned locations for houses, a hospital, a chapel, a shrine, and a fortress.[19] Pedro de Alvarado left
Mexico City for Spain and while he was there obtained the post
of governor and captain-general of Guatemala, being subject only
to the authority of the crown.[20] The appointment was made in
1528, and in 1530 Guatemala became officially a separate *gobierno,*
attaining greater independence from the government in Mexico.
Middle America was governed through several overlapping but
related systems. Politically Guatemala was part of the Viceroyalty
of New Spain, which included territory in Mexico, Central America,
the Caribbean, and northern South America. The *gobiernos* were
subordinate political jurisdictions headed by governors.[21]

By 1528 regular collection of tribute had begun in the Lake
Atitlán area.[22] In 1530 the Cakchiquels went to work in the new
capital as part of their labor requirement. The *Annals* say that "four
hundred men and four hundred women were contributed to work
in *Pangán*[23] on the construction of the city, by order of Tunatiuh
[Alvarado]." The lords as well as the common people paid tribute.[24]

Besides being taken as soldiers, Tzutujils were conscripted to mine gold. Other Tzutujils served as carriers *(tamemes)*. *Mantas,* cacao, honey, turkeys, salt, chili, copper, maguey, and many other items were also delivered to the Spaniards as tribute.[25]

News of Alvarado's excesses reached Spain, and in 1536 the crown ordered an official to Guatemala to examine the state of affairs in the *gobierno*. The official, Alonso de Maldonado, assumed charge of Guatemala in May, 1536, and ordered some reforms to help the Indians. Before Maldonado's arrival Alvarado had left for Honduras and from there had gone to Spain to defend himself against charges made about his conduct while he was governor. He was successful in this and in 1539 returned once again to Guatemala as governor with the full confidence of the crown.[26] "Six months after the death of the Ahtzib [a Cakchiquel lord], Tunatiuh came to [the capital] and at once the lord Mantunalo departed. When he left, Tunatiuh succeeded him."[27]

Not content with settling down to rule a conquered colony, in 1540 Alvarado went off to seek the Spice Islands. He stopped in Mexico to help suppress an Indian rebellion. He was injured in battle when a horse fell on him, and he died in June, 1541, in Guadalajara.[28] His widow, Beatriz de la Cueva, succeeded him as governor, but her rule was cut short when she perished in the eruption of Agua Volcano that destroyed the capital on September 10, 1541.[29] A new capital, today called Antigua, was begun in the Valley of Panchoy soon afterward.

## The Establishment of Royal Authority, 1541-55

The audiencia was created by a royal order of September 7, 1543, and had its seat in Gracias a Dios, on the coast of Honduras. The first audiencia was composed of a president, three judges *(oidores)*, and a scribe *(escribano)*.[30] Audiencias were the highest royal courts of appeal within the limits of their territorial jurisdiction. They also served as councils to advise the viceroy and crown and supervised governors and other Spanish officials in their areas.[31] Alonso de Maldonado became the first president of the Audiencia de los Confines. The first *oidores*, or judges, were Diego de Herrera, Juan Rogel, and Pedro Ramírez de Quiñónes.[32] The audiencia was moved to Santiago de Guatemala in 1549.[33]

The establishment of the audiencia signaled the end of the era of conquistador control in Guatemala and meant that the full force of the Spanish imperial administrative system came to bear on the Guatemalan population. The decisions of the audiencia were final, subject only to crown veto. That did not necessarily mean that the Indians' situation improved, however. In many instances it worsened because with the creation of the audiencia the number of exploiters also increased.[34]

One of the worst aspects of this exploitation, along with excessive tribute, was the Spaniards' practice of taking Indian slaves. Indian lords also continued to enslave other Indians and sold them to Spaniards or among themselves.[35] The crown was against slavery in general but condoned the continuance of the pre-Hispanic custom of taking captives in war.[36] During the Conquest period the Spaniards took many Indians as slaves under this pretext. If they were insufficient, individual Spaniards requested *tandas,* or drafts, of a given number of Indians for a specified length of time from all the groups under their control.[37] The 240 Tzutujils taken every ten days and the 800 Cakchiquel men and women taken to build the capital were part of such forced-labor drafts.

After the end of the period of fighting, Indian lords kept the slaves whom they had owned in pre-Conquest times, and the Spaniards often obtained some of them from the lords. The character of slavery changed after the coming of the Spaniards: it was much harsher.[38] More Indians were used as slaves than before, and many were enslaved who previously had been free.[39] The Spaniards also sent highland Indians, who were accustomed to a cool climate, to tropical areas, where they became ill and died.[40] Along with the great epidemics and excessive tribute, slavery accelerated the population decline at a faster pace than would probably have occurred otherwise.

Some priests in Guatemala, such as Bartolomé de las Casas, were against all forms of slavery and did everything they could to put an end to it. Complaints by the few dedicated priests who were in the country, along with the catastrophic mortalities of the 1520s and the 1530s, convinced the crown of the necessity for laws to protect the remaining Indian population.[41] This was the background of the New Laws decreed in 1542 and 1543. Slavery was to be abolished according to these laws, but it continued in practice until the early 1550s.[42]

The New Laws were not put into effect to any great extent in Guatemala during Maldonado's presidency because he tended to side with the Spanish colonists.[43] The Indians continued to decline to the point of scarcity, and it gradually became necessary for the Spaniards to shift to a less wasteful method of using labor. Gold was soon exhausted, and products, such as cacao, that required the Indians to remain nearer their homelands, rose to importance.[44] By 1548, when Alonso López de Cerrato became presi-

dent of the audiencia, the New Laws had come into wider application: "When he arrived, he condemned the Spaniards, he liberated
the slaves and vassals of the Spaniards, he cut the taxes in two,
he suspended forced labor and made the Spaniards pay all men,
great and small. The lord Cerrado truly alleviated the sufferings
of the people."[45]

An important policy that the Spaniards began putting into effect
in the lake region around 1547 was the congregation of Indians
into focal settlements, where they could be governed and more
readily taught the Catholic religion: "In the fifth month of the
sixth year after the beginning of our instruction . . . the houses
were grouped together by order of the lord Juan Roser. Then the
people came from the caves and the ravines. On the day 8 Caok
[October 30, 1547] this city was founded."[46] The quotation refers
specifically to Tzololá, but in that same year Betanzos and de la
Parra also moved the Tzutujils to their present site and named the
town Santiago Atitlán.[47] Sometime after the congregations the Indian town-government system was set up in the highland area.
It was composed of a town council, or cabildo, and an Indian governor, who was subordinate to a local Spanish magistrate, the
*corregidor.* In 1547 the towns in Alvarado's former holdings, which
included Atitlán, were apportioned into seven *corregimientos,* and
Atitlán became a head town *(cabecera)* of the *corregimiento* of
that name. The pre-Hispanic dependencies were called *sujetos*
and continued to be under the jurisdiction of Atitlán. The *corregimientos* were at a lower level in the political system than the
*gobierno,* and the *corregidor* was subject to the governor and the
audiencia. There were also three larger divisions, called *alcaldías
mayores.* They were Sonsonate, Zapotitlán, and Verapaz. Atitlán
was a *corregimiento* within the *alcaldía mayor* of Zapotitlán.[48]

*Solidification of Spanish Control (1555-1630)*

Presidents of the audiencia who succeeded López de Cerrato were
viewed by the Indians as being less favorable to them.[49] Antonio
Rodríguez de Quesada assumed the presidency of the audiencia
on January 14, 1555, and the Cakchiquels noted that during his
term of office he did not exert himself for their cause: "Some
time later the Doctor Quexata died, without sentencing anyone
or arresting anyone. On the contrary, the Lord Cerrado did indeed
condemn [the Spaniards] and did that which was just."[50] During
Quesada's time a decree was issued requiring the lords to pay
tribute just as they had before López de Cerrato's time, an indi-

cation of a return to more stringent policies against the Indians.[51]

On September 2, 1559, Juan Núñez de Landecho became president of the audiencia. He too favored the Spaniards and was noted for his harshness toward the Indians.[52] He entrusted the regulation of tribute to the *encomenderos* and Indian leaders, which led to increased exploitation.[53] The *Relación Tzutujil* says that the lords of Atitlán asked Landecho to reappraise them in the hope of having their tribute reduced: "He did [reappraise us] and added to our tribute two thousand *pesos* more than we had been giving and besides [that] two hundred *fanegas* of maize and ten *arrobas* of honey."[54] The Cakchiquels blamed the Tzutujils for the increase: "During the second month of this year Doctor Antonio Mexía arrived, sent to these places by the avarice of the Zutuhils." To make matters worse for the Indians of the lake region, in 1560 they were again stricken by plague:

In the sixth month after the arrival of the Lord President in Pangán, the plague which had lashed the people long ago began here. Little by little it arrived here. In truth a fearful death fell on our heads by the will of our powerful God. Many families [succumbed] to the plague. Now the people were overcome by intense cold and fever, blood came out of their noses, then came a cough growing worse and worse, the neck was twisted, and small and large sores broke out on them.[55]

During Landecho's rule (1559-63) Spain separated Central America from the Viceroyalty of New Spain and established a captaincy general composed of Guatemala, Honduras, El Salvador, Costa Rica, Nicaragua, and Chiapas. The president of the audiencia was given the title of governor and captain general. Captain general was the highest military title in Spanish America.[56] This remained the basic structure of colonial government in Guatemala until the Bourbon reforms of the late eighteenth century.

Francisco Briceño, who had been *oidor* of the Audiencia de Bogotá, was ordered to Guatemala to conduct a full inquiry into Landecho's government. For his many abuses Landecho was deposed by royal decree on May 30, 1563. The Audiencia de los Confines was dissolved, and a new audiencia was established in Panama City. The government hoped by doing this to restore royal authority.[57]

Briceño also made a visit to Santiago Atitlán, and the Indians, ever hopeful, again asked to be reappraised in an effort to alleviate their tribute burden.[58] Hostility between the Tzutujils and the Cakchiquels continued because of Landecho's earlier unfavorable assessment, and the Tzutujils killed the Xajil leader of Palopó.[59]

In 1566 two full-time permanent resident priests, Juan Alonso and Diego Martín, arrived in Atitlán.[60] Their arrival initiated a period of strong church influence in the *cabecera*, which in the long run aggravated the financial burdens of the Indians. Organized religion was in force in Atitlán no later than 1566, and possibly as early as 1552, when a school was established in the town to teach the children of the lords and others to read, write, and officiate at mass and divine offices.[61] Gonzalo Méndez, who succeeded Alonso and Martín, presided over the construction of a permanent church, which was not finished until some years later.[62] In 1571 famine struck the lake area, and a few years later the highlands suffered still another attack of plague.[63]

García de Valverde, formerly president of the Audiencia de Quito, assumed the presidency of the Audiencia de Guatemala in 1578. During his term of office the tribute the Indians had to pay was finally reduced. By this time the population had fallen somewhat (see chapter 12), though the area remained fairly lucrative for the Spaniards throughout the sixteenth and early seventeenth centuries.

During García de Valverde's administration, in the monastery at Atitlán there were four Franciscan resident priests under the direction of Pedro de Arboleda.[64] In 1585, Arboleda and the *corregidor* of Atitlán, Alonzo Páez Betancor, collaborated to write the *Relaciones geográficas* of Atitlán and its dependencies in response to a royal command for more information about the New World. In 1579, Juan de Estrada, the *alcalde mayor* of Zapotitlán, had written a *relación* for the Zapotitlán and Suchitepéquez area, which included information on the Tzutujil lowland and highland *sujetos*. These two documents contain much valuable information about the lives of the Tzutujils during the late sixteenth century.

Another component in the Spanish colonial system was the ecclesiastical hierarchy. At the top of the religious structure was the single Archdiocese of Mexico, with its seat in Mexico City. The Diocese of Guatemala was subordinate to Mexico but in reality was practically autonomous (in 1745 it was elevated to archdiocese status). From 1561 to 1607 Verapaz was a separate see.[65]

Within the diocese of Guatemala there were lesser units, or parishes *(doctrinas)*, and the town containing the principal church where the local priest resided was called the *cabecera de doctrina*. Original pioneer churches, like that of Atitlán, became *doctrinas*, and by the end of the sixteenth century the Tzutujils of the *cabecera* were well integrated into the church hierarchy. Around 1600 San Bartolomé was made a separate *doctrina* because of the difficulty of reaching the lowland towns from the *cabecera*. Vásquez reported that, although San Bartolomé was still a *cabecera de doctrina* in his time, the town was reduced to only eighty confessors.[66]

Thus by 1524, following a brief battle, the Tzutujils were brought under Spanish control. Afterward they helped Alvarado put down the Cakchiquel rebellion of 1524. Until the mid-sixteenth century the Tzutujils remained in Chiya' and were visited only sporadically by a few priests. They sent slaves and tribute to Alvarado.

Spanish control extended over the Tzutujils of both the lake and the piedmont as a result of congregation, which began in 1547. Santiago Atitlán became the new Tzutujil capital, and a local system of town government was instituted and supervised by a crown official, called the *corregidor*. There is some information about Tzutujil life from 1550 to 1570. It is known that the Indians paid excessive amounts of tribute before and after Cerrato's time, suffered repeated attacks of disease and plague, and came under closer supervision by the Franciscans. By 1570 the Tzutujils of Atitlán had begun work on a large, permanent church.

## CHAPTER 11

# Tzutujil Territory

Several events occurred after the Conquest that affected the settlement pattern of the Indians of the former Tzutujil kingdom. From 1521 the repeated epidemics that struck the Tzutujils severely reduced their number. The population of pre-Conquest Chiya' was said to have been around 48,000; by 1585 only 1,005 tribute payers were left.[1] Many rural settlements suffered similar drops in population. Xeoj, for example, declined from around 1,600 tributaries in pre-Hispanic times to only 223 in 1585,[2] and those of Quioj declined from 800 to 104.[3] The great Indian capitals, such as K'umarcaaj, Iximché, and Chiya', lost their political independence after the Conquest and were eventually abandoned as their inhabitants were moved to more accessible locations.

### Congregation and Its Effect on Settlement Pattern

Another reason for change in the Indian settlement pattern was the Spanish policy of congregation, which was largely carried out around Lake Atitlán from 1547 to 1550.[4] The main agents of congregation were the priests. Antonio de Remesal, a seventeenth-century priest, described the procedures used by the members of the religious orders in forming congregations. They planned the layout of the town and indicated where the church was to be built. The priest's house stood next to the church, and a plaza was built in front of the church. The town-council house (cabildo) was built facing the plaza, and the jail was next to it, and the inn for travelers (mesón) was nearby. The streets were laid out in blocks north to south and east to west. The priests and the Indian leaders measured off the new site and planted maize next to it. They constructed the buildings while the crop grew. When the maize was ready to be harvested, on a chosen day all the people went to the new town and celebrated with music and dancing, which lasted for several days, to make them forget their old homes.[5]

Concerning the Atitlán region, Pedro de Betanzos wrote in a letter to King Philip II: "We grouped them by towns, which were previously in the hills, elusive and frightened, and in this manner we made towns [of] a thousand, two thousand and three thousand men."[6] The procedure followed in Chiya' was probably typical. The priests reported to the audiencia that the ancient site was difficult to reach and that it was impossible to convert the Indians while they continued to live in the old way.[7] The audiencia issued a decree in the name of the crown ordering the priests to take the Indians from where they were living and settle them in a new town. Smaller towns were probably formed by a general authorization to specific priests. In his letter to Philip II, Betanzos said that he and de la Parra had congregated more than two hundred towns, far more than they could have formed under separate authorizations.

The Indians were settled in towns laid out according to the grid plan, which was based on the design established by the Romans during their occupation of Spain. The clearest statement of Spanish town-planning concepts is found in instructions from Philip II in 1573:

The plaza should be a rectangle, prolonged so that the length is at least half again as long as the width. . . . The size of the plaza should be proportionate to the population, taking into consideration that in Indian towns, since they are new and intended to increase, the plaza should be designed with such increase in mind.[8]

Subdivisions of an Indian town that were integral parts of the town were referred to as barrios, or wards.[9] Santiago Atitlán and other larger towns were divided into wards, today called *cantones.*

Lowland settlements were called *estancias,*[10] *sujetos,*[11] *ranchos,*[12] or *milpas.*[13] Gibson said that the word *estancia* was probably introduced into Mexico from the West Indies, where it was used to designate any cluster of Indian dwellings.[14] Dependent towns in the lowlands were not always built on the grid plan. Xeoj, for example, was composed of houses clustered around the church.[15]

Betanzos and de la Parra congregated the inhabitants of Chiya' in the present town of Atitlán in 1547.[16] They named it Santiago; in 1566 the town was referred to as Santiago Chía in the *Libro primero de bautismos de Santiago Atitlán* for that year.[17] Owing to the natural configuration of the site, however, only a few blocks were laid out by the grid plan. The other blocks, a few yards from the plaza, were haphazardly arranged as they continue to be today. The town is described in the *Relación geográfica Atitlán* in 1585:

This town of Santiago Atitlan . . . is arranged and populated . . . with well laid out streets according to the order and plan of Spanish towns with a square plaza in the middle, although not very large. Toward the east is located the monastery and church. . . . on the north on a side of the plaza is the house of justice[18] where the *Corregidor* . . . has his . . . residence. In the said plaza at the south are the houses of the *Cabildo*.[19]

Near the cabildo was the *mesón*, which was run by Indians and provided food and accommodations for travelers (see fig. 10). It was supervised by an innkeeper *(mesonero)* and officials of the cabildo.[20] The *aposento*, which provided lodgings for Spaniards, and two homes belonging to prominent Indians, probably don Gaspar Manrique, a *principal* who served as interpreter, and don Francisco Vásquez, the governor of Atitlán, were also situated on the plaza (see fig. 10).[21]

Most of the congregations that were carried out around Lake Atitlán involved settling scattered groups of Indians on sites that had been *amak'* in pre-Hispanic times. The overall effect of the congregation policy was to make the highland settlement pattern more compact. This contrasted with the situation in central Mexico, where the Indians were already highly concentrated when the Spaniards arrived.

Congregations were carried out in the lowlands by Gonzalo Méndez and Diego Ordóñez.[22] Owing to the difficulty of the terrain, the internal arrangement of lowland congregations had to be different from that of highland towns. According to Alonso Paéz Betancor and Pedro de Arboleda, San Bartolomé (Xeoj) "is not laid out like the head town because being on a little hill. . . . it is all concentrated in a small area, and the church is in the middle." Traveling from the dependency to the *cabecera* was difficult, for the road lay over a ridge marked by steep gorges on either side and there were three large rivers that could be crossed only in the winter on wooden bridges built by the natives.[23] In his *Relación*, Fray Alonso Ponce vividly described the rigors of traveling in the Tzutujil lowlands in the sixteenth century.[24]

Estrada described the manner of settlement common throughout the lowland area in 1579:

If [they are] not near the sea, then they are in the savannas. The rest . . . is a blur of trees that cover and impede the view of the land so that no town of all this coast from the mountains to the sea can be

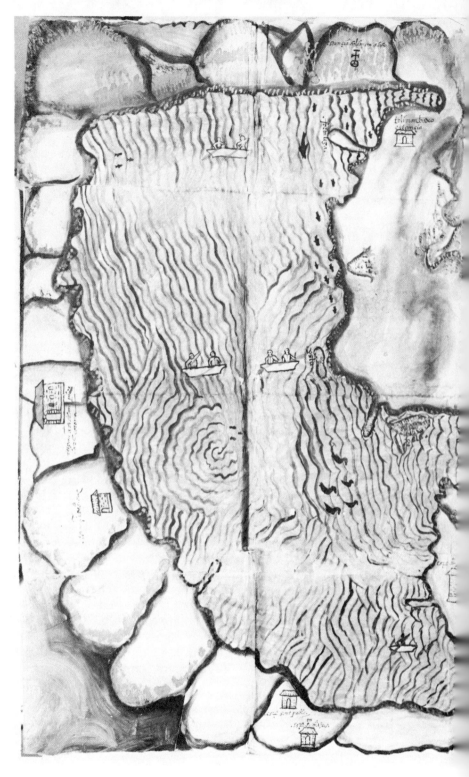

Fig. 10. *Santiago Atitlán, 1585. Colección Joaquín García Icazbalceta, University of Texas, Austin, JGI XX, fol. 306. This map was originally drawn to accompany the* Relación geográfica Atitlán. *The directional*

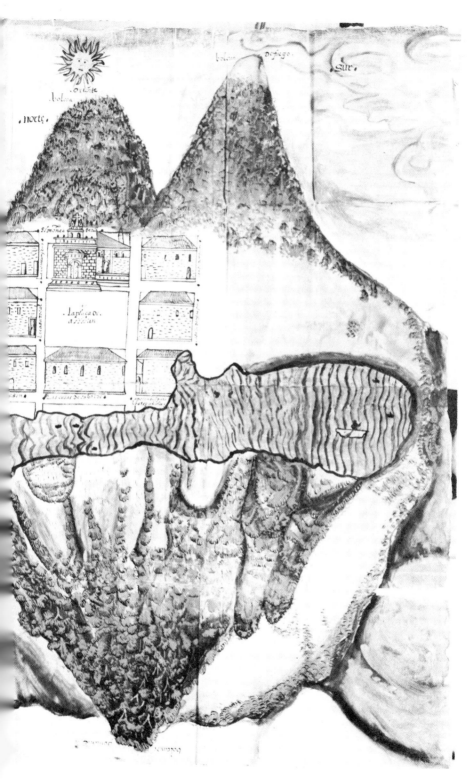

orientation is the east at the top, which is common in sixteenth-century maps. The map is in oblique perspective and is fairly accurate suggesting that the cartographer knew the area well.

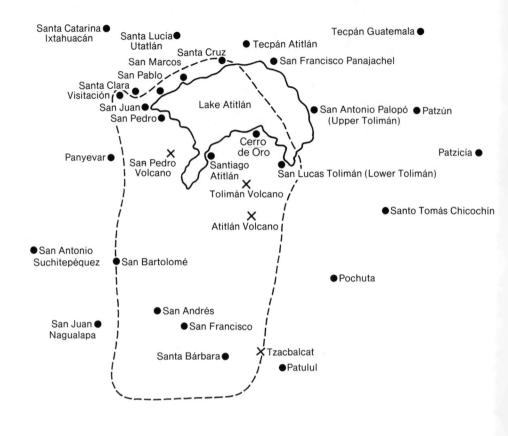

Fig. 11. *The Corregimiento of Atitlán, 1630. Based on documentary material summarized in chapter 11.*

seen from another town, nor road, nor river. . . . The locations of the towns are almost all in some flat parts between small streams . . . and can be seen only when the trees are cut and removed.[25]

Estrada said that by that time the streets were oriented from north to south and east to west, but the houses were interspersed irregularly. Such street orientations were no doubt confined to settlements containing Spaniards, such as Suchitepéquez, because even in modern times McBryde reported that, though lowland towns were generally rectangular, true directional orientation of the streets was unusual.[26]

San Andrés and San Francisco were established in similar terrain. San Andrés was "near a deep gorge, at the top of which is a plain encircled by high mountains, . . . and below the [town] is a wide river . . . that in the rainy season cannot be crossed because of its swollen stream, and for this reason the Indians have constructed a high wooden bridge of large, thick beams." San Andrés, formed around two streets with a plaza in the middle, where the church stood, must have been a fairly typical lowland *estancia.*[27] San Francisco stood on the side of the volcano, where the earth was gravelly and rocky. It was laid out with streets and plazas and also had a church in the middle.[28] Although the *estancias* were fairly close to each other, they remained isolated owing to the lack of good roads.

The Conquest effected some changes in the native settlement pattern. Many *tinamit* were abandoned as Indians were congregated into new settlements. The inhabitants of K'umarcaaj were resettled in Santa Cruz del Quiché; those of Iximché, at Tecpán Guatemala; and the Tzutujils of Chiya', at Santiago Atitlán. Imposition of the Spanish town plan did not always mean a drastic alteration of the ancient settlement pattern; *tinamit* such as Chiya' had been oriented around a central complex. The spatial orientation of ancient sites was often retained or replicated in the congregations. For example, the temple was replaced with a church, and the plaza continued to serve as an area for public gatherings.

Some ancient settlements persisted, possibly being enlarged and serving as centers for congregations, and with hispanicized names. For example, Chi-Tzunún-Choy became San Pedro, and Chupalo became San Pablo. By the seventeenth century most of the lake towns had come to be known primarily by their Spanish names. Lowland areas retained a more dispersed pattern than that of the highlands and one that was basically Indian, though some lowland sites, such as San Antonio Suchitepéquez, became Spanish towns during the cacao boom of the sixteenth century.

The Indians continued to resist congregation throughout the colonial period and constantly returned to the countryside. As late as 1768, Archbishop Cortés y Larraz complained that probably over one-half of them were scattered throughout the rural areas.[29]

Another factor that influenced the location of settlements in the Tzutujil area was that of jurisdictional disputes. Such disputes tended to arise after the congregations were carried out, but some areas had been under contention in the pre-Hispanic period as well. Many of the documents in the archives in Guatemala City concern these disputes. Some are ancient *títulos* justifying ownership of ancestral lands, written in both Spanish and the native language.

By Conquest times the Tzutujils had lost some of their former territory northeast and northwest of Lake Atitlán. The Cakchiquels had also encroached upon Tzutujil lowland territory west of Quioj. The arrival of the Spaniards did not immediately change the pre-Hispanic boundaries because the conquerors tended to respect Indian political entities. The population was redistributed in the mid-sixteenth century, and new settlements were created, but further boundary changes were minimal until the seventeenth century. Betancor and Arboleda described the general boundaries of Atitlán in 1585: "This town of Atitlán to the north part borders on the town and *cabecera* of Tecpán Atitlán [Tzololá], . . . which is a distance of four leagues more or less. Between Atitlán and Tecpán Atitlán is the lake. . . . On the south part this town's borders meet those of Sanct Juan Nahualapa."[30]

## The Highland Territory

In 1579, Estrada named several of the towns belonging to Atitlán and Tecpán Atitlán:

Atitlán . . . has annexes [dependencies] of the towns of San Bartolomé and San Francisco and Tolimán the lower called San Lucas, and the town of San Pedro and San Pablo. Tecpán Atitlán has an administration of the same order and has annexes of upper Tolimán [San Antonio Palopó] and Santo Tomás, San Miguel, and . . . Patulul.[31]

Thus by that time San Antonio Palopó was definitely considered to be Cakchiquel.

In 1583, Santa Cruz was assessed for tribute as an integral part of Atitlán[32] and in 1623 was listed as a *sujeto,* or dependency, of Atitlán and its government.[33] If the site was occupied before that date, the pre-Hispanic name is unknown, but Santa Cruz was probably a congregation. The aboriginal site was Panpatí. Santa Cruz was later moved because of flooding and has occupied its present site for only about one hundred years.[34] By 1583 towns east of Santa Cruz were no longer Tzutujil. Santa Cruz contained a larger proportion of Cakchiquel speakers than Tzutujil speakers, and after it became part of the *alcaldía mayor* of Sololá in the seventeenth century, it lost all Tzutujil affiliations.[35]

San Marcos has changed its location several times since pre-

Conquest days, also owing to flooding. On April 26, 1584, the first mass was said to celebrate the founding of San Marcos in Payán Chocol (now called Jaibalito) by Cakchiquel immigrants from Paquip, a coastal settlement near San Jerónimo.[36] The immigrants had been forced to leave the coast because of a plague of bats. The *oidor* Diego Palacios reported such an attack of bats in 1576, when great herds of cattle were destroyed.[37] Tzutujil speakers also continued to inhabit Payán Chocol and Panpatí, both of which were in the jurisdiction of Atitlán.

In the late sixteenth century there was litigation between Santiago Atitlán and Tecpán Atitlán over the boundary between their respective domains. The boundaries of Payán Chocol, Panpatí, and Pacáon (Coón) were surveyed in 1583. *The Annals of the Cakchiquels* say: "Today, Friday May 10, [1585] the lawsuit ended; the sentence arrived, and the landmarks were surveyed . . . there in Payán Chocol."[38] Estrada's map shows that Paçon, or Coón (or Patzún, as it is called today), was near Upper Tolimán. He stated, "In Paçon begins the jurisdiction of this province of Çapotitlán: from Paçon to Upper Tolimán there are five leagues."[39] Coón had probably been under Cakchiquel control since pre-Hispanic times.

In 1703, San Marcos was moved from Payán Chocol to Panpatí, again owing to flooding. Panpatí was ceded to San Marcos by the inhabitants of Santa Cruz. Under the order of the audiencia dated February 1, 1703, the inhabitants of San Marcos were told "to populate the site . . . named Panpatix."[40]

On December 14, 1724, they received authorization from the audiencia to move again to another area, called Uacujil, for the same reason and yet again in 1881.[41] The last mention of Panpatí was in the document dated 1703; the site was probably permanently abandoned after the flood of 1724.

San Pablo evidently contained a small population in pre-Hispanic times. It was founded as a congregation by Pedro de Betanzos between 1547 and 1550.[42]

Santa Clara was one of the lake towns formed as a congregation after the Conquest, though it probably had a small population in pre-Hispanic times. The town was formed in 1582 to prevent the encroachment of Tzutujils into Quiché territory. The Tzutujils of Santiago Atitlán in turn settled some people in San Juan, which also had a small aboriginal population, to counteract southward movement by Quichés. The town was called San Juan Atitlán, and is now San Juan la Laguna. The Indians who settled at Santa Clara were from Santa Catarina Ixtahuacán, a Quiché town.[43] This, of course, was a pre-Hispanic method of holding frontier areas and was similar in form, if not intent, to the Spanish method of congregation. Both policies resulted in an increase in the number of inhabitants at the two settlements.

The *Título Santa Clara* demonstrates that the Quichés' claims to territory were based on Q'uik'ab's military expedition that had passed along the western side of the lake. The inhabitants of Santa Clara and Panyevar were probably conquered at that time. The Quichés, however, were not successful in retaining Panyevar (which is today a hamlet of San Juan), but Santa Clara remained in their control.

San Juan was officially founded between 1618, when it was not mentioned in a tribute assessment, and 1623, when it was included as "the new town of San Juan."[44] The small population residing in San Juan before 1623 had probably become too insignificant to stem Quiché encroachment.

In 1641 the Indians of San Juan claimed lands occupied by the people of Santa Clara: "Since time immemorial . . . we have owned . . . the lands . . . inherited from our fathers. . . . The Indians of Santa Clara are moving into these lands to our detriment because we do not have other good lands for our fields." Eventually the crown awarded lands to each town on the basis of areas they actually possessed.[45] In 1751, San Pedro and San Juan disputed ownership of the area of Tzan-cal.[46] Today more then half of the land of San Juan is owned by the people of San Pedro. Some people of San Juan pay them rent and farm the land.[47]

Santa María Visitación was also founded by 1583 by the Tzutujils of Atitlán to help forestall movement of Quichés into their territory. The town was listed in the assessment of 1583 as Santa María de Jesús.[48] By 1623 the name had been changed to Santa María Visitación (or Visitación de Nuestra Señora).[49] Both San Pedro and Santa María were often called Atitlán in the early period, but that practice gradually lapsed in favor of the modern names.

Today Santa María Visitación contains both Quiché and Tzutujil speakers and has lost much of its original land. There is still conflict between Visitación and Santa Clara over land lying along the line between Socopache, which is situated just past Paquip, and Chirijajau, the southernmost area of Santa Clara. It is sparsely inhabited, like the lands often disputed among lake towns.[50] The Tzutujils of Atitlán largely succeeded in preventing further movement of Quichés to the western side of the lake by founding San Juan and Santa María.

On the western side of Lake Atitlán congregations had been carried out at San Pedro by 1550. The town was known as San Pedro Patzununá as late as the eighteenth century, but by the mid-eighteenth century San Pedro la Laguna, the modern name, was becoming accepted.[51] The name Patzununá was derived from the aboriginal Chi-Tzunún-Choy.

The date of the founding of San Lucas Tolimán is not known, but it was mentioned as early as 1575.[52] In 1609 it was assessed along with Atitlán.[53] By that year it was referred to as San Lucas Tolimán, rather than Lower Tolimán.

In summary, most of the Tzutujil lake towns were founded by the end of the sixteenth century: Santiago Atitlán, San Pedro, and San Pablo by 1550; San Lucas by 1575; Santa María Visitación and Santa Cruz by 1583; San Marcos by 1584; and San Juan by 1623. These were the towns that were originally assessed tribute along with Atitlán and remained under its jurisdiction. Other settlements controlled by Atitlán in pre-Hispanic times, such as Tzololá, Ajachel, Palopó, and Coón remained under the jurisdiction of Tecpán Atitlán and were never again considered to be Tzutujil.

Today the border between Tzutujil and Cakchiquel speakers is at San Pablo.[54] All towns east of San Pablo are Cakchiquel, continuing on down the east side of the lake to San Lucas, which contains Cakchiquel and Tzutujil speakers. The most significant highland territorial loss in the colonial period was Santa Cruz, but that did not occur until the late seventeenth century.

## The Lowland Territory

In the *Relación Tzutujil* the lords of Atitlán listed the lowland *estancias* under their jurisdiction as San Bartolomé, San Andrés, San Francisco, and Santa Bárbara.[55] In 1571 they were having some trouble maintaining control of these settlements: "We also ask Your Majesty [to aid us] because there are some rebel Indians in our *estancias* who want to be outside our subjection and do not obey our commands to collect tribute."[56] A year earlier the same *estancias* had been listed by Diego de Garcés as belonging to Atitlán: "San Francisco and Santa Bárbara and San Andrés and San Bartolomé, *estancias* of Atitlán, . . . are towns rich in cacao."[57]

The *Relación geográfica Aguacatepec* states that San Bartolomé was "bounded on the south at a distance of two or three harquebus shots by *Sanct Juan Naualapa*, of the *encomienda* of Gaspar Arías de Avila."[58] San Andrés was "bound[ed] on the south

at a distance of seven leagues by Xicalapa, of the *encomienda*
of Juan Rodríques Cabrillo, . . . and on the west four leagues
away more or less by . . . Sanct Juan Navalapa."[59] San Francisco
and the new town Santa Bárbara were nearby:

San Francisco is located between . . . Atitlán, San Andrés, and Santa
Barbola. It is subject to [Atitlán] and thus since they are all one, and
there is no distinction of boundaries between them, nothing is written
here except that the *estancia* of Santa Barbola . . . is bounded from north
to south by Santa María Magdalena Patulul . . . for a distance of two
leagues more or less.[60]

Santa Bárbara was said to have been around forty years old in
1585. Thus it would have been founded around 1545, and that is
probably when the priests formed all the coastal congregations.[61]
All these towns were called Atitlán in the sixteenth century and
de la Costilla in the seventeenth century.

According to a document of 1587, the Cakchiquels of Patulul
tried to take over ancient lands of the Tzutujils at Tzacbalcat.
The lands belonged to Santa Bárbara. A fight erupted over the
lands, and the people of Patulul were driven off. They appealed
to Tecpán Atitlán, their *cabecera*, for help in the conflict.[62] According to *The Annals of the Cakchiquels*, Tecpán Atitlán won the
lawsuit,[63] but according to the document of 1587, a compromise
settlement was agreed upon whereby Atitlán eventually regained
the land.

Vásquez mentioned the existence of San Bartolomé, San Andrés,
San Francisco, and Santa Bárbara in his time,[64] but San Francisco
did not survive the decline of cacao of the eighteenth century.
The population had become so small that on March 17, 1756,
the *alcalde mayor* of Sololá ordered the town abandoned and the
remaining inhabitants moved to Santa Bárbara.[65] Santa Bárbara
is still in existence but was separated from the Department of
Sololá and annexed to the Department of Suchitepéquez on May
22, 1934.[66] San Bartolomé was moved to the modern site of Chicacao (the old location is on the Finca San Bartolo Nanzales).[67]
Chicacao remained under Atitlán's jurisdiction throughout the
nineteenth century, but in 1934 was transferred to the Department of Suchitepéquez.[68] It is not known exactly when San Andrés
died out; a town of San Andrés was still in existence in 1800,
according to the map prepared under the auspices of don José
Rossi y Rubí, the *alcalde mayor* of Suchitepéquez (fig. 12).[69]

San Antonio Suchitepéquez and San Juan Nagualapa were incorporated into different *encomiendas* in the early sixteenth cen-

tury and became completely separate from Atitlán. With the separation of Nagualapa from their influence the Tzutujils lost their most lucrative cacao dependency. Garcés described the town in 1570: "San Juan de Nagualapa is the richest town of this coast, and in all the land there are no Indians who spend and buy more than those of this town because they have a lot of good cacao."[70] Nagualapa was also moved from its original location, probably in the eighteenth century. The town appears to have become extinct sometime between 1762 and 1764, if it is the one mentioned by Cortés y Larraz.[71]

The coast, being valuable for such products as cacao, was eventually removed from Indian control. During the sixteenth and early seventeenth centuries, however, the boundaries of the pre-Hispanic Tzutujil kingdom remained largely intact. After the decline of cacao some *estancias* disappeared, leaving only San Bartolomé and Santa Bárbara. These became *ladino* (non-Indian) towns after coffee production began in the mid-nineteenth century, and Atitlán lost any say in the administration of these former colonies.

The effect of the Spanish Conquest on the Tzutujils was gradually to contract the area of their influence in the highlands and eventually to separate them from their lowland territory. Most of the territorial disputes in the colonial period arose between close neighboring towns that needed more land for subsistence farming. The land was usually sparsely inhabited or vacant and of interest mainly to the Indians. Some of the disputes had their origin in pre-Columbian times, but they increased in frequency after the seventeenth century as individual towns sought to gain local political independence from the *cabecera*. In pre-Hispanic times land had been controlled by the Ajtz'iquinajay and his most important nobles. After the Conquest, as some of these lineages died out, the lines of succession were disturbed. These factors tended to increase jurisdictional disputes and to create pressures that eventually altered the boundaries of the old kingdom.

Basically highland towns that contained a majority of Cakchiquel speakers or were under the Cakchiquels' control at contact continued to remain separate from Tzutujil control after the Spanish administrative structure was set up. East of Santa Cruz, Cakchiquel was mainly spoken at contact, and those towns remained under the control of Tecpán Atitlán. Santa Cruz and towns west of it remained primarily Tzutujil in the early colonial period.

In the lowlands the Tzutujils were effective in keeping jurisdiction of their most important *estancias*, though Nagualapa was

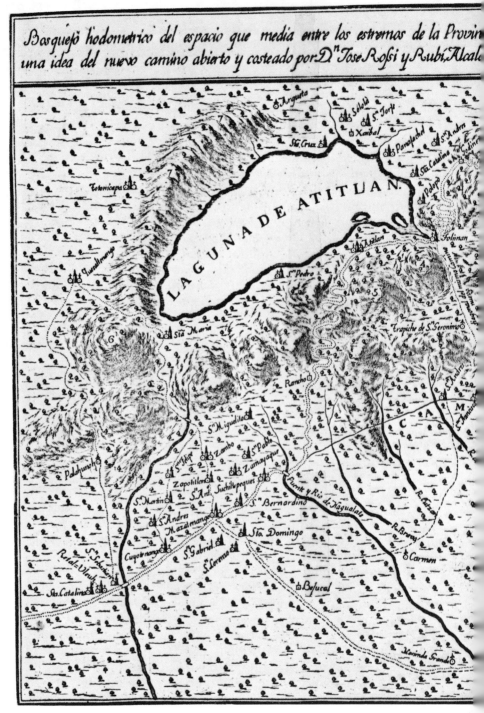

Fig. 12. *The Province of Suchitepéquez, 1800. From AGC A1.22.33* exp. *4,171* leg. *207. Año 1805.*

e Suchiltepeques, y la Capital de Guatemala, para dar
uyor de d'ña Provincia, de Orden Superior. año de 1800

NVA GUATEM.

Paros
Patzicia
Chimaltenango Zumpango
Xoco
Itenar
Villa
Yizapa
AG.A
Amatitlan
Acatenango
2
S.° Christobal
2
S.° Pedro Marti
Ihaguir
Chinas Grande
V O
Escuinta
Sta. Lucia Cosumalguapa
R.Ichacoa
Ziquinala
R.Ichacoa
Garcia
N U E
R.Zungua
R.Chaca
Chipilapa
Sta. Ana Mixtan
Noria

### Explicacion de Señales.

- Ciudad
- Cabezeras de Curatos
- Pueblos
- Haciendas
- Ranchos
1. Volcan de Agua
2. y 2 Volcanes de Fuego
3. Volcan de Acatenango
4. Volcan de Toliman
5. Volcan de Atitlan
6. Volcan de Sunil
7. y 7. Cuesta de la Laja

......... Veredas de transitos
_____ Camino que llaman de
los altos
_._._._ Camino de ábajo llamá
de la Costa

El camino que dice nuebo fui el
avierto por D.ⁿ Jose Rosi y Rubi.

Escala de 5 Leguas de à 25 en Grado.

lost. They also managed to defend frontier lands at Tzacbalcat. It was not until the decline of cacao production that the Tzutujil lost much of their influence in the piedmont area, though they retained jurisdiction over San Bartolomé and Santa Bárbara until modern times.

## CHAPTER 12

# Encomienda *and Tribute*

After the Conquest the first Spanish institution imposed on the Indians was the *encomienda*. This system empowered the conquerors to collect tribute and demand labor from the conquered peoples. Under the system specified groups of Indians were "granted" to Spanish colonists who had performed services for the crown. In return for the Indians' tribute and labor the holders of *encomiendas,* called *encomenderos,* were obligated to render military service to the crown and to provide for the spiritual welfare of the Indians under their control.[1] *Encomenderos* customarily discharged the latter responsibility by paying the salary of the local priest and contributing to the ornamentation of the local church.

The *encomienda* was not a land grant but was sometimes based upon the *cabecera-sujeto* unit.[2] In the sixteenth century the term *encomienda* was not often used in Guatemala; rather, the colonists spoke of *repartimientos* of Indians, a term used to designate the geographical area of an *encomienda* grant.[3] Many *encomenderos* lived in the capital city, far from their Indian subjects;[4] some never visited their *encomienda* Indians.

The earliest *encomiendas* were administered through the local Indian lords, who saw to it that the proper numbers of laborers were available and that tribute demands were met.[5] Lords who were able to supply the tribute stayed in office; those who did not were often removed. An *encomendero* who was busy or absent from the area employed a *mayordomo,* or steward, to manage the *encomienda.* There were also Indian tribute collectors, called *calpixqui* (Nahuatl) or *calpisques* in Guatemalan colonial documents.[6]

Although the *encomienda* was not intended to be harsh and disruptive of Indian society, in practice it allowed for a tremendous amount of exploitation, especially in the first two decades or so after the Conquest. The amount of tribute and labor was not specified in the early *encomiendas,*[7] and the *encomendero* could de-

*137*

mand whatever he felt the grant should provide and relied on the Indian lord to collect it.[8] The lords' procedures for obtaining labor and tribute followed pre-Hispanic custom, but there was a great increase in the amount collected. The *encomienda* placed Indian society under heavy stress, but its basis in the *cabecera-sujeto* unit kept the aboriginal Indian organization intact. The willingness of *encomenderos* to deal with the caciques perpetuated ancient methods of tribute collection.

The conquerors utilized the Indians in several ways. After they had subdued the most important regions, they used the Indians of those lands as warriors in the conquest of secondary areas.[9] The Indians also built cities, acted as carriers, worked in the mines, and paid tribute to their *encomenderos*.[10] Under Spanish law Indians who resisted conquest could be treated as slaves of war (*esclavos de guerra*), as were those who had been slaves of Indian lords (*esclavos de rescate*) before the coming of the Spaniards.[11] The conquerors added slaves captured in warfare to their *encomienda* Indians to enlarge the labor force. The native lords usually sent their own slaves to serve the Spaniards and work in the mines.[12] Many of those Indians died far from their homelands. In pre-Columbian times slaves of the native lords had been treated less severely and had been entitled to some rights.[13] Those taken by the early *encomenderos* worked constantly, often until they died.

### *The* Encomienda *of Atitlán*

The most important *encomiendas* in the Guatemalan highlands were formed in Quiché territory. They had developed a complex administrative structure in aboriginal times, and the Spaniards simply took over that structure.[14]

Pedro de Alvarado was the first *encomendero* of Atitlán, and it was one of the most lucrative *encomiendas* in early times. Alvarado soon granted half of Atitlán to another conquistador, Pedro de Cueto.[15] During Alvarado's absences from Guatemala from 1526 to 1530 and from 1534 to 1535, his brother Jorge acted as governor of the colony. During those periods Jorge made some *encomienda* grants and kept some of his brother's *encomiendas* for himself: "Jorge de Alvarado made grants and took for himself the towns of Attitan, Pantittan, and Quezaltenango which he possessed but were afterward taken from him by this Real Audiencia [Mexico]."[16] Jorge was dispossessed after moving to Mexico because an *encomendero* was not permitted to live outside the province in which the *encomienda* had been granted.[17]

A document detailing the services of Pedro de Cueto states that he held half of the Atitlán *encomienda,* sharing it with Sancho de Barahona el Viejo, another of Guatemala's most prominent conquistadors.[18] In 1529, Jorge granted Barahona "half of the province of Atitlán near [Tecpán] Guatemala with half of the towns called zuquitlan, comilpa, aguantepeque, oçotepeque, and the other towns and *estancias* subject to it with half of the lords and natives of it."[19]

It is not clear whether Jorge granted his half of Atitlán to Barahona, but that is what the document dealing with de Cueto's services seems to imply. If so, both de Cueto and Barahona could have been *encomenderos* of Atitlán at the same time, as the document states. It is much more likely, however, that Jorge granted de Cueto's half to Barahona in 1529. De Cueto held the *encomienda* for only two or three years, until his death, when his half of the *encomienda* escheated to the crown. Jorge then probably regranted it to Barahona. De Cueto's descendants, writing to the crown regarding their esteemed ancestor, probably were confused regarding who owned the other half of the *encomienda.* It must have been Alvarado, not Barahona.

When Pedro de Alvarado returned from his travels, he voided many of the grants that Jorge had made. When he returned to Guatemala in 1530, there were so many complaints and so much quarreling about the division of *repartimientos* that a new distribution was ordered.[20] In 1532, Pedro regranted half of Atitlán to Barahona and kept the other half, temporarily possessed by Jorge during his absence, for himself. Barahona's area was listed as

Half of the Indian lords and *principales* of the towns called Atitan and çucitlan which is also called chupalu and comilpa . . . or xebalo and aguatepeque or xaob and orquetepeque and çanona, çaqualpa, chobes, cinacatepeque, or quiob, and canaquil with all the *estancias* and *sujetos* which in any manner may belong to the said towns.[21]

Alvarado came to possess an enormous *encomienda,* which included "Tequecistlán, Totonicapán, Izquintepeque, and Guazacapán and half of Atitlán."[22]

Alvarado and Barahona quarreled after the grant of 1532 was made, and Alvarado took the other half of Atitlán away from Barahona. He then gave Atitlán and Tequecistlán (or Tecocistlán) to Jorge and left for Peru in 1534. After Jorge moved to Mexico City,

Pedro then took back Atitlán and Tequecistlán and gave his brother some of his own Mexican holdings.[23] In 1537, Barahona lodged a complaint against Alvarado and was eventually successful in regaining his half of Atitlán.[24] Alvarado and his wife, Beatriz de la Cueva, died in 1541 without legitimate heirs, and by 1542 Alvarado's half of Atitlán had passed to the crown.[25] After that time the crown held half of Atitlán, and Barahona held the other half. In 1548, Barahona had five hundred tributaries from his half of Atitlán.[26]

Attempts to regulate the *encomienda* began during the 1530s but were generally unsuccessful until after Alvarado's death. When Maldonado arrived in Guatemala in 1536, having been sent there by the Audiencia of Mexico to investigate Alvarado, he tried to enforce the royal order to assess the Indians so that regular, fixed payments of tribute could begin.[27] After Alvarado resumed control of the government of Guatemala in 1539, the order was ignored, and the *encomenderos* began exacting tribute arbitrarily as before.

The *encomienda* proved to be exploitative wherever it was instituted, but it was particularly harsh in Guatemala during Alvarado's time. He was the governor and prime exploiter, and there was little obstacle to his excesses. Even Indians like the Tzutujils who cooperated after the Conquest were ill-treated along with those who continued to resist. The *encomenderos* used their Indian slaves as domestic servants, *tamemes* (burden bearers, or porters), farmers, miners, and all-purpose laborers, and all Indians were forced to surrender any items of value they owned.

Priests like Las Casas exhorted the crown to halt the abuses and to put an end to slavery, and in 1542–43 the New Laws were decreed. These laws were designed to reduce the power of the *encomenderos* and ameliorate the catastrophic Indian mortality. The laws were not immediately put into effect in Guatemala, however, owing to the extreme opposition to them by the colonists and by audiencia officials, many of whom were practically *encomenderos* themselves.[28] Maldonado with his friends and relatives controlled about one-third of the *encomiendas* in Guatemala in the 1540s.[29] Not until Alonso López de Cerrato took over the presidency of the audiencia in 1548 were some of the New Laws actually put into effect and the suffering of the Indians was alleviated.

López de Cerrato conducted Maldonado's *residencia* and referred to his predecessor's administration as "the golden age of slavery." He stated that the tributes demanded were exorbitant and that "every *encomendero* did as he wished, and although they killed and robbed Indians, or enslaved them, there was no punishment."[30] The New Laws ordered that no Indian could be taken as a slave and that slaves held without legitimate title must be set free.[31] López de Cerrato enforced the articles relating to slavery, but by his time the Indian population was so reduced that less wasteful labor systems had come into use. Moreover, by 1548 many of the gold and silver mines had been abandoned. Fewer Indians were used as *tamemes* by 1550 owing to the growth of the cattle and horse herds.[32]

Not all the Indians favored the elimination of slavery. The lords of Atitlán complained that they were without their services in the coastal cacao plantations: "We have lost our haciendas and cacao plantations and some birds called parrots have destroyed them because there was no one to keep guard over them or to look after them. Because of this we live in poverty and want."[33]

Beginning in 1549, labor service was removed from the native *encomienda* obligation.[34] From that time on Indians were to be paid for whatever labor they performed. After 1550 new tribute schedules *(tasaciones)* were drawn up prescribing the legal amounts that *encomenderos* could demand. From that time on, crown officials prepared the schedules, thereby removing the *encomenderos'* jurisdiction over the Indians.[35] The crown also ordered the *oidores* to make frequent visits to the Indian towns to prevent abuses by the *encomenderos.*[36]

By 1549, Sancho de Barahona, the younger son and namesake of the conquistador, had inherited his father's half of Atitlán.[37] At the time Atitlán was one of the richest *encomiendas* in Guatemala owing to its control of coastal cacao fields.[38] The value of the *encomienda* declined somewhat after 1578 because of the epidemics of disease and plague, which reduced the population of Atitlán and its *sujetos* (see tables 4 to 6).

Even though the income of the *encomienda* was reduced, the expenses of the *encomendero* continued. In 1587, Barahona refused to pay for the ornaments for the church of Atitlán, and the Indians divided up the cost among themselves.[39] Barahona's refusal to pay was probably the result of declining income and increasing royal restrictions placed on *encomiendas.* In 1586 the Franciscan friar Francisco Salcedo said that Barahona could pay a tax of 50,000 *maravedíes,* which would go to the church.[40] In 1587, García de Valverde, president of the Audiencia of Guatemala, fixed the tax to be paid by *encomenderos* at 50,000 *maravedíes* per 400 tributaries. The money was to be paid to the priest of the district in which the *encomienda* was granted.[41]

Table 4. *Populations of Atitlán and the Highland* Sujetos, *ca. 1524-1660*[a]

| Year | Tributaries | Number of Inhabitants | Source |
|---|---|---|---|
| Ca. 1524 | 12,000 | 48,000 | *RGA* 1964, p. 95. |
| 1547 | 1,400 | 5,600 | *RGA* 1964, p. 97. |
| 1570 | 1,500 | 6,000 | *CDI* 1925, 17: 180. |
| 1572 | 1,673 | 6,692 | Solano 1974, p. 91 |
| 1575 | 1,333 | 5,332 | AGI Guatemala *leg.* 169. Año 1575. |
| 1583 | 1,057 | 4,228 | AGI Guatemala *leg.* 171. Año 1592.[b] |
| 1585 | 1,005 | 4,020 | *RGA* 1964, p. 97. |
| 1586 | 1,100 | 4,400 | AGI Guatemala *leg.* 171. Año 1592. |
| 1598 | 1,400 | 5,600 | AGI Guatemala *leg.* 172. Año 1597. |
| 1599 | 1,600 | 6,400 | AGC A3.16 *exp.* 40,491. *leg.* 2,801. Año 1599. |
| 1604 | 1,000 | 4,000 | Solano 1974, p. 107. |
| 1609 | 1,000[c] | 4,000 | AGC A3.16 *exp.* 40,491. *leg.* 2,801. Año 1599.[d] |
| 1630 | 1,000 | 4,000 | Cobo 1944, p. 195. |
| 1660 | 1,000 | 4,000 | Vásquez 1937, 1:170-71. |

[a] The figures for tributaries given in this table from the years 1524 to 1599 and 1609 include the highland *sujetos*. In 1599 and probably in 1598 as well, lowland *estancia* residents are also included in the figure, and for 1630 and 1660 only residents of Atitlán are shown. In this table and tables 5 and 6, widowers, bachelors, widows, and unmarried persons not living at home are considered one-half tributary unit each. A married couple and their children are one tributary unit. *Reservados* are not included here. *Vezinos* are equal to tributaries (Sherman 1979, p. 6).

[b] Francisco Salcedo calculated one tributary as being equal to two widows and two bachelors.

[c] An approximate number.

[d] This document contains tribute censuses for the years 1599 and 1609.

After the death of the younger Barahona, Atitlán reverted to the crown. Because of the services given by the father and son to the monarchy, the *encomienda* was granted a third life *(vida),* and by a royal command dated November 8, 1608, don Pedro Núñez de Barahona, the grandson of Sancho de Barahona el Viejo, received the *encomienda* of Atitlán. He formally took possession in 1623, though he had actually had control of the *encomienda* for several years.[42]

The passing of the *encomienda* from one *encomendero* to the next had little meaning to the Indians. Since the early days the Barahonas had lived in the capital, Santiago de Guatemala, and the lords of Atitlán had taken care of the tribute collection. Atitlán was still supplying a fairly lucrative income at the beginning of

Table 5. *Populations of the Coastal* Estancias, *ca. 1524-1689*

|          | San Bartolomé | | San Andrés | | San Francisco | | Santa Barbara | |
| --- | --- | --- | --- | --- | --- | --- | --- | --- |
| Year | T[a] | I[a] | T | I | T | I | T | I |
| Ca. 1524 | 1,600[b] | 6,400 | 800[c] | 3,200 | 1,000[d] | 4,000 | | |
| 1575[e] | 380 | 1,520 | 160 | 640 | 240 | 960 | 30 | 120 |
| 1583[f] | 252 | 1,008 | 104 | 416 | 198 | 792 | 91 | 364 |
| 1585 | 223[g] | 892 | 104[h] | 416 | 193[i] | 772 | 92[j] | 368 |
| Ca. 1623[k] | 90 | 360 | 83 | 332 | 101 | 404 | 133 | 532 |
| 1689[l] | 25 | 100 | 18 | 71 | 123 | 492 | 39 | 154 |

[a] T = tributaries; I = inhabitants.   [g] *RGAG* 1965, p. 267.
[b] *RGAG* 1965, p. 267.               [h] *RGSA* 1952, p. 104.
[c] *RGSA* 1952, p. 104.               [i] *RGSF* 1952, p. 125; approximate number.
[d] *RGSF* 1952, p. 125.               [j] *Ibid.*, p. 143-44.
[e] AGI Guatemala *leg.* 169. *Año* 1575.   [k] AGC A1.1 *exp.* 10 *leg.* 1. *Año* 1623.
[f] AGI Guatemala *leg.* 171. *Año* 1592.

[l] Vásquez 1944, 4:53-54. Vásquez gave the Population of the *estancias* in confessors (men and women "*de confesión*"); MacLeod (1973, p. 131) estimates that confessors equal around 80 percent of the population; tributaries are given to the nearest whole number.

the seventeenth century, but the 2,867 *tostones* collected by don Pedro equaled 1,433.5 pesos, as compared with the 2,000 pesos his grandfather had received in earlier days.[43] Nevertheless, because Atitlán was one of the most valuable *encomiendas* of the sixteenth century, the Barahona family was able to enjoy a decent living and avoid the abject poverty of less fortunate *encomenderos.* The poverty and isolation from Spanish interest that characterized Atitlán in the late seventeenth and early eighteenth centuries was the result of the virtual abandonment of cacao cultivation in the lowland Zapotitlán-Suchitepéquez area.[44]

In 1629, after don Pedro's death, the Barahona family no longer drew income from the Tzutujil area. The last *encomendero* of Atitlán was the Conde de Oropesa, who retained it until 1707.[45]

## Tribute

At first Pedro de Alvarado divided the revenue of the *encomienda* of Atitlán with Pedro de Cueto. The lord of Atitlán (Chiya'), don Pedro, collected the tribute and saw that it was delivered to both *encomenderos.* Alvarado's initial demands were for money and valuables. No doubt he quickly relieved the Tzutujils of whatever treasure they had, just as he did with the Cakchiquels.[46] The *Relación geográfica Atitlán* describes the tribute services provided by the Tzutujils in the period just after the Conquest:

In the wars[47] that occurred, many Indians from this town died. Many others died in the mines, mining gold. The Indians who went to the mines

Table 6. Populations of the Highland Sujetos, 1599-1689

| | San Juan | | San Pedro | | San Pablo | | San Marcos | | Visitación | | San Lucas | | Santa Cruz | |
|---|---|---|---|---|---|---|---|---|---|---|---|---|---|---|
| | T[a] | I[a] | T | I | T | I | T | I | T | I | T | I | T | I |
| 1599[b] | | | 70 | 280 | 19 | 76 | | | 15 | 60 | 50 | 200 | | |
| 1609[c] | | | 75 | 300 | 22 | 88 | 7 | 28 | 8 | 32 | 55 | 220 | 17 | 68 |
| 1623[d] | 51 | 204 | 102 | 408 | 35 | 140 | 7 | 28 | 16 | 64 | 73 | 292 | 21 | 84 |
| 1689[e] | 125 | 500 | 136 | 544 | 63 | 250 | 81 | 325 | 37 | 149 | 141 | 563 | 94 | 375 |

[a] T = tributaries; I = inhabitants.

[b] AGC A3.16 exp. 40,491 leg. 2801. Año 1599.

[c] Payán Chocol and Panpatí are combined under San Marcos for 1609 and 1623. AGC A3.16 exp. 40,491 leg. 2,801. Año 1599. AGC A1.1 exp. 10 leg. 1. Año 1623.

[d] Ibid.

[e] Vásquez 1944, 4:44-47. The population is given in terms of confessors; tributaries are given to the nearest whole number.

were taken by the *encomenderos* who at that time held this town. According to the Indian lords, the number of Indians taken for the mines every ten days was two hundred and forty. Others died of . . . smallpox, measles, fever, blood which ran from their noses,[48] and other epidemics and hardships which befell them. When the 240 Indians went to the mines to mine gold, they took their wives with them to prepare their food and for other personal services which were needed in the mines. . . . at that time the Spaniards used them as carriers for their trade and profit, . . . and the Indians suffered great hardships.[49]

The *Relación Tzutujil* states that in this time Atitlán gave as tribute, in addition to cacao,

slaves, men and women in the quantity of four hundred and five hundred for service of their persons, and to send to the mines. They also gave tribute of *mantas,* cacao, honey, turkeys, salt, chili, copper, and maguey and many other things that they made them give. They also made them give many Indians in tribute every fifteen days to whom they gave such excessive work that they died.[50]

These were most of the same products that they had paid as tribute in pre-Hispanic times, though some items, such as jade and feathers, were omitted because they had no value to the Spaniards.

The *Annals of the Cakchiquels* state that tribute began in Tzololá on January 12, 1528.[51] That was during the period when Jorge de Alvarado was *encomendero* of Atitlán and represents the beginning of a more regular system of collection. It appears that after this time tribute was collected once a year. In 1530, upon Pedro de Alvarado's order, the Cakchiquels contributed four hundred men and four hundred women for work on the new capital.[52] The Tzutujils may have supplied laborers for this construction as well.

The *Relación Tzutujil* describes the tribute paid by Atitlán to Alvarado and de Cueto: "The first masters we had were the Adelantado D. Pedro de Alvarado and one . . . [Pedro] de Cueto to whom our forefathers gave 1,400 *xiquipiles* of cacao, which was in money 10,000 pesos, with many mantas, turkeys, honey, maize, and other lesser things they ordered to be given every year."[53] In 1537, Sancho de Barahona stated that Jorge de Alvarado demanded from Atitlán 250 slaves, 1,200 *xiquipiles* of cacao, and 2,000 mantas valued at 3,000 to 4,000 pesos. This tribute was demanded in 1534 and 1535, when Pedro de Alvarado was in Peru. Barahona demanded payment of the 4,000 *pesos* that he had lost when his half of Atitlán was taken away from him; thus he was probably collecting around 2,000 pesos a year before Jorge gained Atitlán.[54] It is difficult to say whether Pedro de Alvarado and de Cueto initially extracted 10,000 pesos, as the lords of Atitlán stated, but the value of cacao may well have dropped by 1534.

By 1538, Alvarado owned a *cuadrilla,* or work gang of slaves, from Atitlán that contained only 65 men and women with their tools and canoes.[55] This was a much smaller number than the 250 taken by Jorge de Alvarado in 1534–35, when Pedro was absent from Guatemala. Maldonado arrived in 1536 and was able to effect some reforms:

Soon there was no more washing of gold; the tribute of boys and girls was suspended. Soon also there was an end to the deaths by fire and hanging, and the highway robberies of the Spaniards ceased. Soon the people could be seen traveling on the roads again as it was before the tribute commenced.[56]

Maldonado also tried to put into effect the royal order that the Indians were to be formally assessed so that fixed payments of tribute could begin. In 1536 the governor and the bishop of Guatemala were empowered to make the assessment. The order was not carried out, however, and after Pedro de Alvarado resumed control of the government in 1539, he charged tribute according to his own will as before.[57]

In 1546 the crown, in a continuing effort to revise the tribute system, ordered the Audiencia de los Confines to reassess the tribute of *encomiendas* formerly belonging to Alvarado.[58] In the same year the crown, to stop double payment of tribute, also decreed that Indians assessed in one town could not be assessed in any other town.[59] Diego de Garcés, the *alcalde mayor* of Zapotitlán, described the evils resulting from assessing an Indian twice: "The husband has a cacao milpa with his wife, pays tribute for himself in his town and pays tribute in the town of his wife because of the milpa he has with her. This is such a burden that each day milpas are abandoned, and they would rather lose them than pay so much tribute."[60] Garcés wrote in 1572, indicating that royal legislation halting this practice had not been put into effect.

In 1547 the crown ordered that tribute must be administered by officials responsible for finance.[61] Tribute was not regularly assessed and collected according to a fixed quota, however, until López de Cerrato assumed control of the government of Guatemala in 1548. Between 1548 and 1551 the Indians of Guatemala were assessed by López de Cerrato and his judges, especially Pedro Ramírez de Quiñónes. The assessment gave the name of the *encomendero* and the amount of tribute for most towns of Guatemala.[62]

After López de Cerrato's time tribute was assessed on married Indian households. A married man, his wife, and their children living at home constituted one tributary unit. The tribute was to be paid only in items produced locally; this provision was designed to discourage highland Indians from leaving their homes and going to the coast to obtain money or cacao. The tribute was collected twice a year, in June and December. In 1551 the crown ordered that assessments must be made with all possible moderation.[63] In 1553 the crown requested information on the tribute-payment customs observed among the Indians before the coming of the Spaniards.[64] Alonso de Zorita, an *oidor* under López de Cerrato, described the royal policy concerning the tribute system in the mid-1550s:

> Your Majesty has . . . ordered that assessments should be made, not on the basis of reports concerning the capacity to pay of the towns, but on the basis of personal observation and study of the character and capacities of each town, the fertility of its soil, and the like, in order that a just assessment may be made. . . . They should give only those things that are found in their native lands. . . . the tribute should consist of only two or three kinds of things . . . and must not be indefinite.[65]

The lords of Atitlán described the tribute that López de Cerrato assigned to their town: "Our fathers paid tribute to Y. M. and to Sancho de Barahona until Licenciado Zerrato came, who had us in moderate tribute and stopped the excess which we were used to giving."[66] The López de Cerrato assessment states that Atitlán was to pay 1,200 *xiquipiles* and 9 *zontles* of cacao each year and nothing else, even though the lords said that they also gave 400 turkeys and 400 chickens. Payment of fowl probably began in 1554, when Cerrato reduced the tribute of Atitlán to 600 *xiquipiles* of cacao.[67] Most of Atitlán's tribute was assessed in cacao because it was plentiful throughout the coastal area that was under Tzutujil control.[68] The cacao tribute assigned by López de Cerrato was about the same that had been taken from Atitlán by Jorge de Alvarado in 1534–35, but under López de Cerrato the Indians did not have to give the many other commodities, nor did they have to provide slaves, owing to the termination of labor service as part of the tribute obligation in 1549. López de Cerrato exempted the lords from paying tribute, but in 1557 the audiencia rescinded his order to that effect.[69]

The crown wanted the Indians to pay less tribute to the *encomenderos* than they were accustomed to paying to their caciques. There was a certain contradiction in crown philosophy regarding nobles and the paying of tribute. Zorita pointed this out:

> Your Majesty has ordered that the caciques and natural lords should receive the tribute and services they used to receive in the time of their heathendom, but that the tribute should not be excessive or imposed

tyranically; if it prove to be such, it should be appraised and lowered. On the other hand, Your Majesty orders that the tribute to be paid to the encomenderos should be fixed at such a rate that they may live comfortably, but without prejudice and harassment to the Indians. . . . Your Majesty has also ordered that the tribute be moderate and less than that which they paid in the time of their heathendom, so that they may know Your Majesty's desire to favor them. It appears to me that this implies a contradiction, for if they pay the caciques and lords what is due them, and if the encomenderos receive their due share of tribute, the total cannot be less than the amount they paid their caciques and lords in the time of their heathendom, but more than double as much.[70]

López de Cerrato's policies alleviated the misery of the average Indian tribute payer, but the lords were not entirely pleased about the freeing of the slaves. The assessments of tribute were equalized so that Sancho de Barahona received about the same amount, 2,000 pesos, as the crown. This was not satisfactory to the *encomendero,* and in 1555, Sancho and his older brother Pedro disputed López de Cerrato's assessment of their half of Atitlán.[71] In general, the Indians seemed to believe that López de Cerrato reduced their burdens.[72] There is no further information concerning assessments until Juan Núñez de Landecho's time (1559-63).

After 1557, Indian nobles were included in the tribute rolls unless they were specifically exempted by being designated caciques, and the audiencia tried to tighten up the collection of tribute:

On the tenth day of the fourth month after the day of St. James came the decree issued by Ramírez, in accordance with which the principal lords had to pay tribute as well as the poor people. Control of taxation, which had not been practiced in the old days by the lords, was immediately established. It was known that the tribute was stolen, but they did not know who was guilty. They did not deliver the full measure of corn, they sent old hens, they left off working in the corn fields. In this way they paid only part of the tribute to the lords. On the day of St. Francis, a Monday, Ramírez issued the decree, on the day 7 Camey [October 4, 1557].[73]

After Landecho assumed control of the audiencia in 1559, the lords of Atitlán asked to be reassessed,[74] perhaps because of their reduced circumstances after losing their slaves and the population losses during the epidemic of 1560.[75] Landecho did reassess them but increased their tribute by 2,000 pesos, along with 200 fanegas of maize and 10 arrobas of honey. The Indians protested: "Thus we have a heavy load and excessive tribute although all the Presidents and Judges who came to these parts gave us the understanding that they only came to favor us and help us, but as to our tribute, we are in no way delivered."[76] The Cakchiquels blamed the Tzutujils for the new assessment.[77] The charge was not quite fair, for Landecho had ordered the *oidor* to make an official tour of the provinces. His trip to the lake area was not prompted solely by the Tzutujils' request to be reassessed.

After the new audiencia president, Francisco Briceño (or Brizeño), arrived in 1564, the Tzutujils went to him to ask him to reassess Atitlán. There was a famine in the years 1563 to 1565,[78] which helps explain their new request after their former disappointment. Briceño reassessed them but "added to us more than that which we were accustomed to giving thirty-five loads of cacao, which in money is 750 pesos, and more in money, 250 pesos.[79] All of this added 1,000 pesos to our tribute."

From the year 1564 it is possible to determine the exact amount of tribute charged Atitlán and its *sujetos;* in the book entitled *Libro del cargos al monedas del Real Hacienda,* the values of the amounts collected are listed for each year by crown officials from 1564 until 1599.[80] The book lists only revenues collected by the crown, and they may not have been the same as those that Sancho de Barahona collected. According to Juan de Pineda, who wrote before 1594, some *encomenderos* were receiving more than the crown was receiving.[81]

The *Libro del cargos* (see tables 7 and 8) was begun by Antonio de Rosales, who served as accountant of the audiencia under President Briceño. In 1564, Atitlán gave 100 loads of cacao, 10 loads being removed to pay the *diezmo,* or tithe, to the church. The crown representatives auctioned off the tribute items and received around 882 pesos for 90 loads of cacao, 301 pesos for mantas, 27 pesos for maize, and 8 pesos for honey. The 100 loads of cacao given in 1564 were worth around 1,000 pesos. This was less than the 1,200 *xiquipiles,* or 400 loads, paid to Barahona and the crown in López de Cerrato's time. In the early 1550s, however, the Indians did not pay mantas, maize, or honey as tribute, and by the 1560s the coastal population working the cacao plantations had probably dropped somewhat with a consequent disturbance of cacao production. The value of cacao rose in 1569, beginning a boom period, and remained high until 1574, when a decline set in.[82] The exact amounts of the items are not usually given in the *Libro del cargos,* except for cacao, and in some instances the amounts varied from year to year. Most of the amounts were constant from 1564 to 1570, as table 7 indicates. The value of maize rose in 1570 because of the destruction of the maize crop by a late frost in the lake area, which drove up the price.[83] Con-

Table 7. *Value of Tribute Items Received by the Crown from Atitlán, 1564-84 (In pesos, tomines, and granos)[a]*

| Year | Loads[b] of Cacao | | Mantas | Maize | Hens | Honey | Total Value[c] |
|---|---|---|---|---|---|---|---|
| 1564 | 90 = | 882p 6t 6g | 301p 2t 1g | 27p 1t 7g | . . . . . . . | 8p | 1,219p 2t 2g |
| 1565 | 90 = | 878p 5t 8g | 301p 1t | 27p 1t 9g | . . . . . . . | . . . . . . . | 1,207p 5g |
| 1566 | 90 = | 726p 6t | 301p 3t 10g | 31p 7t | . . . . . . . | 6p 4t | 1,077p 3t 10g |
| 1567 | 90 = | 856p 1t 7g | 301p 3t 9g | 30p 1t 9g | 10p 7t 2g | 7p 2t 2g | 1,206p 1t 5g |
| 1568 | 90 = | 875p 7t 9g | 301p 3t | 27p 1t 6g | 11p 4t | 7p 4t 5g | 1,223p 4t 8g |
| 1569[d] | 107 = | 1,247p 7t | 286p 4t | . . . . . . . | 10p 7t | 6p 1t 6g | 1,550p 5t 1g |
| 1570 | 90 = | 1,030p 1t 7g | 339p 1t | 41p 7t | 10p 1t 6g | 7p 1t | 1,428p 4t 1g |
| 1571 | 107 = | 1,192p 1t 11g | 320p 7t 8g | . . . . . . . | 14p | . . . . . . . | 1,527p 1t 7g |
| 1572 | . . . = | 1,314p 2t 11g | 383p 1t 8g | 58p 6t 7g | 10p 2t 3g | . . . . . . . | 1,766p 5t 5g |
| 1573 | . . . = | 1,321p 5t 7g | 218p 6t 3g | 72p 6t 10g | 16p 3t 9g | 8p | 1,637p 6t 5g |
| 1574 | 138 = | 943p 6t 5g | 392p 4t 9g | 31p 3t 5g | . . . . . . . | . . . . . . . | 1,397p 6t 7g |
| 1575 | 125 = | 840p 5t 3g | 430p 5t 2g | 29p 4t 11g | 9p 1t 6g | 19p 6g | 1,329p 1t 4g |
| 1576 | = | 921p 2t 7g | 428p 5t 6g | 31p 3t 5g | 15p 6t 9g | 6p 2t 9g | 1,403p 5t |
| 1577[e] | . . . | | . . . . . . . | . . . . . . . | . . . . . . . | . . . . . . . | 1,483p 1t 9g |
| 1578[e] | . . . | | . . . . . . . | . . . . . . . | . . . . . . . | . . . . . . . | 924p 1t 8g |
| 1579[e] | . . . | | . . . . . . . | . . . . . . . | . . . . . . . | . . . . . . . | 703p 4t 5g |
| 1580 | . . . = | 936p 5t 10g | 215p 2t 8g | 31p 3t 4g | 16p 6t 11g | 7p 6t 8g | 1,208p 1t 5g |
| 1581 | 76 = | 465p 5t 11g | 430p 5t 3g | 40p 2t 9g[f] | 12p 1t 11g | . . . . . . . | 948p 7t 10g |
| 1582[g] | | | | | | | |
| 1583 | . . . = | 960p 4t 11g | 215p 2t 8g | 28p 5t[h] | 34p 6t 4g | . . . . . . . | 1,239p 2t 11g |
| 1584 | 180 = | 1,397p 1t 3g | . . . . . . . . | . . . . . . . | 55p 3t 5g | . . . . . . . | 1,452p 4t 8g |

SOURCE: *Libro del cargos al monedas del Real Hacienda,* AGI Patronato 82-3-2. Año 1600.

[a] 1 *tomin* (abbreviated *t*) = 1 real, or one-eighth peso (abbreviated *p*); 1 *grano* (abbreviated *g*) = 1 grain, the smallest unit of weight; 20 *granos* = 1 Spanish scruple (Velázquez de la Cadena 1967, pp. 365, 640).

[b] Loads are given in the nearest whole number.

[c] Some of the totals were incorrectly added in the *Libro del cargos;* they have been corrected in this table.

[d] For the year 1569 the text of the *Libro del cargos* says that 1065p 5t 2g were received for 90 loads of cacao, but this is written numerically as 1075p 5t 2g; the numerical figure is probably wrong. Seventeen additional loads of cacao were also paid in that year. It is not known why no maize was collected in that year.

[e] The entries in the *Libro del cargos* for 1577, 1578, and 1579 are difficult to read owing to ink smudging. Therefore, only the totals are given for these years.

[f] This figure includes maize and honey.    [g] There is no entry for this year in the *Libro del cargos.*    [h] This figure includes maize and hens.

Table 8. *Value of Tribute Items Received by the Crown from Atitlán,*
*1585-99 and 1623*[a]
(In pesos, *tomines*, and *granos*)

| Year | Totals | | |
|------|--------|--|--|
| 1585 | 1,154*p* 3*t* | 2*g* | |
| 1586 | 1,697*p* 3*t* | 9*g* | |
| 1587 | 1,325*p* 3*t* | 1*g* | |
| 1588 | 1,384*p* 1*t* | 3*g* | |
| 1589 | 2,126*p* | | |
| 1590 | 2,855*p* 2*t* | | |
| 1591 | 2,199*p* 1*t* | | |
| 1592 | 2,272*p* | 6*g* | |
| 1593 | 2,273*p* 2*t* | 6*g* | |
| 1594 | 2,785*p* 5*t* | 11*g* | |
| 1595 | 2,480*p* 3*t* | | |
| 1596 | 2,375*p* 6*t* | | |
| 1597 | 2,475*p* 2*t* | 1*g* | |
| 1598 | 2,720*p* | | |
| 1599 | 2,720*p* | | |
| 1623[b] | 1,433*p* 4*t* | | |

SOURCES: 1585-99: *Libro del cargos al monedas del Real Hacienda.* AGI Patronato 82-3-2. *Año* 1600. 1623: AGC A1.1 *exp.* 10 *leg.* 1. Año 1623.
   [a] Entries for 1585-94 are long and include hens and cacao collected from Atitlán and the four coastal *estancias.* Those totals are shown in this table 8. For
the years 1595-99 only total amounts are shown in the *Libro del cargos.*
   [b] This is the amount collected by don Pedro Núñez de Barahona.

ditions were so bad in 1571 that no maize was collected as tribute
from Atitlán in that year.

In 1570, Diego de Garcés, the *alcalde mayor* of Zapotitlán, wrote
to the Audiencia of Guatemala concerning the tribute capacity of
the towns in his jurisdiction. He said that highland towns should
not pay tribute in cacao "because they do not have it or raise it,
and if the Indians go in search of it outside their lands, some become sick and die." Garcés, however, was probably referring to
highland towns in which, unlike Atitlán, there were no owners
of cacao *estancias.* He also said that highland towns were paying
tribute in mantas, which produced the same result because the
Indians had to go to the coast to trade for cotton. He believed
that highland Indians could pay in maize and hens because those
two commodities were plentiful in the area.[84]

In his report of 1570, Garcés gave the general values of tribute items. Mantas varied in size and were worth 4 to 8 *tostones* (2 to 4 pesos) each. Somewhat later Juan de Pineda reported that they were worth at least 10 *tostones*. Hens were worth ½ to 1 real each, and maize was worth ½ to 1 real per fanega, though the value of maize could vary from 4 or 8 reales to 2 reales per fanega.[85] In 1569, Atitlán gave 200 hens worth a total of 10 pesos 7 reales, which meant that they were valued at a little less than ½ real each. In Landecho's time Atitlán gave 200 fanegas of maize and 10 arrobas of honey. Assuming that Briceño did not change those amounts, in 1564 maize was worth around 1 real per fanega, and honey was worth about 1½ *tostones* per arroba.

In 1566, Atitlán gave nine *cántaros,* or jugs, of honey worth around 6 pesos, or a little more than ½ peso, per *cántaro.* Francisco Ximénez, a Dominican friar who lived in the Quiché area, said that honey was sold in little ollas that were called "eggs" because one of these "little *ollas* looks like an egg."[86]

Garcés said that Atitlán's coastal *estancias* were very rich in cacao and that Atitlán was also rich because its inhabitants owned coastal cacao plots where they also raised cotton, seeds, and vegetables: "All can give in tribute very well eighteen *contles* [*zontles*] of cacao without anything else but no more because in the cacao towns the Indians all occupy themselves with it and do not understand other cultivation if it is not maize for their sustenance of travelers."[87] Eighteen *zontles* equaled 7,200 beans, or slightly less than 1 *xiquipil* per tributary.[88] According to the population figures for the coast for the year 1575, this would mean that the four *estancias* gave 243 loads. That was probably what they paid. Table 7 shows that the crown received 125 loads in 1575, and Barahona probably received around the same amount, for a total of about 250 loads.

Garcés described some of the evils associated with the tribute system. Indians were encouraged to marry young:

... this causes a lot of harm because by being married, they make them tributaries no matter what age. Because they are children, they do not have strength or ability to provide ... for themselves and their houses and pay their tribute. They go about broken and poor, ragged and seeking relatives to pay their tribute and serving in the houses of others. ... This thing is so bad that children of eight and ten years and less are married.[89]

This abuse was still occurring in 1581, and in that year a royal order was issued prohibiting *encomenderos* from forcing young Indian girls to marry.[90]

In 1571 the crown canceled the order that had declared single Indians *(solteros),* widows, those serving in and caring for the churches *(reservados),* and Indian *alcaldes* exempt from paying tribute.[91] This action was an attempt to place more Indians on the tribute rolls. In 1572, Indians over fifty-five years old, widows over fifty, and single persons living with their parents were exempted from paying tribute.[92] As of 1573 widows fifty years of age and younger were to pay only 5 reales a year.[93] In 1573 the crown also ordered that tribute payments of crown Indians must be equal to those paid by *encomienda* Indians.[94] It appears that by the end of the sixteenth century the latter ruling did not have much effect, and Pineda explained why *encomenderos* continued to receive more tribute than the crown received:

The Indians ask the *encomenderos* to reassess them saying that many deaths have occurred. . . . The royal *audiencia* provides the judges, assessors, and officials. [The] *encomenderos* and [their relatives] go to the president and *oidores* day and night saying that . . . there are more Indians than before, and they are very rich and can give double what they are giving. They [the *encomenderos* and their relatives] . . . ask to be favored because they only have the tribute to sustain themselves. . . . [When the assessment is made], if there are more Indians than before, they increase it. If there are fewer Indians than there were before, they increase it for the living to equal that which would have been paid by those who died. The tribute is always more.[95]

That was exactly what had happened to the Indians of Atitlán during Landecho's and Briceño's times.

By the provisions of legislation of 1571 tribute was supposed to be reassessed every three years.[96] Sometimes, however, fifteen to twenty years elapsed between assessments. In 1574 each Cakchiquel of Tecpán Atitlán was assessed two *tostones,* one-half bushel of maize, and one hen.[97] The Tzutujils paid in cacao, mantas, and maize but apparently did not give hens that year.

In 1580 and again in 1582 it was ordered that tribute due from those who had died or were absent was not to be assessed from the Indians remaining.[98] This problem could not be remedied, however, without careful regular reassessments. The members of the audiencia were responsible for making accurate asessments, but few judges had the time or the willingness to count the Indians and their cacao trees house by house and tree by tree. Ordinarily they questioned a few Indians about population and trees and simply entered those numbers in the tribute registers. Sometimes *encomenderos* told the Indians what to say to the audiencia officials.[99] The tributaries of Atitlán and its *estancias* are given in a document dated 1583 (see the numbers of tributaries in tables 4 and 5). The assessment for Atitlán included San Lucas, San Pedro, San Pablo, Santa Cruz, and Santa María de Jesús, but the four coastal *estancias* were listed separately. Each tributary unit from the highlands was supposed to pay 10 *zontles* of cacao, and married couples were also assessed one hen each.[100] In the *estancias* of San Bartolomé, San Andrés, San Francisco, and Santa Bárbara each tributary was to pay 14 *zontles* of cacao, and married couples one hen.

In a report dated 1584, audiencia president García de Valverde described two kinds of tribute that the Indians in Guatemala had been accustomed to paying. The first was the tribute required of married Indians *(tributo personal)* of two *tostones,* and the other was an assessment on cacao plantations *(tributo real),* based on the plantations' size and productivity.[101] Both kinds of tribute were paid in the Tzutujil area.

The *tributo real* was attached to the cacao land and must be paid by the new owner when the property was sold or inherited. The wealth of these plantations, which had enriched the lords in pre-Hispanic times, was now siphoned off by the *encomendero* and the crown, and the Indian owners were left with little or nothing. The cacao trees were sensitive and in some years were sterile, producing no fruit, but the Indians were obliged to pay tribute despite royal orders exempting payment in those years. Sometimes the *encomendero* took four-fifths of the cacao, and at other times all of it. The Indians were also obliged to deliver cotton even if cotton did not grow in their area.[102]

The collection of tribute was left in Indian hands into the seventeenth century, though in 1553 the crown had prohibited the *encomenderos* from allowing *calpixques* to collect the tribute because of their mistreatment of their people.[103] The English priest and traveler Thomas Gage observed in the early seventeenth century: "The heads of the several tribes have care to gather the tribute, and to deliver it to the *alcaldes* and *regidores* [Indian government officials], . . . who carry it either to the King's exchequer in the city or to the nearest Spanish justice, . . . or to the *encomendero* of the town."[104] In 1588, Alonso de Vides, treasurer of the audiencia, described the manner of tribute collection employed in Tecpán Atitlán and Quezaltenango:

The *gobernador, alcaldes,* and *regidores* of the towns are careful to charge the tributes, and they have *calpules* who are Indian *principales* from each *parcialidad* [lineage], and these *calpuleros* charge the tribute from the inhabitants of their wards, and they go with all that they have charged to the *gobernador, alcaldes,* and *regidores.*[105]

In 1588 the Indian officials sent the tribute to the *encomendero* or the nearest crown officials. The crown, however, charged (through Vides) that local tribute collectors in the two towns had not turned in the full amount of tribute in the previous two years. This demonstrates that it was aware of abuses.[106] The lords were usually careful to deliver the full amount of tribute on time; if they did not, they would be fined or even publicly whipped.[107] The same method of tribute collection described in the Vides document probably existed in Atitlán.

Vides's document is important because it demonstrates that the aboriginal method of collecting tribute was still continuing in Tecpán Atitlán. The *tlatoques* and *cabezas de calpul* collected the tribute according to *parcialidades,* which may have been based on the pre-Hispanic *chinamit* structure, but the estates had no doubt changed considerably since pre-Conquest times. Many former noble families had come to be included in the class of tribute payers during the sixteenth century, and a new group of *reservados* had been created.

In 1592 the *servicio real,* or *tostón del servicio,* was instituted to pay for the Spanish fleet, and owing to the crown's financial straits the tribute was continued to the end of the colonial period.[108] The tribute was 4 *reales,* or 1 *tostón,* per tributary unit a year in addition to personal tribute.[109] Gage wrote: "There is no town so poor, where every married Indian doth not pay at least in money four reals a year for tribute to the King, besides other four reals to his . . . *encomendero.*"[110] The *tostón* payment was collected by the *corregidor,* and Indians who could or would not pay it were jailed until the sum was turned in.[111]

Atitlán and its dependencies were reassessed in 1599, when Alonso Criado de Castilla was president of the audiencia. The census count of Atitlán and its *sujetos* was made by Carlos Vásquez de Coronado, the *alcalde mayor* of Zapotitlán. He claimed that he counted the Indians "house by house" and their cacao plots and that the task took him about two months to complete. He wrote asking the crown for an *ayuda de costo,* a pension granted for service, because the census had entailed a great deal of work, and Atitlán, in his opinion, could afford to pay.[112] According to a prior decree of 1586, expenses incurred by officials making tribute assessments were not to be charged to the Indians, but it is not known whether Vásquez de Coronado received any salary.[113] The tributaries given under this assessment are shown in tables 4 and 6. The Indians continued to pay their tribute in cacao and hens.

Bishop Juan Ramírez of Guatemala stated that in the early seventeenth century the tribute burden was very heavy in Atitlán and Tecpán Atitlán. The Indians paid 12 reales, or 3 *tostones* each, for the personal tribute and two hens a year. "Considering the poverty of the Indians, this tribute was excessive because it was more than an Indian had in his house. Their great poverty could be seen in their manner of dressing, and their children went about nude."[114] Despite this, the bishop maintained that the tribute would have been tolerable if it had not been for the royal tribute paid on cacao lands. It was not levied on lands on which maize, hens, or vegetables were raised, but cacao plantations were more valuable, and Indians growing cacao often paid more than the 12 reales as tribute. They had to pay one-half or one load, which was valued at 25 or 50 *tostones,* or 100 or 200 reales, respectively. No matter how much maize an Indian grew, however, he paid only 12 reales. Many Indians feared inheriting any cacao lands because of this situation.[115]

In 1607 the Indians of Atitlán were called upon to help repair the capital for fifteen-day work periods. Atitlán was assessed thirty men, who were to be paid for their labor. They were not allowed to leave the capital until they were replaced by others.[116] Such forced-labor draft was called *repartimiento.* The primary difference between this obligation and the slavery of earlier times was the shorter period of work and the pay, though low. After the beginning of the seventeenth century, the Indians of Atitlán also supplied labor to wheat farms near Tecpán, Godines, and Argueta.[117] In 1631 four Indian leaders from Visitación complained that don Gaspar de Argüeta was constantly pressing them to give him Indians to work on his land. He was also demanding horses and maize. If they did not pay, they said, Argüeta beat them.[118]

In 1609, Alonso de Vides, who had become *corregidor* of Atitlán, aided by the local priest, Fray Juan Sánchez, assessed the people of the Tzutujil area "who owe the *tostón del servicio* to Your Majesty." The Vides assessment is the first list that gives all the names of the tributaries in Atitlán, listed under heads of *calpul,* and the highland *sujetos.* The costal *estancias* were not given in the lists of 1599 and 1609.[119]

Don Pedro Núñez de Barahona had received half of Atitlán by

1608, and in 1623 he obtained from it an annual tribute of 2,867 *tostones.*[120] In comparison to many other declining *encomiendas,* Atitlán was still producing a considerable amount of income.

In summary, the *encomienda* was basically a transitional institution that presided over the deterioration of pre-Hispanic Indian society. It allowed the Spanish conquerors and their descendants to draw off Indian wealth and to utilize the aboriginal tribute structure for their own advantage. The *encomienda* in New Spain was based on the large numbers of Indians who were to be made available to Spaniards engaged in such activities as subduing new subjects for the crown, colony building, and extracting mineral wealth from local areas. When epidemics reduced the native population, the crown moved to tighten control over the institution, thereby checking the power of many ambitious conquistadors.

Atitlán was initially exploited by Pedro de Cueto and the Alvarados, who took slaves and as much cacao and other items as they wanted in tribute. During most of the sixteenth century the *encomienda* remained divided between the crown and the Barahona family, and was carefully regulated. The Indians were always at the mercy of officials responsible for assessments. Some officials, like López de Cerrato and García de Valverde, tried to moderate tribute payments, while others forced all that they could from the Indians.

Unlike many other early *encomiendas,* Atitlán remained valuable throughout the entire sixteenth and early seventeenth centuries owing to its cacao production. Highland and lowland Indians in the Atitlán region paid cacao, mantas, maize, hens, and honey as tribute from the 1550s until late in the century, when they began paying mainly in cacao and hens. After 1592 the *tostón de servicio* was added to the Indians' tribute. Indians of Atitlán owning cacao plots also paid the *tributo real.*

The tribute was still collected by Indians themselves during the late sixteenth century. It was collected from the inhabitants of the town and taken to the nearest crown official or *encomendero.* After the beginning of the seventeenth century the people of Atitlán were also subject to the *repartimiento.* They worked on wheat farms and in the capital.

The *encomienda* served as an instrument for reducing the social distinctions of pre-Hispanic times. Although Indians continued to collect tribute, little of it remained in their hands. Thus during the sixteenth and early seventeenth centuries the *encomienda* was the major vehicle of exploitation in Guatemala.

## CHAPTER 13

# Production and Exchange

Sometime after the mid-sixteenth century coin money was introduced into the Indian economy and became a form of tribute. This development helped revive local trade and specialization because the Indians had to travel to trade their products to obtain coins. Highland Indians of the lake region who owned lowland cacao plantations need not go to the coast to obtain money but paid their tribute in cacao grown by their grove tenders.

The native-market system functioned much as it had in earlier times and continued to be based on foodstuffs and crafts. Community specialization remained important throughout the colonial period and on into modern times, but some ancient occupations gradually died out as they became irrelevant to post-Conquest lifeways. Painted books were no longer made, featherwork declined, and Indian craftsmen found it difficult to continue such crafts as gold and silverwork owing to Spanish monopolization of the metals.

Among the Indians the lives of the individual buyers and sellers were the least disturbed by the upheaval of the Conquest. They went on conducting business in the local markets much as they had in pre-Conquest days. It appears, however, that even their day-to-day transactions were disrupted somewhat during the first decade or so of Spanish domination. *The Annals of the Cakchiquels* indicate that Maldonado made the roads safe again for travel in 1536.[1] Keeping the roads open was vital to the Indian market system, which was based on regional trade and community specialization.

## Production

During the sixteenth and early seventeenth centuries the Indians continued to own their lands, but, as we have seen, the Spaniards drew off much of the produce of the lands in tribute. The lords of Atitlán still owned lowland cacao plantations in 1571, though after their slaves were freed, they complained of the impoverishment of the area, and the cacao industry suffered from the lack of skilled labor.[2] Simply hiring other Indians was not enough to prevent crop declines, though it did save the plantations from utter ruin. Cacao was very sensitive and required the constant attention of skilled hands, especially during April and May, when rain could destroy the young shoots.[3] With many of those who had knowledge and skill in cacao cultivation dead of disease or gone from the land, the plantations suffered. Atitlán's lowland fields remained fairly productive, which indicates that hired workers must have learned how to care for the cacao or perhaps that older retainers were lured back with high wages.

Few changes were made in farming methods after the Conquest, though new crops introduced by the Spaniards were adopted. The most important change was the replacement of the stone ax and the digging stick with the machete and the *asadón,* a two-sided metal hoe.[4] Indian agriculture continued to be at the mercy of the weather and insects. Locusts were particularly destructive. *The Annals of the Cakchiquels* say that "during this year [1554] the locusts came again. . . . They passed over all parts of the country."[5]

Beginning in the 1550s, the crown attempted to stimulate agricultural production, which had declined from pre-Hispanic levels. In 1550, López de Cerrato was ordered to do all he could to revive production. In the following year the crown issued another order, that the Indians be provided with tools, seed, and funds to increase cultivation, especially maize.[6]

Bad weather brought recurrent famine. In the years 1563 to 1565 famine was followed by a period of drought and epidemic.[7] This siege of misfortunes may have affected the lake area: *The Annals of the Cakchiquels* state that smallpox struck in 1564.[8] In 1571 frost attacked the crops and caused a scarcity of maize and fruit. Fray Gonzalo Méndez, who was in charge of the convent in Atitlán, asked Pedro de Villalobos, president of the audiencia, to send maize to the *cabecera.* A few fanegas of seed maize arrived, and Méndez distributed it for planting in Tecpán Atitlán, Atitlán, and other lake towns. The maize grown from that seed fed the towns.[9]

The Indians of the lake region continued to harvest traditional native staples such as maize, beans, chili, and fruit. In 1585, Betancor and Arboleda reported that little maize was grown in

Atitlán but was purchased in other areas.[10] Around the mid-seventeenth century Fray Diego de Ocaña, a Dominican, said that the
lake Indians grew better maize than that grown in other parts
but grew only enough for themselves and coastal Indians who came
up to look for it.[11] Production appears to have been somewhat reduced from pre-Hispanic levels throughout the early colonial period,
which can probably be attributed to such post-Conquest factors
as disease, population decline, and the loss of slaves.

Besides the traditional native crops, some crops introduced by
the Spaniards were cultivated in the Tzutujil area. Fig, quince,
pomegranate, and apple trees were grown around the lake, though
Betancor and Arboleda said that the Indians had not planted many
trees by 1585.[12] Some lake areas and towns came to specialize
in certain Spanish crops. Ocaña reported that anise was gathered
on the north side of Lake Atitlán along with chickpeas and other
vegetables. He also noted that San Pablo produced very large
avocados.[13] The people of Tolimán continued to specialize in the
traditional tumplines made from the reeds growing near the
shore.[14]

Cacao production continued to dominate lowland Tzutujil agriculture throughout the early colonial period. The industry declined
somewhat after the Conquest but began expanding again as soon
as the *encomenderos* recognized its value in the Indian market.
They sold it to all Indians, nobles and commoners alike, with the
result that the upper class lost its monopoly on cacao.[15] After this
recovery a long-term decline eventually set in, even though cacao
production continued longer in the coastal area dominated by
Atitlán than it did in most other regions.[16] In 1621 most of the
Indians of the coastal *estancias* were planting between 100 and
300 cacao trees each, although a few planted only 60 to 80 trees.[17]
A planting of that magnitude produced a considerable amount of
cacao, but most was taken for tribute, leaving the Indians little
or none to sell.

Fuentes y Guzmán said that the lowland Indians depended too
heavily upon cacao. If the harvest was abundant, the Indians
spent liberally. If the crop failed, they starved.[18] The lowland
Indians, however, did have many native fruits, fish, and wild animals, which, along with some introduced crops, probably served
as supplementary foods.

In the early seventeenth century Bishop Ramírez described how
Spanish officials cheated the Indians in the lowland areas, adding
to the problems caused by the emphasis on cacao. The officials
distributed money among the Indians in advance so that they

would deliver the cacao at harvesttime. The official would pay 30 *tostones* a load, though it was worth 50 *tostones*. If an Indian had a bad harvest in his field, being afraid of the authorities, he went to buy cacao, paying double for what he had received.[19] It is clear from Ramírez's and Fuentes y Guzmán's statements, however, that in the seventeenth century not all of an Indian's harvest of cacao was being taken for tribute.

The pre-Hispanic nobles had worn clothing made of fine cotton cloth, and cotton production continued to be important after the Conquest. The Spaniards established a woolen-cloth industry in New Spain, and the Indian merchants who had the means began wearing wool socks and leather shoes or boots.[20] Bishop Ramírez said that some officials exploited Indian women in cotton-growing areas. They gave each woman four pounds of cotton to burl and spin. The spinning took three or four weeks, and the woman received only one real for her labor.[21]

Estrada remarked that the lowland area would be suitable for sugar mills but thought it doubtful that there was a market for sugar. He also thought that mulberry trees and silk might be produced in the lowland area but was somewhat skeptical because of the prevalence of harmful insects that might eat the silkworms. The region also abounded in nopal cacti, which nurtured the insects from which cochineal was made.[22] At the beginning of the seventeenth century there was a concerted effort to introduce cochineal cultivation into the Tzutujil piedmont area. The effort had failed by 1621 owing to locust attacks and lack of skilled labor to care for the plants. Most of these new industries were initiated in other areas along the coast after the decline of cacao in the seventeenth century.[23]

Salt continued to be collected and processed around Xicalapa in colonial times, but by 1579 it was a small-time, expensive operation.[24] It appears that most of the salt processed at Xicalapa was purchased by those who dealt in salt for sale in highland and piedmont markets.[25]

Fishing continued to provide supplementary food and income for Indians living around Lake Atitlán. Crabs and *olominas* remained important items for food, and *pescaditos* were also caught and traded around the lake. Mojarras were introduced into the lake by Franciscans in 1575. Betancor and Arboleda said that the fish had multiplied by 1585 and that some of them were "large and delicious to eat." By Ocaña's time their numbers had diminished, however, and only a few were caught in Atitlán.[26] The introduction of mojarras into the lake probably did the Indians more harm than good: often the Indians were ordered to take great quantities of fish to the capital and other distant places, especially during Lent.[27]

After the Conquest hunting diminished as the Indians accepted the domestic animals, such as chickens and sheep, introduced by the Spaniards. Moreover, the Indians no longer had much time to hunt, being burdened with the heavy tribute demands.[28] Ocaña said that the Indians of some of the lake towns rarely ate meat because of its scarcity, but they probably did eat some small wild animals.[29] Ocaña did not include Atitlán in his list of places lacking meat, and perhaps the *cabecera* was better off in this regard. Cattle, sheep, and pigs were also introduced into the lowlands and supplemented the natives' sources of meat. The congregation system and the declining population opened large expanses of land for cattle pasturage, but not many Spaniards were interested in stock raising, and wild cattle and pigs roamed these areas.[30]

## Exchange

*Merchants:* In post-Conquest times the distinction between Indian petty merchants and professionals began to disappear. In 1585 some merchants in Atitlán were better off than others: in discussing the variety of clothing worn by the Indians, Betancor and Arboleda said that "some, such as the merchants who are able to afford them, wear woven jackets made in Mexico and woven trousers of different colors."[31] Some of these merchants may have been directly involved in trade with Mexico, but it is more likely that they purchased the articles of clothing on the coast.

Estrada reported that Spanish merchants lived in the coastal piedmont area and made regular journeys to New Spain. They bought cacao, took it to Mexico, and returned with clothes and other items to sell to the Indians. They sold the merchandise in bulk or little by little, exchanging it for cacao and repeating the cycle. Some merchants also took from the capital back to the coast such items as wax, candles, baked bread, biscuits, garlic, and onions. Most of the Spaniards who engaged in this trade were of humble origin.[32] They largely took over the long-distance buying that had formerly been carried out by the Indian professional merchants. It is doubtful that this class continued in existence very long after the Conquest, for the Spaniards rapidly saw the value of conducting such trade with the Indians themselves.

The traveling Spanish merchants gradually came to do more and more business with the Indians. Originally the official view was that Indian commerce was separate from that of the Spaniards, and Indians were exempted from paying the sales tax *(alcabala)* as long as they traded in native products.[33] Trade offered lower-class Spaniards an opportunity to make money, and they often did so by cheating the Indians. The practice was particularly rampant along the coast, where Indians went to get money for tribute or to buy cacao.

The exploitative Spanish merchants were called *quebranta-huesos* ("bone crushers" or "bone breakers") in the early seventeenth century. Bishop Ramírez said that in his time they went about like vagabonds and "were not good for much except teaching vice and evil to the Indians by example." They sold huipils, hats, and other merchandise to the Indians at exorbitant prices. They got maize in return and resold it to other Indians when they were hungry, charging 8 to 10 *tostones* a fanega, when they bought it for 2. Some of the merchants were relatives of Spanish officials and were allowed to live freely among the Indians with official favor.[34]

The closer an Indian town was to a Spanish settlement, the more opportunities there were for exploitation. Gage described how these merchants sold wine to the Indians living near the capital:

There is a strict order against selling wine in an Indian town, with a fine and forfeiture of the wine as punishment. Yet the baser and poorer sort of Spaniards will go out from Guatemala to the towns of Indians about, and carry such wine to sell and inebriate the natives as may be very advantageous to themselves. For of one jar of wine they will make two at least, confectioning it with honey and water, and other strong drugs. . . . This they will sell at the price current for Spanish wine, and they use such pint and quart measures as never were allowed by justice order, but were invented by themselves. . . . they soon intoxicate the poor Indians, and when they have made them drunk, then they will cheat them more, making them pay double for their quart measure.[35]

Other than in the capital, the Tzutujils encountered such practices more often in the coastal area than in the highlands.

Most Indian merchants were petty traders and engaged in trade between the highlands and lowlands. The merchants of Atitlán traded for lowland salt, cotton, and cacao. They carried the goods back to Atitlán on their backs—or, if they were better off, on horseback—and sold them in the marketplaces of lake towns.[36] Fuentes y Guzmán said that the Indians of Atitlán were inclined toward trade and traveled as far as San Salvador, San Antonio, and Soconusco.[37] By Vásquez's time many had also moved to Samayac to engage in trade.[38] Vásquez mentioned that the Indians of Atitlán tended to specialize in one occupation. For example, the merchant was only a merchant, the muleteer only a muleteer, and a fisherman only a fisherman.[39]

Betancor and Arboleda said that the Indians of Atitlán sold cacao for money or exchanged it for clothing of all kinds: "With cacao they buy what they need for their dress, and also for their wives and children for cacao is to them money."[40] Fuentes y Guzmán reported that the Tzutujils traded a great deal of maguey fiber, especially items made from it, such as ropes and halters. They also rented dance costumes at high prices. They bought cotton on the coast and sold it in the plazas of the capital, selling it in bales or in smaller quantities. He also reported that commerce was a principal means by which the Tzutujil area maintained itself and flourished.[41]

Sometimes the demand by Spaniards for certain products was not completely satisfied by tribute payments, or they wished to buy certain common goods that were not given as tribute. Individual Indian traders sold their excess goods to Spaniards and other Indians in the marketplace.[42]

*The Market System:* After the Conquest some of the important pre-Hispanic regional markets, such as K'umarcaaj and Iximché, ceased to exist. Congregation no doubt eliminated some local markets as well. The regional market, usually a pre-Hispanic capital, was replaced by a new Spanish capital and other major cities, but some markets of Indian *cabeceras,* such as Atitlán's, continued to be important. The market at Atitlán remained a focal point in the highland-lowland exchange, especially for cacao and salt.

In general, the Spaniards did not interfere in the exchange of day-to-day items in the Indian markets, especially in remote highland areas like Atitlán. The Indians retained control of the markets, which were regulated by the town council. The council fixed the prices of goods sold.[43] Most of the commodities exchanged in the Indian market (usually called *tianguiz* in early colonial documents) remained the same as in pre-Hispanic times. Cacao continued to be the major medium of exchange among Indians,[44] but barter was also common, especially in small transactions.

In some cases Spanish standards of weight and measurement were adopted by the Indians. Tribute maize was paid by the fanega and honey by the arroba. The almud, a measure equaling one-half fanega, was commonly used for smaller quantities of grain. These measures were probably used in market transactions as well.[45] For cacao the Indian measurements carga, *xiquipil,* and *zontle* continued in use. Most Indian monetary transactions were confined to small amounts involving reales *(tomines)*, but owing to the scarcity of coins in the sixteenth century cacao continued to be an acceptable substitute.

Gage described the Indian *tianguiz* as it existed in the 1630s in the Pokoman area:

. . . some Indians all the day sit selling fruits, herbs, and cacao, but at four in the afternoon, this market is filled for a matter of an hour, where the Indian women meet to sell their country slop (which is dainties to the Creoles) as *atole, pinole* [a drink of parched maize], scalded plantains, butter of the cacao, puddings made of Indian maize, with a bit of fowl or fresh pork in them seasoned with much red biting chile, which they call *anaca tamales.*[46]

The market in Atitlán looked somewhat different from the one Gage described because there were probably no Creole women there. Four in the afternoon was perhaps a busy time for lowland markets too in the 1630s. Except for the decline of some crafts and the introduction of new products and new measures, exchange probably went on as before the Conquest in most Indian markets, with the addition of Spanish itinerant traders. Such traders were far more numerous in the lowlands, where cacao was plentiful, but they probably visited the market of Atitlán from time to time.

*Highland-Lowland Exchange:* As mentioned above, the inhabitants of Atitlán did not grow much maize, only enough to maintain the town and supply coastal dwellers who came to the highlands to get it.[47] The Indians of San Francisco in particular were usually short of maize.[48] The system of exchange between the two areas continued to operate just as it had in pre-Hispanic times. During the seventeenth century Ocaña said that lake towns had many beans, which they took to other towns, especially Suchitepéquez, to trade. Highland products were taken to the coast to trade for cacao and clothing. The traders also brought back such items as sugar cane, cotton, and fragrant red and white flowers.[49]

The lowland Indians' supply of cacao constantly diminished, most of it drawn off by the Spaniards in tribute. Even in pre-Hispanic times, however, the commoners had had little to do with the cacao exchange, which was largely controlled by the lords. Therefore, the post-Conquest scarcity mainly affected the nobles, and their loss of monopoly over the cacao trade contributed to their eventual impoverishment. *Pataxte* continued to be cultivated, but it was traded only within the lowland area. Estrada reported that it was not sent out of the province and in 1579 was worth about half the price of cacao.[50]

The lowlanders continued to grow cotton and traded it to merchants who sold it in highland towns that specialized in weaving mantas, huipils, and skirts. Indians of lowland towns that did not grow cotton also had to buy it from producing settlements. Patulul and Samayac were important in the cotton trade.[51]

Ocaña said that the people of Atitlán were more industrious than their neighbors and went many leagues from their homes to sell merchandise. He also said that they were much inclined to this business. The cacao the highlanders obtained in the lowlands also served them as money to buy items not made in towns around the lake.[52]

After the Conquest the Spaniards monopolized the tribute system, with the result that luxury goods passed from Indian to Spanish control. The agricultural and marketing system was not as seriously affected, except for the lowland cacao exchange, which also passed into Spanish hands. Cacao plantations were initially disrupted by population decline and later by the freeing of the Indian slaves who worked in the groves. Conditions were not as severe in Atitlan's coastal area as in other areas, however. Because cacao was valuable, exploitation of lowland Indians was rampant, and they were often cheated out of their crops by Spanish officials. In the highlands agriculture seems to have been disturbed by the institution of Spanish control as maize production dropped in Atitlán. Both the highlands and the lowlands adopted some Spanish crops and domestic animals.

The professional class of Indian merchants disappeared after the Conquest, but petty merchants specializing in the highland-lowland trade operated in Atitlán and other lake towns. Some of these merchants became wealthy. Spaniards who were often of lower social status than the *encomenderos* and government officials took over the long-distance trade with Mexico. They also cheated the Indians, especially those on the coast, and were an additional annoyance to a people already overburdened with tribute payments.

The Conquest also eliminated some local and regional markets, but the Atitlán market remained important, especially in the highland-lowland trade. Things did not change much for individual buyers and sellers, but coinage and some new Spanish weights and measures were introduced, and some aboriginal craft specializations disappeared. As in pre-Hispanic times, the market system remained a significant factor in cultural integration as Indians circulated throughout various towns exchanging products and coming into contact with different groups.

## CHAPTER 14

# *Class and Lineage*

Pre-Hispanic social structure, especially at the lower levels, tended to persist in the sixteenth and early seventeenth centuries, but was modified by epidemics that struck repeatedly in those years, by the gradual disappearance of the pre-Hispanic nobility, and by Spanish interference.

## *Class Stratification*

*Caciques and Lords:* After the Conquest there were two basic divisions among upper-class Indians. These were the caciques who had been rulers in aboriginal times and other nobles, called *principales,* who were relatives of the caciques or descendants of pre-Conquest nobles.[1] While Alvarado remained in control of Guatemala, these Indian lords continued to govern their people much as they had in former times, subject to Spanish will. The Tzutujil lords stayed in Chiya' until congregation and kept control of their lowland dependencies.

The Spaniards referred to the ruler of a town as the cacique. The title "cacique," a term of Arawak derivation for a local chieftain, was subsequently applied by the Spaniards to all native rulers of conquered towns.[2] The first Tzutujil cacique was Jo'o' No'j Quixcáp, who was the ruler when Alvarado arrived in Guatemala. He was baptized don Pedro; from the time of the Conquest it was customary for Indian lords to take Spanish Christian names.[3] The Spaniards used the caciques to exact tribute and labor from their people. The conquerors did not always understand native patterns of behavior and found it convenient to leave the native system intact and deal only with the caciques. This practice placed the Indian leaders in an intermediary position between the Spaniards and their own people, and they sometimes squeezed the commoners to obtain excess tribute for themselves.[4]

It was Spanish custom to rule through leaders who were in power at the time of the Conquest or through direct descendants, though the Spaniards sometimes put a favorite in office.[5] The crown, however, wanted only legitimate lords to govern:

It was always their royal will that in the towns of Indians which were found to have some form of organized government, or in which such was later set up, . . . there should be maintained to rule and govern them particularly those petty kings . . . who did this in the time of their paganism, or those who may prove to be their descendants.[6]

Alvarado also disturbed the native succession process by dealing harshly with Indian nobles who did not cooperate with him. For example, he hanged the lords of the Cakchiquels to prevent rebellion: "Thirteen months after the arrival of Tunatiuh, the king Ahpozotzil Cahí Ymox was hanged. On the day 13 Ganel [May 26, 1540] he was hanged by Tunatiuh, together with *Quiyavit Caok.*"[7]

In 1630, Fray Bernabé Cobo, a Spanish naturalist who became a Jesuit in Peru, traveled in Guatemala. He wrote a letter to a friend in which he said that he had stopped by Atitlán and had met the cacique, who was the grandson of the ruler of Atitlán at the time of the Conquest (don Pedro).[8] The cacique whom Cobo met in 1630 must have been don Bernabé, who was probably very old at the time of their meeting.[9] His father, don Juan, died in 1547, and if Bernabé was only one year old at that time, he would have been about eighty-four in 1630. Don Bernabé showed Fray Cobo a painted *lienzo* depicting the Tzutujils receiving the Spaniards with gifts in Conquest times. Perhaps it was painted soon after Alvarado and his men subdued Chiya'. The leader of the Tzutujil moiety was probably also a cacique, and many of the leaders of that group had the title "don" throughout the sixteenth century (see table 9). Thus it appears that descendants of aboriginal leaders did rule in Atitlán.

Before the establishment of the Audiencia of Guatemala, the Tzutujil nobles suffered hardships along with their people, especially the forced-labor drafts and the excessive tribute levies:

Thus, lords also left with these Indians. . . . not many of them returned to their lands because they died. . . . our ancestors were much reduced so that the lords were pressed into service. . . . they lost their cacao plantations and everything else which they gave in tribute because they [the Spaniards] asked for much tribute. To fulfill all of this, they spent and sold all they had and came to suffer such need, they and their wives, that they were forced to carry loads and dig and eat fruit and roots of trees owing to the excessive tribute they [the Spaniards] asked.[10]

Table 9. Principales *of Atitlán in Sixteenth- and Seventeenth-Century Documents*

| Ajtz'iquinajay Moiety | Tzutujil Moiety | Source |
|---|---|---|
| Don Bernabé | Don Gonzalo Méndez | Archivo General de |
| Don Pedro Cabinjay | Don Lucas de Escobar | Centroamérica |
| Don Hernando de Soto | Don Alonso (?) | (1563)* |
| Don Andrés Estamal | Don Diego de Mendoza | |
| Francisco de Rivera | Don Pedro de Alvarado† | |
| Pedro de Tapia | Bartolomé Ahrriyu | |
| | Francisco Vásquez | |
| | Pedro de Alvarado | |
| | | |
| Don Francisco de Rivera | | *Relación Tzutujil* |
| Don Joseph de Santa María | | (1571) |
| Don Hernando de Soto | | |
| | Don Lucas de Escobar | |
| Don Gaspar Manrique‡ | | |
| Don Pablo de Aguilar‡ | | |
| Don Toribio de Constantino‡ | | |
| | Don Francisco Vásquez | *Relación geográfica Atitlán* (1585) |
| Don Hernando de Soto | | |
| Don Gaspar Manrique§ | | |
| | Don Pedro de Alvarado | |
| | Don Gonzalo Méndez | |
| Gonzalo Ortiz‡ | | |
| Diego Ramírez‡ | | |
| Juan Elías‡ | | |

*AGC Al *exp.* 52,042 *leg.* 5,946. *Año* 1563.
†There appear to have been two individuals with the same name, one using the title "don," the other untitled.
‡Moiety affiliation is not known.
§Don Gaspar Manrique is not mentioned in *RGA* 1964, but his name does appear in *RGAG* 1965, p. 265; he was probably Ajtz'iquinajay.

Perhaps Jo'o' No'j Quixcáp (don Pedro) was a casualty of this early era of harshness and epidemics: in 1540 his son don Juan succeeded him as cacique of Atitlán.

After Alvarado's rule came to an end, the caciques tried to better their situations, which often meant increased hardship for their people. The Spanish priests acted in behalf of the common Indians and reported actions they considered excessive. Las Casas pushed for stronger royal protection of the Indians and continually decried the evils resulting from Spanish and Indian exploitation of the common people. In the 1520s and 1530s, however, there were not enough priests to do much about existing conditions. Throughout the 1540s the few who were stationed in Guatemala complained about the treatment of the Indians. In 1547, Fray Francisco de la Parra reported: "Every day we see many deaths among the Indians and many thefts, and there is no one to carry out justice, nor is there order among them, nor any one to observe them other than to receive tribute.[11] The caciques of Atitlán continued to exercise their traditional prerogatives of nobility, and until the mid-sixteenth century the pre-Hispanic mode of government continued with little interference from the Spaniards.

In its effort to strengthen the caciques and limit the arbitrary power of the Spaniards, the crown issued orders that only *señores naturales* were to be considered legitimate caciques. The *señor natural* has been defined as

a lord who, by inherent nature of superior qualities . . . attains power legitimately and exercises dominion over all within his lands justly and in accord with divine, natural, and human law and reason, being universally accepted, recognized, and obeyed by his vassals and subjects and acknowledged by other lords and their peoples as one who rightfully . . . wields authority within his territory. The dominion held by such a lord is a *señorío natural.*[12]

According to crown theory, caciques ruled by natural law and, therefore, to some extent, by divine right. If they proved to be loyal vassals of the crown, they could be considered as nobility and receive the privileges of rank. This philosophy was in accord with royal desires to limit the power of the Spanish colonists by means of a strong Indian nobility.[13] It did not materialize in the colonies, however, and the caciques enjoyed the privileges of nobility only when those privileges did not interfere with the economic interests of the colonists.

When the Spanish concept of *señor natural* was applied in the Indies, it designated lords of large empires, provinces, or towns.[14] If the *señores naturales,* most of whom were pre-Hispanic rulers or their direct descendants, proved amenable to the Spaniards, they were allowed the rights and privileges of rank. They used the title "don," and were allowed to ride a horse, have a coat of arms, and bear arms.[15] These Indians built Spanish-style homes. Two such houses belonging to two prominent Indians of Atitlán, one probably of the Ajtz'iquinajay moiety and the other of the Tzutujil moiety, are shown in the map of Santiago Atitlán made in 1585 (fig. 10). Caciques were exempt from tribute, and sometimes they were granted royal coats of arms and other insignia. Don Juan of Atitlán was granted the following rights in 1543:

By word of Bartolomé de las Casas I have been informed that you have

worked in pacifying and bringing to peace the natives of the Provinces
of Tezulutlán who were at war and of the favor and aid that . . . you
have given to Fray Bartolomé de las Casas and to Fray Pedro de Angulo
and to the other religious who have taken part in it. . . . I encharge
you to continue until all the natives of the said provinces come into
knowledge of our Holy Catholic Faith and come under our yoke and service as our vassals, and when Fray Bartolomé de las Casas, Fray Pedro
de Angulo, or any of their companions enter into the said Provinces
which are at war, you will enter with them and carry with you the
persons and principal men with whom you have participated until now
in this pacification. . . . and thus we send order to our Governor of
that Province and to the Bishop of it that they favor you and do not
consent nor let any immoderate services be imposed on you.[16]

Don Juan was promised that he personally would never come
under the rule of an *encomendero* but would always be a direct
vassal of the crown, and he received a coat of arms (fig. 13).[17]
Maldonado and the *oidores* recommended that don Juan and other
caciques who aided the Spanish priests in the pacification of Verapaz be allowed to keep their Indians.[18] The crown reiterated its
favor toward don Juan in 1547.[19]

The practice of favoring *señores naturales* was consistent with
pre-Conquest patterns. The traditional native ruler continued to
be recognized and to perform his role much as he had before.
Tribute and labor services continued to flow into the center, and
the cacique maintained his control over the population residing
in the dependencies.[20] The difference, of course, was that most of
the tribute went to the *encomenderos* or to the crown. Zorita
believed that if caciques were cooperative and maintained their
pre-Hispanic dignity and rank, and if Spaniards could be restrained
from interfering, control of the people would be facilitated. He
gave an idealized description of how smoothly things ran when
the *señores naturales* governed:

When the natural lords governed, then, they kept their people in peace
and subjection. These lords sent for the tribute their subjects were to
give, and took care that the communal fields and those of individuals
were cultivated, and saw to it that each town provided the people needed
for personal service to the Spaniards.[21]

Of course, things did not always go that well, but Zorita hoped
that rule by Indian leaders would be better than allowing Spaniards to remove and replace caciques at will.

In many instances the position of the Indian nobility improved
after the 1550s. López de Cerrato wrote a letter to the crown
in 1552 expressing his concern over the cacique situation:

Fig. 13. *The coat of arms of don Juan of Atitlán. From AGI mapas y planos, escudos y arb. Gen. 24.*

When the Spanish entered this land, they killed some caciques and removed others from their *cacicazgos* to such an extent that in all this province there is almost no natural nor legitimate cacique. And if these have to carry tribute as before and more to the *encomenderos,* it implies a very great contradiction to what Y.M. has ordered, . . . that the Indians pay less tribute to the *encomenderos* than they used to pay to their caciques.

He exaggerated the situation somewhat, for there were many legitimate caciques, including the cacique of Atitlán. López de Cerrato was also worried about the caciques' control over their areas. He was especially concerned about their pre-Hispanic system of justice, which he considered barbaric: "Many still exercise their tyrannies ordering 20 given when 10 are assessed for tribute."

He also feared the possibility of revolt "because anciently they revered them [the caciques] as gods, and if this goes on, the lords will be able to raise the land easily."[22]

In 1557 Philip II enunciated Spanish policy toward caciques:

In the time of their infidelity certain natives of the Indies were caciques and lords of towns, and since it is just that they should preserve their rights after their conversion to our holy Catholic faith, and that their having submitted to us should not lessen their rank: we command our royal *audiencias* that if these caciques or *principales*, descendants of the first ones, claim to succeed to that sort of lordship or *cacicazgo* and attempt to bring an action in the matter, they shall be allowed to do so, and the parties concerned shall be summoned and heard with all dispatch.[23]

In 1557, don Juan Cortés, cacique of Santa Cruz del Quiché, went to Spain to make a personal plea to the crown to restore all of his alleged former kingdom, on the grounds that it had been ruled by his grandfather. At the time of the request his domain was confined to Santa Cruz del Quiché and its dependencies. Pedro de Betanzos was opposed to giving the larger kingdom to don Juan because if the crown gave in to him it would have to accede to the caciques of Atitlán and Tecpán Guatemala, who would certainly make similar requests. No doubt the cacique of Atitlán would have asked for lands that were once part of the Tzutujil kingdom but had been taken away in pre-Conquest times by the Quichés or the Cakchiquels. Don Juan Cortés did not gain control of the wider area that he claimed, but he was reaffirmed in control of the lands he already held. He also continued to authorize elections of other caciques in Quiché towns along with the Cawek cacique, don Juan de Rojas.[24]

None of the nobles of Atitlán went to Spain to petition for privileges, but the lords wrote a letter to the crown in 1571. In their letter they stressed their poverty and asked for the right to bear arms and collect tribute and small rents. They based their request on their fathers' privileges in aboriginal times and described their loyalty as vassals of the crown. They specifically requested arms to put down Indians in some of their *estancias* who were rebelling against their control and also asked that their tribute not be increased.[25] No response from the crown is recorded.

By the 1570s it was becoming harder for the nobles to maintain their social position. Although they kept their lands, they were obtaining less and less of the produce of those lands. The lords faced hostility from the *encomenderos* and crown officials if the assessed tribute was not delivered. They also had to deal with the dissatisfaction of their own people, who were pressed to their limits. The only option left was to reduce the amounts they retained for themselves.[26]

Indians in various parts of Guatemala continued to make requests for special privileges until the nineteenth century, but they were progressively less successful in attaining them, largely because by the 1630s many of the nobles were hardly distinguishable from the rest of the population:

Those that are of the better sort, and richer, and who are not employed as *tamemes* to carry burdens or as laborers to work for Spaniards, but keep at home on their own farms, or following their own mules about the country, or following their trades and callings in their shops, or governing the towns . . . may go a little better apparelled, but after the same manner. For some will have their drawers with a lace at the bottom, or wrought with some colored silk or crewel, so likewise the mantle about them shall have either a lace, or some work of birds on it. . . . And for their beds, the best Indian governor or the richest, who may be worth four or five thousand ducats, will have little more than the poor *tamemes*, for they lie upon boards, or canes bound together, and raised from the ground.[27]

This description of the Pokoman Indians would probably fit those of Atitlán just as well because by the mid-seventeenth century few Indians of means remained there.[28]

Even though some Indians were able to maintain their status as caciques until the early nineteenth century, most of their claims were denied after the beginning of the seventeenth century because of the difficulty of proving direct descent from a pre-Hispanic noble line. By that time the basic reason for attempting to gain cacique status was exemption from paying tribute. The Ajtz'iquina-jay moiety was able to maintain such status until 1630, but beyond that date it is not certain that there were any caciques in Atitlán.

*Middle Class:* We have little information about the middle class after the Conquest, but it is certain that for some life was much altered from that of aboriginal times. It is possible that some of the pre-Hispanic professional merchants became well-to-do petty merchants after the Conquest. Owing to the fluid conditions of the period from 1520 to 1540 and the population decline caused by epidemics, it is likely that some commoners saw their chance to gain in status and filled that role. Atitlán was deeply involved in the highland-lowland trade, and merchants were able to gain some measure of wealth. Some of them probably became *princi-pales,* since wealth brought with it influence, especially in the local town government.

Some craftsmen continued to exercise their occupations, espe-cially those whose skills were also of value to the Spaniards. The *Relación Tzutujil* spoke of carpenters and bricklayers, whose knowledge would have been useful in the construction of the church and other buildings in Santiago Atitlán.[29] Other craftsmen of the upper and lower classes, however, found that there was no raw material or market for their products. Jewelers, silversmiths, and goldworkers had to change media or find other trades.

The scribes ceased to function as they had before the Conquest. Spanish priests were suspicious of the pre-Conquest scribes, who were closely connected with the native religious books and calen-dars, and did not allow them to continue practicing their profes-sion. The scribal tradition did not entirely die out, however. Pineda mentioned good Indian scribes *(escribanos)* in Atitlán during the late sixteenth century.[30] These were Indians who served mainly as clerks for the local government and wrote in Spanish. Feather-workers also were discouraged from practicing their craft. They were seen as encouraging the perpetuation of native religious costumes and, thus, religious practices.

*Commoners:* The social situation became somewhat more fluid after the Conquest, offering enterprising commoners some oppor-tunities for social advancement. Perhaps they took up some of the crafts or became petty merchants and moved into the middle class or even became *principales.* Most still paid tribute to their lords, but in larger quantities, and continued to farm their fields or en-gage in other daily subsistence activities.

One other avenue of social mobility that may have been open to commoners was work for the Catholic church. Indians serving in the church hierarchy did not have to pay tribute. In 1585 there were in Atitlán, according to the *Relación geográfica Atitlán,*

singers who know how to read, write and sing. . . . They officiate at mass, at vespers, and other divine offices. . . . There is a school where the town children gather to learn the Christian doctrine in their native tongue, and to learn to read and write. . . . an Indian who is very well fitted for the purpose and who is a *principal* of the town . . . is the teacher of the children.[31]

Some of the Indian church workers, like the native petty mer-chants, were able to gain prestige and influence. Most Indians serving in the church were probably nobles, but some commoners may have filled some of the positions, rising to become *principales.* The most important social distinction after the Conquest continued to be that between tribute payers and those who did not pay it.

*Serfs and Slaves:* Some of the Quiché lords were able to keep their serfs *(nimak achi)* until the eighteenth century.[32] It is doubt-ful, however, that the lords of Atitlán kept them that long. Most of the serfs became ordinary tribute payers after the 1550s. The same was true for slaves after López de Cerrato freed them.

## The Lineage System

*Lords:* It is impossible to determine how many of the most impor-tant pre-Hispanic Tzutujil lineages continued to exercise authority in Atitlán after the Conquest. By the mid-sixteenth century some of these lineages had died out, while others had combined as their members diminished. Many of the names were still in exis-tence in the seventeenth century,[33] but since it was customary for the *principales* to hispanicize their names, they may have been lesser relatives of the aboriginal lineage heads. It is clear that rivalry between the Ajtz'iquinajay and Tzutujil moieties continued after the Conquest,[34] and we know that a member of the Ajtz'iquina-jay moiety was cacique of Atitlán in 1630.[35] The adjunct lord con-tinued to fulfill his role at least until 1565.[36] In Atitlán the lords of the leading pre-Hispanic lineages of both the Ajtz'iquinajay and the Tzutujil moieties were the ones who had the title "don" throughout most of the sixteenth century (table 9). It is impossible to distinguish the moieties of the *principales* after 1585.

By 1609 there were eighteen *calpules* (probably *chinamit* heads) in Atitlán, some having more than one leader. Nine of these leaders bore the title "don" and could therefore trace their descent back to pre-Hispanic nobles (table 10). In 1647 there were thirteen *chinamit* in San Pedro (table 3). Unfortunately, we have no in-formation about the leaders of these groups or whether any of them used the title "don." In the list of tributaries of San Pedro prepared in 1609, unlike the list of Atitlán, only names are given, not *calpul* affiliations. No one used the title "don." Atitlán is the only town in the list of 1609 for which leaders are listed.[37]

It is difficult to find any information on the lineages in any of the Tzutujil towns after the mid-seventeenth century. Vásquez said that there were eighteen *calpules* in Atitlán in aboriginal times, and that is the same number that existed there in 1609

Table 10. *Calpul Leaders of Atitlán, 1609*

| | |
|---|---|
| *Don Leonardo de Valdivia* | *Jerónimo López and* |
| *Don Lope de Santa María* | *Diego Hernández* |
| *Don Lázaro de Silva* | *Melchor de San Marcos* |
| *Don Jerónimo de Buenaventura* | *Baltasar de (?)* |
| *Don Toribio Constantino* | *Martín Rumán* |
| *Don Jerónimo de Mendoza* | *Juan López* |
| *Don Juan de Escobar* | *Gaspar Pérez* |
| *Don Bonifacio de Silva and* | *Francisco Osorio* |
| *Alcalde Pedro Colmenares* | *Domingo López* |
| *Don Blas de Santa María* | *Francisco de León* |

SOURCE: AGC A3.16 *exp.* 40,490 *leg.* 2,801. Año 1599.

(table 10).[38] Therefore, it is likely that the lineage heads continued their authority until at least that time. In present-day Atitlán there is no evidence of lineage structure. The household group, usually composed of a nuclear family, performs the functions formally handled by the lineage. For example, all expenses for baptisms, ritual offices, celebrations, and marriages are paid by the household.[39]

*Commoners:* It is not clear exactly what unit of social structure is indicated by the term *calpul* in post-Conquest times. The ancient *calpul* was a colony in an area somewhat distant from the *tinamit*. The *calpules* of post-Conquest Atitlán were probably *chinamit* existing in the town at the time. They were not, of course, identical with those of ancient Chiya', and some of the heads of the post-Hispanic *calpules* may have been influential men unrelated to the dominant aboriginal lineages. What is significant is that the modified *chinamit* structure continued to exist and to integrate all levels of Indian society. It remained the unit of tribute collection. Perhaps the judicial and ritual functions of the *chinamit* also persisted.[40]

In 1647 fifteen families composed the Tzununá *chinamit* of San Pedro, and the names of most of these families also appear in the tributary list of 1609. Additional family names belonged to the other *chinamit* noted by Aguirre (table 3), and since there were only seventy-five tributaries in San Pedro in 1609, by 1647 some of the *chinamit* must have been reduced to a family or two. It is not always possible to say which families in the list of 1609 belonged to the Tzununá *chinamit* because by 1609 some of the Indians were using Spanish surnames. Some *chinamit* may have died out by 1647.

*Marriage:* The regulation of marriage continued to be an important function of the lineage leaders in post-Hispanic times. Gage
wrote:

When any is to be married, the father of the son that is to take a wife
out of another tribe goeth unto the head of his tribe to give him warn-
ing of his son's marriage with such a maid. Then that head meets with
the head of the maid's tribe, and they confer about it. The business
commonly is in debate a quarter of a year; all which time the parents
of the youth or man are with gifts to buy the maid. They have to pay
for all that is spent in eating and drinking when the heads of the two
tribes meet with the rest of the kindred of each side, and sometimes
they sit in conference a whole day, or most of the night. After many
days and nights thus spent, and after a full trial has been made of the
affection on one side and the other, if they chance to disagree about the
marriage, then must the tribe and parents of the maid restore all that
the other hath spent and given. They give no portions with their daughters, but when they die, their goods and lands are equally divided among
their sons.[41]

Some of these customs may also have characterized the Tzutujil
area. In modern times, however, although a boy's father may
sometimes arrange an engagement for his son, it has become more
common for young people to find their own mates.[42]

The influence of the lineage leaders continued despite a royal
command of the year 1515 that Indians were to be free to marry
whomever they wished.[43] The law was passed to prevent the
Indian leaders from forcing their people to marry when and whom
they chose. As mentioned earlier, very young boys and girls were
sometimes forced into marriage so that they could be included
on the tribute rolls.[44] Gage's passage indicates that people did not
marry within their own lineage, suggesting a continuation of pre-
Hispanic custom. Bride price was also retained in the colonial
period.

Gage's reference to the Pokomans' division of their goods equally
among their sons may describe not only the custom among commoners in his time but possibly that of aboriginal times as well,
which would have been a deviation from pre-Hispanic practice
among the Quichean nobles. Ordinarily the oldest son of a noble
line inherited the largest part of his father's goods and often his
title as well. Today in Atitlán land is usually divided among all
the children of a household head. Daughters and sons have equal
claims on their parents' estates,[45] and perhaps that has been a
long-standing practice among the commoners.

At the time Gage wrote his account, marriage was almost always an intratown affair arranged by lineage leaders of the bride and groom. After the Conquest most of the caciques and *principales* continued to marry within their own class so that they would not risk losing their privileges. Among the Tzutujils, soon after the Conquest spouses probably came to be chosen from within the town or at least from within the immediate area. Dynastic marriages with Quichés and the Cakchiquels would not have had the advantages of such alliances in earlier times. The most significant change in marriage as far as the upper class was concerned was the Spaniards' prohibition of polygyny, which they regarded as a great sin. Although it was more difficult to support several wives in post-Conquest times, a few well-to-do Indians may have had more than one spouse despite Spanish orders. Even in recent times in Santiago Atitlán some men have had two wives.[46]

Thus the pre-Hispanic social structure persisted during the sixteenth and early seventeenth centuries, but with modifications. In Atitlán the lords endured population losses and a gradual loss of wealth but were able to maintain some privileges. They continued to be exempt from paying tribute, kept their lands, and received some of the trappings of Spanish nobility. They collected tribute from the commoners and kept any excess for themselves. A descendant of the pre-Hispanic Ajtz'iquinajay line continued to fulfill the cacique position. By the 1550s the lords found it harder to keep excess tribute for themselves, and the commoners suffered from their attempts to do so. The result was that the lords eventually lost much of their wealth.

Some middle-class occupations continued after the Conquest and may have been filled by members of traditional craft lineages or by aspiring commoners. Utilitarian crafts were still in demand, but professional Indian merchants and featherworkers tended to disappear. Those who learned to write in Spanish served as scribes.

Commoners remained in such traditional occupations as farming and fishing or moved up socially by becoming petty merchants or perhaps by serving in the church hierarchy. It is not known how long any serfs remained under Tzutujil control, and slaves became ordinary tribute payers after they were freed.

It is impossible to determine how many pre-Hispanic Tzutujil lineage leaders remained in authority. Some died out, while others adopted Spanish surnames. The Ajtz'iquinajay and Tzutujil moieties can be distinguished only until the late sixteenth century. A modified form of the *chinamit* structure seems to have continued and carried out traditional functions. Some of the *chinamit* leaders, called *calpul* heads, used the title of "don," indicating descent from pre-Hispanic nobility, and they were probably members of the most important native lineages.

Marriage became primarily a local matter after the Conquest, and lineage leaders maintained control over it. Bride price was still paid, and some commoners appear to have divided their goods equally among their children. With the decline of native warfare, dynastic marriages were no longer important, but marriage was still a matter of great concern to the nobles because their privileges depended upon maintaining the purity of their lines. Polygyny also continued despite Spanish prohibition of the practice.

Thus, in post-Conquest times the lineage system, the titles "cacique" and "don," and intermarriage of nobles within the local area helped maintain the upper class temporarily. More powerful forces were at work that eventually destroyed them. Population decline and decreasing tribute eroded the nobility, while new bases of social status provided opportunities for some nobles and possibly commoners.

## CHAPTER 15

# Tzutujil Town Government

We have little information about the political system in the Tzutujil region from the time of the Conquest until the mid-sixteenth century. Native warfare ceased after the Conquest, and the only Indians who fought were those used by the Spaniards as auxiliaries. The most significant effect of the Conquest on the various Indian kingdoms was the loss of their status as independent political entities. Indian lords were no longer free to make war with each other, but continuing hostility was expressed in the form of land litigation.

Large Indian empires of the New World, such as that of the Aztecs, were broken down by the Spaniards into their constituent parts. Some smaller kingdoms, like that of the Tzutujils, survived almost intact during the sixteenth century, as described earlier. The head of the Ajtz'iquinajay moiety served as cacique. Alvarado and the Barahonas ruled Atitlán through the cacique, whose main functions, as far as the *encomenderos* and the crown were concerned, was to organize the labor force and deliver tribute. Important decisions and appeals were handled by the *encomendero*, the local priest, or a Spanish official who was passing through, such as an *alguacil* (constable) or a *visitador* (inspector).[1]

In 1547 seven *corregimientos,* or administrative units, were created by the audiencia of Guatemala. Two of these were Atitlán and Tecpán Atitlán, which, after 1560, were placed within a larger political division, the Alcaldía Mayor of Zapotitlán. This structure remained in effect until 1689, when the Corregimientos of Atitlán and Tecpán Atitlán were combined to form the new Alcaldía Mayor of Sololá.[2]

In the Corregimiento of Atitlán Indian control was maintained in the *cabecera* and *sujetos* but was supervised by a local Spanish official, the *corregidor.* The *cabecera-sujeto* unit was fundamental to Spanish political and economic organization. Santiago Atitlán was designated the *cabecera* because the local cacique resided there, and the newly congregated highland and lowland towns were its *sujetos.*

Indians and Spaniards lived in separate towns and were administered by different royal officials, had distinct judicial systems, and worshiped in separate churches. *Alcaldes mayores* and *corregidores* were appointed and controlled by the audiencia.[3] Often the *corregidor* had a staff consisting of a *teniente* (deputy), an *alguacil,* an *escribano* (secretary), and an interpreter.[4] The *corregimiento* was designed to protect Indian society from Spanish interference, to supervise Indian government, to collect the stipulated amount of tribute, to see that the Indians were Christianized, and to adjudicate cases involving Indian crimes and civil litigation.[5]

The *corregimiento* usually conformed to the native political boundaries as they existed at contact. The Corregimiento of Atitlán originally encompassed the area of the aboriginal kingdom, but congregation and population decline eventually altered the settlement pattern somewhat (fig. 11). The crown also favored the establishment of *alcaldes mayores* during the mid-sixteenth century to counteract the abuses of the *encomenderos* and lesser authorities.[6]

The cabildo, or town council, was the basic institution of the *corregimiento.* The principal offices were those of *alcalde* and *regidor.* There were usually two *alcaldes,* or judges, and four *regidores* (councilmen). The local system was supposed to work in the following manner, according to the *Recopilación de leyes de los reynos de las Indias:*

In each town and Reduction [congregation] there shall be one Indian Alcalde from the same Reduction; and if there are more than eighty houses, two Alcaldes and two Regidores, also Indian, and even though the town be very large, there shall not be more than two Alcaldes and four Regidores, and if there are less than eighty, but forty, no more than one Alcalde and one Regidor who are elected annually, in the presence of the priests as is the practice in the towns of Spaniards and Indians.[7]

In practice the number of *alcaldes* and *regidores* in Atitlán varied over time. For example, in 1623 there were six *regidores* (see table 11).

Other local officials were the *mayordomo* (steward), *alguacil mayor* (chief constable), and *alguaciles* (lesser constables). The caciques and *principales* filled the offices of the cabildo, which had one-year terms, and Indian officials elected to the cabildo must be approved by the *corregidor.*[8]

Table 11. *Officers of Santiago Atitlán, 1587-1650*

| Name | Office | Source |
|------|--------|--------|
| Don Francisco Vásquez | *Gobernador* | Document of 1587[a] |
| Don Andrés de Mansilla | *Alcalde* | |
| Don Diego de Mendoza | *Principal* | |
| Bonifacio de Silva | *Regidor* | |
| Pedro Colmenares | *Alguacil mayor* | |
| | | |
| Don Lázaro de Silva | *Alcalde* | 1609 *Residencia* of the |
| Pedro Colmenares | *Alcalde* | Alcalde Mayor Medinilla[b] |
| Pedro de Alvarado | *Regidor pasado* | |
| Bartolomé Pérez[c] | *Regidor* | |
| Don Leonardo de Valdivia | *Cabeza de calpul* | |
| Melchor de San Marcos | *Alcalde pasado* | |
| Gerónimo López | *Alcalde pasado* | |
| | | |
| Don Guillermo López[d] | *Gobernador* | 1623 *Título* of the *encomienda* |
| Don Guillermo de | | of don Pedro Núñez de |
|   Buenaventura | *Alcalde* | Barahona[e] |
| Don Cebrían Rodríguez | *Alcalde* | |
| Don Pedro de Alvarado | *Regidor* | |
| Andrés Colmenares | *Regidor* | |
| Gaspar Enríquez | *Regidor* | |
| Diego de Aguilar | *Regidor* | |
| Bartolomé de Villavicencio | *Regidor* | |
| Gabriel Mejía | *Regidor* | |
| Francisco de Sobre | *Alguacil* | |
| Don Guillermo de Mendoza | *Escribano* | |
| | | |
| Diego de Aguilar | *Alcalde ordinario* | Document of 1650[f] |
| Juan de Alvarado | *Alcalde ordinario* | |
| Antón Blas | *Regidor* | |
| Pedro Pacheco | *Regidor* | |
| Francisco de Buenaventura | *Regidor* | |
| *Bartolomé Ramírez* | *Escribano* | |
| Don Damián de León | *Cabeza de calpul* | |
| Juan Pablo | *Cabeza de calpul* | |
| Baltasar Vásquez | *Cabeza de calpul* | |
| Martín Rodríguez | *Cabeza de calpul* | |
| Gaspar de Sal | *Cabeza de calpul* | |

[a] AGC Al *exp.* 24,781 *leg.* 2,811. *Año* 1587. According to another document dated 1587 (AGC Al *exp.* 31,428 *leg.* 4,055), Francisco Vásquez was still living and was probably still *gobernador*.

[b] AGI Escribania de Camara 344B fols. 125v-127. *Año* 1609.

[c] Bartolomé Pérez was a member of the *calpul* of his brother Gaspar Pérez in 1609. AGC A3.16 *exp.* 40,490 *leg.* 2,801. *Año* 1599.

[d] Guillermo is written for Jerónimo or Gerónimo in this document.

[e] AGC Al.1 *exp.* 10 *leg.* 1. *Año* 1623.

[f] AGC Al.1.14 *exp.* 48,870 *leg.* 5,797. *Año* 1650.

The cabildo was somewhat similar to the pre-Hispanic council that had advised the Indian ruler. Although the term of service was one year, the offices tended to be rotated among the same men, who were usually descendants of the most important nobles of pre-Hispanic times.[9] Their ancestors would have been members of the council. *Caja* (community-treasury) funds were derived from crops grown on communal lands, goods sold in town shops, and community lands rented to private individuals. They were used to defray community expenses and pay salaries of cabildo officials and teachers.[10]

The two titles *gobernador* and "cacique" were sometimes applied to the same individual. Theoretically, the *gobernador* was elected for a two-year term, whereas the cacique kept his title for his lifetime, since it was based on descent. Over time the distinction became blurred because the cacique often served as *gobernador* for many years.[11] Don Pedro Cabinjay was *gobernador* of the Tzutujils in 1565 and probably held the office since don Juan's death, when he took over as regent until the young don Bernabé came of age.[12]

In general, the town council enacted legislation on matters not covered by Spanish law and performed some of the functions formerly carried out by the pre-Hispanic council of the lords. Cabildo officials on occasion petitioned the *alcalde mayor,* the audiencia, and even the crown in such matters as excessive tribute levies and jurisdictional disputes and payment for church ornaments. They also verified wills, as in the *Testament Ajpopolajay,* provided laborers for the Spaniards and local projects, saw that the tribute was collected and delivered, and took care of matters relating to community interest.[13] The *mayordomo* was in charge of communal monies, and the cabildo decided how they were to be used.[14] Gage described the town-government system as it existed among the Pokomans in the early seventeenth century:

From the Spaniards they have borrowed their civil government, and in all towns they have one or two *alcaldes,* with more or less *regidores,* . . . and some *alguaciles,* . . . who are as constables, to execute the orders of the *alcalde.* . . . In towns of three or four hundred families or upwards, there are commonly two *alcaldes,* six *regidores,* two *alguaciles mayores,* and six under . . . *alguaciles.* Some towns are privileged with an Indian governor, who is above the *alcaldes* and all the rest of the officers. These are changed every year by new election, and are chosen by the Indians themselves. . . . The Governor, being some chief man among the Indians, is also commonly continued many years, unless there are complaints of his misdemeanors or the Indians [dislike] him. [The Indian governors] may imprison, fine, whip, and banish, but they may not hang and quarter, but must remit such cases to the Spanish governor.[15]

This is fairly consistent with the structure set forth in the *Recopilación* and is probably similar to the Indian government in the Tzutujil area.

The lineage heads assisted the cabildo by calling their people to work on council projects and delivering up criminals for punishment. Gage reported:

Amongst themselves, if any complaint be made against any Indian, they dare not meddle with him until they call all his kindred, and especially the head of that tribe to which he belongs. If he and the rest together find him to deserve imprisonment or whipping or any other punishment, then the officers of justice, the *alcaldes* . . . , and their brethren the jurats inflict upon him that punishment which all shall agree upon. Yet after judgment and sentence have been given, they have another, which is their last appeal, if they please, and that is to their priest and friar, who liveth in their town, by whom they will sometimes be judged, and undergo what punishment he shall think fittest.[16]

Such practices were probably as widespread in the Quichean region as in the Pokoman area. According to the *Recopilación de leyes de reynos de las Indias,* the *alcaldes* had jurisdiction to punish with one day in jail or six to eight lashes an Indian who missed mass on the day of the fiesta or who became intoxicated or committed other unlawful acts. They could also punish those guilty of habitual drunkenness with greater severity.[17] Thus some of the judicial functions of the pre-Hispanic council of the lords were also retained by the Indian cabildo. Garcés said that the Indian *gobernadores* did much harm and that there was little that a common Indian could do about it.[18] It was difficult to get rid of Indian officials who abused their privileges.

Some idea of the kinds of abuses that were occurring in the mid-seventeenth century can be gained from the set of questions in Cakchiquel prepared by Fray Antonio del Saz (who had also been a priest in Atitlán) to be used in examining the Indians during confession. He asked several questions of the Indian *gobernadores, alcaldes,* and other officials. The questions focused on current deeds, such as taking things from the commoners that they were not obligated to give, adding to the commoners' tribute, and taking some of it for themselves. They were also asked whether they forced commoners to work for them without adequate pay, whipped them, or took bribes from individuals guilty of infractions. *Alguaciles* were asked whether they kept the money of the Indians (presumably those who were serving jail sentences), failed to punish criminals if they offered them bribes, sinned with women who were serving jail sentences or with those known to be at home alone, or gave women to travelers if paid to do so.[19]

During López de Cerrato's time, the Indian officers had some independence from Spanish authorities, but after 1561 they were increasingly restricted by the crown.[20] Despite these restrictions the town-council system allowed the nobles and their descendants to continue to govern their people after the Conquest with a minimum of Spanish interference. The nobles lost ultimate authority, of course, and were subordinate to the local *corregidores,* who confirmed all elections, and to the *encomendero* and the crown, to whom they paid tribute. These Spaniards were usually primarily interested in monetary gain, however, not in the daily affairs of the Indian towns. Thus Indian officials were permitted a good deal of control over the commoners, which they exercised according to aboriginal standards and values as much as possible.

## Succession to Office

Pre-Hispanic modes of selecting officials continued to operate throughout most of the sixteenth century, but with the high death rate among members of all levels of Indian society, elections became more frequent. Unfortunately, it is often impossible to determine from the sources the offices that the pre-Hispanic lineages held in the post-Hispanic system, owing to the hispanicization of names.

Some of the earliest information on the local government and the election process in Atitlán concerns complaints by lords of the Tzutujil moiety against the Ajtz'iquinajay *gobernador,* don Pedro Cabinjay. The line of caciques of Atitlán until 1563 is shown in table 1. The succession passed from father to son among the Ajtz'iquinajay. After the death of don Juan in 1547, don Pedro Cabinjay acted as regent, just as he would have under pre-Hispanic custom, until don Bernabé came of age. Because the cacique was very young, the adjunct lord filled the office of *gobernador.* After that time the office of cacique and *gobernador* remained separate in Atitlán (see below), though it is not possible to determine whether the office of *gobernador* was always filled by members of the Cabinjay lineage. The office of *gobernador* was monopolized by the Ajtz'iquinajay moiety until 1583.

Because don Bernabé was too young to serve as *gobernador,* members of the Tzutujil moiety challenged the succession and tried to increase their own power in the town. The Spanish authorities called several witnesses to testify concerning the succession. Two lords from Tecpán Atitlán—don Jorge, the Ajpoxajil, and his brother don Pedro de Robles—and don Baltasar and don Diego, the caciques of Nagualapa, provided evidence that, while don Bernabé was the legitimate cacique, don Pedro Cabinjay was the legitimate regent until don Bernabé came of age.[21] From this testimony it is clear that the Spaniards followed pre-Hispanic custom in Atitlán in matters relating to political office and that other caciques were considered proper witnesses in validating the succession. Such proceedings were also common in the Quiché area.[22]

The Tzutujil moiety gained something from the challenge. The Spanish authorities ruled that there were to be two *alcaldes,* one for each moiety. President Landecho further ordered in 1563 that in each election one-half of the officers would be named from the Tzutujil moiety and the other half from the Ajtz'iquinajay moiety. It appears that this order was not immediately put into effect; Diego de Garcés, the *alcalde mayor* of Zapotitlán, later ordered that the previous order be followed: that each moiety would have its *alcalde* and *mayordomo* and that the cabildo was to be composed of officials of both moieties.[23]

According to the *Testament Ajpopolajay,* written in 1569, don Francisco de Rivera, a member of the Ajtz'iquinajay moiety, was *gobernador* of Atitlán. He must have succeeded to the office on the death of don Pedro Cabinjay, who had died in 1565. *The Annals of the Cakchiquels* state that in the year 1564 "many people died of smallpox, which was prevalent."[24] Perhaps don Pedro died in that epidemic. Rivera was one of the signers of the *Relación Tzutujil;* thus he was probably still governor in 1571. He was also mentioned in the document of 1563 cited by Carrasco but was not at that time given the title "don." He was using the title by 1569, however, and probably succeeded to it upon the death of don Pedro Cabinjay.

Rivera was succeeded by don Joseph de Santa María, who was an *alcalde* at the time of the signing of the *Testament Ajpopolajay.* Santa María died on September 12, 1583.[25] Upon his death don Francisco Vásquez, a member of the Tzutujil moiety, became *gobernador.* Don Hernando (or Francisco) de Soto and don Pedro de Alvarado were listed as *principales* in the *Relación geográfica Atitlán.*[26] Vásquez was named in the 1563 document as a member of the Tzutujil moiety along with don Pedro de Alvarado.[27] It appears that by the end of 1583 Landecho's ruling was having an effect on the political succession to office in Atitlán and that the monopoly of the Ajtz'iquinajay moiety on the office of *gobernador* had ended.

Vásquez signed a document written in 1587, indicating that he was probably still *gobernador* in that year.[28] Beyond that date it is not impossible to distinguish between the two moieties or to determine whether the office of *gobernador* came to be regularly alternated between them. Interfactional struggles may have diminished by the time Vásquez assumed office because Betancor and Arboleda did not speak of them. By the late sixteenth century some of the direct descendants of Atitlán's pre-Hispanic nobility had died out, and perhaps by then *principales* were also being drawn from among the wealthy men who made their way by trading or by serving in the church hierarchy.

From an examination of the list of *principales* of Atitlán in the period 1563 to 1609 given in tables 9 and 10, it can be seen that Indians with the title "don" were prominent in the government throughout the sixteenth century. Some of the men who were not originally titled, like Francisco Vásquez and Francisco de Rivera, later acquired the title. Some men without titles were also influential and served as *alcaldes* and *regidores* in the late sixteenth century (table 11). *Gobernadores* were always "dons" and were leading members of the Ajtz'iquinajay or Tzutujil moieties during this time.

After 1563 there were always two *alcaldes,* possibly one from each moiety. The practice of having two *alcaldes* continued into the mid-seventeenth century, and in the year 1650, Diego de Aguilar and Juan de Alvarado served in this office. It seems that by 1609 the title "don" was no longer prerequisite for *alcaldes,* and a brother of a *calpul* head served as *regidor,* but the higher offices remained the prerogative of the *principales,* titled or not. Other minor offices may have been filled by descendants of lesser branches of important aboriginal lineages.

Spanish patterns of local government were similar to aboriginal patterns, and the two were effectively blended during the sixteenth century. In Atitlán the leader of the Ajtz'iquinajay moiety served as *gobernador* until 1583, when the leader of the Tzutujil moiety gained the office. The cabildo was composed of *principales* from each moiety, with the highest-ranking leaders monopolizing the offices of *gobernador* and *alcalde* until the early seventeenth century. *Regidores* came to be increasingly drawn from among nontitled men who were *principales.* The rest of the cabildo offices may have been occupied by near relatives of the important lineage heads.

## *Local Government in the* Sujetos

Throughout most of the sixteenth century Atitlán continued to maintain social and political control over its Conquest dependencies. Spaniards preferred to live in the major cities *(ciudades)* and receive tribute sent from their *encomienda* Indians in distant areas. The only Spaniards who lived in Atitlán were the priests and the *corregidor* and his family. Probably none resided in the *sujetos*. As the *cabecera*, Atitlán exercised jurisdiction over the entire *corregimiento*, which in the sixteenth and early seventeenth centuries included the following towns: San Bartolomé, San Francisco, Santa Bárbara, and San Andrés, on the coast; and San Pedro, San Pablo, Santa María de Jesús (Visitación), San Marcos, Santa Cruz, and San Lucas Tolimán around the lake (fig. 11). Suchitepéquez was separated from Atitlán's domination and became the seat of the entire Alcaldía Mayor of Zapotitlán. Nagualapa was also lost.

The *sujetos* sought to obtain some political independence from the *cabecera* after the mid-sixteenth century. As long as they were included in the tribute assessments as integral parts of Atitlán, they were still considered to be politically dependent upon the *cabecera*. The key to greater independence was the existence of a cabildo and cabildo officials.[29]

Before achieving their own cabildos, if a dispute arose between two *sujetos*, they were still dependent upon the *cabeceras* to resolve it. For example, Santa María de Jesús and Santa Clara disputed lands, and sometime between 1581 and 1583, Fray Pedro de Arboleda of Atitlán and Fray Juan Martínez of Tecpán Atitlán (of which Santa Clara was a *sujeto*) came together to settle the dispute: "And the said Padres, seeing the dissension and complaints that the caciques and *gobernadores* of both parts had, called them to the church of Santa Clara, and they agreed that both nations would enjoy the land in common."[30] In this incident the priests dealt not with *alcaldes* and *regidores* but with *gobernadores* and caciques, proving that Santa María de Jesús and Santa Clara were not yet towns formed with their own political authorities and independent of the cabildos of Atitlán and Tecpán Atitlán.

By 1585, the coastal *sujetos* had their own cabildos, and some highland *sujetos* probably established them around the same time.[31] It was after this time that Atitlán and all the *sujetos* were counted separately in tribute assessments. Before that time assessments sometimes gave tributaries for the coastal *estancias* but merely mentioned the names of highland towns being included in the number of tributaries given for Atitlán. In 1623 highland *sujeto* cabildo officers were listed in the *Título de la encomienda de don Pedro Núñez de Barahona* (see table 12).

The cabildos in the *sujetos* could make petitions on behalf of their respective towns and carry out local business instead of having to go through the cabildo of Atitlán. Despite their local political independence, Tzutujil-speaking towns continued to maintain linguistic and cultural ties with Atitlán, which, as *cabecera* of the *corregimiento,* remained in a position similar to that of a county seat. The attaining of local independence and the official founding of towns meant the beginning of a de facto social and political separation which, for the lake settlements, became the basis of the later-nineteenth-century *municipio* system of government.[32]

### Local Spanish Officials

*Corregidores* received stipulated salaries, which were not very high, and their daily food, fodder, and fuel from their Indian charges. They also received personal services from the Indians.[33] During their time of office many *corregidores* no doubt tried to make their fortunes by whatever means possible because they had no assurance of being reappointed to another post. Although *corregidores* were charged by the crown to protect the Indians from abuse, they often proved to be among the most serious offenders in the mistreatment of the Indians, along with the *alcaldes mayores* and the *encomenderos.* Atitlán, in the Alcaldía Mayor of Zapotitlán, was also subject to visits from the *alcalde mayor.* According to Bishop Ramírez, on these visits the *alcalde mayor* brought a chief constable, a secretary, and an interpreter, and the salaries were borne by the Indians whom he visited.[34] The Indians received little protection when the *corregidor* and the *encomendero* collaborated to defraud them. The only recourse the natives had was the local priest.

Soon after the establishment of the *corregimientos,* the crown began issuing legislation to restrict the power of the *corregidores* and the *alcaldes mayores.* In 1552 the latter were prohibited from asking for fodder, maize, beans, firewood, or personal services from the Indians without paying for them.[35] In 1559 the

Table 12. *Officers in the Coastal and Highland Towns, 1585 and 1623*

| Town | Name | Office |
|------|------|--------|
| | | **1585** |
| San Bartolome* | Domingo Elías | *Alcalde* |
| | Baltasar López | *Regidor* |
| | Domingo Ramos | *Regidor* |
| | Marcos Sánchez | *Fiscal* |
| San Andrés† | Tomas Pérez | *Alcalde* |
| | Andrés Martín | *Regidor* |
| | Melchor Martín | *Regidor* |
| San Francisco‡ | Diego Rodríguez | *Alcalde* |
| | Andrés Aguilar | *Regidor* |
| | | **1623§** |
| San Bartolomé | Bartolomé Paz | *Alcalde* |
| | Sebastián Calderón | *Regidor* |
| Santa Bárbara | Diego Méndez | *Alcalde* |
| | Juan Martín | *Regidor* |
| San Francisco | Bernardino Mejía | *Alcalde* |
| | Francisco de Paz | *Regidor* |
| San Lucas Tolimán | Gaspar Pérez | *Alcalde* |
| | Melchor Pérez | *Regidor* |
| San Pedro | Juan Méndez | *Alcalde* |
| | Gaspar Pérez | *Escribano* |
| San Juan | Diego Jirón | *Alcalde* |
| | Melchor Martín | *Regidor* |
| | Gaspar Pérez | *Escribano* |
| San Pablo | Pedro Ramírez | *Alcalde* |
| | Felipe López | *Regidor* |
| | Gaspar López | *Regidor* |
| Visitación | Melchor Sánchez | *Alguacil mayor* |
| | Juan Mejía | *Vecino* |
| | Alonso Matías | *Vecino* |
| Santa Cruz | Diego López | *Alguacil mayor* |
| | Juan López | *Alguacil* |

*RGAG 1965, p. 265.
†RGSA 1952, p. 102.
‡RGSF 1952, p. 122.
§AGC Al.1 *exp.* 10 *leg.* 1, fols. 5v-7. *Año* 1623.

crown prohibited any special district from being assigned on behalf of the *corregidor* or his deputy or family in the general tribute assessment.[36] *Corregidores* and *alcaldes mayores* were often remote from the capital, however, and in practice little was done to check their exploitation of the Indians.

Two means were devised to restrain the misconduct of Spanish officials: the *visita* and the *residencia*. The *visita* was a surprise inspection visit paid by audiencia officials during an official's term of office. In practice it was not always effective because *visita* officials sometimes colluded with *encomenderos* or officials or looked the other way and merely reported minor infractions.[37] The *residencia* was held at the completion of the term of office, by which time the harm was done. Moreover, officials were not usually harshly punished as the result of the *residencia*. The effect was that the *corregidor* and the *alcalde mayor* had a fairly high degree of local autonomy, and the amount of graft depended upon the character of the individuals appointed to the posts. In 1582 the crown again ordered that *alcaldes mayores* who forced Indians to work on their properties without pay were to be relieved of their lands and prosecuted.[38] The order demonstrated that the officials were continuing their abuses.

Bishop Ramírez described the many injustices suffered by the Indians at the beginning of the seventeenth century. Indian males who hired out by the week were ordered to perform services for the *alcaldes mayores,* the *corregidores,* the *jueces de milpas,* or the president of the audiencia. Some of the officials gave these workers to their friends and relatives. The Indians repaired houses, cultivated fields, and worked in the kitchens. Indian women were forced to perform grinding, weaving, sewing, and other tasks in Spanish towns. This forced labor was very detrimental to native family life. The Indians were paid very little for their work and lost time they would have spent cultivating their own fields.[39] The Tzutujils around the lake suffered less from these forms of extortion than did the Indians living close to Spanish settlements, though the *corregidor* of Atitlán and his family no doubt expected and received labor services from the Indians of the *cabecera*. Indians on the coast towns generally suffered more abuses by the Spaniards than did those of the highlands.

Some Spanish officials extorted huge sums from the communities in their charge:

Not being content with what the Indians gave voluntarily, which was four to ten *reales,* they compelled them to give fifteen, twenty, or more.

An *alcalde mayor* in Suchitepéques, in the year 1602, removed in this manner fifteen thousand *tostones* from the province of Zapotitlán, with which he bought one thousand loads of cacao, each load being valued ordinarily at fifty or sixty *tostones*. He sent them to Mexico to be sold, thereby conducting commerce with royal money. All this was publicly known.[40]

Two other common means of defrauding the Indians were the *derrama* and the *repartimiento de efectos.* In colonial times *derrama* referred to extra or unauthorized tributes. In Guatemala the *derrama* system was extended to commerce. The local official acted as a merchant, purchasing goods cheaply in the cities and selling them to the Indians at high prices whether they wanted them or not. The reverse of that practice was to buy goods from Indians at very low prices and then resell them for a profit.[41] This went on despite crown legislation of 1582 that explicitly prohibited the *derrama.*[42]

The *repartimiento de efectos* often involved a *corregidor* who purchased cotton cheaply on the coast or in Santiago and then forced highland Indian women in his jurisdiction to weave it into mantas. The Spanish official sold them back to the Indians or to the cities at a profit.[43] Although in 1609 the crown ordered that *corregidores* were not to engage in commerce,[44] the abuses continued. In 1679 the *corregidores* of Atitlán and Tecpán Atitlán were expressly forbidden to carry out the *repartimiento de efectos* among the Indians of Santa Lucía Utatlán, a town near Lake Atitlán.[45] This practice was evidently still occurring in Atitlán around the end of the seventeenth century, according to Fuentes y Guzmán.[46]

In summary, until the introduction of the *corregimientos* and Indian town government, the Tzutujils remained in their pre-Hispanic locations and maintained much of their aboriginal political structure. In the *cabecera* of Atitlán the *corregidor* supervised the local cabildo, composed of Indian officials who were usually descendants of important aboriginal lineages who had served in the pre-Hispanic council of the lords. Although the *corregidor* was responsible for protecting the Indians, seeing that the correct amount of tribute was delivered on time, and adjudicating cases involving Indians, the Indian *principales* continued to govern town life in areas of less importance to the Spaniards. The lot of the common Indians was often made worse by abuses inflicted by Indian officials and nobles.

In Atitlán, because the cacique of the Ajtz'iquinajay moiety was too young to fill the office of *gobernador* in 1547, the position came to be occupied by the pre-Hispanic adjunct lord, and thus the office of *gobernador* became separated from the office of cacique. Succession, following pre-Hispanic custom, continued from father to son in the office of cacique of the Ajtz'iquinajay moiety, and this group also controlled the office of *gobernador* at least until 1583. Titled men served as *gobernadores* and *alcaldes* throughout the sixteenth and early seventeenth centuries, and lesser offices were filled by important nontitled men who were sometimes near relatives of important aboriginal lineage heads. By the end of the sixteenth century the Tzutujil moiety had achieved political equality with the Ajtz'iquinajay moiety, succeeding in a bid for power that had begun in 1521.

Originally the *sujetos* did not have their own cabildos. Since a town must have a cabildo to become independent, by the 1580s many towns were establishing town councils. However, all the *sujetos* retained cultural and linguistic ties with Atitlán, which continued to serve as *cabecera* of the *corregimiento*.

The Tzutujils' area was somewhat remote from large Spanish towns, and therefore they escaped the continuous demands for labor that fell on Indian settlements closer to the Spaniards. The Tzutujils did not escape exploitation, however. The establishment of the *corregimientos* opened the door to additional extortion of Indian wealth as the *corregidor*, charged with protecting the Indians against the *encomenderos*, often colluded with them to augment their low salaries. The *alcalde mayor* of Zapotitlán also toured his province from time to time, which brought additional expense to each town he passed through.

The *derrama* and the *repartimiento de efectos* were adopted by Spanish officials to extort money from the Indians and no doubt adversely affected the Tzutujil area. While the highland area achieved more local autonomy and freedom from Spanish interference than many Indian areas closer to Spanish towns, on top of all the other burdens imposed by the conquerors, the *encomenderos*, and the crown, extortion by officials severely strained the native economy.

## CHAPTER 16

# *Religion*

As mentioned earlier, the first Roman Catholic priests to make contact with the Tzutujils may have been Bartolomé de Olmedo and Juan Díaz, who, according to the *Título San Bartolomé,* arrived in Guatemala in 1522-23 as emissaries of Cortés. After the Conquest a few priests traveled throughout Guatemala, and perhaps some visited Chiya' and the lowland Tzutujil settlements. Catholicism was formally established in 1534, when the Diocese of Guatemala was created,[1] with Francisco Marroquín as bishop. His first goals were to build a church in the capital and to persuade more clergy, especially members of the orders, to come to the country to convert the natives.

The first priests in Guatemala, lacking churches, said mass in temporary buildings or in the open. All the priests' altar appointments were portable.[2] Their primary goal was to baptize the Indians, which they often did in large groups,[3] and to destroy any remnants of "idolatry" and "paganism." They made special efforts to convert the caciques and the *principales,* reasoning that the other Indians would follow their leaders' examples. Few Indians were converted by the first priests who visited their towns, and when the clerics moved on, they continued to practice their native religion.

## The Introduction of Catholicism into the Tzutujil Region

Fray Rodrigo de Ladrada, a Dominican, preached in Chiya' and Tecpán Atitlán in 1538, and by that time the caciques and some other nobles were already Christians. It was probably Fray Luís Cancer, another Dominican, who brought to the faith don Juan of Atitlán and the inhabitants of the other lake towns.[4] Fray Luís arrived in Guatemala with Bartolomé de las Casas, Pedro de Angulo, and Rodrigo de Ladrada in 1535.[5] They supported the

Indians against the *encomenderos,* and Las Casas was instrumental in gaining passage of the New Laws.[6]

Don Juan of Atitlán learned that the Dominicans intended to go on a mission to convert the Indians of Sacapulas, Rabinal, and Verapaz. Several caciques, including don Juan, *principales,* and their vassals accompanied the priests in the pacification and conversion of the Indians of that area. In 1540, don Juan was rewarded by the crown for his part in that effort.[7] Such rewards explain why some of the caciques and *principales* were willing to be converted and participate in such drives for conversion of other Indians. After adopting Catholicism, the lords gained the protection of the priests and could become a part of Spanish society. This allowed them to retain some of the privileges they had enjoyed in pre-Hispanic times and receive concessions from the crown.

According to *The Annals of the Cakchiquels,* religious instruction began in Tecpán Atitlán early in 1542, when Pedro de Angulo and another Dominican, Juan de Torres, arrived and began teaching in the Cakchiquel language. Although the account states that until that time "no one had preached the word of God to us,"[8] as noted above, the caciques and *principales* had previously accompanied Dominicans to Verapaz, and Rodrigo de Ladrada had preached in Tecpán Atitlán as well. By 1542, however, instruction was probably more regularized in both Atitlán and Tecpán Atitlán and was better remembered (it is also possible that the author or authors of the *Annals* remembered the date incorrectly).

In 1538 the crown had ordered the construction of churches in Indian towns or their suburbs.[9] Owing to the shortage of priests and the lack of funds, the first churches in Guatemala were huts with straw roofs. Such churches probably stood up on top of Chuitinamit and in Santiago Atitlán after congregation in 1547. Construction of a permanent monastery *(convento)* and church required the supervision and commitment of a full-time resident priest, and none lived in the Tzutujil region at the time.

Sometime after the town was moved to the other side of the lake, priests took up residence there. In 1552, Fray Juan de Mansilla wrote in a letter to the crown that he had set aside three houses in Atitlán and Tecpán Atitlán in which the children of the lords and others were to be taught. He had selected priests who knew Indian languages to teach the natives Spanish and to read.[10] Betancor and Arboleda wrote that sometime after the town was congregated the priests ordered that a school was to be established in Atitlán. The schoolchildren were to learn to read, write, sing, and serve at masses and divine offices.[11] The clerics who established the school were Pedro de Betanzos and Francisco de la Parra, who congregated Atitlán and were probably the first religious to reside there.

In the school in Atitlán:

The town children come to learn the Christian doctrine in their native tongue, and to learn to read and write, in all of which the *guardián* [priest in charge] and the religious apply themselves with great diligence. They have chosen and named an Indian who is very well fitted for the purpose and who is a *principal* of the town, to be the teacher of the children. . . . He is paid a salary out of the goods of the community.[12]

By 1550 the Tzutujils were under Franciscan jurisdiction. Congregation was essentially complete, providing the concentrated pool of native labor that was necessary for the construction of a permanent church. The Indians learned Catholic ritual and began serving in the office of the church.

## The Church in the Late Sixteenth Century

The Diocese of Guatemala was divided into *doctrinas*, or parishes, based on the original permanent missions established to Christianize the Indians. The head town of the parish was called the *cabecera de doctrina*, and the local priest resided there with his assistants. Until the mid-seventeenth century such a priest was referred to as a *guardián doctrinero*.[13] Smaller towns within the parish, called *visitas* or *anexos*, had simple churches *(iglesias de visitas)*, unlike the more elaborate churches that were eventually built in the *cabeceras*. In the Tzutujil area the head town of the *corregimiento* was also the *cabecera de doctrina*, and the lake and coastal *sujetos* were *visitas*. The *visitas* were attended to as often as possible, usually by one of the assistant priests.[14]

Little information is available on the practice of the Catholic religion among the Tzutujils before 1570. In 1566 two full-time resident priests, Juan Alonso and Diego Martín, were living in Atitlán, but nothing is known of their administration.

Fray Gonzalo Méndez was elected *guardián* of Atitlán in 1570.[15] Somewhat earlier he and his companion, Fray Diego Ordóñez, had been responsible for congregating the coastal Tzutujil towns. Méndez put together catechisms, dictionaries, and explanations of the Christian doctrine in the Tzutujil language and began construction of a permanent church in Atitlán.[16] In 1571 the lords of Atitlán described it:

In all the land our fathers . . . founded, in no other part is there a church of hewn stone and worked wood covered with straw and a floor of brick and lime. In this work we spent by ourselves a lot of money for all the necessary tools for the work without the *encomenderos* giving us anything to help with the church.

The lords stated that they had received for the church only four hundred pesos altogether since the earliest times of Alvarado and Pedro de Cueto, though the crown had contributed a bell and a chalice.[17] That the *encomenderos* did not contribute much money helps explain why construction was slow. Fray Bernardino Pérez, writing in 1574, said that the Franciscans had begun building monasteries and churches in the Indian towns but needed more funds and more priests. He said that Sancho de Barahona, the *encomendero* of Atitlán, had not given any money to the church for years.[18]

By 1582 the church of Atitlán was finally finished, and President García de Valverde had the monastery enlarged, adding a room and several classrooms.[19] The monastery was behind and at the side of the church, as shown in the map of Atitlán of 1585 (fig. 10). Soon afterward Fray Alonso Ponce described the church: "The monastery is fair, . . . with its cloister high and low, dormitories, cells, and church. It is very old, all made of stone and clay with some lime."[20] By 1585, Fray Pedro de Arboleda was *guardián* of Atitlán, and four other priests also resided there:

[Atitlán] is the *cabecera de la doctrina* of the natives because in it is founded a monastery . . . of the religious friars of the order of St. Francis. . . . They also have in their charge the other small towns which are subject to this *cabecera* and which are small and are located down the southern coast at four, five, and six leagues.[21]

In 1630, Fray Bernardino Cobo was impressed by the church of Atitlán and described it as "very sumptuous, with a stone tower."[22]

It was always somewhat difficult for the priests living in the *cabeceras* to journey to the *visitas*. Betanzos and de la Parra actually moved the inhabitants of Chiya' because it was hard to reach their location.[23] Sixteenth-century writers, such as Ponce[24] and Estrada,[25] testified to the bad roads and hardships endured in traveling to the coastal *visitas*, particularly during the rainy season. In Ponce's time two priests were living in San Bartolomé and also had San Andrés and two or three others in their charge because these *visitas* were so far from Atitlán.[26] Around 1590, San Bartolomé became an independent *cabecera de doctrina*, with San Andrés, San Francisco, and Santa Bárbara as *visitas*. San Francisco became a separate *doctrina* in 1596.[27] That did not, however, interfere with the *cabecera-sujeto* relationship, and the coastal *estancias* continued to be under the jurisdiction of Atitlán.[28]

## Exploitation of the Indians by the Church

The church provided the Indians with some protection from excessive tribute payments and other abuses by greedy Spaniards, but it also placed heavy demands on them. Initially the *encomendero* was supposed to pay the stipend of the *doctrina,* provide a church bell, and furnish ornaments. The Indians were to provide labor for building the church. After 1565 the church was to be built with a fourth of the tribute of the *encomendero.*[29] After 1562 the crown supplied the priests with holy oil and wine.[30] As noted above, Sancho de Barahona failed to give his share of money for the church in Atitlán, and the inhabitants had to pay for all the construction materials themselves. This was contrary to royal legislation of 1533 and 1553, which stated that *encomienda* Indians were not obliged to contribute to the construction of the local church other than their labor or to the maintenance of the local priest.[31] In 1587 the Indians of Atitlán lodged a formal complaint against Sancho de Barahona for his failure to pay for the church ornaments, but in the end they paid the 2,125 *tostones* 1 real owed for the items.[32]

Fortunately, the Indians were skillful in construction work and did not need to pay Spaniards to do the carpentry and bricklaying. Gage said that the Indians were as good builders as the Spaniards, adding that "they are much inclined to painting, and most of the pictures and altars of the country towns are their workmanship."[33] Such skills had been developed by the Tzutujils in pre-Hispanic times.[34] The caciques, who were responsible for collecting tribute, were also given the task of supplying labor for the building of the church.[35] In important native settlements the construction of large churches placed additional burdens on the caciques and *principales,* who were constantly being pressed by the Spaniards for labor and tribute while their own people simultaneously resisted the exactions. In smaller towns church construction did not place such a strain on the Indian population.

Pineda blamed the heavy burden of church building for the decline in the Indian population. He said that the work was so laborious that in his time the only church that was completed was the one in Cobán. While the permanent church was being built, the Indians continued to use the one made of wood, clay, and

thatch. Pineda noted that all the churches contained rich ornaments, costly silks and brocades, much worked silver, and crosses
that cost five hundred pesos and more.[36] Pineda was opposed to
the church because he represented crown interests and felt that
the church competed for Indian revenues, but his description of
the wealth of the religious establishment was probably accurate.
In 1574, because of the burden that church construction had placed
upon the Indians, the crown forbade erection of any new monasteries without express royal consent.[37]

Besides church building and furnishing, constant repairs and
maintenance depleted the Indians' resources and time. The earthquakes and fires that plagued the Tzutujil region eventually took
their toll on the churches: in 1683 witnesses testified that the
church of Atitlán needed to be rebuilt because it was no longer
serviceable. The wood had rotted, and the walls were broken in
places. According to the Indians, repeated earthquakes had caused
the church to fall into that state. They asked that one-fourth of
their tribute revenues for four years be allocated to make the
needed repairs. By 1735, they still had not received the money.[38]
The smaller churches in the *visitas* also had to be rebuilt from
time to time, as when lightning struck during the rainy season
and started fires in the towns.[39]

From the earliest times Indians were expected to give gifts to
prelates who arrived on inspection tours. One of the most celebrated visits of the sixteenth century was that of Fray Alonso
Ponce, who passed through the Tzutujil area: "In San Bartolomé
he was received with much celebration and piety because all the
Indians, men and women . . . came out in procession to see him
and receive his benediction, and all of the people are very de-
vout; they offered him a thousand hens, bananas, and colored
zapotes." He received "fish, hens, bananas, nances, and a large
gourd of pinole . . . from the people of San Francisco."[40] Such
gift giving, very similar to the offerings made to the pre-Hispanic
ruler Q'uik'ab when he arrived at the frontiers of the Tzutujil
domain, was another survival of the aboriginal tribute system.

Priests living in Indian settlements were mainly supported by
the Indians. In 1676 a royal order gave official sanction to a
custom that had prevailed for years:

And by being customary . . . that the priests of *doctrinas* are given
service and supplies among all the towns of their *doctrinas*, . . . I order
the *alcaldes* of the said towns to give to the priests of their *doctrinas* a
person who will prepare their food, another who will make tortillas,

and one who will receive wages to bring firewood for the kitchen . . .
and grass for his mule.[41]

Gage described some of the payments of the Pokoman Indians to
their priest:

There . . . is a monthly maintenance in money allowed the priest, and
brought to him by the *alcaldes* . . . and jurats. This he has to write
a receipt for in a book of the town's expenses. This maintenance . . . is
either gathered about the town, or taken out of the tribute which they
pay unto the King, or from a common plot of ground which with the
help of all is sowed and the produce gathered in and sold for that
purpose.[42]

In the early years clerical salaries were paid by the *encomendero*
or by the crown, but the *encomendero* was often in arrears with
his payments. In 1553 the crown ordered that the Indians living in
*encomiendas* were not to be obliged to contribute to the support
of the resident priests.[43] The order indicates that the priests were
supported by the Indians when the *encomendero* failed to do so.
In 1565 a cleric's salary was fixed at 50,000 *maravedies* a year
for each four hundred Indians.[44] If the tithe *(diezmo)* collected
by the town was not enough to cover the salary, the rest was to
be paid by the royal treasury.[45] Aguirre, who was supportive of
the clergy, said that this salary scarcely equaled that of a brick-
layer.[46]

The *diezmo*, a tax of 10 percent on income or commodity increase, was collected from each town.[47] The *diezmo* was usually
divided into four parts. One-fourth went to the bishop, and one-
fourth went to the ecclesiastical chapter *(cabildo eclesiástico)*. The
other two parts were divided into nine portions, called *novenas.*
Seven of the nine portions went for church construction and sustenance of the hospital, and the other two portions *(novenas reales)*
were reserved for the crown.[48] After 1562 the audiencia had charge
of administering the *novenas reales.*[49] Beginning in 1564, the
tribute paid by the Indians of Atitlán was one hundred loads of
cacao, ten loads of which were removed for payment of the
*diezmo.*[50] This was collected despite legislation of 1549 that ordered that only the Spaniards were to pay the *diezmo* of cacao.[51]
Besides the *diezmo*, the Indians had to pay fees *(derechos)* for
almost all the services provided by the church, such as weddings,
funerals, and special masses.[52]

The Indians also brought reales, candles, and fruit to the saints
during mass. Similar offerings have been made to images in San-

tiago Atitlán in recent times.[53] Gage, who wrote with some bitterness against the Catholic church, said that after mass the priest and *mayordomos* took such offerings and then resold the candles to the Indians. He also said that every communicant gave at least one real during mass and that the Indians gave offerings for souls in purgatory and on All Souls' Day.[54] In 1578 priests were prohibited from collecting goods or personal services during mass,[55] but this order appears to have had little effect by Gage's time, at least in the Pokoman area. Such abuses may have occurred from time to time in the Tzutujil area as well, but it seems doubtful that priests were uniformly as mercenary as Gage suggests.

Priests sometimes tried to supplement their incomes by selling goods. They bought items from the Indians at low prices and resold them at higher prices elsewhere. In 1560 they were specifically prohibited from dealing in cacao,[56] and in 1588, from engaging in any commerce.[57] The *guardián* of Atitlán, Gonzalo Méndez, received tortillas, chilis, herbs, and fruit from the Indians of the towns. Vásquez said that while it was scant sustenance he gave some of it away to the children to attract them to the faith.[58] Perhaps the early priests were less exploitative, especially those belonging to the orders, than those who arrived later, after Catholicism had been firmly implanted. The priests probably always received food from the Indians, but by Gage's time the quality of the clergy was not as high as it had been in the sixteenth century, and abuses may have been more common.

In 1577 the crown recommended that the Indians cultivate their lands on festival days with the object of forming community funds *(cajas de comunidad).*[59] *Caja* funds were used for town- and church-related expenses. They also provided funds for paying off sudden exactions from priests, merchants, and local officials.[60] Such supplies of cash seem to have tempted unscrupulous priests from the beginning. Pineda, who was also anticlerical, said that priests forced highland Indians to go to the coast to sell mantas to get money for tribute and for the *caja,*[61] which the priests controlled, but it is not known that this occurred in the Tzutujil highlands. *Caja* funds were used for town fiestas in the early eighteenth century, and the expenditures were probably similar in earlier times.[62] By the late sixteenth century the salary of the schoolteacher was also paid out of *caja* funds.[63]

By the mid-1560s the crown had become concerned about the drop in the Indian population and issued legislation to curb harmful activities of the clergy. Some of the royal orders represented efforts to reduce the power of the priests living in Indian areas. In 1565 the crown ruled that clergy residing in the towns could not have their own jails or stocks in the monasteries for punishment of the Indians and that they could not cut the Indians' hair as punishment.[64] This order aimed at preventing the priests from competing with the civil-justice system. The crown was also concerned about the Indians who were performing jobs for the priests without pay, but primarily because such duties kept them from tribute-generating activities. It was also ordered in 1565 that singing and instrument playing were to be regulated owing to the "harms and vices" of those brought up in the church as musicians.[65] These groups were ordinarily exempt from paying tribute, and after the population decline the crown moved to reduce the number of *reservados.*

It is difficult to evaluate the precise extent of church exploitation in the Tzutujil region, but the drain of church construction and maintenance, *diezmo,* and *caja* expenses must have been considerable. The amount of exploitation by individual priests is not known, but it is clear that opportunities were numerous.

### Indian Church Officials

By 1585 the church was well established among the Tzutujils. It was reported that priests living in Atitlán "say mass, preach the Holy Gospel to the natives in their own tongue, marry [the Indians], baptize them, and administer the other sacraments."[66] They kept a record of marriages and baptisms[67] and instructed Indian church officials in the essentials of the faith. The Indians were reportedly responsive to the instruction:

The natives of this town are intelligent, docile, and favorably inclined to understand and learn all that they are taught. This is particularly true of those connected with the church, such as the singers, who know how to read, write, and sing. They have learned to sing the *canto y organo* [*canto de organo,* or polyphony], are used to officiate at mass, at vespers, and during other divine offices. They know how to play . . . the organ, trumpets, flutes, sackbuts [trombones], oboes [*cheremías*], and other instruments used in church for the service and adoration of the divine cult.[68]

Indian church officials were referred to as *pilhuanes* (from *pilguanejo,* "servant in a convent or monastery").[69] In all towns of more than one hundred tributaries there were two or three *cantores* (singers) and a *sacristán* (sexton) whose duties included caring for the ornaments and sweeping the church.[70] In Mexico the *cantores* often taught Christian doctrine on Sunday and holidays, and Gibson pointed out that the office of *cantor* was a prestigious office and a continuation of the regard accorded to pre-Hispanic groups of noble singers.[71] That may have been true in the Tzutujil area as well. The *Testament Ajpopolajay* refers to a *maestro de capilla* in Santiago Atitlán in 1569,[72] and in recent times in San Pedro this office was the same as first *cantor*.[73]

The *fiscal*, another important Indian church official, assisted the priest and called the people to mass. In towns of more than one hundred Indians there were two *fiscales*, who must be fifty or sixty years old.[74] (Vásquez said that the word *fiscal* was derived from *theopixcal*, which meant "guard or caretaker of the church," and the Indians, pronouncing *p* as *f*, said *"fiscal"* for *"pixcal."*)[75] Gage described the role of the *fiscal* and other Indian officials among the Pokomans:

The *fiscal* has a white staff with a little silver cross on the top to represent the church and shew that he is the priest's clerk and officer. When any case is brought to be examined by the priest, this *fiscal* or clerk executes justice by the priest's order. He must be one that can read and write, and is commonly the master of music. He is bound upon the Lord's Day and other saints' days, to gather to the church before and after service all the young youths and maids, and to teach them the prayers, sacraments, commandments and other points of catechism allowed by the Church of Rome. In the morning he and the other musicians, at the sound of the bell, are bound to come to church to sing and officiate at Mass, which in many towns they perform with organs and other musical instruments. . . . So likewise at evening at five of the clock they are again to resort to the church, when the bell calleth, to sing prayers. . . . This *fiscal* is a great man in the town, and bears more sway than the mayors, jurats, and other officers of justice, and, when the priest so wishes, attends him, goes about his errands, and appoints such as are to wait on him when he rides out of town. Both he and all that belong to the church are exempted from the common weekly service of the Spaniards, and from giving attendance to travellers, and from other officers of justice. But they have to attend with their waits, trumpets, and music, upon any great man or priest that comes to their town, and to make arches with boughs and flowers in the streets for their entertainment.[76]

Gage's description of the functions of the *fiscal* is similar to that given by Vásquez, who described the routine of the Indian church in the late seventeenth century. He referred specifically to towns that, like Atitlán, were under Franciscan jurisdiction:

Every day . . . the bell was rung for Mass, which was either sung or prayed. The *cofradía* officials and *texeles* . . . attended, some with lighted candles in their hands. . . . The organ was played even if the Mass was not sung. Other prayers were said according to the number of priests there were in the monastery. . . . After Mass the church doors are closed, and they pray all the prayers of the Christian doctrine, . . . and they make an exercise with the catechism questions (all in the native language). . . . Every day . . . the [unmarried] girls gather in the church, and for two hours they pray all the doctrine . . . and go over the catechism, two old principal Indians attending [who are] *Teopixcales*. . . . At four vespers are sung every day, and at sunset the young men congregate on the porch of the church and have the same doctrinal exercise until they play Ave María.[77]

In the *visitas* the routine was much the same except that the priest came only once a week or so. The *fiscales* were in charge between visits, and the Indians directed church ritual to a greater degree than did those in the *cabeceras*.

The local priests also had several helpers, such as cooks, gardeners, stable boys, and fishermen, who provided for their tables.[78] Other helpers, called *chajales*, served as the priests' butlers—a post that still exists in Atitlán today.[79] Young boys called *semaneros* ran errands for the priest, and Gage said that they took turns sleeping in the house of the priest.[80] In pre-Hispanic times young boys had resided in houses near the temples and worked in them as servants.[81] Therefore, such service represented a continuance of ancient custom. In recent times in Santiago Atitlán, Indians served as cooks and ran errands for the priests, just as their forebears did in colonial times.

Service in the various church offices provided a means of gaining prestige and status in colonial society. While these offices were ordinarily occupied by members of the upper strata of Indian society, commoners probably filled some of the offices and may have worked their way up to positions of importance. Gaining status and becoming a *principal* were strong motives for serving in the church hierarchy, but since most Indian church officials were already important men in the town, the exemptions from tribute and personal services that went with the positions must be seen as more important reasons for doing so. After 1571 the number of *reservados* was reduced.[82] The most important church officials, however, seem to have maintained their exemption as late as the eighteenth century.[83]

### Native Tzutujil Religion After the Conquest

The Spaniards were horrified by Indian religious beliefs and practices, especially human sacrifice and idolatry. The early priests sought to destroy the native religion as quickly as possible and replace it with Catholicism. During the first two decades after the Conquest they managed to eradicate or drive underground those aspects of the Indian religion that were the most obvious or offensive to them. The power and prestige of the upper strata of the native religious hierarchy were attacked, and many idols were destroyed. Between 1545 and 1550 idols that the priests found in Tecpán Atitlán, Atitlán, and other towns were burned.[84] Gonzalo Méndez publicly burned many idols in the Tzutujil area.[85] Aboriginal worship was not destroyed, but by 1570 remaining practices were carried out secretly.

Méndez suspected that the Indians of Atitlán continued to practice ancient religious rituals covertly. One night he climbed a road leading to the hills and discovered the Indians about to sacrifice a girl. One of the sacrificers was the Ajaw Jun Tijax (Lord One Flint), possibly a descendant of the priest of the aboriginal idol cult. Méndez saved the girl and soundly berated her captors. They promised to end volcano sacrifice,[86] and it is not mentioned again in the literature until the eighteenth century. In 1767, Pedro Cortés y Larraz, archbishop of the Diocese of Guatemala, said that he had heard that the Indians had performed such sacrifices "a few years back." He was not sure that the story was true, however, and it is likely that someone had read the account in Vásquez and passed it on to him.[87]

Native ritual dances continued to be performed after the Conquest in some Tzutujil towns. The dance that caused the most concern to the Spaniards was the *tun*. In 1623 the *tun-teleche* was prohibited in Mazatenango "for being bad and superstitious and reminiscent of the harms and perverse sacrifices with which they in their gentility venerated the demon, resolving to him and worshiping him with sacrifice of men and women which in the said dance they practiced, removing the heart while they were still alive and offering it to the demon." The *tun* was danced in Nagualapa and other coastal towns.[88] Orders prohibiting it seem not to have had much effect; Fuentes y Guzmán reported that the dance called *oxtun* was still being performed in his time,[89] and Cortés y Larraz reported that it was prohibited in Santa Bárbara as late as 1749.[90]

The Indians continued to believe in nagualism in colonial times. Gage reported:

Many are given to witchcraft, and are deluded by the devil to believe that their life dependeth upon the life of such and such a beast (which they take unto them as their familiar spirit) and think that when that beast dieth, they must die. When he is chased, their hearts pant; when he is faint, they are faint.

Because of their belief in nagualism, the Indians regarded the images of the saints as deities accompanied by their naguals. Gage described how they viewed specific saints:

. . . they see some of them painted with beasts—Jerome with a lion, Anthony with an ass, . . . Dominic with a dog, Blas with a hog, Mark with a bull, and John with an eagle—they are more confirmed in their delusions, and think verily those saints were of their opinion, and that those beasts were their familiar spirits, and that they also were transformed into those shapes when they lived, and when they died, their beast died, too.[91]

Estrada also mentioned the existence of nagualism in Suchitepéquez in 1579.[92] In 1684 an order was issued to the priests in San Pedro to "remove from the images of San Miguel and the other saints, the figures of the devil and of the animals that they have at their feet."[93]

Owing to the scarcity of Catholic priests, the rural highland area was still basically pagan as late as the latter part of the sixteenth century. Indeed, images of Catholic saints were regarded as a pantheon of anthropomorphic deities by the Indians throughout New Spain.[94] After the Conquest the Christian saints were not substituted; instead both concepts continued to exist as two manifestations of the same power.[95] The fact that the Spanish religious orders taught a primitive form of Catholicism to the natives of the New World facilitated the continuation of paganism beneath a façade of Christianity. Only the essentials of the Catholic faith were taught by the early priests to a generally uncomprehending Indian population, and even by the 1630s Gage believed that Indian Catholicism was mostly "sights, shows, and formalities," lacking true substance.[96] The Indians initially accepted the exterior forms of the simplified Catholicism but later incorporated Catholic beliefs and structures that were at times compatible with pre-Hispanic structures and at others in contradiction to them. As is true with many other facets of the Spanish domination, the Tzutujils attempted to cope with the incongruities as best they could.

One problem in the early phase of missionization was the language barrier, and that situation did not change until the priests mastered the native languages. Another problem was the scarcity of priests and their frequent moves; they did not stay in one place for very long. New teachings were often confused by the Indians or forgotten as soon as the priests left. When images of the Catholic saints were installed in Indian shrines in place of the native idols, old rituals and beliefs sometimes became associated with the new images after the clerics moved on. At times churches were erected on top of ancient native temples; it has been reported by contemporary priests that ancient foundations underlie the church in Atitlán. The clergy hoped that pagan beliefs and practices would wither away after a time, but they did not, much to the dismay of the priests.

Many objects and elements of Catholic religious practice, such as the cross, altars, baptism, confession, incense, fasting, celibacy, pilgrimages, visual representations of sacrifice, and the ceremonial consumption of wine, had parallels in aboriginal highland religion. In some instances the Indians made use of these parallels and merely exchanged one set of terms for another, continuing ancient beliefs as before. Gage said: ". . . they yield unto the Popish religion, especially to the worshipping of saints' images, because they look upon them as much like unto their forefathers' idols."[97] The result was an amalgam in which Jesus Christ and the saints were gradually intertwined with ancient Maya deities.

## Hermandades *and* Cofradías

The *cofradía* system of religious brotherhoods was instituted in many Indian towns during the sixteenth century help implement the Catholic faith.[98] The *cofradía* with its hierarchy of officers, image of the patron saint, house, and ritual activity was similar to the *chinamit* structure of pre-Hispanic times. During the seventeenth century the *cofradía,* along with the cabildo, emerged as a fundamental vehicle for the ongoing process of confrontation and adjustment of native and Spanish culture. The Indians showed great enthusiasm for the *cofradías,* and they rapidly proliferated throughout Guatemala. Official *cofradías* were sanctioned by the church, but other, unofficial ones, called *hermandades,* were formed without the approval of church authorities.[99] The origin of the *hermandades* can be traced back to early sodalities, which were responsible for Indian *barrio* fiestas, or *guachibales,* as they were known in colonial times.[100] The words *guachibal* and *hermandad* came to be used interchangeably.

The earliest Indian *cofradías* were founded in Guatemala after the mid-sixteenth century, when there were more priests in the country and the congregations were completed. The first *cofradía* for Spaniards in Guatemala, Santa Veracruz, was founded in 1533 by Bishop Marroquín, who was its first *cofrade,* or brother.[101] This *cofradía* was established in the capital. In 1552, Fray Juan

Mansilla gave license to the Brothers of the Cofradía of Santa
Veracruz so that they could have a chapel in the Church of San
Francisco in that city. By 1559 another *cofradía*, Nuestra Señora
del Rosario, had been founded in the capital.[102] The Indians worshiped separately from the Spaniards and had separate *cofradías*.[103]
Even today in Atitlán the Indians have separate *cofradías* from
those of the *ladinos*.

It is not known when the first sodalities were established in the
Tzutujil area. A *cofradía* had been established in Cobán by 1569.[104]
In 1584, *The Annals of the Cakchiquels* made reference to what
may have been a *cofradía* office, that of *mayordomo*,[105] which,
however, was a civil office as well. The *mayordomo* of the *cofradía*
was responsible for the income and properties of the brotherhood.
The earliest documented reference to *cofradías* in the Tzutujil area
is to the establishment of the Cofradía Concepción in San Pedro
on January 7, 1613.[106]

Cortés y Larraz speculated about the history of the establishment of *cofradías* in Indian towns. He blamed the carelessness
of the Indians and the local priests for the loss of early *cofradía*
books. He said that some of the *guachibales* were founded by
the Indians but that most were set up by the early priests. He
believed that the *cofradías* and *hermandades* had their origins
in early post-Conquest years, probably beginning around the time
that the *doctrinas* were established or soon afterward.[107] In any
case, during the seventeenth century there was a great rise in the
popularity of the *cofradías*. Legally authorized *cofradías* were established in the *sujetos* as well as in the *cabeceras*.

Part of the reason for the great success of the *cofradías* was
that they facilitated the working out of contradictions and encouraged the homogenization of native and Spanish beliefs and
practices. The main function of all the brotherhoods, official and
unofficial, was to celebrate the fiestas of the various patron saints:

As for *Guachivales* or *hermandades*, those are no different from *cofradías*
because the main activity is to celebrate the day of the saint of their
devotion which is kept in the house of an Indian. . . . He and others
who give alms gather there, and he feeds them and serves drinks. . . .
on the whole they do not have as much expense as *cofradías*, though it
depends on the priests.[108]

This description of *hermandad* functions is from the eighteenth
century, but the only change from earlier times was that by the
later period the patron saint was kept in the *cofradía* house instead
of the church. It is not clear just when the saints were removed

to the *cofradía* houses. Gage stated that they were kept inside the church in the 1630s, and Cobo said that he saw saints' effigies on litters inside the church in Atitlán in 1630.[109] It appears that some images remained in the church, and today in Atitlán some are in the church and some in the *cofradía* houses. The *cofradía* members are also responsible for the care of the corresponding altar in the church.[110] This is probably an example of an attempt to evolve a satisfactory solution to native and Spanish desires respecting the residence of the images. The Indians wished to have them in the *cofradía* houses, and the priests preferred them in the churches. In Atitlán both seem to have got their way.

Fuentes y Guzmán said that the Indians used various kinds of feathers to decorate the litters *(andas)* used in their *guachibales* and that there was no day of the year without a *guachibal* celebration involving a procession, sermon, and mass. The processions were similar to ancient ones in which idols were carried through the towns on specified celebration days. Inside the *guachibal* house were decorations, incense, and flowers, and the image of the saint was placed there. Therefore, the images seem to have been taken into the *cofradía* houses by the late seventeenth century in the Quiché area, but it is not clear whether some of them remained there permanently. Fuentes y Guzmán said that such celebrations took place all over Guatemala.[111] Except for the feathered litters, this description fits *cofradía* celebrations held in Tzutujil towns today.

Besides celebrating the fiesta of their patron saint, the *cofrades* attended mass daily, visited the sick, and celebrated a monthly mass for living and dead members.[112] Fuentes y Guzmán described the *cofradía* routine in Tecpán Guatemala: "It is a custom that every day the devotees of the *cofradías* go forth to visit all the houses of the place, dividing this work among themselves by *calpules*, where they ask if there is anyone who is sick, and if so, they enter to visit him and ask him if he wants and needs to receive the sacraments."[113] Such customs were probably widespread throughout the Quiché area.

*Cofradía* officers usually included the head *mayordomo,* or *alcalde,* lesser officials, who were also called *alcaldes* or *mayordomos,* and a scribe, who kept the *cofradía* books under the supervision of the priest.[114] Women assistants, called *tijxeles* in Tzutujil,[115] usually wives of officials, helped in such tasks as preparing food for the celebrations and washing the clothes of the saints. The election of new officers took place on the saint's day or the day after.[116] This organization characterizes *cofradías* of lake towns today.[117]

The members paid dues to defray *cofradía* expenses and to pay the priest for services performed. Thomas Gage reported that the owner of a saint in the Pokoman area held a feast on the saint's day and presented the priest with money, "sometimes two or three, sometimes four or five, crowns for his Mass and sermon, besides a turkey and three or four fowls, with as much cacao as will serve to make him chocolate for . . . eight days following."[118] It is not known whether this practice was widespread. Gage also reported that "every company or sodality of the saints or of the Virgin has two or three *mayordomos* who collect from the town alms for the maintaining of the sodality. They also gather eggs about the town for the priest every week, and give him an account of their gatherings, and allow him every month, or fortnight, two crowns for a Mass to be sung to the saint."[119] How common such forms of payment were is not known.

*Cofradía* funds were kept locked in a chest and, along with municipal funds, provided revenue for group functions.[120] Each *cofradía* and *hermandad* kept books, in which were recorded income and expenditures for such items as candles, incense, and fees. In Atitlán income came from membership dues, contributions *(limosnas)*, and fees charged for certain services.[121]

The oldest extant *cofradía* book thus far discovered for Santiago Atitlán is that of San Juan Bautista, which begins in 1712 and ends around 1885. An earlier document contains some information on the coastal *sujetos* and their *cofradías* in 1683.[122] In 1683–84 the bishop of Guatemala conducted a *visita* to the highlands and coast. He listed the names of the *cofradías* of each town and summarized the contents of their books—mainly lists of the officers elected annually, expenses, debts, and goods owned by the *cofradía*. The books were periodically reviewed by the bishop.

Aguirre listed *cofradía* books dating from the middle and late seventeenth century for San Pedro, San Juan, San Pablo, Santa Clara, and Visitación, whose existence was recorded in 1683 by the bishop. Aguirre noted that only fragments of one of these books, from the Cofradía Concepción of San Pablo, has survived until modern times. It is still kept in San Pablo. He found several books from the eighteenth century in San Pedro.[123]

The *cofradía* soon became a focal point of Indian life. It allowed both maintenance of continuity with the aboriginal past and incorporation of some of the fundamentals of the Spanish Catholic tradition. Because it was mainly an Indian-documented institution with little or no outside participation or interference, the *cofradía* gradually became shaped in form and function primarily along native lines.

In pre-Hispanic times general ritual had been a state concern, and the ceremonies involved feasting, dancing, and human sacrifice, especially sacrifice of noble captives taken in war. Religious celebrations were also held at the local level; each *chinamit* had its own communal buildings, temples, gods, and ceremonies.[124] After the Conquest state-level religion was abolished, but the lineage structure and the local religious personnel remained. The *cofradía* system, with its officers, *cofradía* house, and cult devoted to the images of the saints, was very similar to the aboriginal religious structure. Lineage leaders "adopted" the saints and sponsored religious ceremonies similar to those of past times.[125] In some instances *chinamit, cofradía,* and ward may have been coterminous in Indian towns.[126] Unfortunately, there is no evidence supporting this arrangement among the Tzutujils, and it is not possible to determine whether there was one ward and *cofradía* for each former *chinamit* in Tzutujil settlements. In Santiago Atitlán there are a few *cofradías* that are privately owned and transmitted in family lines. These *cofradías* honor native deities and may represent remnants of the aboriginal ancestor idol cults, as well as the lineage organization of such cults.[127]

Fuentes y Guzmán compared the *cofradía* rituals of his time with those of aboriginal days: "They . . . celebrate today the festivals of the saints which they call *Guachibales,* dancing around . . . adorned with the same dress that they used in that . . . time, but their songs are reduced to the praise of the saints, referring to and representing their miraculous histories composed by their ministers."[128] Dancing was regarded as a religious act in aboriginal times, and the Indians continued to follow such pre-Hispanic customs as confession and sexual abstinence before dancing. Today the *nabeysil,* an official of the Cofradía San Juan, must remain unmarried and celibate as long as he holds office.[129] He dances with the sacred bundle of San Martín. The officials of the Cofradía Santa Cruz dance with Maximón, and this may be a continuation of ancient custom.[130]

Pre-Hispanic dances encountered their equivalent in *autos sacramentales* as well as in new dances introduced by the Spaniards, such as "Baile de moros y cristianos" ("Dance of the Moors and Christians"), "Baile del torito" ("Dance of the Little Bull"), and "Baile de los viente-cuatro diablos" ("Dance of the Twenty-four

Devils"). Native dances continued too and were performed by *cofradía* members. Such dances as "Palo Volador" ("Flying Stick"), "Venado" ("Deer"), and "Culebra" ('Snake") have persisted in the highlands to modern times.[131]

The Indians drank *chicha*, or maize beer, during pre-Hispanic ceremonies, and heavy ritual drinking continued after the Conquest. As in aboriginal times, drinking, like dancing, was viewed as a religious act that would be pleasing to the gods, who would then remember the group.[132] Post-Conquest ceremonies resembled aboriginal ones and had a similar format.

During the seventeenth century concerned clergy often complained about prolonged *cofradía* celebrations, called *zarabandas,* in which the Indians indulged in drunken orgies for several days and did not work. The *cofradía* celebrations were described by observers during this period and later:

In leaving the church they gather in the house of the *mayordomo*, where there is food and drink, . . . which they eat and drink until they are drunk. They have music and dancing . . . in which they spend the whole day and night in heavy excess. To this, and nothing else, are the fiestas of the Indians reduced. . . . Although they appear so poor and miserable, for their own ideas, orgies and caprices, they spend money generously and abundantly. I do not know where they get it. . . . Being so ancient and sought after, [the *cofradías*], although without any idea of Christianity, cannot be suppressed, reformed, or changed in any manner because this would stir up the Indians who would abandon their towns. . . . Having removed them in the *alcaldía* of Sololá (according to an account of the *Cura* of that *parroquia*), the Indians did not even want their children baptized until they were reinstituted.[133]

On March 20, 1637, an order was sent out by the audiencia to suppress illegal *cofradías* in an effort to reduce their number and the harm they were bringing to the natives:

In view of the growing number of *cofradías* in the Indian towns and of the excesses committed during dances and feasts celebrated during the day of the patron saint, it is ordered in the confines of the Audiencia . . . that all *cofradías* not authorized by the bishops be suppressed . . . for the offenses which are made against God our Lord with drunkenness and feasts which are celebrated the day and night of the fiesta when it is customary for many drunken Indians to gather together in the house of the Indian *mayordomo* of the *cofradía*, . . . where with dances and fiestas they recall their antiquity and idolatry in scandalous form which devalues their devotion before the images, . . . and without more authority than their own [the *principales*] found and institute . . . *cofradías* and . . . make the poor Indians pay, taking their hens away

from them . . . so that they are unable to pay tribute to their *encomenderos.*
. . . it is an excess so great that in most of the towns where there are
no more than one hundred Indians there are ten or twelve *cofradías*
so that all year long they are occupied and impeded from working in
their fields.[134]

It is clear from these descriptions that the process of religious
inculcation did not always proceed smoothly. The priests were
angered and disgusted by behavior in the *cofradías,* and many Indians were determined to conduct religious ceremonies according
to their own system of values. As is presently true in Santiago
Atitlán, some Indians, especially those serving in the church, may
also have been opposed to *cofradía* excesses. By Vásquez's time
there were ten *cofradías* in Atitlán, two in Tolimán, eleven in
the Doctrina of San Pedro, seven in the Doctrina of San Bartolomé,
and twelve in the Doctrina of San Francisco.[135] These numbers
were excessive, given the small populations of those towns reported by Vásquez (see tables 4 to 6).

Individual and group private rituals also continued after the
Conquest and into modern times. The pre-Hispanic calendar,
divining rituals, offerings at ancient shrines in the hills and at
the crossroads, witchcraft, and curing were mentioned by several
writers.[136] Such references were numerous enough to demonstrate
the continued importance of aboriginal religious practices and
beliefs in the life of the colonial Indians. Today diviners, witches,
and curers sometimes operate through the *cofradía* system, but
often they do not. In pre-Hispanic times some of these practitioners
had been members of the established religious hierarchy, while
others may have functioned autonomously.[137] Cortés y Larraz com-
mented that it was difficult to discover exactly what went on in
the privacy of Indian homes.[138]

After the Conquest an entirely new religious structure was imposed on the Tzutujil Indians. The Indians accepted some elements
of the Catholic faith but retained many aspects of aboriginal religion. The more objectionable the practices were in Spanish eyes,
the more hidden they became. There were contradictions as well
as compatibilities as a result of the introduction of Catholicism.
The Tzutujils developed a strategy for coping with this situation,
which saw some individuals casting their lot with the official church,
others becoming involved with the *cofradías,* and perhaps others
performing rituals alone. For some, the three roles were probably
not mutually exclusive, and they engaged in more than one dimen-
sion of religious behavior.

Early priests in the Tzutujil area performed mass baptisms and converted a few nobles to the Catholic faith. Don Juan, the cacique of Atitlán, helped the clerics convert Indians in other areas. After congregation, schools were established in Atitlán, and work was begun on a permanent church. With the establishment of more formal church authority, Atitlán became *cabecera* of the *doctrina*, and the *sujetos* became *visitas*. Priests resided in Atitlán by 1552, and the church was completed in 1582.

Church building and maintenance, along with celebrations and gifts to visiting prelates, placed a heavy burden on the Indians of Atitlán. The local priests were supported by the Indians, who also paid a tithe to the church. There were many opportunities for unscrupulous priests to take advantage of their native charges, but it is not known how much of this occurred in the Tzutujil region. Priests also provided some measure of protection to the Indians from *encomenderos* and other Spanish officials. Indians served in the church hierarchy, for such offices as *fiscal* and *sacristán* conferred much prestige and exemption from paying tribute.

Although some practices of the aboriginal religious system were driven underground or eradicated by the Spaniards, many of them remained during the sixteenth and seventeenth centuries. Human sacrifice and the worshiping of pagan idols were practiced covertly, but the *tun*, a dance involving human sacrifice, continued to be performed publicly in the seventeenth century in some coastal towns. Ancient beliefs, such as nagualism and witchcraft, also continued, as did idol worship and native-style worship of saints' effigies.

The *cofradía* was the focal institution of native religious life during the sixteenth and early seventeenth centuries. The system of religious brotherhoods was tolerated and even encouraged by many priests because it provided financial support for the church and extra income for local clergy. This helps account for their proliferation. *Cofradías*, though a burden on the Indian economy, were enthusiastically accepted by many Indians.

This popularity cannot be explained merely on the basis of the usefulness of the *cofradías* to the church. The brotherhoods allowed the Indians to retain some aspects of native customs, beliefs, and practices and some privacy from the Spanish institutions that otherwise controlled their existence. As Indians found that participation as equals in the major institutions of colonial society was closed to them, they were forced to actualize their values and ideals in the local arena. The two main channels were the cabildo and the *cofradía*. The similarity of the *cofradía* to the pre-Hispanic *chinamit* structure facilitated the Indians' adaptation.

Fig. 14. *The curate of Atitlán, 1768. 1: Atitlán; 2: Tolimán. From AGI mapas y planos, Guatemala 183. Años 1768-70; Cortés y Larraz.*

Fig. 15. *The curates of San Pedro, Sololá, Panajachel, and Atitlán, 1768. From AGI mapas y planos, Guatemala 157. Años 1768-70; Cortés y Larraz. 1: San Pedro; 2: San Juan; 3: San Pablo; 4: San Marcos; 5: Santa Clara; 6: Visitación; 7: Sololá; 8: San Jorge; 9: Santa Cruz; 10:*

San José Chacayá; 11: Santa Lucía Utatlán; 12: Argueta; 13: Panajachel; 14: San Andrés; 15: Concepción; 16: San Antonio Palopó; 17: Santa Catarina Palopó; 18: Tzukún; 19: Chuacorral; 20: Godínez; 21: Atitlán; 22: Tolimán.

The *cofradía* became a focus of ritual activity that followed the Catholic ceremonial calendar but preserved the ancient religion. Fasting, ritual purification, abstinence from sexual relations, incense burning, drinking, and dancing characterized aboriginal general religious celebrations, as well as those of the *cofradías.* Burning candles and incense and giving gifts to the saints came to replace blood sacrifice.

In general, wherever Indians were allowed a certain amount of freedom from Spanish control, aboriginal religious practices proved to be one of the most enduring aspects of the former native way of life. Many of these practices are still important in the Tzutujil region today.

## CHAPTER 17

# Tzutujil Acculturation

Contact between the Tzutujil Mayas and the Spaniards initiated a process of acculturation involving two very distinct cultures that had no previous knowledge of each other. The Spanish culture was the dominant one, and Part Two of this book has focused on the changes that occurred in the subordinate Indian society. Important changes also took place among the conquerors, however, as Foster has demonstrated.[1]

Acculturation resulted from continuous interaction between the dominant Spaniards and the subjugated Tzutujils and was not merely a transfer of traits from one culture to another. The Spaniards rejected some Tzutujil cultural practices, such as warfare, idolatry, and human sacrifice. These patterns of behavior died out, were practiced in secret, or were transformed into more acceptable practices, such as land litigation and worship of the saints. The Indians, of course, rejected or resisted many Spanish cultural impositions.

The acculturation process proceeded with many confrontations between the two cultures. Indians accepted, at least publicly, what they felt they had to accept, but individuals and groups must have constantly tried to form satisfactory accommodations of opposing cultural beliefs, practices, and world-views. That could sometimes be done by maintaining the exterior form of any behavior favored by the Spaniards. At other times the Indians blatantly practiced native customs until prevented from doing so. Such behavior worked well in areas like the western highlands that had few Spanish inhabitants by the beginning of the seventeenth century.

Even when Spanish patterns were adopted, whether grudgingly or enthusiastically, the intent behind them was often transformed or lost. The Spaniards did not intend that the *cofradías* should be the means of what many of them perceived to be drunken orgies. They also attempted to prevent worship of animal effigies associated with certain saints. The Spanish were highly successful in bending the native economy to their will, but the Indians were more capable of resistance when it came to their social and religious beliefs and customs.

A few studies have attempted to identify stages of acculturation.[2] The models presented encompass a long time span, however, and do not clearly distinguish the microlevels of acculturation that occurred in various local areas. In this book I have presented the acting out of acculturation in a local arena, and it may be useful, with other such studies, to illuminate the general patterns of this process. In the following pages a summary of Tzutujil acculturation is presented. In this analysis I have found Beals's model most useful.[3] I have made some modifications of his general categories to achieve a better fit of the Tzutujil situation and have assigned dates to them.

Tedlock points out that the categories used by Beals and others present static, nonprocessual schemes which treat acculturation as diagnostic traits that may be present or absent during particular episodes of history.[4] Beals's scheme is used here as a framework for discussing major changes that occurred in Tzutujil life from 1524 to around 1630. Many developments that began in one period continued on into succeeding ones, and in some instances are still unfolding among the Tzutujils today. Acculturation is seen here as an open-ended process.

Native views regarding ideal behavior probably conflicted with actual behavior in some instances, but it is often difficult to find data on these conflicts in local areas during the sixteenth and seventeenth centuries.[5] Disagreements among individuals about proper conduct must have occurred from time to time in the colonial period. These incompatible points of view gave rise to different patterns of adjustment which remained in force until conditions changed and new configurations were again worked out.

When the Spaniards arrived in Guatemala in 1524, they encountered highly civilized and sophisticated native cultures. The Quichean groups were the most advanced but were not as wealthy as the peoples of central Mexico and Peru. Their civilization had attained a high degree of cultural and organizational development, and the population was fairly dense, having attained around 50,000 in the Tzutujil highlands alone. The sociopolitical organization was complex, and the area was ruled by dynasties related through marriage and a common cultural inheritance. The lineage system provided the basis of social organization and political offices. Rulers of separate kingdoms led their people in warfare and religion and controlled the upper levels of administration.

Considerable acculturation had taken place in the Guatemala highlands before the arrival of the Spaniards.[6] Several migrating groups appear to have entered the area from the east in Classic and Postclassic times, bringing Mexican cultural patterns to Maya groups. Existing data allow a fairly thorough discussion of Quichean culture for only Late Postclassic times. During that period the Tzutujils were incorporated into the Quiché state and thereby lost some wealth and independence. The Tzutujils, however, do not seem to have been devastated by this conquest by a closely related group with whom they shared common behavioral patterns. Eventually internal problems brought the collapse of the Quiché state, and the Tzutujils regained their independence. Whatever stresses they experienced from Quiché control were not severe enough to cause any serious cultural disintegration, probably because subjugated highland groups were allowed quite a bit of autonomy, and tribute demands were not excessive.

*Period 1: Contact and Consolidation, 1524-47*

At first, contact with the Spaniards was not destructive or psychologically traumatic to the highland Mayas. Cortés was regarded as a great leader from a powerful kingdom beyond the sea, and in traditional fashion the Tzutujils sought his judgment in a dispute. When warfare between the Spaniards and Indians began in Guatemala at the beginning of 1524, the Indians initially viewed the intruders as potential allies. In its earliest phase the Quichés, Cakchiquels, and Tzutujils saw the Conquest as a continuation of the pre-Hispanic political situation. Of course, the superior Spanish military strategy and technology soon led to the defeat of the highland Indians.

Even defeat, however, did not immediately signal profound changes in native life. The conquerors demanded tribute, but that was customary in the highlands, and the Spaniards kept the native organization intact. The most important *encomiendas* in Guatemala were those in the Quichean area owing to the sophisticated structure of pre-Hispanic society. The Spaniards continued to use this structure to draw off tribute. The lineage heads were responsible for tribute collection, just as they had been before the Conquest. They delivered the tribute to the ruler or cacique, who sent it to the *encomendero.* The Tzutujil lords kept their lands, and retainers continued to be responsible for cultivating cacao.

The owners, however, reaped less profit from their produce, since most of it was taken by the Spaniards as tribute. The situation must have been similar to the period of Quiché dominance, when the Tzutujils sent tribute to K'umarcaaj—except that the Spaniards took more. As far as the common Indians were concerned, the *encomendero*, like the old lords, was remote. Life was not much different for those farming milpas or tending cacao groves.

The Indians delivered most of the same tribute items that they had offered before the Conquest. The important change was in the excessive amounts demanded by the conquerors, for the *encomiendas* were not closely regulated in the early period. The *encomenderos* asked for tribute more frequently than the former lords had; took all the gold, silver, and precious gems the Indians owned; and thereby destroyed native crafts that had utilized those items. The nobles were also forced to increase the amount of tribute to be able to keep some for themselves. These demands added to the commoners' burden, and this was a period of increased stress on the Indian population.

Labor service under the Spaniards was more severe than it had been in previous times. Slaves were used in mining, construction, and farming, and they had no rights as they had had in aboriginal times. Many formerly free persons became slaves, especially those captured in warfare. Some of these captives were nobles. *Encomienda* Indians who were not slaves served the *encomendero* much as they had their former lords, except that the work was harder.

Community markets continued to concentrate on foodstuffs and simple crafts, but even local buying and selling seems to have suffered some disruption until 1536, when the roads were safe again. Community specialization was still important, but some large Indian markets, such as those at Iximché and K'umarcaaj, ceased to exist, and possibly some local markets disappeared as well. The Tzutujil area was not as seriously affected as those of the Quichés and the Cakchiquels, and the market at Chiya' maintained its role in the highland-lowland trade.

After the fighting ceased, few of the Indians had direct contact with Spaniards other than the wandering priests who preached to them and tried to convert them. The cacique did business with the *encomenderos*. Other than the exorbitant amount of tribute and superficial mass baptisms, for a time Tzutujil life went on much as before. Some nobles, like don Juan of Atitlán, began to adopt Spanish customs in an effort to maintain their privileges of rank. They were exempt from paying tribute, and quite early the basic social distinction in post-Conquest, as in aboriginal, Indian society was that between those who paid tribute and those who did not pay it. Incorporation of some of the native nobility into Spanish society was a key factor in Indian acceptance of Spanish rule.

In general, there was little acculturation in the immediate post-Conquest period. Priests were few and usually did not know the Indian languages well enough to advance Catholicism effectively. Most other Spaniards lived in the capital and rarely if ever visited remote highland towns. While some of the Indian nobles tried to adopt Spanish ways and gain entrance into the conquering society, the vast majority of the natives had little direct contact with non-Indians. The common Indians suffered the most—from excessive tribute demands, harsh labor service, and the expansion of slavery.

By 1547 the Tzutujils had begun adjusting to the Spanish social system, although the process was to intensify in the succeeding period. During the early years after the Conquest adjustment to Spanish rule was not unlike that which occurred in response to the earlier Quiché domination, the major difference being the excessive amount of tribute and labor service demanded by the Spaniards.

*Period 2: The First Colonial Indian Period: The Establishment of Spanish Institutions, 1547–82*

After the establishment of the audiencia, the *corregimiento*, and the congregations, the stage was set for a more comprehensive adaptation of native life to European institutions. The first Colonial Indian Period was one of intense and, in part, directed acceptance of Spanish culture. The *corregidor*, his family, and the several priests who resided permanently in the newly established *cabecera* of Atitlán were able to exercise a greater amount of control and influence over the day-to-day lives of the Indians. The Tzutujils were forcibly removed from their ancient homes, the idol cults were attacked and destroyed or driven underground, and population decline accelerated.

Spanish interference altered the Tzutujils' settlement pattern. In general, it became more compact, and the Indians became less isolated. Lowland towns were more informally arranged than were highland ones, but the Spaniards designed the *cabeceras* according to a standard plan. Many *tinamit*, including Chiya', were abandoned, and some less important pre-Hispanic centers were augmented. Congregated towns usually had hispanicized names. The

Spanish town plan was successfully implemented, at least in the
central portion of Indian towns, because it was not a drastic alteration of the native settlement pattern. The central plaza remained,
with important buildings around it and a church in place of the
aboriginal temple. Despite the similarities to the native settlement
pattern, during the sixteenth and early seventeenth centuries some
of the Indians resisted congregation and returned to their old
homes. Congregation aided acculturation but also proved harmful
in that it accelerated the decline of the native population. Congregation was not new to the highland peoples—it had also been an
aboriginal method of holding frontier areas—but it was probably
not always successful in pre-Columbian times either.

In post-Conquest times jurisdictional disputes represented a continuation of aboriginal native land claims, and the Tzutujils used
congregation to settle people in San Juan and Visitación to prevent
encroachment by the Quichés. Claims for land were often based
upon pre-Hispanic *títulos,* and the Spaniards tended to respect
aboriginal political units. Some Tzutujil territory was lost, especially in the lowlands, where more Spaniards settled.

Tribute became more regularized but remained heavy, and the
assessments were not revised often enough to accord with the
population drop. Tribute, church building, and extortion by Spanish officials and visiting priests fell on a declining number of tributaries, though the Tzutujil area did not lose as much population
during this period as did some other areas. The nobles became
impoverished, especially after López de Cerrato freed the slaves,
and they found it harder to keep excess tribute for themselves.
Population decline and the *encomienda* proved to be the major
factors in destroying social distinctions in Indian society.

To gain more tribute, the Spaniards sometimes resorted to drastic means to place more Indians on the tribute rolls. They encouraged them to marry at very young ages, levied tribute on Indians
who had died, and included on the rolls those who could not prove
direct descent from aboriginal noble lineages.

The Spaniards also set up new political structures. They instituted the *corregimiento,* which roughly encompassed the pre-Hispanic Tzutujil kingdom, and the cabildo to supervise town government. The cabildo was a successful means of administering local
Indian government because it was similar to the pre-Hispanic
council and allowed some native political control. Spanish patterns of local government proved to be fairly consistent with native
ones. The nobles tended to dominate the offices of the cabildo.
The Spaniards also gave the Tzutujil moiety equality with the

Ajtz'iquinajay moiety, a position it had been struggling to achieve since Late Postclassic times.

In some ways the Spanish philosophy of Indian rule served as a buffer to acculturation, based as it was upon the concept of separate populations. Spaniards were not supposed to reside in Indian towns or to stay in them for any length of time. The only exceptions were the *corregidores* and the priests. This policy worked fairly well in the remote highlands but was unworkable in the coastal cacao region. There intinerant traders sold their wares and cheated the Indians. Population decline was rapid, and parts of the area became more Spanish than Indian. San Antonio Suchitepéquez became a Spanish town, and the lowlanders in the Tzutujil dependencies did not even have the protection of a permanent resident priest until the turn of the century. Abuses and constant contact with unscrupulous petty traders took a heavy toll on the lowland Indian communities.

Highland Indians who went to the coast to trade were also subject to increased contact with Spaniards. Some of the Indians became traders and prospered, while others suffered. The pre-Hispanic professional traders were replaced by the more humble class of Spaniards, but the Tzutujils continued to act as petty merchants in the highland-lowland trade. This period saw the beginning of cabildo regulation of local markets, the introduction of some Spanish weights and measures, and increased use of coins as a medium of exchange. New crops introduced by the Spaniards were sold in the markets, and the Indians adopted European agricultural implements that made farming a little easier.

With the decline of native warfare, political alliances became less important, and dynastic marriages ceased. The end of warfare was a very significant change for all the highland peoples. It had been the most important factor in a noble's life in pre-Hispanic times and the major means of social advancement. Individuals were forced to actualize their desires for status in the town framework after the Conquest, when there was less power attached to offices than there had been in former days.

The lineage, *chinamit,* and moiety systems remained after the Conquest, but modifications occurred as several lineages combined owing to the reduction in population. Some formerly important noble houses may have become weak or disappeared, allowing others to gain in status and prestige. It is not clear how closely the post-Hispanic *calpules* adhered to aboriginal *chinamit,* but the continuation of these groups represented an attempt by the natives to maintain a basic feature of pre-Conquest social organization. The profound changes in lineage rankings that must have accompanied the population loss from Late Postclassic times was a significant factor in leveling the old noble class. Nevertheless, the lineage structure itself survived and continued to be important locally in the regulation of marriages and settling disputes.

Church building added to the burdens of the Tzutujils during this period, especially in the *cabecera*. The resident priests saw that the Indians were taught the fundamentals of Catholic doctrine in their own language and founded schools in which to teach them. Some Indians, mainly of the noble class, were effectively integrated into the church hierarchy, but opportunities for advancement through the church were limited, and few Indians really understood Catholicism. Although forced to attend mass, they kept many of their own traditions alive by adopting the externals of the Catholic faith while giving them native meanings. The priests of Guatemala did not attempt to modify Indian religious practices radically as long as the people attended mass and did not openly practice idolatry and human sacrifice.

The Indians made offerings to the saints just as they had to pre-Hispanic idols and associated old rituals with the new images. In many ways the church facilitated Indian acculturation, and there was a remarkable compatibility in certain aspects of the Indian and Spanish religions, particularly since the priests had introduced a simplified Catholicism.

Even the church offices that were open to Indians were similar in some respects to aboriginal religious offices. The *cantores* may have been a continuation of pre-Hispanic noble singers; the *sacristán*, who held office for life, performed tasks similar to those of temple officials, and the *fiscal* may have replaced the high priest. Young boys served in the church just as they had in ancient times, and commoners supported the priest and performed services for him. Important visiting priests and church dignitaries were given gifts and feted much as temple officials must have been welcomed in the past.

Much of the native religion survived despite the efforts of Spanish priests to eliminate paganism. Volcano worship, aboriginal dances, idol-cult priests, diviners, curers, and sacrifices continued in the Tzutujil area after the mid-sixteenth century. Some aspects of native religion were eradicated, however. Sacrifice of war captives, many idols, and much of the pre-Hispanic cult structure had disappeared or been transformed by the late sixteenth century. As Indians came into the church to escape tribute obligations and maintain their status in society, acculturation was hastened. The priests also deliberately designed ceremonies and dances with similarities to pre-Hispanic rituals and thereby attracted participation by the Indians.

In the second phase of post-Conquest acculturation the Tzutujils came under more comprehensive Spanish institutional and cultural influence. Their contacts with Spaniards became more numerous, especially in the lowlands, and increasing numbers of Spaniards settled in the country. More aspects of Spanish culture were forced on the Indians, especially those relating to religion and economics, and Tzutujil culture experienced some changes as individuals tried to adjust to the changes imposed on them. There was some resistance, but in the end Indian society adjusted as best it could. Tighter control by the administrative and ecclesiastical branches was necessary to ensure that the tribute was properly collected and conversion of the Indians was effected. The priests and *corregidores* were sent to live in Indian towns to fulfill these important goals of crown policy.

Although the Indians were congregated to ensure conversion and tribute collection, it was impossible for the priest, his assistants, and the *corregidor* to control all the elements of day-to-day Indian life. Moreover, the crown policy of separate populations allowed the Indians to maintain many aspects of their former way of life, especially those behaviors that the Spaniards did not consider to be harmful. Some ancient beliefs and practices that the Spaniards considered evil also continued, but in secret.

### Period 3: The First Colonial Indian Period: Accommodation and Restructuring, 1582-1630

By the opening of the third period, most of the major innovations in native life had been initiated, and much of the work of building an Indian society acceptable to the Spanish philosophy of separate populations had been completed. Many of the Indians were congregated, and much of the work of town building was finished.

There was a gradual, continuing economic and social decline in the Tzutujil area. The tribute rolls were revised in the 1580s, but the Tzutujil population continued to pay large amounts of tribute throughout the entire period. The value of the *encomienda* of Atitlán was still fairly high in 1630 owing to the piedmont cacao plantations. Ancient methods of grove tending must have continued to some extent, but population decline and abuses of the Indians in Suchitepéquez also took their toll because by the early seventeenth century the value of the *encomienda* had dropped.

By 1630 few nobles were left in Atitlán, though don Bernabé, a direct descendant of the old Ajtzi'iquinajay ruling class, was still the cacique. The decrease in nobles meant that few people in Atitlán could prove direct descent from the pre-Hispanic noble lineages and therefore claim exemption from tribute. The decline of the pre-Hispanic noble lines also tended to increase jurisdictional disputes.

The decline of the noble class, especially after 1590, also affected the cacao plantations. The nobles had owned the groves and had seen that they were properly cultivated. More remote descendants came to inherit these plantations and were subject to the *tributo real*. Many must have tried to avoid such inheritances. In any case, the descendants may not have understood the process of cacao tending and its supervision, and by the turn of the century the forces had been initiated that would eventually lead to the destruction of the primary basis of Tzutujil wealth. In this case the process of accommodation and restructuring failed to produce a successful pattern of maintaining wealth. The failure was also the result of the Spaniards' disinterest in developing new means of plantation maintenance and supervision in face of Indian inability to maintain pre-Hispanic levels of production.

By the beginning of the seventeenth century the *calpul* was the main unit of social organization, and the tributaries of Atitlán were listed under *calpul* heads. This probably represents a synthesis of the pre-Hispanic *chinamit-calpul* structure; in fact, in some documents of the period the term *chinamit* is used in place of *calpul*. Such groups represented a reworking of the aboriginal concept and were composed of pre-Hispanic lineages that had declined in number and had incorporated members of other lineages. Many lineages must have completely died out. The lineage structure survived and carried out some traditional functions, such as the regulation of marriage. It is not known when the *chinamit-calpul* structure was abandoned in the Tzutujil area.

During the late sixteenth century many Tzutujil towns achieved de facto political independence from Atitlán. Atitlán, however, remained the *cabecera* of the *corregimiento* and was the most influential town in the Tzutujil area. In Atitlán it appears that the distinction between the Ajtz'iquinajay and Tzutujil moieties had become less significant by the end of the sixteenth century, probably because many pre-Hispanic noble lines were dying out. New bases of wealth and power also allowed new men to achieve power and finally end this aboriginal conflict.

The most significant development of this period was the rise of the *cofradías*. As the sixteenth century drew to a close, sodalities had probably been established in most Tzutujil towns. They were originally regarded by priests as instruments for aiding in the conversion of the Indians. They were enthusiastically taken up by the natives, probably because of their similarity to the old *chinamit* structure of aboriginal times and because, being separate from Spanish *cofradías*, they provided some privacy for native religious rituals and celebrations. The *cofradía* was a profoundly successful feature of native life because it allowed the Indians to maintain some segments of aboriginal existence and incorporate them into post-Conquest town living. It provided an institution in which the reworking of native values could occur.

*Cofradía* rituals were similar in many ways to pre-Columbian rites. Processions, drinking, dancing, feasts, divination, curing, and the use of the ancient calendar proceeded under *cofradía* auspices along with the worship of the Christian saints. Lineage leaders also functioned within the *cofradías* just as they had within the old *chinamit* structure. They sponsored ceremonies and cared for the images. *Cofradía* rituals provided a satisfactory alternative to human sacrifice and the worship of idols. By this time many of the major ancient priests and idol cults were gone, but the simpler beliefs in nature gods remained, and the Catholic saints took on many characteristics of aboriginal gods.

Tzutujil society experienced a profound reorganization after the mid-sixteenth century and was deeply modified by incorporation into the Spanish governmental and religious systems. The Spaniards ruled the Indians by implanting institutions that were often similar in form to indigenous structures. Pre-Hispanic cultural institutions were not totally destroyed, however, and some of these, such as the modified *chinamit-calpul* continued to operate throughout much of the colonial period.

The Tzutujil acculturation experience involved many psychological and physical hardships. The Indians had to cope with changes in many areas of life which entailed constant reworking and readaptation. At any given time the situation was not entirely satisfactory to some, if not all, individuals, and this discontent provided a constant stimulus to improve the situation as much as possible. Some Tzutujils may have been more resigned than others to uncomfortable situations, but others saw new opportunities in the changes brought about by the Conquest and acted upon them. This process eventually led to a new class structure. By 1630 the Tzutujils had accomplished a comprehensive reorganization of their culture in reaction to the imposition of Spanish culture and institutions. The first one hundred years after the Conquest involved the most arduous and profound changes highland Tzutujil culture had ever had to confront, but the Tzutujils were able to effect necessary changes and maintain their basic cultural identity. Such changes among the Tzutujil and other highland Guatemalan groups have never completely ceased.[7]

# Glossary

*Achiote.* Annatto *(Bixa orellana);* in pre-Hispanic times, a small tree from which a red food coloring or dyestuff was obtained. The coloring was often mixed with cacao to make a chocolate beverage.

*Ajaw.* Pre-Hispanic Tzutujil lord.

*Ajkun.* Native curer and part-time religious specialist.

*Alcabala.* Sales tax.

*Alcalde.* Magistrate and officer of a town council.

*Alcalde mayor.* Spanish official in charge of a province.

*Alcalde pasado.* Former *alcalde.*

*Alcalde ordinario.* One of the grades of the office of *alcalde* established in the seventeenth century.

*Alcaldía mayor.* Province governed by an *alcalde mayor.*

*Aldea.* 1. Political division in the modern *municipio* system. 2. Hamlet.

*Alguacil.* Constable or lower-grade police officer.

*Almud.* Unit of measure; 1 almud equals one-half fanega.

*Amak'.* 1. Territorial group that was also a lineage. 2. Small, permanent town.

*Anexo.* Dependent church or town subject to the main church of a *doctrina,* or parish.

*Arancel.* 1. List of prices to be charged for services performed by the clergy. 2. Tariff of duties or fees.

*Arroba.* 1. Dry measure of weight; 1 arroba equals about 11 kilograms. 2. Liquid measure; 1 arroba equals about 4.26 gallons.

*Atole.* Thick maize beverage served hot with seasonings.

*Audiencia.* 1. Court or governing body of a region, or the area of the court's jurisdiction. 2. In colonial times, an advisory and judicial body that ruled on behalf of the crown. It was composed of judges *(oidores)* and was subordinate judicially to the Council of the Indies in Spain.

*Auto sacramental.* Allegorical or religious play.

*Ayuda de costo.* Pension granted by the crown to a Spaniard for services performed.

*Boca costa.* Pacific Coast foothills, or piedmont, of Guatemala.

*Cabecera.* Head town of a district, usually with several towns under its jurisdiction.

*Cabeza de calpul.* Leader of a *calpul.*

Cabildo. Town council.

Cacaxtle. From Nahuatl *cacaxtli;* boxlike carrying frame worn on the back and usually held in place with a tumpline; often spelled *cacaste* in Guatemala.

*Cacicazgo.* Territory ruled by a cacique. The institution of cacique rule was based on hereditary rights.

*Cacique.* Indian leader, usually of noble descent.

*Caja de comunidad.* Community treasury.

*Caldera.* Crater caused by the collapse of a volcano or by continuous eruptions.

*Calpixque.* From Nahua *calpixqui;* Indian tax collector or administrative agent; often spelled *calpisque* in Guatemalan colonial documents.

*Calpul.* From Nahuatl *calpulli.* 1. Group of houses. 2. Territorial unit or the group of families occupying such a unit. 3. Garrison or colony.

*Cántaro.* Jug.

*Captain general.* Highest military office in the New World. The captain general was usually the viceroy, governor, or president of the audiencia.

*Carga.* Load, unit of measure. 1 carga equals about 24,000 cacao beans, or 23 kilograms.

*Caserío.* Group of houses, the smallest division within a *municipio.*

*Chajal.* 1. Guardian. 2. In pre-Hispanic times, an idol that was the guardian of the house. 3. In colonial times, a man or boy who performed minor tasks in a church. 4. Today, *cofradía official.* 5. Municipal official with minor police duties.

*Chia.* Lime-leaved sage (*Salvia hispanica* L).

*Chicha.* Fermented beverage made from maize or fruits.

*Chinamit.* From Nahua word meaning "fenced-in place." 1. Territorial unit, usually within a large town, separated by a wall. 2. Persons living in such a unit.

*Cochinilla.* Cochineal, a dye made of the dried bodies of a female scale insect *(Dactylopius coccus).*

*Cofradía.* Sodality; religious brotherhood of laymen dedicated to the care of a patron saint.

*Comal.* Griddle used for cooking tortillas.

*Congregación.* Concentration of groups of Indians in a centralized town.

*Convento.* Monastery.

*Corregidor.* Spanish official in charge of a *corregimiento.*

*Corregimiento.* Administrative-judicial unit or district governed by a *corregidor.*

*Cura.* Parish priest.

*Derecho.* Fee charged by the clergy.

*Derrama.* Extra or unauthorized tribute assessment or burden imposed on the Indians by unscrupulous Spanish officials.

*Diezmo.* Tithe.

*Doctrina.* 1. Originally a town of Christianized Indians in which a parish had not been established. 2. Parochial jurisdiction.

*Encomendero.* One possessing an *encomienda.*

*Encomienda.* Originally a grant of a specific number of Indians to a Spanish colonist with the right to collect labor and tribute. After 1549, a grant mainly for the right to tribute.

*Escribano.* Town clerk.

*Estancia.* Subordinate Indian settlement.

*Fanega.* Unit of measure; 1 fanega equals about 1.6 bushels, or 55.5 liters.

*Finca.* Plantation on which coffee is the major crop.

*Fiscal.* Indian church official who convoked the Indians to mass and taught them church doctrine.

*Grano.* Grain, the smallest unit of weight; 12 *granos* equal 1 real; 20 *granos* equal 1 Spanish scruple.

*Guachibal.* Indian fiesta held by a ward of a town; the word came to be used interchangeably with *hermandad.*

*Guardián doctrinero.* Head priest of a church and mission district.

*Harquebus.* Heavy matchlock gun.

*Hermandad.* Unofficial local sodality.

*Huipil.* Short blouse worn by Indian women. Two holes are left at the sides for the arms.

*Juez de milpa.* Spanish official who supervised Indian agriculture.

*Ladino.* 1. Non-Indian. 2. Spanish-speaking resident of Guatemala.

*League.* Measurement of distance; in Guatemala, 1 league equals about 5 kilometers.

*Lienzo.* Linen cloth, often painted.

*Limosna.* Alms.

*Macana.* From Nahuatl *macuahuitl;* war club containing sharp pieces of obsidian glued in with an adhesive.

*Mano.* Stone grinder shaped like a rolling pin and used with a metate.

*Manta.* Blanket composed of strips of cotton cloth *(piernas)* woven on a backstrap loom and sewn together along the edges.

*Maravedí.* Spanish coin; 1 maravedí equals one-thirty-fourth real.

Mayeque. From Nahuatl; group of bondsmen and tenant farmers.

*Mayordomo.* 1. Steward, overseer, or manager. 2. Civil or *cofradía* official.

*Metate.* Large stone used in grinding maize.

*Milpa.* From Nahuatl; maize field, often containing other interspersed crops. 2. In Guatemala, any cultivated land. 3. Small town.

*Moiety.* Family group; one of two units of a larger group.

*Mojón.* Boundary marker.

*Nimak Achi.* Quiché term meaning "Big People." In pre-Hispanic times, serfs inhabiting conquered lands. Important men among them came to occupy positions of trust in Quichean society.

Oidor. Judge of the audiencia.

*Parroquia.* Parish.

*Pataxte.* From Nahuatl *patlaxtli.* 1. Tree *(Theobroma bicolor)* bearing fruit similar to cacao but of lesser quality. 2. Fruit of the tree.

*Parcialidad.* Group composing a lineage or faction.

*Peso.* Spanish coin; 1 peso equals 8 reales, or *tomines.*

*Petate.* Rush mat.

*Pilguanejo.* Servant in a convent or monastery.

*Pinole.* Beverage made of ground, toasted maize and seasoning.

*Principal.* Member of the native upper class.

*Quintal.* Unit of weight; 1 quintal equals 46.1 kilograms.

*Quval.* Green stone.

*Rancho.* Small settlement, usually in the countryside.

*Real.* Coin; 1 real equals one-eighth peso.

*Regidor.* Officer of the town council.

*Repartimiento.* 1. Labor draft. 2. Sales or purchases forced on Indian communities by Spaniards. 3. *Encomienda.*

*Reservado.* Person exempt from paying tribute.

*Residencia.* Investigation of an official held at the end of his term of office.

*Roza.* Farming method in which trees and brush are cut down in a field, left to dry, and then burned; planting is done in the burned area.

*Sacristán.* Sexton.

*Señor natural.* "Natural lord," a term applied to a legitimate native ruler or his descendant.

*Señorío.* Territorial unit, including a *tinamit,* its dependencies, and conquered lands, under the direct control of an Indian ruler.

*Sujeto.* Subject town.

*Tablón.* Small garden plot, usually irrigated and used for intensive crop cultivation.

*Talud-tablero.* Teotihuacán architectural feature in which the base of the platform slopes upward *(talud)* to meet a recessed vertical panel *(tablero).*

*Tameme.* From Nahuatl *tlamama;* Indian carrier or porter.

*Tanda.* Gang of laborers, usually Indians called to serve by a *repartimiento.*

*Tecpán.* From Nahua; Indian palace, government building, or community house.

*Tequitlato.* From Nahuatl; Indian tribute collector who also delivered laborers.

*Tijxel.* Woman who assists the brothers of a *cofradía,* usually in preparing food for celebrations and caring for the garments of the saints.

*Tinamit.* From Nahua; fortified center, usually an important Indian capital.

*Tlatoani.* From Nahuatl; Indian ruler; Plural, *tlatoque.*

*Tomín.* Spanish coin; 1 tomín equals one real, or one-eighth peso.

*Tostón.* Monetary unit; 1 *tostón* equals one-half peso.

*Tul.* Reed.

*Tun* (or *tum*). From Nahuatl *teponaztli.* 1. In Guatemala, a percussion tube or drum, made from a hollow log and beaten with sticks. 2. Trumpet. 3. A dance portraying human sacrifice.

*Vara.* Unit of measurement; 1 vara equals approximately 1 meter.

*Vecino.* 1. Inhabitant of a town. 2. Citizen.

*Vida.* Granting of an *encomienda* to a specific person. The original grantee was said to have a first *vida,* or life. If regranted to a legitimate heir, it was a second *vida,* etc.

*Visita.* 1. Town with a small church but no full-time resident clergy. 2. An official tour of inspection or inquiry.

*Visitador.* One who made a *visita.*

*Xiquipil.* Nahua measure; 1 *xiquipil* equals about 8,000 cacao beans, or 7.5 kilograms.

*Zacate.* Grass, hay, or fodder for animals.

*Zarabanda.* Sixteenth-century Spanish dance characterized by picaresque character and lascivious movements. The Spanish missionaries referred to all lascivious dances as *zarabandas.*

*Zontle.* Nahua measure; 1 *zontle* equals about 400 cacao beans, or 0.4 kilogram.

# Abbreviations Used in Notes

| | |
|---|---|
| AGC | Archivo General de Centroamérica |
| AGI | Archivo General de Indias, Seville |
| *Anales* | *Anales de los Cakchiqueles* |
| *Annals* | *The Annals of the Cakchiquels* |
| CDI | *Colección de documentos inéditos* |
| CF | *Crónica franciscana* |
| DG | *Diccionario geográfico* |
| FyG | Francisco Antonio de Fuentes y Guzmán |
| PV | *Popol Vuh* |
| *Recopilación* | *Recopilación de leyes de los reynos de las Indias* |
| RC | *Relación Cerrato* |
| RG | *Relación Garcés* |
| RGA | *Relación geográfica Atitlán* |
| RGAG | *Relación geográfica Aguacatepec* |
| RGSA | *Relación geográfica San Andrés* |
| RGSF | *Relación geográfica San Francisco* |
| RGZ | *Relación geográfica Zapotitlán y Suchitepéquez* |
| RT | *Relación Tzutujil* |
| SB | *Título San Bartolomé* |
| SC | *Título Santa Clara* |
| TA | *Testament Ajpopolajay* |
| *Tamub* | *Título Tamub* |
| TC | *Título C'oyoi* |
| TN 1 | *Título Nijaib 1* |
| TN 2 | *Título Nijaib 2* |
| TT | *Título Totonicapán (Title of the Lords of Totonicapán)* |
| TX 1 | *Título Xpantzay 1* |
| TX 2 | *Título Xpantzay 2* |
| TX 3 | *Título Xpantzay 3* |

# *Notes*

## Preface

1. Carmack 1973.
2. For a discussion of this subject see Carmack 1971.
3. See Cline 1972a, pp. 14-15.
4. Scholes and Roys 1968; Spores 1967; Roys 1972.
5. Miles 1957; Carmack 1965 and 1981; Wallace and Carmack 1977.
6. Gibson 1952 and 1964; Solano 1974; Zavala 1944.

## Chapter 1

1. Edmonson 1965, p. 137.
2. Ibid., p. 131.
3. The spelling *Amak'* is consistent with modern orthography. See Carmack et al. 1975, p. 16.
4. *RT* 1952, p. 435.
5. Campbell 1971, p. 3; see also Grimes 1968.
6. Campbell 1971, p. 239.
7. In the rest of this book "la Laguna" is omitted from the names of the lake towns.
8. *RGA* 1964, p. 96.
9. Ibid., p. 97.
10. Carrasco 1967, p. 323.
11. FyG 1972:2; 23; *Annals* 1967, p. 24. Although Ajtz'iquinajay designates the leader of the Tz'iquinajay lineage, in the documents Ajtz'iquinajay is also used as the equivalent of the lineage name Tz'iquinajay for the Tzutujils.
12. Williams 1960, pp. 43-44.
13. McBryde 1947, p. 180.
14. Williams 1960, p. 45.
15. *RGA* 1964, p. 101.
16. Ximénez 1967, p. 153.
17. Williams 1960, p. 45.
18. *RGA* 1964, pp. 101-102 (translation mine).
19. Aguirre 1972, p. 5.
20. McBryde 1947, p. 132 and map between pp. 10 and 11.
21. Vivó Escoto 1964, p. 199.
22. Vivó Escoto 1964, p. 198.
23. McBryde 1947, p. 133.
24. *RGA* 1964, p. 94.
25. Alvarado 1954, p. 36; McBryde 1947, p. 99.
26. Vivó Escoto 1964, p. 213.
27. McBryde 1947, p. 131.
28. Ibid., p. 150.
29. Ibid., pp. 4-5.
30. Portig 1965, p. 74.
31. Stevens 1964, p. 308, map.
32. See Madigan 1976, pp. 26-27, for a soil survey of Santiago Atitlán.
33. McBryde 1947, p. 132; Madigan 1976, p. 25.
34. *DG* 1961, 1:30.
35. Williams 1960, p. 29.
36. Atwood 1935, p. 259.
37. Williams 1960, pp. 29-31.
38. McBryde 1947, p. 132.
39. Lothrop 1933, p. 3.
40. Heights of geological features are taken from Tax 1968, map of the towns of Lake Atitlán.

239

41. See ibid., map at the front; Williams 1960, p. 44.
42. Lothrop 1933, p. 3.
43. Madigan 1976, p. 22.
44. *RGAG* 1965, p. 266; McBryde 1947, pp. 23-24.
45. The avocado was the major source of vegetable fat in pre-Hispanic times.
46. The *nahuazapote* came from Mexico. McBryde (1947, p. 146) discusses the varieties of sapotes in the highland and coastal areas.
47. *RGA* 1964, p. 103.
48. Feldman 1971, pp. 112-13.
49. See McBryde 1947, map between pp. 10 and 11, p. 133.
50. *RGA* 1964, p. 103.
51. Ibid.; Ocaña 1932-33, p. 302; McBryde 1947, pp. 28, 147.
52. *RGA* 1964, p. 102.
53. FyG 1972, 2:40-41.
54. Tax 1946, p. 20.
55. Vásquez 1938, 2:33.
56. Ibid., 4:46.
57. McBryde 1947, p. 120.
58. Lothrop 1928, p. 392.
59. Madigan 1976, pp. 95-96.
60. Lothrop 1928, p. 392; Madigan 1976, p. 96.
61. *RGA* 1964, pp. 101-104.
62. McBryde 1947, p. 121.
63. Tax 1946, p. 213; See Feldman 1971, pp. 104-105, for a discussion of ancient hunting techniques.
64. McBryde 1947, pp. 132-33.
65. Parsons 1969, 1:22.
66. Shook 1965, p. 180.
67. McBryde 1947, p. 4.
68. See McBryde 1947, map between pp. 10 and 11.
69. *RGA* 1964, p. 104.
70. *RGSF* 1952, p. 140.
71. FyG 1972, 2:39.
72. *RGAG* 1965, p. 266.
73. Some varieties of banana, including the *plátano,* or plantain, were probably pre-Columbian, but the best varieties were introduced after the Conquest (McBryde 1947, p. 36). The place of origin of the pineapple is not known, but it may be Central America or Mex-

ico (McBryde 1947, p. 141).
74. *RGSA* 1952, pp. 104, 115.
75. *RGA* 1964, p. 104; *RGAG* 1965, pp. 273-74.
76. *RGSF* 1952, pp. 124-25.
77. Estrada 1955, pp. 71, 74-75, 77.
78. McBryde 1947, p. 30.
79. Estrada 1955, p. 77.
80. *RGAG* 1965, p. 267; *RGSA* 1952, p. 115; *RGSF* 1952, p. 137.
81. Feldman 1971, pp. 174-79.
82. *Annals* 1967, pp. 66-67; Miles 1957, p. 768.
83. *RGZ* 1955, p. 78; *RGAG* 1965, pp. 271-74; *RGSA* 1952, pp. 116-17.
84. *RGSA* 1952, p. 113.
85. Ibid., p. 117.
86. *RGZ* 1955, p. 78; Carmack 1965, p. 75.
87. *RGZ* 1955, p. 80.
88. McBryde 1947, p. 94.
89. *RGAG* 1965, p. 267; *RGSA* 1952, p. 113.
90. McBryde 1947, p. 22.

CHAPTER 2

1. See Bernal 1962, pp. 219-25.
2. Nicholson 1955, p. 596.
3. *RGA* 1964, p. 97.
4. Alvarado 1954, p. 36.
5. Díaz del Castillo 1927, p. 398.
6. *RGA* 1964, p. 105.
7. *RGSF* 1952, p. 141.
8. *RGAG* 1965, p. 268.
9. FyG 1972, 2:12-44.
10. Ibid., p. 28.
11. Quoted in Villacorta Calderón 1927, pp. 125-28.
12. Lothrop 1928, p. 381.
13. Lothrop 1933, p. 1.
14. See Borhegyi 1965, pp. 3-58, for a complete archaeological synthesis of the Guatemalan highlands, which incorporates this sequence.
15. Shook 1965, 2:180-94; Thompson 1948; Parsons 1969.
16. *RGA* 1964, p. 95.
17. Ibid.
18. Lothrop 1933, p. 68.

19. *RGA* 1964, p. 95.
20. FyG 1972, 1:70.
21. Carlos Orellana 1972.
22. FyG 1972, 2:34-35; Carmack 1973, p. 154.
23. *RG* 1973, pp. 380-81; McBryde 1947, map between pp. 32 and 33.
24. McBryde 1947, p. 132.
25. See Lothrop 1933.
26. *RGAG* 1965; *RGSA* 1952; *RGSF* 1952.
27. Carrasco 1967b, pp. 319-21; AGC A1 *leg.* 5,946 *exp.* 52,042. *Año* 1563.
28. Stone 1972, pp. 19-20.
29. Coe and Flannery 1967.
30. Baudez 1971, p. 83. Lothrop 1933, pp. 47-51, mentioned finding Usulután sherds at Chukumuk. Usulután pottery is Middle to Late Preclassic.
31. Coe and Flannery 1967, pp. 89-91.
32. Borhegyi 1965, p. 9.
33. Lothrop 1933, pp. 18-22.
34. Stone 1972, pp. 49, 51.
35. Lothrop 1933, p. 49.
36. Ibid., p. 21.
37. Ibid., p. 55.
38. Ibid., pp. 48-49; Borhegyi 1965, p. 14.
39. Lothrop 1933, pp. 29, 45-47.
40. Shook 1965, map between pp. 184 and 185.
41. Miles 1965, pp. 242, 247.
42. Shook 1965, p. 191.
43. Borhegyi 1965, p. 19.
44. Lothrop 1933, pp. 22-26.
45. Ibid., pp. 33-34.
46. Stone 1972, p. 112.
47. Shook 1965, pp. 182-83.
48. Ibid., p. 191.
49. Parsons 1969, 1:101.
50. Lothrop 1933, p. 40.
51. Parsons 1969, 1:134, 139-40.
52. Lothrop 1933, pp. 66-67.
53. Ibid., p. 29.
54. Borhegyi 1965, p. 37.
55. Ibid., p. 38.
56. Parsons 1969, 2:146.
57. Borhegyi 1965, p. 39.
58. Shook 1965, p. 187.

59. Ibid., pp. 192-93.
60. Borhegyi 1965, p. 32.
61. FyG 1972, 2:24, 36.
62. Fox 1980, p. 45.
63. Borhegyi 1965, p. 42.
64. Fox 1978, p. 118-19.
65. Ibid., p. 119.
66. Miles 1965, p. 270; Lothrop 1933, pp. 85-86.
67. Ibid.
68. See Wallace and Carmack 1977, pp. 98-99.
69. Fox 1980, pp. 50-51.
70. Lothrop 1933, p. 92.
71. Ibid., p. 97.
72. Fox 1978, p. 117.
73. Robert M. Carmack, personal communication, 1979.
74. Shook 1965, p. 190.
75. Ibid., p. 189.
76. Carmack 1981, pp. 44-45.
77. Borhegyi 1965, p. 73; Stewart 1977, p. 73.
78. Lothrop 1933, pp. 73, 88.
79. Guillemín 1965, p. 14.
80. Lothrop 1933, p. 75.
81. *RGA* 1965, p. 268.
82. Lothrop 1933, p. 75; in 1977 Guillemín also reported finding the remains of a ball court at Chiya', at the edge of the eastern slope, off the main plaza. Guillemín 1977, p. 258.
83. Lothrop 1933, p. 79.
84. Ibid., p. 81.
85. Guillemín 1965, pp. 16-17.
86. Lothrop 1933, pp. 67-68.
87. Ibid., pp. 18-21.
88. Personal communication, 1979.
89. Lothrop 1933, pp. 98-99.
90. Lothrop 1928, p. 377.
91. Lothrop 1933, p. 69.
92. Ibid.
93. Rojas Lima 1968, p. 313.
94. Cited in Lothrop 1933, p. 71.
95. Secondary centers in the highlands were situated on volcanic plateaus but were smaller than Chiya' and were dominated by it in the Late Postclassic Period.
96. Aguirre 1972, p. 40; Lothrop 1933, pp. 71, 100-101.

97. Lothrop 1933, p. 99.
98. Aguirre 1972, p. 72.
99. Lothrop 1933, pp. 100-101.
100. FyG 1972, 2:34.
101. Shook 1965, pp. 188-89, legend for fig. 4.
102. Ibid., p. 191.

CHAPTER 3

1. *SB* 1956, pp. 12-13; Carmack (1965, 1968, 1977, 1981) has dealt extensively with aboriginal Quichean life, and this reconstruction of Tzutujil history draws from these important works.
2. Tula (or Tollan—Nahua for Reed or Rush) was the capital of the Toltecs of Mexico and the mythical source of the traditions of the highland Maya elite. The Tula of the Quichean peoples was probably a second capital, possibly Chichén Itzá. Carmack 1981, p. 46.
3. See *Título Tzutujil* in Carmack 1973, pp. 377-78.
4. *Annals* 1967, pp. 47-59; *PV* 1971, pp. 161-66.
5. Carmack 1981, pp. 44-45.
6. Ibid., p. 122.
7. Fox 1977, p. 82; Carmack 1981, p. 49.
8. *Annals* 1967, p. 49; the Seven Settlements (Wuk Amak') were the native peoples of the Guatemala highlands. There were actually more than seven groups; the name Amak' was used to describe various peoples. Carmack 1981, pp. 59-60.
9. *Annals* 1967, pp. 48-49.
10. Carmack 1973, p. 378.
11. *Annals* 1967, p. 49; *PV* 1971, p. 166.
12. *RGA* 1964, pp. 98-99; Carmack (1981, p. 62) translates Sakibuk as Steam.
13. *Annals* 1967, p. 50.
14. Ibid., pp. 57-59; Carmack 1981, p. 46.
15. Fox 1977, pp. 82-83, 86.
16. Wallace and Carmack 1977, p. 99.
17. Borhegyi 1965, p. 53.
18. Carmack 1981, p. 45-46.
19. This mountain can be identified as a hill on the border between San Bartolomé Jocotenango and San Andrés (Carmack et al. 1975, p. 30).
20. *PV* 1971, p. 172.
21. *Tamub* 1957, p. 39; Carmack 1981, pp. 63-65.
22. Carmack 1965, pp. 182-83.
23. *Annals* 1967, p. 60.
24. Jakawitz has been identified as the archaeological site of Chitinamit, south of the hill called Mamaj, in the Quiché region (Carmack et al. 1975, p. 34).
25. Carmack 1981, pp. 123-25.
26. *PV* 1971, pp. 190-91.
27. *Annals* 1967, p. 77.
28. Ibid., p. 63.
29. Carmack 1981, p. 122.
30. *TT* 1967, p. 176.
31. Carmack 1965, p. 201; *Annals* 1967, pp. 64-65. Campbell (1972) disagrees with this interpretation and doubts that there were any pre-Hispanic Nahuas in the Motagua Valley.
32. *PV* 1971, pp. 219-20.
33. Carmack et al. 1975, pp. 21-22.
34. *Annals* 1967, p. 49.
35. Carmack et al. 1975, pp. 22-23.
36. Carmack 1981, pp. 68, 150.
37. *Annals* 1967, pp. 76-78.
38. *TX 3* 1957, p. 155.
39. Carrasco 1964, p. 329.
40. Carmack 1981, p. 69.
41. *Annals* 1967, pp. 80-81.
42. Carmack 1981, p. 126.
43. Ibid., p. 131.
44. *TX 3* 1957, p. 161.
45. Wallace and Carmack 1977, p. 4.
46. Fox 1977, p. 85.
47. Carmack 1981, p. 122; Carmack 1968, p. 74.
48. *Annals* 1967, pp. 85-86.
49. *TT* 1967, pp. 184-85.
50. Carmack 1981, pp. 130-31.
51. *TT* 1967, pp. 185-86.
52. FyG 1972, 2:18-20; see also *CF* in Carmack 1973, p. 376.

53. Carmack 1981, p. 131.
54. FyG 1972, 2:285.
55. FyG 1969, 1:10; *CF* in Carmack 1973, p. 377.
56. Carmack et al. 1975, p. 87 (see map).
57. Carmack 1981, pp. 122, 135.
58. "Qikab-Cavizimah" refers to the ruler Q'uik'ab and to the assistant ruler.
59. *TT* 1967, pp. 188-89.
60. *TX 2* 1957, p. 149.
61. *Annals* 1967, p. 97.
62. Carmack 1981, p. 137.
63. FyG 1972, 2:20-21.
64. Fuentes y Guzmán refers to the Tzutujil ruler as Zutuhilepop, but this is a contraction of the office title Ajpop Tzutujil, or Tzutujil Pop. Ajpop (He of the Mat) was the title of a ruler.
65. *Annals* 1967, p. 106.
66. Carmack 1965, p. 347; Paul and Paul 1963, pp. 138-40.
67. FyG 1972, 2:16-37.
68. See a discussion of these documents in Carmack 1973, pp. 71-79.
69. FyG 1972, 2:20; Carmack 1981, p. 139.
70. Carmack (1981, p. 140) says that this ruler may have been Tecum, one of Q'uik'ab's sons. Balam Acam should be Balam Ak'ab.
71. FyG 1972, 2:20.
72. Ibid., p. 23.
73. Ibid.; Carmack 1965, p. 344.
74. FyG 1972, 2:24-30.
75. Ibid., pp. 31-32.
76. *Annals* 1967, pp. 106, 110.
77. FyG 1972, 2:32-34.
78. *Annals* 1967, p. 110; there appears to be a copying error in the *Annals* text. In a subsequent passage Jo'o' Cawok (Voo Caok) is called "lord of the Akajals," a Cakchiquel group. It should say "lord of the Tzutujils."
79. FyG 1972, 2:35.
80. Ibid., pp. 35-36.
81. *Annals* 1967, p. 111.
82. FyG 1972, 2:36.
83. Carmack 1965, p. 338.
84. FyG 1969, 1:96-99.
85. *Annals* 1967, pp. 116-17.

86. Ibid., p. 117.
87. Ibid.
88. Carmack 1981, pp. 136-37.
89. *Annals* 1967, pp. 117-18; Pavacal may have been Pachavaj or the site of present-day Santiago Atitlán.
90. FyG 1972, 2:37.

CHAPTER 4

1. Smith 1955, p. 48.
2. Borhegyi 1965, p. 42.
3. Miles 1957, p. 751; Borhegyi 1963, p. 43.
4. Carmack et al. 1975, pp. 16, 19-20.
5. Ximénez 1929, 1:130.
6. *RGAG* 1965, p. 269; *RGSA* 1952, p. 108; *RGSF* 1952, p. 128; *RT* 1952, p. 435.
7. Aguirre 1972, p. 59n.
8. *TX 2* 1957, pp. 147, 149.
9. *SC* 1957, p. 175.
10. Carmack 1965, p. 281.
11. *TX 2* 1957, p. 147.
12. *SC* 1957, p. 175.
13. *TT* 1967, p. 188.
14. *TX 2* 1957, p. 149.
15. Carmack 1965, p. 447.
16. *Annals* 1967, p. 76.
17. Aguirre 1972, pp. 111-13.
18. Ibid., p. 72.
19. Carrasco 1967b, pp. 318-19.
20. Carmack 1981, p. 138.
21. Carmack 1965, p. 363.
22. *Annals* 1967, p. 109.
23. "Qizqab," or Quixcáp, is the modern San Jorge.
24. The pre-Hispanic name of Santa Clara is not known.
25. Aguirre 1972, p. 97; Carmack 1965, p. 283.
26. *SC* 1957, pp. 175, 177.
27. See Aguirre 1972, pp. 41-43, for a discussion of the name Tzununá.
28. Estrada 1955, p. 73.
29. Edmonson 1965, p. 127.
30. Estrada 1955, p. 80; Estrada (1966, p. 99) says that Upper Tolimán was five leagues from "Paçon," which

would be the approximate location of Palopó.

31. *Annals* 1967, p. 117.

32. Edmonson, 1965, p. 4.

33. *SC* 1957, p. 175; it is not clear whether Xequiakabaj was a Tzutujil settlement or a Cakchiquel settlement under Tzutujil rule.

34. *Annals* 1967, p. 81.

35. *TX 3* 1957, p. 157.

36. Thompson 1948, p. 6.

37. Estrada 1955, p. 71.

38. *RT* 1952, p. 435.

39. *RGAG* 1965, p. 267.

40. *RGSA* 1952, p. 104, 107.

41. *RGSF* 1952, pp. 127, 129.

42. *SB* 1956, pp. 12-13.

43. Thompson 1948, p. 9; in later colonial times the name Suchitepéquez was loosely applied to much of the territory formerly known as Zapotitlán.

44. Juarros 1823, p. 169.

45. Estrada Monroy 1972, p. 66; Solano 1969, p. 150, 158. Estrada Monroy (1972, p. 65) also found evidence that there were Tzutujil speakers in San Felipe Quezaltenango and San Martín Zapotitlán in 1769.

46. *TN 2* 1957, pp. 102n., 103.

47. *RGAG* 1965, p. 268; *RGZ* 1955, p. 72.

48. Carrasco 1967b, p. 321; AGC A1 *leg.* 5,946 *exp.* 52,042. *Año* 1563.

49. *TT* 1967, p. 185; *TC* in Carmack 1973, p. 299.

50. *SC* 1957, p. 173.

51. FyG 1972, 2:17. As late as 1818, Tolimán was trying to claim piedmont lands called Santo Tomás, in San Jerónimo. Tolimán did not have title to the lands but claimed possession on the basis of use (see AGC A3.15 *exp.* 40,455 *leg.* 2,796 fol. 2). Perhaps this is the location of ancient Malaj.

52. *El común de Santiago Atitlán con el de Santa María Magdalena Patulul sobre deslinde de ejidos* (AGC A1 *exp.* 24,781 *leg.* 2,811. *Año* 1587).

53. FyG 1972, 2:3-37.

54. Thompson 1948, p. 11.

55. Ibid., p. 9.

56. *SC* 1957, p. 177.

## Chapter 5

1. *PV* 1971, pp. 118-209; *Annals* 1967, pp. 66, 72; Carmack 1968, p. 78.

2. *PV* 1971, pp. 191-94.

3. Carmack 1968, p. 77.

4. *Annals* 1967, p. 91; *PV* 1971, pp. 236-40.

5. *TX 3* 1957, pp. 157-59; *PV* 1971, p. 174.

6. *RGA* 1964, p. 99.

7. *Annals* 1967, p. 102.

8. *TX 3* 1957, p. 159.

9. *PV* 1971, pp. 204-206.

10. FyG 1972, 2:24.

11. Ibid., pp. 31-32.

12. Ibid., p. 27.

13. *TT* 1967, p. 186.

14. *RT* 1952, p. 435.

15. Las Casas 1967, 2:13.

16. *RT* 1952, p. 436; *TN 2*, p. 107.

17. *TX 2* 1957, p. 135.

18. *Annals* 1967, p. 57.

19. *RGA* 1964, pp. 99-100.

20. In Nahuatl, *ichcahuipilli*.

21. Estrada 1955, p. 74.

22. FyG 1972, 2:15; see also *PV* 1971, p. 208, for a reference to poisoned spears. Edmonson (1971, p. 201n.) said that the reference is textually uncertain. Fuentes y Guzmán referred to poisoned wounds.

23. FyG 1972, 2:29.

24. *RGA* 1964, p. 100.

25. Las Casas 1967, 2:513.

26. FyG 1972, 2:23; *RT* 1952, p. 435.

27. Wallace and Carmack 1977, p. 8.

28. FyG 1972, 2:26.

29. Ibid., p. 27.

30. Those of K'umarcaaj, Iximché, Tezulutlán, and Chiya'.

31. *RGA* 1964, p. 94.

32. FyG 1972, 2:38.

33. *TT* 1967, p. 186.

34. See FyG 1972, 2:26.

35. *Annals* 1967, pp. 110-11.

36. *TC* in Carmack 1973, p. 298.

37. Wallace and Carmack 1977, p. 8.

38. *Annals* 1967, p. 57n.

39. Las Casas 1967, 2:513.

40. The spear tipped with an obsidian point, possibly the *dardo de chameychay* mentioned by Fuentes y Guzmán (1972, 2:22), was propelled by the spear-thrower (in Nahuatl *atlatl*). Landa (1966, pp. 31-32) described the spear-thrower used in Yucatán: "And they had a certain method of throwing darts by means of a piece of wood about three fingers thick, pierced to about the third of its length, and six palms long and with this and with cords they threw with force and accuracy."

41. FyG 1972, 2:24, 30.

42. *TN 2* 1957, pp. 105, 109.

43. Wallace and Carmack 1977, p. 17.

44. FyG 1969, 1:77.

45. *RGA* 1964, p. 99.

46. Las Casas 1967, 2:502-503; Wallace and Carmack 1977, p. 7.

47. FyG 1969, 1:71.

48. *Annals* 1967, p. 117; FyG 1972, 2:24-37.

49. The green feathers were from the quetzal bird; the blue, from *cotinga amabilis*.

50. A reference to the ritual calendar *(tzolkin)* of 13 months of 20 days (260 days). The Cakchiquels and possibly the Tzutujils also had a calendar of 400 days, called the *jun may* (Miles 1957, p. 748).

51. *Annals* 1967, pp. 48-49.

52. Lime plaster used to paint the face.

53. *Annals* 1967, p. 50.

54. *Tlacaxipehualiztli* (Nahuatl), a month in the Aztec calendar.

55. The Tzutujils, who had no mines in their territory, may have obtained the metal from the Pipils, east of their lowland territory. The Pipils could have obtained the metal through trade networks with southern Central America.

56. *Annals* 1967, p. 85.

57. *PV* 1971, p. 233.

58. Ibid., pp. 246-47.

59. Las Casas 1967, 2:510.

60. *SC* 1957, p. 175.

61. *TN 2* 1957, pp. 105, 107.

62. FyG 1972, 2:24-31; in the account of FyG the Tzutujils were often the losers.

63. Las Casas 1967, 2:509.

64. *RGA* 1964, p. 98.

65. *RGAG* 1965, p. 269.

66. *RT* 1952, p. 435.

67. Ibid., p. 436.

68. Carrasco 1967b, pp. 328-29.

69. Las Casas 1967, 2:509.

70. Ibid., p. 511.

71. *RT* 1952, p. 435.

72. *SB* 1956, p. 12.

## Chapter 6

1. *RGA* 1964, p. 98.

2. Garcés in Carmack 1973, p. 380.

3. *TA* in Carmack 1973, pp. 373-74.

4. McBryde 1947, p. 94; Douglas 1969, p. 34.

5. Wallace and Carmack 1977, p. 12.

6. *RT* 1952, p. 437; *RGA* 1964, p. 98.

7. McBryde 1947, pp. 17-19, gives a detailed description of slash-and-burn farming in the highlands.

8. *Annals* 1967, p. 81.

9. McBryde 1947, p. 19.

10. Ibid., p. 17.

11. Ibid., pp. 22-23.

12. *RGAG* 1965, p. 266.

13. Feldman 1971, pp. 90-91.

14. McBryde 1947, p. 23.

15. Tax and Hinshaw 1969, p. 75.

16. *RGA* 1964, p. 104.

17. Lothrop 1929b, pp. 216-21; McBryde 1947, p. 68.

18. Feldman 1971, p. 221; *RT* 1952, p. 436.

19. *RGZ* 1955, p. 73.

20. McBryde 1947, p. 142.

21. Tax and Hinshaw 1969, p. 84.

22. *RT* 1952, p. 435.

23. *RGAG* 1965, p. 273.
24. McBryde 1947, pp. 33-34, 92, discusses cacao cultivation.
25. *RGAG* 1965, p. 266; see McBryde 1947, p. 131, for a discussion of piedmont rains.
26. *RGSA* 1952, p. 103.
27. Feldman 1971, p. 201.
28. *RGAG* 1965, p. 272.
29. *SC* 1957, p. 175.
30. *RGZ* 1955, p. 80.
31. *AGAG* 1965, p. 274; *RT* 1952, p. 436 (the office of featherworker is mentioned).
32. Feldman 1971, p. 208; *RGAG* 1965, p. 274; *BGSA* 1952, p. 117; *RGSF* 1952, p. 139.
33. Wallace and Carmack 1977, p. 8; Carmack 1981, p. 154.
34. Feldman 1971, p. 72.
35. *RGZ* 1955, p. 70.
36. Feldman 1971, p. 245.
37. Tax 1946, p. 31.
38. Wallace and Carmack 1977, p. 9.
39. *Annals* 1967, p. 96.
40. Las Casas 1967, 2:514.
41. Wallace and Carmack 1977, p. 8.
42. Lothrop 1948, p. 86.
43. Nash 1967, p. 96.
44. Tax and Hinshaw 1969, p. 86.
45. Las Casas 1967, 2:514.
46. *RT* 1952, p. 436.
47. Las Casas 1967, 2:514.
48. McBryde 1947, p. 11; MacLeod 1973, p. 70.
49. Carmack 1977, p. 9.
50. McBryde 1947, p. 60.
51. Feldman 1971, p. 185.
52. *RGZ* 1955, p. 78.
53. Feldman 1971, p. 140.
54. Nash 1967, p. 87.
55. Paul 1968, p. 95.
56. Woods 1968, p. 209.
57. *RGA* 1964, p. 95.
58. McBryde 1947, pp. 23-24.
59. *Annals* 1967, p. 101; Vásquez 1932, 2:33.
60. *RGAG* 1965, p. 266.
61. Ibid., p. 269.
62. FyG 1969, 1:70.
63. McBryde 1947, pp. 148 and n.

64. *TT* 1967, pp. 184-85.
65. Ibid., p. 185.

CHAPTER 7

1. *Annals* 1967, p. 86. "Lord" is spelled *Ahauh* in the *Annals;* the correct spelling is *ajaw.*
2. Carmack 1981, p. 149.
3. *RGA* 1964, pp. 98-100.
4. Ibid., p. 100.
5. *PV* 1971, pp. 217-18.
6. *RGA* 1964, p. 100; *RGAG* 1965, p. 269.
7. *RGAG* 1965, p. 268.
8. Carmack 1981, p. 153.
9. *RGA* 1964, p. 100.
10. *PV* 1971, p. 22.
11. Carmack 1981, pp. 154-55.
12. *Annals* 1967, p. 103; the spellings have been changed to conform to modern orthography.
13. *PV* 1971, pp. 21-22.
14. *Ajxom* (*ah xom* in Miles 1957, p. 768) denoted a master stonecutter and mason among the Pokomans, according to the sixteenth-century Spanish writers Diego de Zúñiga and Pedro Morán. Perhaps the Tzutujil term was similar.
15. *RT* 1952, p. 436.
16. *TT* 1967, p. 188.
17. Carmack 1965, p. 446; these names are spelled Atzib and Atzcot in the list.
18. *RGA* 1964, pp. 98, 101.
19. Las Casas 1967, 2:511.
20. *RT* 1952, p. 436; *RGA* 1964, p. 98.
21. Carrasco 1967a, pp. 262-65.
22. Zorita 1971, p. 92.
23. Aguirre 1972, p. 41n.
24. Carmack 1981, p. 156.
25. *RT* 1952, pp. 436-37. Carmack 1981, p. 151, explains that *munib* was a general term meaning "slaves" or "captives" and usually referred to domestic servants.
26. Carmack 1981, p. 151.
27. Ibid.; see also Miles 1957, p. 768.

28. Las Casas 1967, 2:514.
29. *RT* 1952, p. 436.
30. Wallace and Carmack 1977, p. 10.
31. Carrasco 1967b, p. 320.
32. Carmack 1981, p. 157.
33. *Annals* 1967, p. 117; Carrasco 1967b, pp. 320, 329-30.
34 Ibid., p. 320; AGC Al *leg.* 5,946 *exp.* 52,042. *Año* 1563.
35. *RT* 1952, p. 435. In the *Relación Tzutujil* these names are spelled Natzti-hay, Aquibihai, Acuhai, Quicihay, and Acaboxul.
36. Carrasco 1967b, p. 322.
37. *TT* 1967, p. 188.
38. Carmack 1965, pp. 446-47.
39. Aguirre 1972, p. 41n.
40. *PV* 1971, pp. 156-57.
41. *Annals* 1967, p. 78.
42. *PV* 1971, p. 157.
43. *TX 3* 1957, p. 155.
44. *TT* 1967, p. 188; Carrasco 1967b, p. 325.
45. *Annals* 1967, p. 117.
46. Carrasco 1967b, p. 323; *Annals* 1967, p. 145; AGC A1 *leg.* 5,946 *exp.* 52,042. *Año* 1563; *Annals* 1967, p. 145.
47. Carmack 1981, pp. 158-59.
48. *PV* 1971, p. 156.
49. Edmondson 1971, p. 156n.; *TC* in Carmack 1973, p. 309.
50. Ibid., p. 287.
51. *TX 2* 1959, p. 149.
52. Aguirre 1972, p. 41n.
53. *TA* in Carmack 1973, pp. 372-74.
54. Carrasco n.d., p. 6.
55. Carmack 1981, p. 159.
56. Ibid., pp. 264-81; Carmack et al. 1975, pp. 17-18.
57. *RGAG* 1965, p. 269; *RGSA* 1952, p. 108.
58. Paul and Paul 1963; Gross 1974.
59. Carmack 1981, p. 164; see also Carmack 1966, p. 43.
60. Carmack 1981, p. 165.
61. Ibid.
62. Ibid., pp. 165-66.
63. Ibid., p. 157.
64. Las Casas 1967, 2:503, 516-18.

65. Paul and Paul 1963, pp. 132-33; Gross 1974, pp. 134-35; Gross and Kendall 1983, p. 207.
66. Gross 1974, p. 37.
67. Ibid., p. 82.
68. Las Casas 1967, 2:510-11.
69. Wallace and Carmack 1977, p. 10.
70. Las Casas 1967, 2:503.
71. Personal observation, 1979.
72. By "lesser Indians" the elders probably meant wealthy commoners.
73. *RGA* 1964, pp. 99-101.
74. *TT* 1967, p. 185.
75. Las Casas 1967, 2:515.
76. *TT* 1967, pp. 184-85.
77. Gage 1969, p. 221.
78. Las Casas 1967, 2:517.
79. *TX 3* 1957, p. 165.
80. *Annals* 1967, p. 117.
81. Ibid.
82. *Anales* 1950, pp. 198, 204.
83. FyG 1972, 2:20.
84. Paul and Paul 1963, pp. 138-40; As Gross and Kendall point out, however, elopment is an institutional mechanism. Before a boy can elope with a girl, it is necessary for him to have his father's approval, for it is the father who will suffer any legal reprisal. Bringing in spouses adds to the potential power and authority of the father in the community (Gross and Kendall 1983, pp. 222, 224, 225).

CHAPTER 8

1. See for example *Annals* 1967, pp. 88-89; *PV* 1971, pp. 230-31.
2. Carrasco 1967b, p. 322; AGC A1 *leg.* 5,946 *exp.* 52,042. *Año* 1563.
3. *PV* 1971, pp. 216-17.
4. *RT* 1952, p. 435.
5. Carraso 1967b, pp. 328-29.
6. Ibid., p. 328; *lolmet* is translated as "Overseer of Cotton of the Lords" in the *Popol Vuh* (*PV* 1971, p. 254).
7. *TT* 1967, p. 188.
8. *Annals* 1967, p. 145.
9. Carrasco 1967b, pp. 321-22.

10. *PV* 1971, p. 254.
11. Carrasco 1967b, p. 328.
12. Las Casas 1967, 2:500.
13. *TX 1* 1957, p. 129.
14. Carrasco 1967b, p. 329; Guillemín 1977, p. 245.
15. Carmack 1981, p. 175; Wallace and Carmack 1977, p. 16.
16. *TA* 1973, p. 374.
17. *RT* 1952, p. 435.
18. Carmack 1981, p. 171.
19. *Annals* 1967, p. 88.
20. Carmack 1981, p. 171; Carrasco 1967b, p. 328.
21. *RGA* 1964, pp. 98-99.
22. Vásquez 1938, 2:29.
23. Carmack 1981, p. 175.
24. Wallace and Carmack 1977, pp. 14-15; AGC A1 *leg.* 5,946 *exp.* 52,042. *Año* 1563.
25. *RT* 1952, p. 435; AGC A1 *leg.* 5,946 *exp.* 52,042. *Año* 1563. These documents mention the lords who would have composed the council.
26. Las Casas 1967, 2:512-13.
27. The council was probably composed of the main lords subordinate to the Ajtz'iquinajay. Carrasco 1967b, pp. 322-23.
28. *RT* 1952, p. 435.
29. *RGA* 1964, p. 99; *RT* 1952, p. 435.
30. Las Casas 1967, 2:502.
31. AGC A1 *leg.* 5,946 *exp.* 52,042. *Año* 1563.
32. Las Casas 1967, 2:512.
33. Ibid., p. 501.
34. Carmack 1981, p. 177.
35. *RGA* 1964, p. 93.
36. Carrasco 1967b, p. 329.
37. Ibid., p. 328.
38. *Annals* 1967, pp. 87-88; Carrasco 1967b, pp. 320-21.
39. Zorita 1971, p. 92.
40. *Annals* 1967, pp. 87-88.
41. Carrasco 1967b, pp. 320-21; AGC A1 *leg.* 5,946 *exp.* 52,042. *Año* 1563.
42. Wallace and Carmack 1977, p. 13; *TT* 1967, pp. 177-78.
43. FyG 1969, 1:72.

44. *Annals* 1967, p. 80; Carrasco 1967a, pp. 260-61.
45. Lothrop 1933, p. 86.

## CHAPTER 9

1. See for example *PV* 1971.
2. Carmack et al. 1975, p. 17.
3. *TX 3* 1956, p. 159; *Annals* 1967, p. 102.
4. Edmonson 1971, p. 213, says that they are called *camahuiles,* from *kavabil* ("deity"); see also Wauchope 1948, pp. 162-63.
5. Las Casas 1967, 2:223; Las Casas gives the spelling as *chalhalhar.*
6. Orellana 1975a, pp. 862-63.
7. *Annals* 1967, p. 49.
8. *PV* 1971, p. 162.
9. Carmack 1981, p. 201.
10. *PV* 1971, pp. 246-47; Las Casas 1967, 2:510.
11. *RGA* 1964, p. 98.
12. *TX 3* 1957, p. 159.
13. Vásquez 1938, 2:29.
14. *RGAG* 1965, p. 269; *RGSA* 1952, p. 109.
15. *RGSF* 1952, p. 129.
16. *RGAG* 1965, p. 268; *RGSA* 1952, pp. 106-107.
17. *RGA* 1964, p. 99.
18. *RGAG* 1965, p. 269; *RGSA* 1952, p. 109.
19. *TX 3* 1957, p. 159.
20. Las Casas 1967, 2:216; Gage 1969, pp. 281-82.
21. Lothrop 1933, pp. 81-83.
22. Thompson 1970, p. 315.
23. Miles 1965, p. 279.
24. Las Casas 1967, 2:216.
25. Ibid., pp. 223-24; Thompson 1970, p. 183.
26. Las Casas 1967, 2:215.
27. McDougall 1955, p. 67; personal observation, 1971.
28. Ordóñez Chipín 1973, p. 149; Mendelson 1957, p. 116.
29. *RGA* 1964, p. 99; Las Casas 1967, 2:216.
30. Thompson 1970, p. 181.

31. *RGA* 1964, p. 99; *RGAG* 1965, p. 270.

32. Thompson 1970, p. 170.

33. Las Casas 1967, 2:225-26.

34. Ibid., p. 214.

35. Carrasco 1967a, p. 260.

36. *PV* 1971, pp. 246-47.

37. Las Casas 1967, 2:221.

38. Personal observation, 1971.

39. *Tun* is the highland Maya term for the Nahuatl word *teponaztli,* a slit drum made from a hollow log and beaten with sticks (O'Brien 1975, p. 95n.). In Guatemala this drum was called a *tun.* However, Miles (1957, p. 768) gives *ah tun* ("trumpeter") in Pokoman; thus the dance may have been named for the trumpets. See Chinchilla Aguilar 1963, pp. 13-15, for a discussion of the *loj-tum* as it was performed in colonial times.

40. FyG 1969, 1:77-78.

41. *RGAG* 1965, p. 269.

42. Mendelson 1957, pp. 268-69.

43. Las Casas 1967, 2:215.

44. Borhegyi 1959, p. 45.

45. See, for example, Gage 1969, p. 281.

46. *PV* 1971, pp. 243-44.

47. Paul and Paul 1975, p. 712.

48. Mendelson 1957, pp. 222-23.

49. *RGAG* 1964, p. 270.

50. *RGSA* 1952, p. 109.

51. Douglas 1969, pp. 154-55.

52. Vásquez 1938, 2:28.

53. *RGA* 1964, p. 102.

54. Lothrop 1929, pp. 5-9; Ordóñez Chipín 1970, pp. 147-49.

55. Mendelson 1957, p. 212.

56. Lothrop 1929a, pp. 2-5.

57. *TC* in Carmack 1973, p. 311; Wallace and Carmack 1977, p. 16.

58. Las Casas 1967, 2:519.

59. Vásquez 1938, 2:26, 28.

60. Wallace and Carmack 1977, p. 16.

61. *RGSA* 1952, p. 109.

62. Douglas 1969, p. 159.

63. Carmack 1965, p. 446.

64. Miles 1957, p. 748.

65. Carmack 1973, p. 17.

66. Douglas 1969, pp. 116-21.

67. Ibid., pp. 146-47.

68. Ibid., pp. 160-61.

69. Las Casas 1967, 2:502.

70. Douglas 1969, pp. 134, 173.

71. Las Casas 1967, 2:225-26; see Orellana (1977) for a more detailed discussion of pre-Hispanic and colonial highland Indian medicine.

72. Douglas 1969, p. 141; Paul 1976, pp. 77-81.

73. Miles 1957, p. 768.

74. Las Casas 1967, p. 225.

75. Estrada 1955, p. 74.

76. Adams and Rubel 1967, p. 341.

77. *Annals* 1967, p. 76.

78. Douglas 1969, pp. 92-93, 98-99.

79. Mendelson 1967, p. 397.

80. FyG 1969, 1:279-80.

81. *TT* 1967, p. 169; the spelling *nahuales* is taken from *TT.*

82. Mendelson 1957, p. 42.

83. *Annals* 1967, pp. 53-54.

84. *PV* 1971, pp. 65-66.

85. Edmonson 1965, p. 127.

86. Vásquez 1938, 2:25.

87. *PV* 1971, p. 17; the spellings of the terms for these diviners are Edmonson's.

88. Douglas 1969, p. 107.

89. Paul and Paul 1975, p. 719.

90. Mendelson 1959, p. 58.

91. Mendelson 1958b, pp. 4-5.

92. Ibid. 1957, p. 477.

93. Carmack et al. 1975, p. 18.

94. Douglas 1969, pp. 68-75.

CHAPTER 10

1. *Annals* 1967, pp. 115-16.

2. MacLeod 1973, p. 40; *TN 1* 1957, pp. 84-85.

3. *SB* 1956, pp. 12-13. The Quichean groups had previously learned of the coming of the Spaniards when the Aztec ruler Montezuma sent a message to urge them to prepare to fight the Spaniards. *TN1* 1957, pp. 84-85.

4. Aguirre 1972, pp. 437-41.

5. *Annals* 1967, pp. 131, 136.
6. Carmack 1973, p. 67. According to Estrada Monroy (1968, p. 565), the document is ancient, probably dating from the sixteenth-century. It is also important because it is the only example of sixteenth-century Tzutujil writing in existence. Carmack agrees that the *título* is of sixteenth-century origin.
7. Alvarado 1954.
8. Carmack 1965, p. 372; Rodríguez Becerra 1977, p. 3.
9. Alvarado 1954, pp. 30-31, 35-37; *Annals* 1967, pp. 120-22.
10. FyG 1972, 2:13, 37.
11. Alvarado 1954, pp. 36-38.
12. FyG 1962, 2:18.
13. Alvarado 1954, p. 38.
14. Sanchíz Ochoa 1976, pp. 19-20. There is a misprint in the text: the year of the founding of the first capital should be 1524, not 1523.
15. *Annals* 1967, pp. 123-25. Bricker (1981, p. 34) points out that some Spanish historians give a later date for this uprising. Ximénez (1929, 1:152) says 1527, but Alvarado was not in Guatemala then.
16. *RGA* 1964, p. 95.
17. *Annals* 1967, pp. 124-26.
18. Ibid., p. 126; Sanchíz Ochoa 1976, p. 20; Kelly 1932, p. 175.
19. Bancroft 1886, 2:96-97.
20. Kelly 1932, p. 173.
21. Cline 1972b, pp. 23-24.
22. *Annals* 1967, p. 127.
23. Pangán is the Indian name for the early Spanish capital of Guatemala.
24. *Annals* 1967, p. 129.
25. *RGA* 1964, p. 95; *RT* 1952, p. 436.
26. *Annals* 1967, pp. 130-31; Kelly 1932, pp. 204-208.
27. Ibid., p. 132.
28. Kelly 1932, pp. 212-14; Sherman 1969, p. 200.
29. *Annals* 1967, p. 134; Sanchíz Ochoa 1976, pp. 22-23.
30. Sanchíz Ochoa 1976, pp. 26.
31. Cline 1972b, pp. 24-25.

32. Sáenz de Santa María 1963, pp. 112-15.
33. Villacorta Calderón 1942, p. 60.
34. MacLeod 1973, pp. 83-84.
35. Zavala 1944, p. 22.
36. See *Dispone su majestad que solamente los indios que hagan guerra, sean reducidos a la esclavitud,* AGC A1.2-4 *exp.* 15,752 fol. 17v. *Año* 1530.
37. MacLeod 1973, p. 57.
38. See Sherman 1979.
39. MacLeod 1973, pp. 46-63, discusses slavery in Central America during the early Conquest period.
40. *RG* in Carmack 1973, p. 380.
41. MacLeod 1973, pp. 107-108.
42. Ibid., p. 56; Zavala 1944, p. 23.
43. MacLeod 1973, pp. 83-84.
44. Ibid., pp. 58-60, 64.
45. *Annals* 1967, p. 137.
46. Ibid., p. 136; *Su majestad indica que el gobernador y el obispo de la provincia de Guatemala, dicten todas las medidas a fin de reducir a poblado a los naturales.* AGC A1.23 *exp.* 1,511 *leg.* 10, *Año* 1540.
47. *RGA* 1964, p. 97; Aguirre 1972, pp. 38-39.
48. Cline 1972b, pp. 23-24; Gerhard 1972, pp. 130-31.
49. See MacLeod 1973, pp. 390-92, for a list of presidents and captains general of the Audiencia of Guatemala from 1542 to 1724.
50. *Annals* 1967, p. 139.
51. Ibid., p. 141.
52. Ibid., p. 142 and n.
53. Bancroft 1886, 2:367.
54. *RT* 1952, p. 437.
55. *Annals* 1967, p. 143.
56. Dombrowski et al. 1970, p. 15; Gerhard 1972, p. 66.
57. MacLeod 1973, p. 85.
58. *RT* 1952, p. 437.
59. *Annals* 1967, p. 146.
60. Aguirre 1972, pp. 175-78, provides a list of all the priests who resided in Atitlán from 1566 to 1638.
61. Ibid., p. 371; *RGA* 1964, p. 97.
62. *RT* 1952, p. 437.
63. Vásquez 1937, 1:33; *Annals*

1967, p. 149.
  64. *RGA* 1964, p. 98.
  65. Cline 1972b, pp. 26–27.
  66. Vásquez 1944, 4:53.

CHAPTER 11

  1. *RGA* 1965, p. 95. Tribute payers were heads of households; a rough estimate of the population can be made by multiplying the number of tribute payers by four. Spores 1967, p. 74.
  2. *RGAG* 1965, p. 267. The *Relación* says that there were 219 tributaries and 8 bachelors, who are customarily counted as half-tributary units.
  3. *RGSA* 1952, p. 104. There were 101 tributaries and 6 bachelors.
  4. Aguirre 1972, pp. 31–33, 37–39; *Annals* 1967, p. 136.
  5. Remesal 1932, 2:244–46.
  6. Aguirre 1972, p. 33.
  7. *RGA* 1964, p. 97.
  8. Stanislawski 1947, pp. 101–103.
  9. Gibson 1964, p. 33.
  10. *RG* in Carmack 1973, pp. 380.
  11. *Testimonio y Autos del Proceso que en esta Real Audiencia se . . . entre los frailes de St. Francisco del Fiscal Sancho Barahona sobre la limosna de tres guardianas acrecentadas.* AGI Guatemala *leg.* 171. *Año* 1592.
  12. *RGZ* 1955, p. 72.
  13. *Título de la encomienda de don Pedro Nùñez de Barahona.* AGC A1.1 *exp.* 10 *leg.* 1. *Año* 1623.
  14. Gibson 1964, p. 33.
  15. *RGAG* 1965, p. 267.
  16. Aguirre 1972, p. 39.
  17. Ibid., addenda page.
  18. The house of justice is called *la casa real* on the 1585 map of Atitlán (fig. 10).
  19. *RGA* 1964, pp. 95–96.
  20. See, for example, Gibson 1952, p. 125.
  21. *RGAG* 1965, p. 265.
  22. Ibid., p. 268; *RGSA* 1952, pp.

104–105.
  23. *RGAG* 1965, pp. 266–67.
  24. Ponce 1873, pp. 306–309. Ponce visited the various Franciscan convents in New Spain to help put their affairs in order and report on conditions he found there (Carmack 1973, p. 132).
  25. Estrada 1955, pp. 74–75.
  26. McBryde 1947, p. 86.
  27. *RGSA* 1952, pp. 103, 105.
  28. *RGSF* 1952, pp. 124, 126.
  29. Cortés y Larraz 1958, 2:199–201.
  30. *RGA* 1964, pp. 96–97.
  31. Estrada 1955, p. 80.
  32. Aguirre 1972, p. 53 and n.; towns were actually founded twice: once as a congregation and again officially when the citizens established their own town councils (see chapter 15).
  33. Ibid., p. 48.
  34. McBryde 1947, pp. 120–21.
  35. Solano 1969, p. 155.
  36. Aguirre 1972, p. 108–10.
  37. McBryde 1947, p. 120 and n.
  38. *Annals* 1967, pp. 152, 155.
  39. Estrada 1966, pp. 97–99.
  40. AGC A1.24 *exp.* 10,217 *leg.* 1,573 fol. 123. *Año* 1703.
  41. Aguirre 1972, p. 116; McBryde 1947, p. 120.
  42. Aguirre 1972, p. 52.
  43. *Sobre el deslinde de las tierras reclamadas por el común del pueblo San Juan Atitlán.* AGC A1 *exp.* 51,997 *leg.* 5,942 fol. 10v. *Año* 1641.
  44. *Autos de los indios y común del pueblo de Atitlán . . . sobre pago del tostón del servicio de Su Majestad.* AGC A3.16 *exp.* 40,490 *leg.* 2,801. *Año* 1618. See also *Tasación del pueblo de Atitlán y sus estancias.* AGC A1.1 *exp.* 10 *leg.* 1. *Año* 1623.
  45. AGC A1 *exp.* 51,997 *leg.* 5,942 fol. 1. *Año* 1641.
  46. Ibid., *exp.* 52,739 *leg.* 5,995 fol. 11. *Año* 1751.
  47. Paul 1968, p. 99.
  48. AGI Guatemala *leg.* 171. *Año* 1592.
  49. AGC A1.1 *exp.* 10 *leg.* 1 fol. 20.

*Año* 1623.
50. Guatemala Project 1970.
51. Aguirre 1972, pp. 40-43.
52. *Memoria de los pueblos que la Ordena de San Francisco tiene en administración y doctrina, y los pueblos que tiene a cargo así el Convento de San Francisco de Huatimala como los demás de esta Provincia.* AGI Guatemala *leg.* 169. *Año* 1575.
53. AGC A3.16 *exp.* 40,490 *leg.* 2,801. *Año* 1609.
54. Rojas Lima 1968, p. 295-96.
55. *RT* 1952, p. 435.
56. Ibid., p. 438.
57. Garcés in Carmack 1973, p. 380.
58. *RGAG* 1965, p. 268.
59. *RGSA* 1952, p. 106.
60. *RGSF* 1952, p. 127.
61. Ibid., p. 144.
62. AGC A1 *exp.* 24,781 *leg.* 2,811. *Año* 1587.
63. *Annals* 1967, pp. 156-57.
64. Vásquez 1944, 4:53-54.
65. *Diligencias echas en virtud del despacho del Govo. Supr. de la translación del residuo de los naturales tributarios del Puo. de Sn. Franco. de la Costilla al de Santa Bárbara, incorporación y padrón.* AGC A1.20 *exp.* 4,063 *leg.* 201. *Año* 1756.
66. *DG* 1962, 2:244.
67. Aguirre 1972, p. 49n.
68. McBryde 1947, p. 93.
69. On the map San Francisco is given, but it should be Santa Bárbara, for the former town had long been abandoned. The location of San Bartolomé is probably at the *rancho* marked southeast of Atitlán Volcano.
70. Garcés in Carmack 1973, pp. 380-81.
71. Cortés y Larraz 1958, 2:275.

CHAPTER 12

1. Gibson 1964, p. 58.
2. Ibid., pp. 63-65.
3. Lockhart 1969, p. 415.
4. See MacLeod 1973, pp. 132-33.

5. Gibson 1966, p. 57.
6. MacLeod 1973, p. 89; Gibson 1964, p. 182.
7. Ibid., p. 62.
8. Carmack 1981, p. 306.
9. *RGA* 1964, p. 95.
10. Ibid.; *Annals* 1967, p. 129; *RT* 1952, p. 436.
11. Zavala 1944, pp. 11-12.
12. *RT* 1952, p. 436.
13. Wallace and Carmack 1977, p. 7.
14. Carmack 1973, pp. 88-89.
15. *RT* 1952, p. 437.
16. *Servicios de Jorge de Alvarado, Alonso de Estrada y del adelantado don Pedro de Alvarado.* AGC A3.10 *exp.* 3,096 *leg.* 160. *Año* 1584.
17. AGC A1.2-4 *leg.* 2,195 fol. 69. *Año* 1535.
18. *Información de méritos y servicios de Pedro de Cueto con el Adelantado Alvarado.* AGI Patronato 82-3-2. *Año* 1600.
19. Carrasco 1967b, p. 318, quoting from AGI Justicia 295. *Año* 1537.
20. Bancroft 1886, 2:118-19.
21. Carrasco 1967b, pp. 318-19, quoting from AGI Justicia 295. *Año* 1537.
22. Aguirre 1972, p. 45.
23. Sherman 1969, p. 205n.
24. *Sancho de Barahona con el adelantado dn. Pedro de Alvarado.* AGI Justicia *leg.* 295. *Año* 1537.
25. Aguirre 1972, p. 46.
26. Solano 1974, p. 33.
27. AGC A1.2-4 *exp.* 15,752 *leg.* 2,197 fol. 35v. *Año* 1536; ibid., A1.24 *leg.* 2,195 fol. 257. *Año* 1536.
28. MacLeod 1973, p. 83.
29. Bancroft 1886, 2:308.
30. Sherman 1971, pp. 29-30.
31. Madigan 1976, p. 230.
32. MacLeod 1973, pp. 110, 116; Madigan 1976, p. 232.
33. *RT* 1952, p. 437.
34. AGC A1.23 *leg.* 1,511 fol. 95. *Año* 1549.
35. Gibson 1966, p. 60.
36. AGC A1.23 *leg.* 1,511 fol. 154. *Año* 1550.

37. Aguirre 1972, p. 46n; *Un Libro de Tasaciones de las naturales de las Provincias de Guatemala, Nicaragua, Yucatán y Pueblos de Comayagua, años 1548-1551.* AGI Guatemala *leg.* 128.
38. MacLeod 1973, p. 117.
39. *Pleito sostenido por la Guardianía de Atitlán con el encomendero don Sancho de Barahona por negarse este a contribuir para los ornamentos de la iglesia.* AGC A1.11.3 *exp.* 31,428 *leg.* 4,055. *Año* 1587.
40. AGI Guatemala *leg.* 171. *Año* 1592.
41. Pardo 1944, p. 29.
42. AGC A1.1 *exp.* 10 *leg.* 1. *Año* 1623.
43. Ibid. AGI Patronato 82-3-2. *Año* 1600; MacLeod 1973, p. 117.
44. Cortés y Larraz 1958, 2:262, 275. By the late eighteenth century Cortés y Larraz said that in Suchitepéquez nothing was grown, and the entire territory was forest, even inside the town. Maize and cacao were still gathered there, however. Given the state of the area, it is unlikely that much cacao was produced.
45. See Aguirre 1972, p. 45n.
46. *Annals* 1967, p. 123.
47. The lords of Atitlán said that the Tzutujils fought in Verapaz, Gracias a Dios, San Miguel, and Leon; *RT* 1952, p. 436.
48. Probably pulmonary bubonic plague.
49. *RGA* 1964, p. 95.
50. *RT* 1952, p. 436.
51. *Annals* 1967, p. 127.
52. Ibid., p. 129.
53. *RT* 1952, p. 437.
54. AGC Justicia *leg.* 295. *Año* 1537. The testimony of witnesses regarding the number of slaves taken by Jorge is somewhat conflicting, but the number was between 200 and 270. Barahona had around 100 to 120 Indians whom he worked in mining gold (Sherman 1979, p. 71).
55. AGI Justicia *leg.* 295 fols. 510-11v. *Año* 1535. *Cuadrillas* frequently

consisted of 100 to 120 Indians, and sometimes as many as 150. The most common size was about 100. Sherman 1979, p. 72.
56. *Annals* 1967, p. 131.
57. Rodríguez Becerra 1977, pp. 115-17. AGC A1.2-4 *exp.* 15, 752 *leg.* 2,197 fols. 35v, 38. *Año* 1536.
58. AGC A1.23 *leg.* 1,511 fol. 34. *Año* 1546.
59. AGC A1.2-4 *exp.* 15,752 *leg.* 2,197 fol. 62. *Año* 1546.
60. Garcés in Carmack 1973, p. 385.
61. AGC A1.2-4 *leg.* 2,196 fol. 186. *Año* 1547.
62. AGI Guatemala *leg.* 128. *Años* 1548-1551.
63. AGC A1.23 *leg.* 1,511 fol. 162. *Año* 1551.
64. Ibid., fol. 201. *Año* 1553.
65. Zorita 1971, pp. 237-38.
66. *RT* 1952, p. 437.
67. AGI Guatemala *leg.* 128. *Años* 1548-1551; AGC A3.16 *exp.* 40, 466 *leg.* 2,792. *Años* 1553-55.
68. Sherman 1969, p. 205; MacLeod 1973, p. 129.
69. Gibson 1964, p. 62; *Annals* 1967, p. 141.
70. Zorita 1971, p. 237.
71. *Los hijos de Sancho de Barahona . . . con el Liz. de Cerrato sobre cierta tasación que hizo a los indios de la mytad del pueblo de Atitlán en Residencia contra de dicho Cerrato.* AGC Justicia *leg.* 983. *Año* 1555.
72. *Annals* 1967, p. 137.
73. Ibid., p. 141.
74. *RT* 1952, p. 437.
75. *Annals* 1967, p. 143.
76. *RT* 1952, p. 437.
77. *Annals* 1967, p. 143.
78. MacLeod 1973, p. 99.
79. *RT* 1952, p. 437.
80. AGI Patronato 82-3-2 fols. 76-84v. *Año* 1600.
81. Pineda 1925, pp. 354-58.
82. See MacLeod 1973, pp. 91-92 for a discussion regarding this boom period in other cacao areas in Guatemala.

83. Vásquez 1938, 2:33.
84. Garcés in Carmack 1973, p. 380.
85. Ibid.; Pineda 1925, p. 350.
86. Ximénez 1967, p. 110.
87. Garcés in Carmack 1973, p. 380.
88. MacLeod 1973, p. 70.
89. Garcés in Carmack 1973, pp. 384-85.
90. AGC A1.23 *leg.* 1,513 fol. 591. *Año* 1581.
91. Ibid., *leg.* 1,512 fol. 384. *Año* 1571.
92. Ibid., fol. 407. *Año* 1572.
93. Ibid., fol. 431. *Año* 1573.
94. Ibid., fol. 437. *Año* 1573.
95. Pineda 1925, p. 354.
96. AGC A1.23 *leg.* 1,512 fol. 385. *Año* 1571.
97. *Annals* 1967, pp. 147-48.
98. AGC A1.23 *leg.* 1,513 fol. 577. *Año* 1580; Ibid., fol. 610. *Año* 1582.
99. MacLeod 1973, p. 90.
100. AGI Guatemala *leg.* 171. *Año* 1592.
101. AGI Guatemala *leg.* 10 fols. 5-6. *Año* 1584; MacLeod 1973, pp. 87-88.
102. Bishop Juan Ramírez in Sherman 1968, pp. 19-20.
103. AGC A1.2-4 *leg.* 2,195 fol. 345. *Año* 1553.
104. Gage 1969, p. 233.
105. AGC 3.16 *exp.* 40,485 *leg.* 2,800. *Año* 1588.
106. Carmack 1973, p. 148.
107. Bishop Ramírez in Sherman 1968, pp. 15-16.
108. AGC A1.23 *exp.* 1,513 fols. 717, 719. *Año* 1591.
109. Solórzano F. 1970, p. 133.
110. Gage 1969, p. 233.
111. Bishop Ramírez in Sherman 1968, p. 20.
112. AGC A3.16 *exp.* 40,491 *leg.* 2,801. *Año* 1599.
113. AGC A1.23 *leg.* 1,513 fol. 664. *Año* 1586.
114. Bishop Ramírez in Sherman 1968, pp. 18-20. In 1603 the personal tribute for Indian males was raised to 3 *tostones* each. AGC A1.23 *leg.* 4,588 fol. 99. *Año* 1603.
115. Bishop Ramírez in Sherman 1968, p. 19.
116. AGC A1.1 *leg.* 1 *exp.* 1. *Año* 1610.
117. AGC A3.12 *leg.* 2,776 *exp.* 40,122. *Año* 1609; ibid., *leg.* 2,774 *exp.* 40,031. *Año* 1631.
118. Sherman 1979, p. 290.
119. AGC A3.16 *exp.* 40,491 *leg.* 2,801. *Año* 1599.
120. AGC A1.1 *exp.* 10 *leg.* 1. *Año* 1623; Aguirre 1972, pp. 47, 50.

CHAPTER 13

1. *Annals* 1967, p. 131.
2. *RT* 1952, p. 437.
3. *RGAG* 1965, p. 266.
4. Madigan 1976, p. 87.
5. *Annals* 1967, p. 138.
6. AGC A1.23 *leg.* 1,511 fol. 142. *Año* 1550; ibid., fol. 176. *Año* 1551.
7. MacLeod 1973, p. 99.
8. *Annals* 1967, p. 145.
9. Vásquez 1938, 2:33.
10. *RGA* 1964, p. 95.
11. Ocaña 1932-33, pp. 301-302. Even in modern times people of Atitlán have had to buy supplementary maize (Douglas 1968, p. 247).
12. *RGA* 1964, p. 95.
13. Ocaña 1932-33, p. 302.
14. *RGZ* 1955, p. 73.
15. MacLeod 1973, pp. 70-71.
16. Madigan 1976, p. 109.
17. AGI Contaduría 971B fol. 103. *Año* 1612.
18. FyG 1972, 2:41.
19. Bishop Ramírez in Sherman 1968, p. 23.
20. Gibson 1964, p. 243; *RGA* 1964, p. 100.
21. Bishop Ramírez in Sherman 1968, p. 24.
22. Estrada 1955, p. 77.
23. Madigan 1976, pp. 110-11; MacLeod 1973, pp. 171-73.
24. *RGZ* 1955, pp. 78-79.

25. *RGA* 1964, p. 104.
26. Ibid., p. 102; Ocaña 1932-33, p. 297.
27. Vásquez 1938, 2:33.
28. MacLeod 1973, pp. 215-16.
29. Ocaña 1932-33, p. 302.
30. Madigan 1976, p. 145; MacLeod 1973, pp. 127-28.
31. *RGA* 1964, p. 100.
32. *RGZ* 1955, pp. 70, 79. See MacLeod 1973, pp. 82-83, for a discussion of merchants trading in this fashion with Indians in Izalcos.
33. Gibson 1964, p. 360.
34. Bishop Ramírez in Sherman 1968, p. 10.
35. Gage 1969, pp. 225-26.
36. *RGA* 1964, pp. 104-105; Pineda 1925, p. 340.
37. FyG 1972, 2:41.
38. Vásquez 1944, 4:52.
39. Ibid., p. 46.
40. *RGA* 1964, p. 105.
41. FyG 1972, 2:43-44.
42. See, for example, Gage 1969, p. 186.
43. Kitchen 1955, p. 12.
44. See MacLeod 1973, p. 249, for the value in reales of cacao per load in Guatemala from 1524 to 1682.
45. Gibson 1964, p. 357; *RT* 1952, p. 437.
46. Gage 1969, p. 186.
47. Ocaña 1932-33, pp. 301-302.
48. FyG 1972, 2:39.
49. Ocaña 1932-33, p. 302; *RGA* 1964, p. 105.
50. Estrada 1955, pp. 76-77.
51. *RGSF* 1952, p. 140.
52. Ocaña 1932-33, pp. 301-302.

CHAPTER 14

1. Gibson 1964, pp. 154-55.
2. Spores 1967, p. 110.
3. Carrasco 1967b, p. 321; AGC A1 *exp.* 52,042 *leg.* 5,946. *Año* 1563.
4. *RC* in Carmack 1973, p. 379; *RG* in ibid., pp. 383-84.
5. Ibid., pp. 20-21, *RC* in ibid., p. 379.
6. Solórzano Pereira 1972, 1:406.
7. *Annals* 1967, p. 132.
8. Cobo in Vásquez de Espinosa 1944, pp. 195-96.
9. Carrasco 1967b, p. 321; AGC A1 *exp.* 52,042 *leg.* 5,946. *Año* 1563.
10. *RT* 1952, p. 436.
11. De la Parra 1889, p. 195.
12. Chamberlain 1939, p. 130.
13. MacLeod 1973, p. 137.
14. Chamberlain 1939, p. 131.
15. MacLeod 1973, p. 138.
16. Ximénez 1929, 1:216.
17. Ibid., 1:244.
18. Bancroft 1886, 2:325n.
19. *Ordena su Majestad que a los indios de Atitlán, se les trate bien y así mismo a su cacique don Juan.* AGC A1.23 *exp.* 1,511 *leg.* 62. *Año* 1547.
20. *RT* 1952, p. 438.
21. Zorita 1971, p. 115.
22. López de Cerrato in Carmack 1973, pp. 378-79.
23. Roys 1972, p. 132, quoting from the *Recopilación de leyes de las reynos de las Indias.*
24. Carrasco 1967a, pp. 251-59.
25. *RT* 1952, pp. 436-38.
26. MacLeod 1973, p. 141.
27. Gage 1969, p. 220.
28. In a document dated 1650 only one Indian is mentioned using the title of "don." *Autos creados en virtud de la queja del Corregidor del Po. de Santiago Atitlán contra de P. Guardían fray Gabriel de Amaya. . . .* A1.1 *exp.* 48,870 *leg.* 5,797. *Año* 1650.
29. *RT* 1952, p. 436.
30. Pineda 1925, p. 341.
31. *RGA* 1964, p. 96.
32. Carrasco 1967a, pp. 262-65.
33. Carmack 1965, pp. 446-47.
34. AGC A1 *exp.* 52,042 *leg.* 5,946. *Año* 1563.
35. Cobo in Vásquez de Espinosa 1944, pp. 195-96.
36. *Annals* 1967, p. 145.
37. AGC A3.16 *exp.* 40,490 *leg.* 2,801. *Año* 1599.
38. Vásquez 1937, 1:70.

39. Gross 1974, pp. 37–39, 49.
40. See, for example, Gage 1969, pp. 221-22.
41. Ibid.
42. Paul and Paul 1963, pp. 132-33.
43. *Recopilación* 1971, 2:190.
44. *RG* in Carmack 1973, p. 384.
45. Gross 1974, p. 53. Whether or not a child receives an inheritance, however, depends to a large extent on whether filial obligations have been met during the parents' lifetime (Gross and Kendall, 1983, p. 209).
46. Personal observation, 1979.

CHAPTER 15

1. Gerhard 1972, p. 75.
2. Ibid., pp. 130-31.
3. Ibid., p. 129.
4. Gibson 1964, p. 84.
5. Ibid., pp. 90-91.
6. AGC A1.23 *leg.* 1,512 fol. 270. *Año* 1559.
7. *Recopilación* 1971, 2:210-11.
8. Gibson 1964, pp. 181-83; Gage 1969, p. 227. For Atitlán the offices of *alcalde* and *mayordomo* are mentioned in AGC A1 *exp.* 52, 042 leg. 5, 946. *Año* 1563.
9. Gibson 1964, p. 175.
10. Kitchen 1955, p. 17; and see, for example, *RGA* 1964, p. 96.
11. Gage 1969, p. 227.
12. *Annals* 1967, p. 145.
13. See for example *RT* 1952; AGC A1.11.14 *exp.* 31,428 *leg.* 4,055. *Año* 1587; ibid., A1 *exp.* 51,997 *leg.* 5,942 fol. 1. *Año* 1641.
14. Gibson 1964, pp. 181-82.
15. Gage 1969, pp. 227-28.
16. Ibid., p. 229.
17. *Recopilación* 1971, 2:211.
18. Garcés in Carmack 1973, pp. 383-84.
19. Chinchilla Aguilar 1963, pp. 27-36.
20. AGC A1.23 *leg.* 1,512 fol. 396. *Año* 1561.
21. Carrasco 1967b, pp. 320-23;

AGC A1 *exp.* 52,042 *leg.* 5,946. *Año* 1563.
22. See, for example, *TN* 2 1957.
23. Carrasco 1967b, pp. 329-30.
24. *Annals* 1967, p. 145.
25. Ibid., p. 152.
26. *RGA* 1964, p. 93.
27. AGC A1 *exp.* 52,042 *leg.* 5,946. *Año* 1563.
28. AGC A1 *exp.* 31,428 *leg.* 4,055 fol. 35. *Año* 1587.
29. Gibson 1964, p. 188; Aguirre 1972, pp. 52-53.
30. AGC A1 *exp.* 51,997 *leg.* 5,942 fol. 11. *Año* 1641; Aguirre 1972, p. 83.
31. *RGAG* 1965, p. 265; *RGSA* 1952, p. 122; Aguirre (1972, p. 53) mentions San Pedro and San Pablo as being officially founded by 1575 San Juan by 1623.
32. After independence from Spain a new political system was established, the department-township system, which kept the old *alcaldía mayores* largely intact. The *alcaldía mayor* of Sololá became the Department of Sololá. Each department was divided into a number of *municipios,* which are similar to the townships of the United States. Most of the towns around Lake Atitlán became *cabeceras,* or head towns, of their respective *municipios.* The *municipios* are presently composed of *aldeas* (hamlets) and *caseríos* (small rural communities or groups of houses), which are subordinate to the *cabecera* of the *municipio* (Dombrowski et al. 1970, pp. 51, 53).
33. Gibson 1964, p. 83.
34. Bishop Ramírez in Sherman 1968, p. 10.
35. AGC A1.23 *leg.* 1,511 fol. 186. *Año* 1552.
36. Ibid., *leg.* 1,512 fol. 253. *Año* 1559.
37. See, for example, MacLeod 1973, pp. 90-91, who discusses the *visita* of García de Palacios to Izalcos in 1575.
38. AGC A1.23 *leg.* 1,513 fol. 608. *Año* 1582.
39. Bishop Ramírez in Sherman

1968, pp. 11-12.
40. Ibid., p. 25.
41. Gibson 1964, p. 93; MacLeod 1973, p. 316.
42. AGC A1.23 *leg.* 1,513 fol. 620. *Año* 1582. In 1636 the *alcalde mayor* was prohibited from carrying out such practices in San Antonio Suchitepéquez. AGC A1.2 *exp.* 16,190 *leg.* 2,245 fols. 97v, 168v. *Año* 1636.
43. MacLeod 1973, p. 316.
44. AGC A1.23 *leg.* 4,576. *Año* 1609.
45. *Sobre carta a la real provisión librada el 23 de febrero de 1679 prohibiendo a los alcaldes mayores de Atitlán y Tecpán Atitlán repartan algodon entre los indígenas del pueblo Sta. Lucia Utatlán.* AGC A1.24 *exp.* 10,232 *leg.* 1,588 fol. 226. *Año* 1679.
46. FyG 1972, 3:116.

CHAPTER 16

1. Cline 1972b, p. 27.
2. Remesal 1932, 1:431.
3. Gibson 1964, p. 98.
4. Ximénez 1929, 1:197, 511.
5. Ibid., p. 178.
6. MacLeod 1973, pp. 107-108.
7. Ximénez 1929, 1:216-17; see Saint-Lu 1968 for a discussion of the role of the Dominicans.
8. *Annals* 1967, pp. 134-35.
9. AGC A1.24 *leg.* 15,752 fol. 41. *Año* 1538.
10. *Carta al príncipe Don Felipe II, 30 de enero de 1552.* AGI Guatemala *leg.* 168.
11. *RGA* 1964, p. 97.
12. *RGA* 1964, p. 96.
13. See Aguirre 1972, pp. 175-79, for a list of the *guardianes* of Santiago Atitlán from 1566 to 1638. After the mid-seventeenth century, priests were referred to as *curas doctrineros* in the Tzutujil area (ibid., pp. 196-203).
14. *RGA* 1964, p. 98.
15. Ibid., pp. 175-76.
16. Vásquez 1937; 1:87; Vásquez

1938, 2:20; *RT* 1952, p. 437.
17. *RT* 1952, pp. 437-38.
18. AGI Guatemala *leg.* 169. *Año* 1575.
19. Aguirre 1972, p. 170.
20. Ponce 1873, p. 446.
21. *RGA* 1964, p. 98.
22. Cobo in Vásquez de Espinosa 1944, p. 195.
23. *RGA* 1964, p. 97.
24. Ponce 1873, pp. 309-10.
25. Estrada 1955, p. 72.
26. Ponce 1873, p. 433.
27. Vásquez 1937, 1:250-51, 318.
28. Santa Bárbara eventually became an *anexo* of the Curate of Patulul. Cortés y Larraz 1958, 2:283.
29. Aguirre 1972, pp. 62, 103.
30. AGC A1.23 *leg.* 1,512 fol. 306. *Año* 1562.
31. Ibid., *leg.* 4,588 fol. 46. *Años* 1533, 1553.
32. AGC A1.11.3 *exp.* 31,428 *leg.* 4,055. *Año* 1587.
33. Gage 1959, p. 230.
34. *RT* 1952, p. 436.
35. MacLeod 1973, p. 139.
36. Pineda 1925, p. 350.
37. Vásquez 1944, 4:292.
38. *Instancia del común del pueblo de Atitan piden fondos para reconstruir el templo Parroquial.* AGC A1.11.25 *exp.* 47,525 *leg.* 5,505. *Año* 1683; AGC A1.10.3 *exp.* 31,308 *leg.* 4,047. *Año* 1735.
39. *RGAG* 1965, p. 267.
40. Ponce 1873, pp. 308-309, 431.
41. AGC A1.23 *leg.* 1,520 fol. 262. *Año* 1676.
42. Gage 1969, p. 232.
43. AGC A1.23 *leg.* 4,588 fol. 46. *Año* 1553.
44. Aguirre 1972, p. 201; AGC A1.2-4 *leg.* 2,195 fol. 211. *Año* 1565.
45. AGC A1.23 *exp.* 1,513 fol. 529. *Año* 1570.
46. Aguirre 1972, pp. 201, 202n.
47. Gibson 1964, p. 123.
48. Villacorta Calderón 1942, p. 158.
49. AGC A1.23 *leg.* 1,512 fol. 303. *Año* 1562.

50. AGI Patronato 82-3-2. *Año* 1600.
51. AGC A1.23 *leg.* 1,511 fol. 105. *Año* 1549.
52. Madigan 1976, p. 61.
53. See, for example, McDougall 1955, p. 67.
54. Gage 1969, pp. 236, 238.
55. AGC A1.23 *leg.* 1,513 fol. 558. *Año* 1578.
56. Ibid., *leg.* 1,512 fol. 269. *Año* 1560.
57. Ibid., *leg.* 1,513 fol. 698. *Año* 1588.
58. Vásquez 1938, 2:31.
59. AGC A1.23 *leg.* 1,513 fol. 525. *Año* 1577.
60. MacLeod 1973, p. 327.
61. Pineda 1925, p. 348.
62. Among the religious expenses defrayed by *caja* funds in Atitlán in the eighteenth century were the following: 12 *tostones* for candles on the Day of Apparition and 50 *tostones* for candles on the Day of Corpus; 71 *tostones* a year as salary for eight *cantores* and two cooks; 4 *tostones* as alms for Jerusalem and 4 *tostones* to the Redempción de Capillas (*Cuentes rendidas por los justicias de los partidos de Atitlán Tecpanatitlán del movimiento habido en los fondos de comunidades indígenas, durante 1709.* AGC A1.73 *exp.* 48,424 *leg.* 5,766. *Año* 1710).
63. *RGA* 1964, p. 96.
64. A1.2-4 *leg.* 2,195 fol. 215v. *Año* 1565.
65. AGC A1.2-4 *leg.* 2,195 fol. 214v. *Año* 1565.
66. *RGA* 1964, p. 96.
67. See, for example, Aguirre 1972, addenda page.
68. *RGA* 1964, p. 96.
69. *RGAG* 1964, p. 268.
70. *Recopilación* 1971, 2:208-209.
71. Gibson 1964, p. 185.
72. *TA* in Carmack 1973, p. 373.
73. Paul 1968, pp. 135-36.
74. *Recopilación* 1971, 2:209.
75. Vásquez 1938, 2:39.
76. Gage 1969, pp. 230-31.
77. Vásquez 1944, 4:343.

78. Gage 1969, pp. 231-33; Aguirre 1972, p. 202.
79. Personal observation, 1971.
80. Gage 1967, p. 231.
81. Miles 1965, p. 286.
82. AGC A1.23 *leg.* 1,512 fol. 384. *Año* 1571.
83. AGC A3.16 *exp.* 17,723 *leg.* 951. *Año* 1768.
84. Vásquez 1937, 1:110.
85. Ibid., 2:20.
86. Ibid., pp. 28-29.
87. Cortés y Larraz 1958, 2:281.
88. Chinchilla Aguilar 1963, pp. 11, 13.
89. FyG 1969, 1:78.
90. Cortés y Larraz 1958, 2:286.
91. Gage 1969, p. 234.
92. Estrada 1955, p. 74.
93. Aguirre 1972, pp. 412-13n.
94. See Gibson 1964, p. 100, who refers specifically to Mexico.
95. See Bunzel 1967, p. 268.
96. Gage 1969, p. 240.
97. Ibid., p. 234.
98. See Orellana 1975b, p. 847.
99. Aguirre 1972, p. 343.
100. Mendelson 1958b, p. 6; Mendelson 1967, p. 400.
101. FyG 1969, 1:187.
102. Pardo 1944, pp. 12, 15.
103. Gibson 1964, p. 127.
104. Bremme de Santos 1965-66, p. 94.
105. *Annals* 1967, p. 154.
106. Aguirre 1972, p. 343. The only other information available on early *cofradías* is an inscription on a chalice in the church of Santiago Atitlán indicating that the Cofradía San Nicolas dates back at least to 1631 (Mendelson 1957, pp. 148-49).
107. *Cortés y Larraz, razon del instituto y advocación de las enunciadas cofradías y hermandades, del aprovechamiento y perjuicio que resulta a los fieles, y de si deben reformarse en todo, o en parte, y en que terminos.* AGI Guatemala *leg.* 948. *Año* 1775.
108. *Autos tramitados a instancia del Obispo de Guatemala, para reglamen-*

*tar los estipendios de cofradías y gua-chivales.* AGC A1.11.2 *exp.* 48,536 *leg.* 5,776 fol. 118. *Año* 1740.

109. Gage 1969, p. 235; Cobo in Vásquez de Espinosa 1944, p. 195.

110. Mendelson 1957, p. 98.

111. FyG 1969, 1:331-32.

112. Aguirre 1972, p. 347.

113. FyG 1969, 1:362.

114. *Libro de hermandad de San Juan de Bautista de Santiago Atitlán.* *Año* 1712 (part of this book is still in the Cofradía of San Juan; William Douglas has the other part).

115. Vásquez 1944, 4:343.

116. Aguirre 1972, p. 346.

117. See Sharon 1971.

118. Gage 1969, p. 235.

119. Ibid., p. 232.

120. Aguirre 1972, p. 352.

121. See, for example, *Libro de hermandad de San Juan Bautista. Año* 1712.

122. *Auto de Visita de Mons. Navas y Quevedo. Año* 1683 (William Douglas has this document).

123. Aguirre 1972, pp. 402-403.

124. Carmack 1966, p. 44.

125. FyG 1969, 1:332.

126. Bremme de Santos 1965-66, pp. 93-95.

127. Personal observation, 1971.

128. FyG 1969, 1:77.

129. Mendelson 1958a, p. 122.

130. Personal observation, 1973.

131. Mendelson 1965, p. 57; Mendelson 1957, p. 566; Ordóñez Chipín 1970, pp. 147-49; Lothrop 1929a, pp. 2-9.

132. Gage 1969, p. 243.

133. AGI Guatemala *leg.* 948; fols. 12v, 14v. *Año* 1775.

134. AGC A1.11.2 *exp.* 16,190 *leg.* 2,245 *fol. 169. Año* 1637.

135. Vásquez 1944, 4:46-47, 53-54; Vásquez mentions only approved *cofradías.* In 1829 there were eight *cofradías* and five *hermandades* in Atitlán. There were three *cofradías* in Tolimán. *(Ingreso del curato de Atitan según consta del Quadrante que fue reformado y el año de 1829 siendo provisor y Governador del Arzobispado el Dr. D. Antonio Alcayago;* William Douglas has this document). In 1971 there were ten *cofradías* in Atitlán: Santa Cruz, Santiago, San Juan, San Antonio, Concepción, San Nicolas, San Gregorio, San Felipe, Ánimas, and Rosario (Sharon 1971).

136. See, for example, Vásquez 1938, 2:20, 25, 28 and the *Relaciones geográficas* of Atitlán and its dependencies. Douglas 1969 discusses the existence of many of these practices in contemporary Atitlán.

137. Miles 1957, pp. 750-51. For a discussion of religious practitioners among the Quichés in the late seventeenth century, see Chinchilla Aguilar 1963, pp. 67-69.

138. Cortés y Larraz 1958, 1:260.

## CHAPTER 17

1. Foster 1960.

2. See, for example, Herskovitz 1938; La Farge 1940; Beals 1967; Schwerin 1970.

3. Beals 1967.

4. Tedlock 1983, p. 237.

5. Ibid., pp. 238-43, presents a case study of such a conflict in the Quiché town of Momostenango in recent times.

6. Beals 1967, p. 449.

7. See, for example, Tedlock 1983, p. 243.

# Bibliography

## ARCHIVAL SOURCES

Many unpublished archival sources have been used in the preparation of this book. Most of these documents are in the Archivo General de Indias, Seville, and in the Archivo General de Centroamérica, Guatemala City. Other manuscripts used are in the Cofradía of San Juan in Atitlán and in the collection of William Douglas, who rescued them from being discarded while he was doing fieldwork in Santiago Atitlán.

### Archivo General de Indias (AGI)

Four divisions of the archive provided information: Audiencia de Guatemala, Justicia, Patronato, and Contaduría. One of the most important documents, in the Patronato division (82-3-2), lists the tribute collected in the Tzutujil region from 1564 to 1599. Another, Justicia 295, which pertains to Pedro Alvarado's *residencia,* is important in the reconstruction of early Tzutujil *encomienda* history.

### Archivo General de Centroamérica (AGC)

In citations to works in this archive the letter *A* refers to colonial documents, the letter *B* to postindependence documents. Almost all sources used were colonial. In citations to these documents *exp.* refers to *expediente* (proceedings), *leg.* to *legajo* (file), and "fol." to folio. The colonial documents are subdivided into four parts: A1, Superior Gobierno; A2, Capitanía General; A3, Real Hacienda; and A4, Eclesiástica. Most of the documents used come from the Superior Gobierno group, but several from Real Hacienda were also consulted. Documents of particular importance to the study of the Tzutujils are A3.16 *exp.* 40,490 *leg.* 2,801, which gives a long list of tributaries for Atitlán and its dependencies; and A1 *exp.* 52,042 *leg.* 5,946, which gives detailed information concerning the Tzutujil political organization in 1563.

PUBLISHED SOURCES

Adams, Richard N., and Arthur J. Rubel
1967    Sickness and social relations. In Manning Nash, ed. *Social anthropology*. Handbook of Middle American Indians, 6: 333-56. Austin: University of Texas Press.
Aguirre, Gerardo G.
1972    *La cruz de Nimajuyú: Historia de la Parroquia de San Pedro la Laguna*. Guatemala City.
Alvarado, Pedro de
1954    *Relación hecha por Pedro de Alvarado a Hernando Cortés, en que se refieren las guerras y batallas para pacificar las provincias del antiguo reino de Goathemala (1524)*. Mexico City: Jose Porrúa e Hijos.
*Anales de los Cakchiqueles [Anales]*
1950    *Memorial de Sololá: Anales de los Cakchiqueles, Título de los señores de Totonicapán*. Mexico: Fondo de Cultura Económica.
*Annals of the Cakchiquels [Annals]*
1967    *The Annals of the Cakchiquels*. Translated from the Cakchiquel Maya by Adrián Recinos and Delia Goetz. *Title of the Lords of Totonicapán*. Translated from the Quiché text into Spanish by Dionisio José Chonay, English Version by Delia Goetz. Norman: University of Oklahoma Press.
Arboleda, Pedro de    See *Relación geográfica*
Atwood, Wallace W.
1935    Lago de Atitlán. *Anales de la Sociedad de Geografía e Historia de Guatemala* 11:259-63. Guatemala City.
Bancroft, Herbert Howe
1882-87 *History of Central America*. 3 vols. In *Works*. San Francisco: History Co.
Baudez, Claude F.
1971    Commentary on: Inventory of some Pre-Classic traits in the highlands and Pacific Guatemala and adjunct areas. In Robert F. Heizer and John A. Graham, eds. *Observations on the emergence of civilization in Mesoamerica*. Contributions of the University of California Archaeological Research Facility, no. 11, pp. 78-84. Berkeley: Department of Anthropology, University of California.
Beals, Ralph L.
1967    Acculturation. In Manning Nash, ed. *Social anthropology*. Handbook of Middle American Indians, 6:449-68. Austin: University of Texas Press.
Bernal, Ignacio
1962    Archaeology and written sources. *Akten des 34 Internationalen Amerikanistenkongresses*, pp. 219-25. Vienna.
Betancor, Alonso Páez    See *Relación geográfica*

Borhegyi, Stephan F.
1959      Culto a la Imagen del Señor de Esquipulas en Centro America y Nuevo México. *Antropología y historia de Guatemala* 11, no. 1:44-49. Guatemala City.
1965      Archaeological synthesis of the Guatemalan highlands. In Gordon R. Willey, ed. *Archaeology of southern Mesoamerica.* Handbook of Middle American Indians, 2:3-58. Austin: University of Texas Press.

Bremme de Santos, Ida
1965-66   La cofradía en Guatemala. *Cuadernos* 5:91-99. Buenos Aires: Instituto Nacional de Antropología.

Bricker, Victoria Reifler
1981      *The Indian Christ, the Indian King: The historical substrate of Maya myth and ritual.* Austin: University of Texas Press.

Bunzel, Ruth
1967      *Chichicastenango: A Guatemalan village.* Seattle: University of Washington Press.

Campbell, Lyle R.
1971      Historical linguistics and Quichean linguistic prehistory. Ph.D. dissertation, University of California at Los Angeles.
1972      A note on the so-called Alaguilac language. *International Journal of American Linguistics* 38, no. 3:203-207.

Carmack, Robert M.
1965      The documentary sources, ecology, and cultural history of the prehispanic Quiché Maya. Ph.D. diss., University of California at Los Angeles.
1966      La perpetuación del clan patrilineal en Totonicapán. *Antropología e historia de Guatemala* 18, no. 2:43-60. Guatemala City.
1968      *Toltec influence on the Post-Classic culture history of highland Guatemala.* Middle American Research Institute, Tulane University, Publication no. 26, pp. 49-92. New Orleans.
1971      Ethnography and ethnohistory: Their application in Middle American studies. *Ethnohistory* 18:127-45.
1973      *Quichean civilization: The ethnohistoric, ethnographic, and archaeological sources.* Berkeley and Los Angeles: University of California Press.
1977      Ethnohistory of the central Quiche: The community of Utatlan. In Dwight T. Wallace and Robert M. Carmack, eds. *Archaeology and ethnohistory of the central Quiche.* Institute for Mesoamerican Studies, State University of New York, Publication no. 1, pp. 1-19. Albany.
1981      *The Quiché Mayas of Utatlán: The evolution of a highland Guatemala kingdom.* Norman: University of Oklahoma Press.

———, Juan Fox, and Rosalio Stewart
1975      *La formacion del reino Quiche.* Instituto de Antropología

e Historia, Publication no. 7. Guatemala City.

Carrasco, Pedro
1964 Los nombres de persona en la Guatemala antigua. *Estudios de cultura maya* 4:323-34. Mexico City.
1967a Don Juan Cortés, cacique de Santa Cruz Quiché. *Estudios de cultura maya* 6:251-66. Mexico City.
1967b El señorío Tz'utuhil de Atitlán en el siglo XVI. *Revista mexicana de estudios antropológicos* 21:317-31. Mexico City.
N.d. Kinship and territorial groups in pre-Spanish Guatemala. Manuscript.

Chamberlain, Robert S.
1939 The concept of *señor natural* as revealed by Castilian law and administrative documents. *Hispanic American Historical Review* 19:130-37.

Chinchilla Aguilar, Ernesto
1963 *La Danza del Sacrificio y otros estudios.* Ministerio de Educación Pública. Guatemala City: Central Editorial José de Pineda Ibarra.

Cline, Howard F.
1972a Introduction: Reflections on ethnohistory. In Howard F. Cline, ed. *Guide to ethnohistorical sources.* Handbook of Middle American Indians, 12:3-16. Austin: University of Texas Press.
1972b Introductory notes of territorial divisions of Middle America. In Howard F. Cline, ed. *Guide to ethnohistorical sources.* Handbook of Middle American Indians, 12:17-62. Austin: University of Texas Press.

Cobo, Bernabé
1944 Cartas del P. Bernabé Cobo de la Companía de Jesús (1630). In *Descripción de la Nueva España en el siglo XVII por padre fray Antonio Vásquez de Espinosa,* pp. 195-206. Mexico City: Editorial Patria.

Coe, Michael D., and Kent V. Flannery
1967 Early cultures and human ecology in south coastal Guatemala. Washington, D.C.: Smithsonian Press.

*Colección de documentos inéditos* [*CDI*]
1925 *Colección de documentos inéditos relativos al descubrimiento, conquista y organización de las antiguas posesiones españoles de ultramar.* 2d ser. 25 vols. Madrid, 1885-1932.

Cortés y Larraz, Pedro
1958 *Descripción geográfico-moral de la diocesis de Goathemala (1768-1770).* 2 vols. Biblioteca Goathemala, vol. 22. Guatemala City.

Crespo, Mario M.
1956 Títulos indígenas de tierras. *Antropología e historia de Guatemala* 8, no. 2:10-15. Guatemala City.

*Crónica Franciscana* [*CF*]
1973    Crónica franciscana [?] In Robert M. Carmack. *Quichean civilization: The ethnohistoric, ethnographic, and archaeological sources,* pp. 374-77. Berkeley and Los Angeles: University of California Press.

Díaz del Castillo, Bernal
1927    *The true history of the conquest of Mexico, written in the year 1568 by Captain Bernal Díaz del Castillo.* Translated by Maurice Keatinge. New York: R. M. McBride Co.

*Diccionario geográfico* [*DG*]
1961-62    *Diccionario geográfico de Guatemala.* 2 vols. Guatemala City: Dirección General de Cartografía.

Dombrowski, John, et al.
1970    *Area handbook for Guatemala.* Washington, D.C.: U.S. Government Printing Office.

Douglas, William G.
1968    Santiago Atitlán. In Sol Tax, ed. *Los pueblos del Lago de Atitlán,* pp. 229-76. Seminario de Integración Social Guatemalteca. Guatemala City: Tipografía Nacional.
1969    Illness and curing in Santiago Atitlán: A Tzutujil Maya community in the southwestern highlands of Guatemala. Ph.D. dissertation, Stanford University.

Edmonson, Munro
1965    *Quiche-English dictionary.* Middle American Research Institute, Tulane University, Publication no. 30. New Orleans.
————, trans.
1971    *The Book of Counsel: The Popol Vuh of the Quiche Maya of Guatemala.* Middle American Research Institute, Tulane University, Publication no. 35. New Orleans.

Estrada, Juan de
1955    Relación geográfica Zapotitlán y Suchitepéquez: Descripción de la Provincia de Zapotitlán y Suchitepéquez (1579) por su alcalde mayor capitán Juan de Estrada y el escribano Fernando de Niebla. *Anales de la Sociedad de Geografía e Historia de Guatemala* 28:68-83. Guatemala City.
1966    Mapa de la costa de Suchitepéquez y Zapotitlán (1579). *Anales de la Sociedad de Geografía e Historia de Guatemala* 39:96-99. Guatemala City.

Estrada Monroy, Augustín
1968    Los primeros españoles que llegaron a Guatemala. *Anales de la Sociedad de Geografía e Historia de Guatemala* 41: 565-68. Guatemala City.
1972    Lenguas de 12 provincias de Guatemala en el siglo XVIII. *Guatemala indígena* 7, no. 4, pp. 23-70. Guatemala City.

Feldman, Lawrence H.
1971    A tumpline economy: Production and distribution systems of early central-east Guatemala. Ph.D. dissertation, Pennsyl-

vania State University.

Foster, George
1960      *Culture and conquest: America's Spanish heritage.* Viking
          Fund Publications in Anthropology, no. 27. New York.

Fox, John
1977      Quiche expansion processes: Differential ecological growth
          bases within an archaic state. In Dwight T. Wallace and
          Robert M. Carmack, eds. *Archaeology and ethnohistory of
          the central Quiche.* Institute for Mesoamerican Studies,
          State University of New York, Publication no. 1, pp. 82-97.
          Albany.

1978      *Quiche conquest: Centralism and regionalism in highland
          Guatemalan state development.* Albuquerque: University
          of New Mexico Press.

1980      Lowland to highland Mexicanization processes in southern
          Mesoamerica. *American Antiquity* 45, no. 1:43-54.

Fuentes y Guzmán, Francisco Antonio de
1969-72   *Obras históricas de don Francisco Antonio de Fuentes y
          Guzmán: recordación Florida.* Edited by Carmelo Sáenz de
          Santa María. Biblioteca de Autores Españoles. Madrid: Edi-
          ciones Atlas.

Gage, Thomas
1969      *Thomas Gage's travels in the New World.* Edited by J. Eric
          S. Thompson. Norman: University of Oklahoma Press.

Garcés, Diego de    See *Relación Garcés*

Gerhard, Peter
1972      Colonial New Spain, 1519-1786: Historical notes on the
          evolution of minor political jurisdictions. In Howard F.
          Cline, ed. *Guide to ethnohistorical sources.* Handbook of
          Middle American Indians, 12: 63-137. Austin: University
          of Texas Press.

Gibson, Charles
1952      *Tlaxcala in the sixteenth century.* New Haven, Conn.: Yale
          University Press.

1964      *The Aztecs under Spanish rule: A history of the Indians of
          the Valley of Mexico, 1519-1810.* Stanford, Calif.: Stanford
          University Press.

1966      *Spain in America.* New York: Harper and Row, Harper
          Torchbooks.

Grimes, James Larry
1968      *Cakchiquel-Tzutujil: Estudio sobre su unidad lingüística.*
          Estudios centroamericanos, no. 4. Seminario de Integración
          Social Guatemalteca. Guatemala City: Ministerio de Edu-
          cación.

Gross, Joseph J.
1974      Domestic group structure in a Mayan community of Guate-
          mala. Ph.D. dissertation, University of Rochester.

———, and Carl Kendall
1983      The analysis of domestic organization in Mesoamerica: The
          case of postmarital residence in Santiago Atitlán, Guate-
          mala. In Carl Kendall, John Hawkins, and Laurel Bossen,
          eds. *Heritage of conquest: Thirty years later*, pp. 201-228.
          Albuquerque: University of New Mexico Press.
*Guatemala Project*
1970      *Guatemala project: Guatemalan research and field training
          project.* Los Angeles: Department of Anthropology, Univer-
          sity of California.
Guillemín, Jorge F.
1965      *Iximché: Capital del antiguo reino cakchiquel.* Instituto de
          Antropología e Historia de Guatemala. Guatemala City:
          Tipografía Nacional.
1977      Urbanism and hierarchy at Iximché. In Norman Hammond,
          ed. *Social Process in Maya prehistory*, pp. 227-64. New
          York: Academic Press.
Herskovits, Melville
1938      *Acculturation: The study of culture contact.* New York: J. J.
          Augustin.
Juarros, Domingo
1823      *A statistical and commercial history of the kingdom of Gua-
          temala in Spanish America.* Translated by J. Baily. London.
Kelly, John E.
1932      *Pedro de Alvarado, Conquistador.* Princeton, N.J.: Prince-
          ton University Press.
Kitchen, James D.
1955      Municipal government in Guatemala. Ph.D. dissertation,
          University of California at Los Angeles.
La Farge, Oliver
1940      Maya ethnology: The sequence of cultures. In *The Maya
          and their Neighbors*, pp. 281-91. New York: D. Appleton-
          Century Co.
Landa, Bishop Diego de
1966      *Landa's relación de las cosas de Yucatán.* Edited by Alfred
          M. Tozzer. Papers of the Peabody Museum of American
          Archaeology and Ethnology, Harvard University, vol. 18.
          Reprint. New York: Kraus Reprint Corp.
Las Casas, Bartolomé de
1967      *Apologética historia sumaria.* Edited by Juan O'Gorman. 2
          vols. Mexico City: Instituto de Investigaciones Históricas,
          Universidad Nacional Autónoma de México.
*Lienzo de Tlaxcala*
1892      *Homenaje a Cristóbal Colón: Antiguedades mexicanas
          publicadas por la Junta Colombina de México en el cuarto
          centenario del descubrimiento de América.* Mexico City:
          Oficina Tipográfica de la Secretaria de Fomento.

Lockhart, James
    1969        Encomienda and hacienda: The evolution of the great estate
                in the Spanish Indies. *Hispanic American Historical Review*
                49, no. 3:411-29.
López de Cerrato, Alonso
    1973        Relación Cerrato. In Robert M. Carmack. *Quichean civili-
                zation: The ethnohistoric, ethnographic, and archaeological
                sources*, pp. 378-79. Berkeley and Los Angeles: University
                of California Press.
Lothrop, Eleanor
    1948        *Throw me a bone: What happens when you marry an ar-
                chaeologist*. New York: Whittlesey House, McGraw-Hill
                Book Co.
Lothrop, Samuel K.
    1928        Santiago Atitlán, Guatemala. *Indian Notes* 5, no. 4:370-
                95. New York: Museum of the Americana Indian, Heye
                Foundation.
    1929a       Further notes on Indian ceremonies in Guatemala. *Indian
                Notes* 6, no. 1:1-25. New York: Museum of the American
                Indian, Heye Foundation.
    1929b       Canoes of Lake Atitlán, Guatemala. *Indian Notes* 6, no. 3:
                216-21. New York: Museum of the American Indian, Heye
                Foundation.
    1933        *Atitlan: An archaeological study of ancient remains on the
                borders of Lake Atitlan, Guatemala*. Carnegie Institution of
                Washington, Publication no. 444. Washington, D.C.
McBryde, Felix W.
    1947        *Cultural and historical geography of southwest Guatemala*.
                Smithsonian Institution, Institute of Social Anthropology,
                Publication no. 4. Washington, D.C.
McDougall, Elsie
    1955        *Easter ceremonies at Santiago Atitlan in 1930*. Carnegie
                Institution of Washington, Notes on Middle American Ar-
                chaeology and Ethnology, no. 123. Washington, D.C.
MacLeod, Murdo J.
    1973        *Spanish Central America: A socioeconomic history, 1520-
                1720*. Berkeley and Los Angeles: University of California
                Press.
Madigan, Douglas G.
    1976        Santiago Atitlán, Guatemala: A socioeconomic and demo-
                graphic history. Ph.D. dissertation, University of Pittsburgh.
Mendelson, E. Michael
    1957        *Religion and world view in a Guatemalan village*. Microfilm
                Collection of Manuscripts of Middle American Cultural An-
                thropology, 8th ser., no. 52. Chicago: University of Chicago
                Library.
    1958a       A Guatemalan sacred bundle. *Man* 58:121-26. London.

1958b    The king, the traitor, and the cross. *Diogenes* 21:1-10. Chicago.

1959    Maximón: An iconographical introduction. *Man* 59:57-60. London.

1965    *Los escándalos de Maximón.* Seminario de Integración Social Guatemalteca, Publication no. 19. Guatemala.

1967    Ritual and mythology. In Manning Nash, ed. *Social anthropology.* Handbook of Middle American Indians, 6:392-415. Austin: University of Texas Press.

Miles, S. W.
1957    The sixteenth-century Pokom-Maya: A documentary analysis of social structure and archaeological setting. *Transactions of the American Philosophical Society* 47:731-81. Philadelphia.

1965    Summary of preconquest ethnology of the Guatemala-Chiapas highlands and Pacific slopes. In Gordon R. Willey, ed. *Archaeology of southern Mesoamerica.* Handbook of Middle American Indians, 2:276-87. Austin: University of Texas Press.

Nash, Manning
1967    Indian economies. In Manning Nash, ed. *Social anthropology.* Handbook of Middle American Indians, 6:87-102. Austin: University of Texas Press.

Nicholson, H. B.
1955    Native historical traditions of nuclear America and the problem of their archaeological correlation. *American Anthropologist* 57 no. 3:594-613.

1967    A "royal headband" of the Tlaxcalteca. *Revista mexicana de estudios antropológicos* 21:71-106. Mexico City.

O'Brien, Linda
1975    Songs of the face of the earth: Ancestor songs of the Tzutuhil-Maya of Santiago Atitlán, Guatemala. Ph.D. dissertation, University of California at Los Angeles.

Ocaña, Diego de
1932-33    Descripción de la laguna de Atitlán (1662). *Anales de la Sociedad de Geografía e Historia de Guatemala* 9:297-302. Guatemala City.

Ordóñez Chípin, Martín
1970    El Baile de la Culebra en Santa Cruz del Quiché. *Guatemala indígena* 4, no. 4:147-49. Guatemala City.

1973    La figura de Judas Iscariote en el medio guatemalteco. *Guatemala indígena* 8, no. 1:143-72. Guatemala City.

Orellana, Carlos L.
1972    Migration and habitation patterns of the Maya of Santiago Atitlán, Guatemala. Manuscript.

Orellana, Sandra L.
1975a    Folk literature of the Tzutujil Maya. *Anthropos* 75, nos.

                    5-6:839-76.
1975b       La introducción del sistema de cofradía en la región del
                    lago de Atitlán en los altos de Guatemala. *América indígena*
                    35, no. 4:845-56. Mexico City.
1977         Aboriginal medicine in highland Guatemala. *Medical An-
                    thropology* 1, no. 1:113-56.
Pardo, J. Joaquín
1944         *Efemérides para escribir la historia de la muy noble y muy
                    leal ciudad de Santiago de los caballeros del reino de Gua-
                    temala.* Publicaciones de la Sociedad de Geografía e His-
                    toria. Guatemala City: Tipografía Nacional.
Parra, Francisco de
1889         Carta de fray Francisco de la Parra (1547). In Joaquín
                    García Icazbalceta, ed. *Nueva collección de documentos para
                    la historia de México,* pp. 193-96. Mexico City: Francisco
                    Díaz de León.
Parsons, Lee A.
1969         *Bilbao, Guatemala: An archaeological study of the Pacific
                    Coast Cotzumalhuapa region.* Milwaukee Public Museum,
                    Publications in Anthropology, no. 12. 2 vols.
Paul, Benjamin D.
1968         San Pedro la Laguna. In Sol Tax, ed. *Los pueblos del lago
                    de Atitlán,* pp. 93-158. Seminario de Integración Social
                    Guatemalteca. Guatemala City: Tipografía Nacional.
1976         The Maya bonesetter as sacred specialist. *Ethnology* 15,
                    no. 1:77-81.
Paul, Lois, and Benjamin D. Paul
1963         Changing marriage patterns in a highland Guatemalan
                    community. *Southwestern Journal of Anthropology* 19:
                    131-48.
1975         The Maya midwife as sacred professional. *American Eth-
                    nologist* 2, no. 4:707-26.
Pineda, Juan de
1925         Relación Pineda: Descripción de la provincia de Guatemala
                    (1594). *Anales de la sociedad de Geografía e Historia de
                    Guatemala* 1:327-63. Guatemala City.
Ponce, Alonso
1873         *Relación Ponce: Relación breve y verdadera de algunas
                    cosas de las muchas que sucedieron al padre fray Alonso
                    Ponce en las provincias de la Nueva España (1584).* 2 vols.
                    Madrid.
*Popol Vuh* [PV]
1971         *The Book of Counsel: The Popol Vuh of the Quiche Maya
                    of Guatemala.* Translated by Munro S. Edmonson. Middle
                    American Research Institute, Tulane University, Publica-
                    tion no. 35. New Orleans.
Portig, W. H.

1965        Central American rainfall. *Geographical Review* 55, no. 1:
            68-90.
Ramírez, Juan    See Sherman 1968.
*Recopilación*
1971        *Recopilación de leyes de los reynos de las Indias (1791).*
            3 vols. Mandados Imprimir y Publicar por la majestad Ca-
            tólica del Rey Don Carlos II. Madrid.
*Relación Cerrato [RC]*
1973        Relación Cerrato (1552). In Robert M. Carmack. *Quichean
            civilization: The ethnohistoric, ethnographic, and archaeo-
            logical sources,* pp. 378-79. Berkeley and Los Angeles: Uni-
            versity of California Press.
*Relación Garcés [RG]*
1973        Relación Garcés (1570-72). In Robert M. Carmack. *Quichean
            civilization: The ethnohistoric, ethnographic, and archaeo-
            logical sources,* pp. 379-85. Berkeley and Los Angeles: Uni-
            veristy of California Press.
*Relación geográfica Aguacatepec [RGAG]*
1965        Descripción de San Bartolomé del Partido de Atitlán (1585),
            por Alonso Páez Betancor and fray Pedro de Arboleda.
            *Anales de la Sociedad de Geografía e Historia de Guate-
            mala* 38:262-76. Guatemala City.
*Relación geográfica Atitlán [RGA]*
1964        Relación de Santiago Atitlán (1585), por Alonso Páez Be-
            tancor y fray Pedro de Arboleda. *Anales de la Sociedad de
            Geografía e Historia de Guatemala* 37:87-106. Guatemala
            City.
*Relación geográfica San Andrés [RGSA]*
1952        Ranch of San Andrés, Dependency of Atitlán, by Alonso
            Páez Betancor and fray Pedro de Arboleda. In Ray Brous-
            sard, trans. Description of Atitlán and its dependencies
            (1585), pp. 101-21. Master's thesis, University of Texas.
*Relación geográfica San Francisco [RGSF]*
1952        San Francisco, Dependency of Atitlán, by Alonso Páez Be-
            tancor and fray Pedro de Arboleda. In Ray Broussard, trans.
            Atitlán and its dependencies (1585), pp. 122-45. Master's
            thesis, University of Texas.
*Relación geográfica Zapotitlán y Suchitepéquez [RGZ]*
1955        Descripción de la Provincia de Zapotitlán y Suchitepéquez
            (1579), por su alcalde mayor capitán Juan de Estrada y el
            escribano Fernando de Niebla. *Anales de la Sociedad de
            Geografía e Historia de Guatemala* 28:68-83. Guatemala
            City.
*Relación Tzutujil [RT]*
1952        Relación de los caciques y principales del Pueblo de Atitlán
            (1571). *Anales de la Sociedad de Geografía e Historia de
            Guatemala* 26:435-38. Guatemala City.

Remesal, Antonio de
  1932      *Historia general de las indias occidentales, y particular de gobernación de Chiapa y Guatemala.* Biblioteca Goathemala, vols. 4–5. Guatemala City.
Rodríguez Becerra, Salvador
  1977      *Encomienda y conquista: Los inicios de la colonización en Guatemala.* Publicaciones del Seminario de Antropología Americana, vol. 14. Seville: Universidad de Sevilla.
Rojas Lima, Flavio
  1968      Los otros pueblos del lago. In Sol Tax, ed. *Los pueblos del lago de Atitlán,* pp. 277–340. Seminario de Integración Guatemalteca. Guatemala City: Tipografía Nacional.
Roys, Ralph L.
  1972      *The Indian background of colonial Yucatan.* Introduction by J. Eric S. Thompson. Norman: University of Oklahoma Press.
Sáenz, C. de Santa María
  1963      Vida y escritos de don Francisco Marroquín, primer obispo de Guatemala (1499–1563). *Anales de la Sociedad de Geografía e Historia de Guatemala* 36:85–366. Guatemala City.
Saint-Lu, André
  1970      *Condition coloniale et conscience créole au Guatemala.* Paris: Presses Universitaires de France.
Sanchíz Ochoa, Pilar
  1976      *Los hidalgos de Guatemala: Realidad y apariencia en un sistema de valores.* Publicaciones del Seminario de Antropología Americana, vol. 13. Seville: Universidad de Sevilla.
Scholes, France V., and Ralph L. Roys
  1968      *The Maya Chontal Indians of Acalan-Tixchel: A contribution to the history and ethnography of the Yucatan Peninsula.* Norman: University of Oklahoma Press.
Schultze-Jena, Leonhard
  1933      Leben, Glaube und Sprache der Quiché von Guatemala. In *Indiana,* vol. 1. Jena: Verlag von Gustav Fischer.
Schwerin, Karl H.
  1970      The mechanisms of culture change. In *The social anthropology of Latin America: Essays in honor of Ralph Leon Beals,* pp. 283–305. Los Angeles: Latin American Center, University of California.
Sharon, Douglas
  1971      Santiago Atitlán. Unpublished field notes, Guatemala Project. Guatemalan Research and Field Training Project. Department of Anthropology, University of California at Los Angeles.
Sherman, William L.
  1968      Abusos contra los indios de Guatemala (1602–1605). Relaciones del Obispo. Cahiers du monde hispanique et Luso-

Brésilien. *Caravelle* 11:5-28. Toulouse.

1969     A conqueror's wealth: Notes on the estate of don Pedro de Alvarado. *Americas* 26:199-213.

1971     Indian slavery and the Cerrato reforms. *Hispanic American Historical Review* 51:25-50

1979     *Forced native labor in sixteenth-century Central America.* Lincoln and London: University of Nebraska Press.

Shook, Edwin M.

1965     Archaeological survey of the Pacific Coast of Guatemala. In Gordon R. Willey, ed. *Archaeology of southern Mesoamerica.* Handbook of Middle American Indians, 2:180-94. Austin: University of Texas Press.

Smith, A. L.

1955     *Archaeological reconnaissance in central Guatemala.* Carnegie Institution of Washington, Publication no. 608. Washington, D.C.

Solano y Pérez Lila, Francisco de

1969     Áreas lingüísticas y población de habla indígena de Guatemala en 1772. *Revista española de antropología americana* 4:145-200. Madrid.

1974     *Los Mayas del siglo XVII: Pervivencia y transformación de la sociedad indígena guatemalteca durante la administración borbónica.* Guatemala City.

Solórzano F., Valentín

1970     *Evolución económica de Guatemala.* Seminario de Integración social Guatemalteca. Guatemala City.

Solórzano Pereira, Juan de

1972     *Política indiana (1776).* Biblioteca de autores españoles. 5 vols. Madrid: Ediciones Atlas.

Spores, Ronald

1967     *The Mixtec kings and their people.* Norman: University of Oklahoma Press.

Stanislawski, Dan

1947     Early Spanish town planning in the New World. *Geographical Review* 37, no. 1:94-105.

Stevens, Rayfred L.

1964     The soils of Middle America and their relation to Indian peoples and cultures. In R. C. West, ed. *Natural environment and early cultures.* Handbook of Middle American Indians, 1:265-315. Austin: University of Texas Press.

Stewart, Russell

1977     Classic to Postclassic period settlement trends in the region of Santa Cruz del Quiche. In Dwight T. Wallace and Robert M. Carmack, eds. *Archaeology and ethnohistory of the central Quiche.* Institute for Mesoamerican Studies, State University of New York, Publication no. 1, pp. 68-81. Albany.

Stone, Doris

1972    *Pre-Columbian man finds Central America.* Cambridge, Mass.: Peabody Museum Press, Harvard University.

Tax, Sol
1946    The towns of Lake Atitlán. Microfilm Collection of Manuscripts of Middle American Cultural Anthropology. 2d ser., no. 13. Chicago: University of Chicago Library.

———, ed.
1968    *Los pueblos del Lago de Atitlán.* Seminario de Integración Social Guatemalteca. Guatemala City: Tipografía Nacional.

———, and Robert Hinshaw
1969    The Maya of the midwestern highlands. In Evon Z. Vogt, ed. *Ethnology.* Handbook of Middle American Indians, 7: 69-100. Austin: University of Texas Press.

Tedlock, Barbara
1983    A phenomenological approach to religious change in Highland Guatemala. In Carl Kendall, John Hawkins, and Laurel Bossen, eds. *Heritage of conquest: thirty years later,* pp. 235-46. Albuquerque: University of New Mexico Press.

*Testament Ajpopolajay* [*TA*]
1973    Testament Ajpopolajay. In Robert M. Carmack. *Quichean civilization: The ethnohistoric, ethnographic, and archaeological sources,* pp. 372-74. Berkeley and Los Angeles: University of California Press.

Thompson, Sir J. Eric S.
1948    *An archaeological reconnaissance in the Cotzumalhuapa region, Escuintla, Guatemala.* Carnegie Institution of Washington, Publication no. 574. Washington, D.C.
1970    *Maya history and religion.* Norman: University of Oklahoma Press.

*Título C'oyoi* [*TC*]
1973    A case study: Título C'oyoi (ca. 1550-70). In Robert M. Carmack. *Quichean civilization: The ethnohistoric, ethnographic, and archaeological sources,* pp. 265-345. Berkeley and Los Angeles: University of California Press.

*Título Nijaib 1* [*TN 1*]
1957    Título de la Casa Ixquin-Nehaib, señora del Territorio de Otzoya (ca. 1550-60). In Adrián Recinos, ed. *Crónicas indígenas de Guatemala,* pp. 71-94. Guatemala City: Editorial Universitaria.

*Título Nijaib 2* [*TN 2*]
1957    Título Real de don Francisco Izquín Nehaib (1558). In Adrián Recinos, ed. *Crónicas indígenas de Guatemala,* pp. 96-117. Guatemala City: Editorial Universitaria.

*Título San Bartolomé* [*SB*]
1956    Uno de los escasísimos documentos zutujiles. In M. M. Crespo. Títulos indígenas de tierras. *Antropología e historia de Guatemala* 8 no. 2:12-13. Guatemala City.

*Título Santa Clara* [*SC*]
1957    Título de los Indios de Santa Clara la Laguna (1583). In Adrián Recinos, ed. *Crónicas indígenas de Guatemala*, pp. 172-81. Guatemala City: Editorial Universitaria.

*Título Tamub* [*Tamub*]
1957    Historia Quiché de don Juan de Torres (1580). In Adrián Recinos, ed. *Crónicas indígenas de Guatemala*, pp. 24-67. Guatemala City: Editorial Universitaria.

*Título Totonicapán* [*TT*]
1967    *Title of the Lords of Totonicapán*. Translated from the Quiché text into Spanish by Dionisio José Chonay. English version by Delia Goetz. Norman: University of Oklahoma Press.

*Título Tzutujil*
1973    Título Tzutujil. In Robert M. Carmack. *Quichean civilization: The ethnohistoric, ethnographic, and archaeological sources*, pp. 377-78. Berkeley and Los Angeles: University of California Press.

*Título Xpantzay 1* [*TX 1*]
1957    Historia de los Xpantzay de Tecpán Guatemala (ca. 1550). In Adrián Recinos, ed. *Crónicas indígenas de Guatemala*, pp. 120-29. Guatemala City: Editorial Universitaria.

*Título Xpantzay 2* [*TX 2*]
1957    Guerras comunes de Quiché y Cakchiquel (ca. 1550). In Adrián Recinos, ed. *Crónicas indígenas de Guatemala*, pp. 132-49. Guatemala City: Editorial Universitaria.

*Título Xpantzay 3* [*TX 3*]
1957    Testamento de los Xpantzay (ca. 1550). In Adrián Recinos, ed. *Crónicas indígenas de Guatemala*, pp. 152-69. Guatemala City: Editorial Universitaria.

Vásquez, Francisco
1937-44    *Crónica de la provincia del Santísimo Nombre de Jesús de Guatemala de la orden de nuestra seráfico padre San Francisco (1714-17)*. Biblioteca Goathemala, vols. 14-17. Guatemala City.

Velázquez de la Cadena, Mariano
1967    *New revised Velázquez Spanish and English dictionary*. London: Heinemann Educational Books.

Villacorta Calderón, José Antonio
1927    *Arqueología guatemalteca*. Guatemala City: Tipografía Nacional.
1938    *Prehistoria e historia antigua de Guatemala*. Guatemala City: Sociedad de Geografía e Historia de Guatemala.
1942    *Historia de la capitanía general de Guatemala*. Guatemala City: Tipografía Nacional.

Vivó Escoto, Jorge A.
1964    Weather and climate of Mexico and Central America. In

R. C. West, ed. *Natural environments of early cultures.* Handbook of Middle American Indians, 1:187-215. Austin: University of Texas Press.

Wallace, Dwight T., and Robert M. Carmack
    1977        See Carmack 1977.

Wauchope, Robert
    1948        *Excavations at Zacualpa, Guatemala.* Middle American Research Institute, Tulane University, Publication no. 14. New Orleans.

Williams, Howel
    1960        *Volcanic history of the Guatemalan highlands.* University of California Publications in Geological Sciences 38, no. 1. Berkeley and Los Angeles: University of California Press.

Woods, Clyde
    1968        San Lucas Tolimán. In Sol Tax, ed. *Los pueblos del lago de Atitlán,* pp. 201-27. Seminario de Integración Social Guatemalteca. Guatemala City: Tipografía Nacional.

Ximénez, Francisco
    1929-30     *Historia de la provincia de San Vicente de Chiapa y Guatemala.* Biblioteca Goathemala, vols. 1-3. Guatemala City.
    1967        *Historia natural del reino de Guatemala (1722).* Guatemala City: Editorial José de Pineda Ibarra.

Zavala, Silvio
    1944        Contribución a la historia de las instituciones coloniales en Guatemala. *Jornada* no. 36, pp. 1-88. Mexico City: El Colegio de México.

Zorita, Alonso de
    1971        *Life and labor in ancient Mexico: The brief and summary relation of the lords of New Spain.* New Brunswick, N.J.: Rutgers University Press.

# Index

278                                                        *The Tzutujil Mayas*

120, 145, 168; *encomienda* grants of, 52,
  138-39, 140; and Tzutujils, 114, 115,
  138-40, 145-46, 157, 167, 168, 181,
  198; *see also* Barahona, Sancho
*Amac-tzutuhile: see amak'*
*Amak':* 3, 42, 49, 55, 78, 84, 123, 239n.,
  242n.
Andes: 2, 21, 32
*Anexo: see visita*
Angulo, Pedro de: 171, 195, 196
Animals: 70, 77, 102, 129, 141, 160;
  hunting of, 9-12, 162, 240n.; as tribute,
  10, 64, 65, 71, 115, 145, 147, 148, 150-
  54, 156, 157, 200, 211, 213-14; intro-
  duced, 10, 162, 166; and trade, 16, 17,
  71, 73, 76; dances of, 103, 212-13; as
  omens, 105; and nagualism, 105, 206-
  207, 221-22; *see also tonal*
Antigua: 51, 115
*Aposento:* 123
Arboleda, Pedro de: 119, 189, 198
Argüeta: 156, 218-19
Argüeta, don Gaspar de: 156
Arias de Avila, Gaspar *(encomendero):* 131
Artisans (craftsmen): 65, 71, 77, 79, 87,
  158, 166, 175, 179, 199, 224, 246n.: in
  Verapaz, 73; and tribute, 78, 88
Atitan: *see* Atitlán
Atitlán: 2-4, 7, 9, 10, 16, 29, 33, 50, 54,
  68-70, 72, 77, 79, 93, 101, 103, 106,
  124-26, 170, 216-19, 243n., 254n.;
  name defined, 4-5, 61; ruins of, 15, 18,
  20, 21, 23, 30; church of, 52, 119, 120,
  123, 141, 159, 175, 196-200, 203-205,
  208, 210, 214-15, 258n.; lords of, 55,
  80-83, 118, 131, 139, 141-43, 145, 147,
  148, 159, 173-74, 176, 179, 188, 194,
  197-98, 224, 253n.; versus Tecpán
  Atitlán, 55, 129, 131-32; Battle of, 60,
  61; market of, 73, 74, 164-66; *cabezas
  de calpul* of, 84, 156, 176, 177, 183, 188,
  230; marriage in, 85, 178; governor of,
  94, 123, 183, 184, 186-88, 194; idols in,
  98, 99, 206, 212; *cofradías* in, 99, 100,
  103, 209, 211, 212, 214, 258n., 259n.;
  divination in, 102-104; *cabecera* of, 117,
  119, 123, 133, 159, 162, 164, 181, 182,
  189, 190, 192-94, 199, 225, 228, 230;
  congregation of, 17, 117, 122, 127, 129-
  30, 196-98, 215; *corregimiento* of, 117,
  126, 181, 189, 193, 194, 197, 230; and
  tribute, 118, 128, 131, 143, 145, 147-57,
  173, 190, 201; *corregidores* of, 119, 120,
  123, 156, 189, 192, 193, 225; school of,
  119, 175, 184, 196, 197, 215; Spanish
  priests in, 119, 159, 185, 189, 196-98,
  202, 203, 206, 215, 250n., 257n.;
  *cabecera de doctrina,* 119, 197, 198,
  215; *principales* of, 123, 139, 169, 171,
  183, 187-89, 197; *cabildo* of, 123, 182,
  183, 186-90, 193, 194, 226, 256n.;
  *encomienda* of, 138-43, 145, 147-57,
  229; tributaries of, 140, 142, 153-54,
  156, 190, 230; population of, 142, 214;

and *repartimiento,* 156; merchants of,
  162, 163, 174-75; *caciques* of, 167-74,
  176, 179, 181, 182, 186, 187, 194, 215,
  224, 230; *regidores* of, 182, 183, 188;
  *repartimiento de efectos* in, 193; *see also*
  Chiya', tribute, Tuztujils
Atitlán, Lake: 2, 3, 10, 12, 14, 15, 17, 19,
  22-24, 28, 31, 32, 46, 50, 51, 56, 64,
  72, 82, 84, 114, 126, 134-35, 149, 160,
  193, 256n.; settlements of, 4, 49-54,
  124-31, 189; topography of, 5, 7, 8;
  climate of, 6; markets of, 6, 73, 74, 163;
  description of, 7; formation of, 7; population of, 8, 16, 17; vegetation of, 9, 70;
  fishing in, 9, 161-62; Cachiquels arrive
  at, 39, 40; Tzutujils arrive at, 39, 47;
  divided, 40, 52; *see also* congregation
Atitlán Volcano: *see* volcanoes
Atzihuinac: *see atzij winak*
*Atzij winak:* 90, 91, 95
Atziquinijai: *see* Chiya'
Audiencia de los Confines: *see* Audiencia
  of Gutemala
Audiencia of Bogotá: 118
Audiencia of Guatemala: 117, 140, 141,
  149, 154, 155, 159, 168, 173, 181, 182,
  184, 192, 201, 225, 250n.; creation of,
  115; functions of, 115; and exploitation,
  116; and congregation, 122; and tribute,
  146-48, 153; and *cofradías,* 213-14;
  *see also* López de Cerrato, offices
  (Spanish)
Audiencia of Mexico: 138, 140
Audiencia of Quito: 119
Aztec: calendar, 38, 245n.; empire, 112,
  181; ruler, *see* Montezuma

Balam Acam (Quiché ruler): 44, 60, 87,
  243n.
Barahona family: 157, 181; Pedro de, 148;
  Sancho de *(el Viejo),* 139, 142, 147,
  253n.; versus Alvarados, 140, 145;
  Sancho de, *el Menor,* 141, 142; and
  tribute, 148, 149, 152; and church 198,
  199
Belehé Quih (Belejeb Quej): 45
Bernabé of Atitlán, don (Tzutujil *cacique*):
  48, 168, 169, 230; and succession, 94,
  184, 186, 187
Betanzos, Pedro: and congregation, 117,
  122, 129, 198; and school of Atitlán, 197
Bilbao: 2, 15, 23
Bitol: 36
*Boca costa: see* piedmont
Boundaries: 21, 44, 54-56, 68, 83, 108,
  111, 128, 129, 131-33, 182; *see also*
  piedmont
Brasseur de Bourbourg, Charles Étienne: 35
Briceño, Francisco: 118, 149, 152, 153

*Cabecera:* 49, 134-35, 137, 138, 205, 209,
  256n.; *see* Atitlán, Sololá
*Cabildo* (town council): 117, 121, 164, 182,
  184-86, 190, 208, 215, 227, 251n.; *see*

Tezulutlán: *see* Verapaz
Ticanlu, Finca: 2, 21, 24
Tikal: 22
Tilapa River: 2, 55
*Tinamit:* 49, 78, 84, 85, 88, 127, 177, 225; defined, 5
Tiquisate: 2, 19, 26, 33; ware, 23, 24
Tithe: *see diezmo*
*Tlatoques:* 155
Tlaxcalans: 61
Tohil Plumbate: 26, 33
Tojil: *see* Quichés
Tolimán: *see* San Lucas Tolimán
Tolimán, Finca: 2, 21, 22, 24
Tolimán, Lower: *see* San Lucas Tolimán
Tolimán, Upper: *see* San Antonio Palopó
Tolimán Volcano: *see* volcanoes
Tollan: *see* Tula
Toltec: 26, 37, 39, 98; influence on highlands, 24, 47; capital, 35, 36, 242n.
*Tonal:* 103, 105; *see* nagualism
Torres, Juan de: 196
*Tostón del servicio:* 155-57
Totonicapán: 2, 51, 139; attacked by Tzutujils, 44
Trade: 33, 37, 42, 68, 71-76, 145, 158, 174, 188, 245n., 255n.; of maize, 8, 17, 72-75, 160, 163, 254n.; of fish, 9, 12, 71; highland-lowland, 11, 17, 70-72, 74-76, 78, 162-64, 165-66, 174, 224, 227; of animals, 16, 17, 71, 73, 76; ware, 20, 21, 23, 26, 33, 241n.; of cacao, 42, 72, 75, 160-61, 162-66, 193, 202; *see also* markets, merchants
Traps: fish, 8; animal, 11-12
Tributaries (tribute payers): 66, 87, 108, 146, 148, 152, 155, 175, 176, 203, 226, 251n.; of Chiya', 121; of *estancias,* 121, 143, 153-54, 190; of Atitlán, 140, 142, 153-54, 156, 190, 230; and tax of *encomenderos,* 141; of highland *sujetos,* 144, 156, 177; *see also* tribute, vassals
Tribute: 59, 63-68, 74, 76, 95, 108, 119, 162-64, 178, 180, 185, 202, 225; of animals as, 10, 64, 65, 71, 115, 145, 147, 148, 150-54, 156, 200, 211, 213-14; of cacao, 17, 36, 63-66, 70, 111, 115, 116, 145, 147, 149-54, 156-58, 160, 201, 211; in Tula, 36, 63, 64; and Quichés, 38, 41-42, 47, 52, 57, 64-67, 98; to Q'uik'ab, 52, 64, 65, 71, 200; collection of, 41, 64, 66, 90, 137, 138, 142, 143, 145, 146, 154-57, 177, 182, 184, 193, 199, 223, 229; time of payment of, 64, 65, 147; assessment of, 118, 128, 130, 131, 140, 141, 146-49, 153-57, 189, 190, 192, 226; and Atitlán, 118, 128, 131, 143, 145, 147-57, 173, 190, 201; and *encomenderos,* 118, 137-38, 140-41, 143, 146-49, 153-55, 157, 172-74, 181, 186, 214, 223-24; double payment of, 146, 153, 226; exemptions from, 147, 148, 153-55, 170, 175, 179, 203-205, 215, 228; *tributo personal,* 154-56, 254n.; *tributo real,* 154, 156, 157, 230;

*see also caciques,* lords, Tzutujils
Tucurú: 71
Tukuchés: 46, 52
Tula: 57, 242n.; founded by migrants, 35; migrants in, 36, 37; idols given in, 36, 37, 98; visit of C'ocaib to, 39-41, 77, 89; omens in, 105; *see also* Chichén Itzá, tribute
Tulán: *see* Tula
Tulimán: *see* San Lucas Tolimán
*Tun (tum):* see *loj-tum*
Tunatiuh: *see* Alvarado, Pedro de
Tzacbalcat: 50, 55, 126, 132, 136
Tz'akol: 36
Tzala: 40, 53; *see* Sololá
Tzanchalí: 17, 18, 29
Tzanchichám: 17, 18, 28, 29
Tzantziapá, Finca: 4, 28
Tz'iquinajá: capital, *see* Chiya'; lineage, *see* Ajtz'iquinajay, Tz'iquinajay
Tz'iquinajay (Quiché lineage): 37, 81
Tz'iquinajay (Tzutujil lineage): *see* Ajtz'iquinajay
Tzololá: *see* Sololá
Tzotzils: 46; *see also ajpotzotzil*
Tzununá: *chinamit,* 83, 177; lineage, 82, 243n.; town, 4, 10, 53
Tzunúaa: *see* San Pedro
*Tzutujil pop:* 48, 60, 89-92, 243n.; *see also* Ajtz'iquinajay
Tzutujil region: 3, 68, 70, 73, 75, 76, 84, 85, 99, 102, 120, 160, 161, 164, 173, 178, 181, 185, 194, 196, 200, 202, 203, 204, 206, 209, 214, 215, 220, 224, 226, 229, 230, 257n.; topography of, 5-8, 10; climate and vegetation of, 6-7, 9; soils of, 7, 55, 69, 239n.; ruins in, 13-34; settlement pattern of, 13, 16-20, 26, 27, 32, 108, 121-28, 182, 225; excavations in, 14-16, 20, 23, 27, 32; archaeological sequence, 15; *see also* crops, trade
Tzutujils: 5, 12, 119, 184, 193, 214, 221, 222, 227, 228, 231, 232; and Nahua, 3; name defined, 3; language of, 3, 4, 19, 35, 53, 55, 56, 72, 77, 105, 128-31, 190, 197, 210, 244n.; and Cakchiquels, 3, 13-14, 18, 40-42, 44-48, 52-54, 56, 58, 62, 72, 81-82, 87, 108, 112-14, 118, 120, 128, 173, 179, 189; and Quichés, 3, 28, 32, 33, 37, 39, 41, 42, 47, 49, 55, 56, 62, 64-67, 72, 75, 86, 87, 98, 112, 129, 130, 179, 196, 223, 224; merchants, 8, 72, 78, 162, 163, 174-75; and tribute, 10, 36, 41-42, 47, 49, 52, 57, 64-68, 70, 71, 75, 78, 90, 95, 115, 120; fight Spaniards, 13, 59-61, 112-13, 120, 143, 224; fight Quichés, 16, 42-46, 48, 49, 52-54, 57, 58, 66, 108, 130; *caciques,* 19, 55, 167-74, 176, 179, 181, 182, 186, 187, 189, 194-96, 215, 224, 230; and Pipils, 24, 26, 44-46, 48, 56; and Tula, 35-37, 63-64, 98; fight in Tabasco-Veracruz, 35, 37; fight in Tula, 36; idols of, 37, 57, 58, 63, 98, 100, 107, 242n.; migrate to Guatemala, 36-38, 47, 82; and Sakiribal, 38,

*The Tzutujil Mayas,*

designed by Bill Cason, is set in a version of Caledonia by the University of Oklahoma Press and printed offset on 55-pound Glatfelter B-31, a permanized sheet, by Cushing-Malloy, Inc., with case binding by John H. Dekker & Sons.